Date label over →

KT-471-833

NORTHERN NORRLAND
See pp262–75

KIRUNA

LAPPLAND

NORR-BOTTEN

NORTHERN NORRLAND

Luleå

GULF OF BOTHNIA

VÄSTER-BOTTEN

Umeå

ÅNGERMAN-LAND
Örnsköldsvik

...nd

...HERN
...LAND
...EDELPAD

Sundsvall

GULF OF BOTHNIA

...LSING-
...LAND
Hudiksvall

GÄSTRIKLAND
Gävle
...un

UPPLAND
Uppsala
...AN-D **EASTERN SVEALAND**
Västerås
SÖDER-MANLAND **STOCKHOLM**
Nyköping

Linköping
...GÖTLAND

...RN
...AND
Visby
GOTLAND

...nar ...ÖLAND

BALTIC SEA

...E
Karlskrona

...RN GÖTALAND

STOCKHOLM
See pp44–117

SOUTHERN NORRLAND
See pp246–61

EASTERN SVEALAND
See pp122–39

GOTLAND
See pp158–69

EYEWITNESS TRAVEL GUIDES

SWEDEN

EYEWITNESS TRAVEL GUIDES

SWEDEN

LONDON, NEW YORK,
MELBOURNE, MUNICH AND DELHI
www.dk.com

PRODUCED FOR DORLING KINDERSLEY BY
Streiffert Förlag AB, Stockholm

SENIOR EDITOR
Bo Streiffert

PROJECT AND PICTURE EDITOR
Guy Engström

ASSISTANT PICTURE EDITOR
Ebba Mörner

MAIN CONTRIBUTORS
Ulf Johansson, Mona Neppenström, Kaj Sandell

PHOTOGRAPHERS
Peter Hanneberg, Erik Svensson, Jeppe Wikström

CARTOGRAPHER
Stig Söderlind

ILLUSTRATORS
Stephen Conlin, Gary Cross, Urban Frank, Claire Littlejohn,
Jan Rojmar, John Woodcock

ENGLISH TRANSLATION
Kate Lambert, Stuart Tudball

EDITOR OF ENGLISH EDITION
Jane Hutchings

Reproduced by Colourscan, Singapore
Printed and bound by South China Printing Co Ltd, China

First published in Great Britain in 2005
by Dorling Kindersley Limited, 80 Strand, London WC2R 0RL

A CIP catalogue record is available from the British Library.
ISBN 1-4053-0875-3

**Summer-flowering cottongrass in
the mountains of Sylarna**

CONTENTS

INTRODUCING SWEDEN

STOCKHOLM AREA BY AREA

**Erik XIV's crown in the Treasury
at Stockholm's Royal Palace**

◁ **Skogavik nature reserve on Bullerö in the Stockholm Archipelago**

Cross-country skiers resting on
Åreskutan mountain *(see p259)*

TRAVELLERS' NEEDS

SURVIVAL GUIDE

Cheesecake with cloudberries, a
traditional Swedish dessert

Inner courtyard of Läckö Slott,
Västergötland *(see p220)*

SWEDEN AREA BY AREA

Royal Palace, Stockholm
(see pp54–7)

INTRODUCING SWEDEN

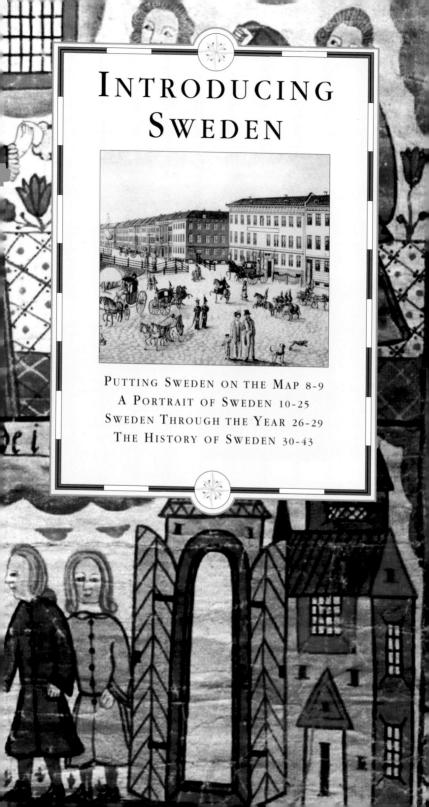

Putting Sweden on the Map

T HE KINGDOM OF SWEDEN is one of the largest countries in Europe, covering 449,964 sq km (173,730 sq miles). The most southerly point, Smygehuk, lies at about the same latitude as Edinburgh in Scotland, and the northernmost tip, Treriksröset, is nearly 300 km (186 miles) north of the Arctic Circle. Much of the country is habitable thanks to the warming effects of the Gulf Stream. As the crow flies, Sweden is 1,572 km (977 miles) from south to north – the same distance as from Smygehuk to Rome. Sweden shares a border with Norway to the west and Finland to the east. Denmark lies across the Kattegat to the southwest.

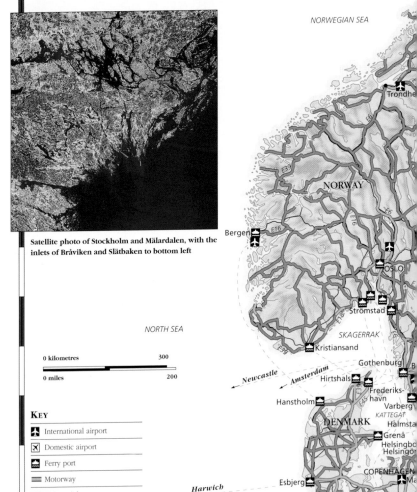

Satellite photo of Stockholm and Mälardalen, with the inlets of Bråviken and Slätbaken to bottom left

NORWEGIAN SEA

NORTH SEA

Trondhe

NORWAY

Bergen E16

OSLO

Strömstad

SKAGERRAK

Kristiansand

Gothenburg

Newcastle　Amsterdam　Hirtshals

Frederiks-
havn

Hanstholm

Varberg

KATTEGAT

DENMARK

Halmsta

Grenå

Helsingbo
Helsingor

COPENHAGEN

Harwich

Esbjerg

Kiel

KEY

✈	International airport
☒	Domestic airport
⛴	Ferry port
▬	Motorway
▬	Major road
—	Train line
–·–	International border

0 kilometres　　　　300

0 miles　　　　　　200

A PORTRAIT OF SWEDEN

SWEDES ARE PASSIONATE ABOUT NATURE *and the outdoors, and justly so since their country contains some of Europe's last surviving areas of wilderness. As a nation, Sweden has built its wealth on its natural resources and the ingenuity of its engineers. It has a heritage rich in music, literature and folk traditions and its people have a deep-rooted sense of peace and democracy.*

Few nations in Europe offer such an exceptionally diverse landscape, rich in flora and fauna, as Sweden. From north of the Arctic Circle the country stretches a lengthy 1,572 km (977 miles) south, a distance equal to almost half the length of Europe.

Elk

The extreme north is the land of the midnight sun, where daylight lasts for 24 hours in high summer, but is almost non-existent in mid-winter. Here, the mountains and tundra are home to the Sami (Lapp) people and their herds of reindeer. Moving southwards, the forests and wetlands of Norrland provide habitats for large numbers of elk and a thriving birdlife. In the far south, the rolling plains of Skåne and the area around the great lakes make good arable land. To the east, the green islands of the Stockholm archipelago contrast with the bare rocky outline of the west coast, but the waters around both offer a wide variety of marine life.

A COUNTRY SHAPED BY ICE

The mountain chain which runs along part of Sweden's border with northern Norway has several peaks more than 2,000 m (6,500 ft) high. It was formed when the ice which covered the country until 10,000 years ago retreated northwards, leaving its mark on the landscape as it shaped mountains and created

Start of the annual Vasaloppet race, which attracts more than 16,000 skiers

◁ Crown Princess Victoria and Princess Madeleine in national costume on Swedish Flag Day

L M Ericsson, setting Sweden on the path to industrialization by founding Ericsson in 1876

ridges. Several glaciers from this time still linger in the north.

THE CLIMATE

The warming effect of the Gulf Stream on Scandinavia gives Sweden a relatively mild climate for its northerly location. Cucumbers grow in the Torne Valley bordering Finland at a latitude which in Greenland is covered by ice.

However, because of the length of the country, the temperature in autumn and spring can vary by more than 20° C (68° F) from one end to the other. Northern Sweden holds the record for the coldest temperature of -53° C (-63° F), while Ultuna, near Uppsala, has recorded the highest summer temperature of 38° C (100° F).

Although there are occasional green winters in southern Sweden, heavy snowfalls can occur. The worst snowstorm took place in Skåne in February 1979, while the heaviest snowfall of 150 cm (5 ft) was on 4–5 December 1998 in Gävle in central Sweden.

SPACE FOR ALL

Sweden covers an area of 449,964 sq km (173,731 sq miles) and with just 9 million inhabitants and 20 people per sq km (52 per sq mile), Swedes have plenty of space. In the under-populated forested areas,

towns can be few and far between. Yet from the 1850s onwards, when increasing numbers of people were dependent on the land and a primitive agricultural system, Sweden couldn't feed its population. Emigration to North America was the way out and more than one million Swedes crossed the Atlantic.

Towards the end of the 19th century and thanks largely to the coming of the railways, Sweden began to exploit her rich natural resources. Forestry and copper industries were established and the rivers were harnessed to produce hydroelectricity. Large manufacturing companies began to develop, such as Ericsson, Volvo and Scania, all of which are still in operation today. The needs of industry led to a massive shift in population. Today 85 per cent of the Swedish population lives in the cities and less than 2 per cent is employed in agriculture.

In the post-war period the need for labour led to immigration rather than emigration. Flows of immigrants became even greater at the end of the 20th century with the arrival of refugees from the world's trouble spots. Sweden is now the most multicultural of the Nordic countries.

GOVERNMENT AND POLITICS

The Swedes have a strong sense of democracy and equality. Sweden is both a parliamentary democracy and a hereditary monarchy. As the head of state, the king has no political power, but he is considered to be an important representative of Sweden to the rest of the world and popular support for the monarchy is high. Carl XVI Gustaf is the descendant of one of Napoleon's marshals, Jean-Baptiste Bernadotte, who was chosen as the heir to the

Emblem of state

throne of the last of the Vasa kings, the childless Karl XIII. The Frenchman was crowned in 1818 as Carl XIV Johan, King of Sweden and Norway. Carl XVI Gustaf came to the throne in 1973 and married the German Silvia Sommerlath. Despite doubt over the king's choice of a commoner for his bride, Swedes soon took Queen Silvia to their hearts. The couple's eldest daughter, Crown Princess Victoria, is the heir to the throne.

Sweden's parliament, the Riksdag, has 349 members and is Sweden's legislative assembly. Elections are held every four years. At the same time, representatives are elected for 21 regional county councils and almost 300 municipalities.

Since World War II, a balance has prevailed between the socialist and non-socialist parties in parliament. With only a few exceptions, the Social Democrats, as the largest group, have governed, either alone or with smaller supporting parties. Generally, policy decisions such as neutrality and non-alliance, social welfare and equality between the sexes have had cross-party support. Taxation has reached record levels, but the majority of Swedes tend to believe that they get value for money. However, dramatic increases in welfare costs have forced cuts in health, education and social care.

The environment is a key issue. Swedes have a deep-rooted love of

Berry- and mushroom-picking in rural areas, with permission under Sweden's Right to Roam

nature, enshrined in the Right to Roam, which guarantees free access to the forests and the countryside and the right to pick berries and mushrooms. There is widespread support for combating pollution. After the 1986 Chernobyl disaster in the former USSR, some parts of Sweden were affected by radioactive fallout, which for a time halted the consumption of reindeer meat and fish. This fuelled an already heated debate on nuclear power and a decision was taken to decommission nuclear power stations, but this has proved difficult to implement in a country so dependent on energy.

On the issue of religion, the link between church and state was dissolved in the year 2000. Sweden's Evangelical Lutheran Church is now one faith among several. Although 85 per cent of Swedes remain members, church visits are largely restricted to weddings, funerals and festivals. The Free Church movement is strong in parts of the country. Immigration has also led to many Catholic and Muslim communities being formed.

LANGUAGES AND DIALECTS

While Swedish is the dominant language, Finnish, Tornedalsfinska (the dialect of Finnish spoken in the Torne Valley), Sami and Romany are all official minority languages. The

The Swedish Parliament's plenary chamber in Stockholm, accommodating 349 members

largest of these is Finnish with around 20,000 speakers, while Sami is spoken by about 10,000 people. The majority are multilingual and Swedes in general are often fluent in English. Among immigrants, around 100,000 people have Arabic or Persian as their main language. Other major languages are Turkish, Serbo-Croat and Spanish.

Roxette, one of Sweden's most successful pop exports over the years

Despite the general use of standard Swedish, dialects flourish. Historical links with neighbouring countries can often be detected, for example between Skånska, the dialect spoken in Skåne, and Danish, and between Jämtska, the dialect heard in Jämtland, and Norwegian.

AN INFORMATION SOCIETY

Sweden has long been a nation of readers. Early investment in education and libraries provided a firm foundation and many of Sweden's most renowned 20th-century writers came from humble beginnings. Among those known internationally is the children's author Astrid Lindgren *(see p24)*.

Astrid Lindgren's Pippi Longstocking

Although radio, television and the Internet have become the main means of receiving news, 75 per cent of households take a daily newspaper. Swedes became keen users of the telephone early on, and today almost 90 per cent of the population has a mobile phone. Computer ownership and Internet usage are also among the highest in the world.

RICH CULTURE

Besides the many specialist museums in the cities, there are more than 1,000 rural museums reflecting local history and popular culture. Great interest is shown in art and handicrafts which can be seen in the countless galleries and shops.

Swedes are keen musicians: many play in local orchestras and large numbers sing in choirs. The country claims to have enough world-class opera soloists to form a choir of their own. Folk music and dancing enjoy a natural high season from Midsummer to the end of August. Recent decades have seen Swedish pop go global with Abba, the Cardigans and Roxette. Music producers and songwriters also attract international artists to Sweden and have turned pop music into a major export industry. The story of film history also has a Swedish chapter, thanks to stars such as Greta Garbo and Ingrid Bergman, and the director Ingmar Bergman.

A SPORTING NATION

Swedes enjoy being active and getting out into the countryside for recreation. Fishing is the nation's biggest hobby. More than half of all Swedes have access to a holiday cottage, with coastal and mountain areas the most popular locations. The long coastline, glorious archipelagos and numerous waterways have made Sweden a nation of sailors.

Interest in sport goes without saying, and for a small nation Sweden has proud traditions, especially in winter sports. Skiing and ice hockey as well as football, handball, tennis, table tennis and golf, all set Swedish pulses racing, while swimming, athletics, boxing, water sports and motorsports also number several stars at international level *(see p25)*.

SWEDEN ON THE WORLD STAGE

The neutrality which protected Sweden from two world wars has remained a guiding principle. Sweden did not join NATO, choosing instead to focus on its own defence and related industry. Despite its policy of non-alliance, the country's export of weapons is considerable.

Sweden has been a member of the EU since 1995 and elections to the European Parliament are held every five years. The attitude to the EU is divided: many people dislike the fact that laws and regulations are dictated increasingly from Brussels. In a referendum in 2003, the Swedes voted "no" to adopting the euro by a considerable majority.

Sweden is an enthusiastic advocate for the work of the UN. Its own Dag Hammarskjöld was a celebrated Secretary-General (1953–61), and Swedish troops have been involved in peace initiatives worldwide.

There have been many myths about the Swedes, who have done their best to shake off their image as a silent,

Ideal conditions for Sweden's sailing enthusiasts in sheltered archipelagos

boring, sex-mad nation. Honesty and inventiveness are considered among their most positive characteristics, and EU membership has made Swedes more outgoing internationally. The country comes under the global spotlight at the end of each year when the prestigious Nobel Prizes *(see p69)* for science and literature are awarded in Stockholm amid great pomp and ceremony.

In the years following World War II Sweden had an advantage over those European countries that had suffered during the conflict. It was then that the country's transformation into a welfare state became an example that others were to follow. The "Swedish model" of understanding and collaboration between employers, employees and trade unions also attracted attention.

Talk of cracks in the welfare system do little to cloud the fact that Swedes experience a high standard of living of which they are proud.

Nadine Gordimer receiving the Nobel Prize for Literature from King Carl XVI Gustaf in 1991

Landscape and Wildlife

SWEDEN HAS A REMARKABLY varied landscape. The flat arable land of Skåne in the south gives way to lakes and forests, rugged mountains, fast-flowing rivers and wild open moorland further north, leading to the Arctic tundra. Plant and animal species from both continental Europe and the Arctic thrive. Large areas of wilderness have become enclaves where endangered species such as bears and wolves, snakes and owls have been able to survive the pressure from civilization. The coastline, too, is immensely varied. Marine life is unique, as North Sea fish make their way into the brackish water of the Baltic and mix with species normally only found in fresh water.

Wolves are a threatened species and, despite migration from neighbouring countries, there are only around 100 in Sweden.

COASTS AND ISLANDS

Smooth rocks and sandy beaches dominate the west coast, where marine life includes saltwater fish such as cod and haddock. Freshwater pike and whitefish can be found off the northerly stretches of the east coast. On the limestone islands of Öland and Gotland orchid meadows flourish.

THE ARABLE SOUTH

The flat lands of Skåne with their fields of crops, willow windbreaks and half-timbered houses topped by storks' nests are a familiar image of Sweden. But just as typical are the stony pastures and juniper slopes of Småland surrounding red cottages, and the meadows and pasture lands of Mälardalen.

Seals declined in number as a result of hunting, pollution and disease. But now populations of grey seals, ringed seals and harbour seals (pictured) are increasing, thanks to their protected status.

Roe deer were almost extinct in the early 19th century. Now they are so common in southern and central Sweden that they are known to raid local gardens in search of food.

Sea eagles, with a wing span of up to 250 cm (8 ft), are Sweden's largest birds of prey. They nest along the east coast and also on lakes in Lappland.

Hedgehogs rely on their 5,000 spines for protection and curl into a ball at the approach of danger. But this is of little effect against cars, and the popular doorstep guest is in decline.

SWEDEN'S FLORA

Considering Sweden's unusually rich flora, it is not surprising that the father of botany, Carl von Linné *(see p128)*, was born here. There are more than 2,000 species of flowers alone. After a long cold winter, nature explodes into life with a profusion of blooms, as in the orchid meadows of Öland. Swedes' love of wild flowers is illustrated by the maypoles and garlands used to celebrate Midsummer.

Wood anemones *carpeting the forests signal the arrival of spring.*

The red water-lily *can only be found in some lakes in Tiveden National Park.*

King Karl's Spire *can grow 1 m (3 ft) tall – an impressive height for an orchid. It is most common in swampy mountain areas.*

FORESTS

More than half of Sweden's land area is covered by forests, with deciduous trees in the south, coniferous forests with pines and spruce further north. Here lingonberries, blueberries and chanterelles grow. This is the home of elk and beaver, and forest birds such as capercaillies and black grouse.

THE FAR NORTH

The mountains and moorlands are characterized by their proximity to the Arctic. With late spring come the migratory birds such as hooper swans and the lesser white-fronted goose, and the mountain flora bursts into flower. Wolves, bears, wolverine and lynx inhabit the national parks.

The elk *is the big game of the forest. Around 100,000 elk are killed in the annual hunting season and, despite the road warning signs, others die in accidents involving cars.*

Reindeer *live as domesticated animals in northern Sweden, farmed by Sami in the mountains and forests. In winter the herds move further south to graze.*

The brown bear *is the largest of Sweden's predators and can weigh up to 300 kg (660 lb). It may look slow, but it moves quickly and is dangerous if disturbed.*

The ptarmigan *lives above the tree line and is often encountered, as it is unafraid of mountain hikers. It follows the changing seasons with up to four changes of plumage.*

Sweden's Wooden Houses

THE QUINTESSENTIAL IMAGE OF SWEDEN is the red-and-white painted wooden cottage. Originally, wooden houses were not considered attractive so they were painted red to make them look as though they were built of brick, or yellow to represent stone, and this tradition has continued. Every building from the humblest hut to the most majestic mansion was made of timber from the large tracts of forest. Wood triumphs in the grandiose manor houses of Hälsingland and the decoratively carved merchants' homes of the Stockholm Archipelago. Even today, architects are developing innovative ways of using this classic material.

Bell Tower
Many 18th-century churches had wooden bell towers: Delsbo's, with its elegant onion cupola, dates from 1742.

Hut in Härjedalen
This simple log-built hut in the mountain pasture of Ruändan incorporates the centuries-old tradition of a grass roof.

Interlocking posts bind together the external and interior walls, while the façades are often boarded.

Skogaholm Manor
Built in the 1680s, this Carolian timber house from Närke was originally painted red. In the 1790s, it was given a yellow plaster façade and large windows in line with Gustavian style. More recently it was moved to the museum at Skansen.

The façade is clad in pine and painted with a copper-vitriol paint, known as Falu red, to prevent rotting.

HÄLSINGLAND'S MANOR HOUSES

Reaping the benefits from the lucrative 19th-century timber industry, the forest-owning farmers of Hälsingland built themselves extravagant manor houses. The size of house and magnificence of the painted portico reflected the owner's wealth and status. The interiors were often decorated with wall paintings.

Swedenborg's Pavilion
The miniature manor house of philosopher Emanuel Swedenborg (1688–1772). It is now at Skansen (see p92).

Societetshuset
Decorative wooden buildings, such as this club house for wealthy visitors to the seaside town of Marstrand (see p216), were a feature of the fashionable west coast bathing resorts in the late 19th century.

Modern Wooden Architecture

The Nordic Watercolour Museum in Skärhamn on the west coast opened in 2000. The Danish architects Bruun/Corfitsen have clad the building's steel and concrete shell with vertical wooden panels in red, using this traditional material in a public setting.

Wooden Lighthouse
Dating from 1840, the wooden lighthouse at Bönan also served as a pilot station. It marked the shipping route into Gävle. The building is now a museum.

Two-storey houses are common in Hälsingland. The finest have an attic floor with half-windows.

Merchant's House in the Archipelago
In the late 19th century Stockholm's upper middle classes spent their summers in the archipelago, where they built magnificent wooden villas with verandas, summer houses, bathing huts and boat houses.

Foundations are a course of cobblestones.

Porticoes and outer doors are particularly richly ornamented and painted. Other details include turned pillars, intricate woodcarving and elegant roofs. The designs vary from parish to parish.

Fishing Cottages at Kungshamn
In fishing villages on the rocky islands of Bohuslän, where space is tight, timber-clad houses in pastel shades crowd in higgledy-piggledy fashion around the harbours.

Decorative Woodwork
More expensive wooden houses dating from around 1900 were often a riot of fretwork and rich ornamentation, known as "carpenter's joy", on verandas, entrances and gables.

Traditions, Customs and Folklore

Folk musician

GLOBALIZATION AND THE gradual erosion of regional identity over the last 50 years have had a major impact on Swedish traditions and lifestyle. Much of the formerly rigid etiquette has been relaxed and today Swedes are more informal when it comes to dress and manners. At the same time, Swedes have become more interested in their roots, local customs, history and traditions. They are passionate about their little red cottages, the countryside, eating herring at Midsummer and the first fresh strawberries.

Sami in traditional costume for a celebratory occasion

FEASTS AND FESTIVITIES

CELEBRATING the high points of the year within the family has again become increasingly important, after a dismissive attitude towards tradition in the 1960s and 70s.

Many traditions have pagan origins, most of them related to the coming and going of seasons, and are an excuse to eat special treats and play games. The most important is Midsummer, the summer solstice feast. Along with dancing and games around the maypole, the light, short night (when all sorts of magic is in the air) can be marked by watching the sun set and rise a few hours apart (or hardly at all in the north). For those who go to bed it is the custom to pick seven different flowers in silence and place them under their pillow; their future partner will appear in their dreams. Walpurgis night, 30 April, is when the last day of winter is chased away with

huge bonfires, and songs and speeches welcome spring. Lucia Day, in December, is an intricate mix of pagan and Christian, a festival of light at the onslaught of darkness, which has adopted a Christian martyr as its symbol of hope and bringer of light. Every school, office and church has a Lucia, a girl dressed in white with a red ribbon around her waist symbolizing the martyr's blood, and a crown of candles on her head (see p29).

Easter also has elements of old folk beliefs. Maundy Thursday is the day witches fly to Blåkulla (see p154) to dance with the devil. Today, children dress up, broomsticks and all, and give handmade Easter greetings cards in exchange for sweets. Christmas is preceded by the hectic run-up of Advent, when Swedes go partying and consume vast quantities of glögg (mulled wine usually mixed with cognac or vodka), lussebullar (saffron buns) and pepparkakor (ginger snaps).

DRESS AND ETIQUETTE

THOSE WHO OWN a folk costume take it out for midsummer, folk dances, weddings and other formal occasions. Each region has its own historic style and there is also a national dress (see p10). The Sami have their own elaborate costumes.

At weddings people are expected to dress up, as specified on the invitation (white tie, black tie or suit). In everyday life, style is more casual, especially in summer.

Although Swedes are more easy-going these days, they are still fond of etiquette. It is important to know how to "skål". Swedes first raise their glass to their female partner at the table, and then to the hostess. People look each other in the eye while raising their glass and saying "skål", looking down as they drink and then re-establishing eye contact before putting down their glass. If the skål is communal, everyone has to look each person around the table in the eye before drinking.

Despite this interest in etiquette, Swedes tend not to observe minor courtesies such as holding open doors or apologizing when they bump into someone. They are very informal when addressing one another; everyone is on first name terms from the start, even when doing business.

SINGERS AND MUSICIANS

MORE THAN half a million Swedes sing in a choir, and their passion for song is reflected not just in singing

Midsummer celebrations with games and dancing round the maypole

at parties and the ever-increasing repertoire of drinking songs, but also in the popularity of singing together. There are few 50th birthday parties where each plate doesn't come with a songbook or where friends don't perform songs they have written themselves. Everyone is expected to know works by troubadour Carl Bellman and ballads by Evert Taube *(see p60)*.

Folk music is played at clubs and there are festivals dedicated to folk instruments such as the accordion and hurdy-gurdy. Pageants and history plays have also seen a huge upturn in popularity in recent years.

CLOSE TO NATURE

THE SWEDES' LOVE of nature is deeply rooted. Many feel, subconsciously, an almost spiritual affinity with the forest, mountains or the sea. Legends and folklore are often linked to nature and many mythical beings are part of country lore. Trolls dwell in the forest, as does the Skogsvrå or Huldra (siren), a beautiful young woman who lures men deeper and deeper into the woods and then, once they are lost, she turns around and all there is to be seen is a hollow tree. Women who stroll too far might hear a lovely tune drifting among the trees – that is Näcken, a handsome naked man, playing his fiddle in the middle of gushing streams

Painting depicting mythical beings in the forest

A tournament during Medieval Week, a popular pageant in Visby

and, needless to say, it is best to stay away from him. Giants and dwarfs roam the mountains while elves dance in the meadows and marshlands. Some beings have adopted modern guises. The Tomte, who traditionally is a stern, grey little man guarding farmers' barns and livestock, has been transformed into a kindly distributor of Christmas gifts. In the countryside, however, a plate of Christmas porridge is left for him on the doorstep, just to be safe.

There is a strong awareness of the changing seasons, linked to how deeply Swedes long for the bright summer. Spring is a slow affair, building up with the blossoming of one flower at a time, each one eagerly awaited. People know when each bloom is due, hence expressions like "between bird cherry and lilac" (ie "at end of May").

On a more practical note, it is easy to be physically close to nature thanks to the Right to Roam. This grants everyone access to all land, apart from the immediate surroundings of a house or farm *(see p314)*. Many make the most of this resource, walking, camping, or going mushroom or berry-picking.

A COUNTRY COTTAGE

THE LITTLE RED cottage is the symbol of paradise. Maybe it is the Swedes' farming roots combined with the

brief summer which makes having a holiday house in the countryside or out on an island such a major ambition.

When spring comes, people head out to tend their cottage gardens, and as the autumn nights draw in they are still at their cottages, curled up by the fire. Almost half the population have access to a summer cottage and 20 per cent own one of their own.

CULINARY TRADITIONS

PEOPLE ARE rediscovering old Swedish dishes and there has been something of a revival in *husmanskost* ("home-cooking"). Few, however, have time to prepare these at home on a daily basis, so childhood favourites such as *kalops* (a slow-cooked meat stew), *köttbullar* (meatballs, *see p293*) and freshly cleaned and fried herring fillets are now often enjoyed in restaurants.

Strawberry cream cake

Swedes drink lots of coffee, and at work the *fika paus* (coffee break) is strictly observed. In fact, *fika* is something everyone does, as proven by the large number of cafés even in small towns. To accompany coffee there is a great variety of *bullar* (buns), cakes, gateaux and biscuits. Home-made sponge cake layered with lots of whipped cream and strawberries is a summer favourite, especially for birthdays.

Swedish Design

SWEDISH DESIGN first attracted international attention at the 1925 World Exhibition in Paris, when glassware in particular took the world by storm and the concept of "Swedish Grace" was launched. The nation's design tradition is characterized by simplicity and functionality, with a major emphasis on natural materials. Swedish designers and architects are renowned for creating simple, attractive, "human" objects for everyday use. The 20th century marked the beginning of a new golden age, in which Swedish design has won worldwide acclaim.

Stoneware, Hans Hedberg
Swedish ceramics from the 1940s, 50s and 60s , such as t* stoneware egg, are popular wi* collectors around the world.

Armchair (1969), Bruno Mathsson
Bruno Mathsson, one of Sweden's most famous 20th-century furniture designers, is one of the creators of the style that became known as "Swedish Modern". He designed the first version of the Pernilla armchair in 1942.

Pale wood and simplicity is the concept most closely associated with Swedish style.

Rag rugs are an old Swedish weaving tradition adopted by Karin Larsson, whose skill as a textile designer is widely recognized.

Cabinet (1952), Josef Frank
Frank was born in Austria, but worked in Sweden, and was another disciple of the "Swedish Modern" style. He is best known for his printed textiles, but he also designed furniture.

Carpet (1931), Märta Määs-Fjetterström
From 1919, Märta Määs-Fjetterström wove her famous rugs at her studio in Skåne. Her work was inspired by folklore and nature, and she created a design concept that was new but still firmly rooted in tradition.

Silver jug (1953)
Sigurd Persson
Persson has an unrivalled ability to handle metal. He made his mark on the history of design with his everyday industrial pieces and exclusive artworks.

Chair (1981), Jonas Bohlin
The Concrete *chair was the most talked about piece of Swedish furniture in the 1980s. A graduation project, it represented an entirely new approach to furniture design.*

flowers and plants on a windowsill and no curtains typifies the Larssons' ideas on interior decoration.

Bookshelf (1989), John Kandell
The Piliaster *bookshelf stores books horizontally instead of vertically. The lines are simple and typically Scandinavian. The maker, Källemo, is one of Sweden's most unconventional furniture companies.*

Gustavian late 18th-century style elements have remained a strong feature in Swedish design through the centuries, but made an international comeback in the 1990s.

CARL LARSSON'S SUNDBORN

The home created by the artist Carl Larsson (1853–1919) and his wife Karin *(see p237)* became a inspiration around the world when featured in his watercolours series *A Home.* The mixture of old and new, pure clear colours, light and space and lots of plants was a clear expression of the "Beauty for All" movement.

Vase, Ann Wåhlström
Wåhlström is one of Kosta Boda's new generation of glass designers. Organic, warm and beautiful, Cyklon (1998) is an excellent example of contemporary Swedish glass.

WHERE TO SEE SWEDISH DESIGN

Asplund
Sibyllegatan 31,
Stockholm. **Map** 2 E3.

DesignTorget
Vallgatan 14,
Gothenburg.

Nationalmuseum
Södra Blasieholmshamnen,
Stockholm. **Map** 4 D2.

Röhsska Museet
Vasagatan 37–39,
Gothenburg.

Nordiska Museet
Djurgårdsvågen 6–16,
Stockholm. **Map** 4 F1.

David Design
Stortorget 5,
Malmö.

Svenskt Tenn
Strandvägen 5, Stockholm.
Map 2 E4.

Glassworks shops
Various, Småland.
(See pp152–3).

Famous Swedes

For a nation with only 9 million inhabitants, a surprisingly large number of Swedes have made names for themselves abroad. They include scientists such as Anders Celsius, who gave us the temperature scale, Alfred Nobel, founder of the prize that bears his name, Dalarna artists Anders Zorn and Carl Larsson, the playwright August Strindberg and peacemaker Dag Hammarskjöld. In recent years, tennis players such as Björn Borg and Stefan Edberg, skiers, film-makers, writers of children's books and pop stars have all gained international acclaim.

Carl Larsson (1853–1919), loved for his paintings of Sundborn

August Strindberg, Sweden's influential dramatist and author

LITERATURE

The first Swedish authors to achieve international recognition were the late-19th-century writers Selma Lagerlöf *(see p232)* and August Strindberg. Lagerlöf's *Gösta Berling's Saga* (1891), set in her home province of Värmland, marked a turning point in modern Swedish novel-writing. She won the Nobel Prize in 1909, an honour not granted the titan August Strindberg (1849–1912), whose groundbreaking naturalistic plays, including *The Father* (1887), *Miss Julie* (1888), *The Dance of Death* (1901) and *A Dream Play* (1902), are still performed around the world.

In contemporary literature it is mainly detective and thriller writers who have gained an international readership. Jan Guillou's Carl Hamilton spy novels have attracted a wide audience largely thanks to films starring Stellan Skarsgård, while the detective stories of Henning Mankell (b. 1948), featuring Inspector Kurt Wallander, have become bestsellers in a number of countries. Astrid Lindgren heads the list of renowned Swedish children's authors, with characters such as Pippi Longstocking and Emil.

ART & ARCHITECTURE

Sweden's age of greatness as the dominant power in northern Europe in the 17th century produced a flowering of art and architecture. Three generations of the Tessin family made their mark: Nicodemus Tessin the Elder (1615–81), who created the Baroque palace of Drottningholm, his son Nicodemus the Younger (1654–1728), who designed Stockholm's Royal Palace, and his grandson, Carl Gustaf (1695–1770), who was an artistic mentor to Gustav III and introduced the Rococo style to Sweden with Carl Hårleman. The sculptor and artist Johan Tobias Sergel (1740–1814) is another influential figure from the Gustavian period.

The period around 1900 was a golden age in Swedish painting. The best-known National Romantic artist was Anders Zorn (1860–1920) from Dalarna, whose paintings of female nudes in the landscape won acclaim. The Stockholm Archipelago featured in the work of Bruno Liljefors (1860–1939), whose lifelike animal paintings are beloved by Swedes. Carl Larsson's idyllic scenes from his Dalarna home, Sundborn, documented in the book *A Home* (1899), have become firm favourites in Sweden and abroad *(see p237)*.

Carl Milles (1875–1955) was one of Sweden's best-known sculptors internationally and several of his monumental works are on public display around Stockholm and at his former home, Millesgården, on the island of Lidingö *(see p95)*.

Architect Gunnar Asplund (1885–1940) was a pioneer of the Functionalist style in the 1920s and 30s, with works such as Stockholm's City Library *(see p99)* and Skogskyrkogården cemetery's crematorium *(see p105)*.

MUSIC

Classical Swedish music has not attracted major attention abroad, but opera singers have become big

ABBA, the most internationally successful Swedish pop group

names on the international stage. The "Swedish nightingale" Jenny Lind (1820–87) and Christina Nilsson (1843–1921) won international acclaim. They were followed by Birgit Nilsson (b. 1918), renowned for her interpretation of Wagner, while Jussi Björling (1911–60) was the great tenor of his age *(see p237)*.

Swedish pop music became a major export industry in the late 20th century, with the advent of groups such as ABBA, the Cardigans, Ace of Base, and the duo Roxette, all of which have had considerable success abroad.

FILM & PHOTOGRAPHY

SILENT FILMS soon became an important art form in Sweden and directors such as Victor Sjöström *(The Phantom Carriage,* 1920), and Mauritz Stiller *(Song of the Scarlet Flower,* 1918), got breaks in Hollywood. Stiller was responsible for launching the enigmatic Greta Garbo *(see p105),* later to star in *Anna Karenina* (1935) and *Camille* (1937). The next big star was Ingrid Bergman, forever remembered for her role in *Casablanca* (1943).

The film genius and multi-Oscar-winning director Ingmar Bergman became internationally synonymous with Swedish film in the 1950s and 60s. *The Seventh Seal* (1957), *The Virgin Spring* (1960), *The Silence* (1963) and *Fanny and Alexander* (1982) are among his masterpieces.

The art of photography has always played an important role in Sweden. Lennart Nilsson, with his voyages of discovery into the inner workings of mankind, such as in *A Child is Born* (1965), has attracted much attention.

Anna Lindh (1957–2003), murdered foreign minister

POLITICS OF PEACE

DAG HAMMARSKJÖLD was one of a line of Swedish peacemakers who have made their mark on world affairs. He became Secretary General of the United Nations in 1953 and was awarded the Nobel Prize for Peace in 1961 after his death in a plane crash during the Congo crisis.

Another Swedish diplomat who met an unfortunate fate was Raoul Wallenberg, who organized the rescue of 100,000 Hungarian Jews in World War II. In 1944 he was captured by the Russians and never seen again.

More recently, the gunning down in Stockholm of two prominent politicians and peace campaigners shocked the nation: prime minister Olof Palme in 1986 and foreign minister Anna Lindh in 2003.

Ingrid Bergman (1915–82)

SCIENCE & TECHNOLOGY

FOR A SMALL COUNTRY, Sweden has an unusually large number of genius inventors. The 18th century produced the father of botany, Carl von Linné *(see p128)*; Anders Celsius, the man behind the temperature scale; and chemists Carl Wilhelm von Scheele, who discovered elements such as oxygen, nitrogen and chlorine, and Jöns Jacob Berzelius, who systematized chemistry and introduced chemical symbols.

Inventors included John Ericsson (1803–89),

locomotive and screw-propeller designer and creator of the first modern naval war vessel *Monitor (see p235);* the telephone pioneer L M Ericsson (1846–1926); and the inventor of dynamite Alfred Nobel (1833–96), whose fortune was used to establish the prestigious Nobel Prize.

SPORT

INTEREST IN SPORT has always been strong in Sweden and the nation has had many international successes. Cross-country skiers such as Mora-Nisse Karlsson, Sixten Jernberg, Gunde Svahn and Per Elofsson have Olympic medals under their belts; and in alpine skiing, no-one has yet eclipsed Ingemar Stenmark. Women's skiing was long dominated by Pernilla Wiberg, whose mantle has now been taken by Anja Pärsson. Professional ice hockey players such as Peter Forsberg and Markus Näslund are among the foremost players in the North American National Hockey League.

Tennis greats have included Björn Borg, Mats Wilander and Stefan Edberg, while in table tennis Jan-Ove Waldner holds his own against the top Chinese players. The world's best woman golfer in 2003 was a Swede, Annika Sörenstam.

Swedish athletes have also reached the top, including high jumpers Kajsa Bergkvist and Stefan Holm.

Annika Sörenstam, the world's top female golfer, 2003

SWEDEN THROUGH THE YEAR

THANKS TO SWEDEN'S geographical location, it experiences wide variations in seasons and climate. Winter retains its icy hold on the north until May, when in the south Skåne is already basking in sunshine. Once spring gets going in the north and the days lengthen, nature soon catches up. Summers are pleasantly warm throughout Sweden and that is when Swedes head off into the countryside to swim and enjoy the

The crocus, a sign of spring

outdoor life, often staying in a summer cottage.

The holiday period from June to August is the height of the tourist season, with the widest range of attractions on offer. In winter, Swedes make for the mountains, which see the first snowfall as early as November. They value their festivals, and events such as Christmas, New Year, Easter, Midsummer's Eve and Walpurgis are celebrated with enthusiasm.

An April start for the salmon fly-fishing season in Mörrum

SPRING

AFTER THE LONG, dark Swedish winter, spring makes a welcome appearance. In Skåne the migratory birds return and spring flowers bloom in March, while in the north it's mid-May before winter releases its hold. Traditionally eaten before Lent, the *semla* cream bun is a tempting treat. Walpurgis Night, on the last day of April, marks a farewell to winter with folk dancing, torchlight processions, student choirs, bonfires and fireworks.

Semla bun

MARCH

Vasa Ski Race *(early Mar)*. World famous long-distance ski race *(see p245)*.
Stockholm International Boat Show *(early Mar)*. The spring's major boat exhibition at Stockholm International Fairs in Älvsjö.

Spring Salon *(Mar)*. Annual art exhibition featuring new artists at Liljevalchs Konsthall in Djurgården, Stockholm.
Åselenappet *(end of Mar)*. Ice-fishing competition, the high point of the winter market in Åsele, Lapland.

APRIL

Start of Salmon Fishing Season, Mörrum *(1 Apr)*, Sweden's main salmon river *(see p187)*.
The "crane dance", Hornborgasjön *(mid-Apr)*. Several thousand cranes gather on the fields around this lake in Västergötland for their annual mating dance.
Walpurgis Night *(30 Apr)*. Around the country bonfires welcome spring, with students donning their white caps and making merry. In the student town of Uppsala, Walpurgis Night also includes fine student choirs, a river-rafting carnival and many other events.

MAY

May Day *(1 May)*. Workers' processions countrywide.
Linné's birthday, Stenbrohult *(23 May)*. The father of botany is commemorated at his childhood home in Småland.
Gärdet Kite Festival, Stockholm *(last weekend in May)*. The Arts College's spectacular kite competition. Great day for a picnic.
Elite Race *(last weekend in May)*. International trotting competition at Solvalla.
"Tjejtrampet", Gärdet *(last weekend in May)*. The 40-km (25-mile) women-only cycling competition.
Trollhättan waterfalls *(weekends in May)*. Magnificent falls, usually tamed by the power station, burst into life.

Walpurgis Night bonfire, at Riddarholmen, Stockholm

Midsummer celebrations at Skansen open-air museum, Stockholm

SUMMER

THE SCHOOL YEAR finishes in early June and summer comes into its own with Midsummer celebrations and dancing round the maypole. Evenings are often warm and the nights light, encouraging parties round the clock. In the far north the sun doesn't even set. July is traditionally the main holiday month and favourite spots can become crowded. But Sweden is big and there's room for everyone. The start of the school term at the end of August coincides with two popular culinary festivals celebrating crayfish and fermented Baltic herring.

JUNE

Stockholm Marathon (*first Sat in Jun*). One of the world's 10 biggest marathons with around 15,000 runners.
Archipelago Boat Day, Stockholm (*first Wed in Jun*). Classic steamboats assemble at Strömkajen for a round trip to Vaxholm.
National Day (*6 Jun*). Not a public holiday, National Day is celebrated around the country as Swedish Flag Day. The royal family attend the celebrations at Skansen in Stockholm.
Postrodden Mail Boat Race, Grisslehamn (*Sat before Midsummer*). Rowing race to the Åland islands following the old mail route.
"Vätternrundan" (*mid-Jun*). Classic cycling race 300 km (190 miles) round Lake Vättern with up to 17,000 participants, starting and finishing in Motala.

Midsummer's Eve (*penultimate Sat in Jun*). A major Swedish festival celebrated by dancing around a flower-bedecked maypole. Midsummer in Dalarna, Rättvik and Mora is especially rich in tradition with folk music and the wearing of colourful national costumes.

JULY

Gotland Race (*first week in Jul*). Major international sailing race around Gotland, starting and finishing in Sandhamn in the Stockholm Archipelago.
Skule Song Festival (*first weekend in Jul*). One of Sweden's largest singing festivals, held at the foot of the Skule mountain on the High Coast.
Hälsinge Hambo (*early Jul*). Folk-dancing competition in Hårga, Bollnäs and Arbrå, with the finals in Järvsö.
Vansbro Swim (*mid-Jul*). Up to 5,000 people take part in the 3-km (2-mile) swim in the Vanån and Västerdalälven rivers, starting in Vansbro.
Stånga Games, Gotland (*mid-Jul*). Events featuring Gotland sports such as Square-and-border-ball, The Stone, Gotlandic Pole Throwing and "Hook the Bottom".
Gammelvala Brunnskog, Värmland (*end of Jul*). Week-long festival celebrating the domestic skills of the past. Music, exhibitions, drama and local food.
Storsjöyran Festival (*end of Jul*). Week-long festival in "the Republic of Jämtland" with drama, exhibitions, films, and concluding with a

huge pop and rock festival.
Music in the Kingdom of Crystal, Småland's Glassworks (*end of Jul*). Folk music, choral singing, opera, wind bands and jazz in a charming setting.
Kukkolaforsen Whitefish Festival (*last weekend in Jul*). Celebrations in Sweden and Finland to mark the whitefish reaching the Torneälven river, which forms the border between the two countries. The fish are caught in large nets and eaten grilled or smoked.

AUGUST

Skänninge Market, Östergötland (*Thu after first Wed in Aug*). One of Sweden's most traditional markets, attracting 100,000 visitors to this medieval city.
Royal Philharmonic Orchestra Outdoor Concert, Stockholm (*2nd Sun in Aug*). This concert on the lawn outside Sjöhistoriska Museet is one of the highlights of the season.
Gotland Medieval Week (*early Aug*). Visby once more becomes a 14th-century Hanseatic city with tournaments, plays and music and participants in colourful medieval costumes.
Hjo Accordion Festival (*2nd weekend in Aug*). Accordion players meet in Hjo on the shores of Lake Vättern.

Crayfish

Crayfish and Fermented Herring (*end of Aug*). Although there is no longer a statutory start date for eating these national delicacies – accompanied by ice-cold schnapps, cheese and silly paper hats – this is when Swedes party the most.

Medieval Week tournament in Visby, Gotland

Beech forest in autumn at Söderåsen, Skåne

AUTUMN

THE NIGHTS may be drawing in, but the mornings are light and the days often crisp and clear. In late autumn deciduous trees provide a stunning display of colours. It's harvest time in the forests and countryside, and a wide variety of delicious edible mushrooms, as well as blueberries, lingonberries and the red-gold cloudberries of the northern marshes are all ripe for the picking.

SEPTEMBER

Oxhälja Market, Filipstad *(early Sep)*. Traditional market in eastern Värmland.

Riddarfjärden Regatta *(first weekend in Sep)*. Stockholmers line the quay to watch hundreds of fine old wooden boats compete.

Chanterelles

Swedish Trotting Derby, Jägersro *(Sep)*. Sweden's top four year-olds compete for the derby title on the trotting track in Malmö.

Halland Salmon Festival *(end Sep)*. In celebration of salmon, the pride of the province, the festival includes fishing, best salmon dish competitions and the crowning of the Salmon King.

OCTOBER

Lidingö Race *(first weekend in Oct)*. The world's largest cross-country race, with tens of thousands of competitors, including elite runners, senior citizens and children.

Harvest Festival, Öland *(early Oct)*. Sweden's biggest harvest festival takes place over four days around Michaelmas, with more than 1,000 events attracting 200,000 visitors to enjoy local food, concerts and exhibitions.

Umeå International Jazz Festival *(end Oct)*. Leading jazz festival, first staged in the 1960s.

Climate

Considerable variations in climate from north to south sometimes result in southern Sweden having no snow and temperatures above freezing in winter, while the north is blanketed in thick snow. The differences are less extreme in summer. The effect of the North Atlantic and the Gulf Stream is felt on the west coast in mild damp winds and the highest rainfall.

STOCKHOLM

°C/°F	Apr	Jul	Oct	Jan
Max	9/48	22/76	10/50	-1/30
Min	1/34	13/55	5/41	-5/23
☀ hours	6	8	3	1
☂ mm	30	72	50	39

GOTHENBURG

Average maximum temperature
Average minimum temperature
Average daily hours of sunshine
Average monthly rainfall

°C/°F	Apr	Jul	Oct	Jan
Max	10/50	21/70	12/54	1/34
Min	2/36	13/55	6/43	-3/27
☀ hours	6	8	3	1
☂ mm	41	68	83	61

MALMÖ

°C/°F	Apr	Jul	Oct	Jan
Max	10/50	21/70	12/54	2/36
Min	2/36	13/55	7/45	-3/27
☀ hours	6	7	3	1
☂ mm	38	61	57	49

ÖSTERSUND

°C/°F	Apr	Jul	Oct	Jan
Max	5/41	19/66	6/43	-6/21
Min	-3/27	10/50	1/34	-13/9
☀ hours	6	7	2	1
☂ mm	32	86	45	36

LULEÅ

°C/°F	Apr	Jul	Oct	Jan
Max	4/39	20/68	6/43	-7/19
Min	-4/25	11/52	0/32	-16/3
☀ hours	7	10	7	0.6
☂ mm	29	50	50	40

WINTER

WHILE CHRISTMAS does not always go hand in hand with snow in southern Sweden, there are plenty of opportunities for ice-skating and there's always a chance of a white January. The mountains become a paradise for skiers, while snow cannons help out elsewhere if nature isn't up to the job. From the first day of Advent, the Christmas season is in full swing, culminating in present-giving on Christmas Eve. Restaurants enjoy their busiest time and Lucia processions brighten the winter darkness.

NOVEMBER

Gustav Adolf Day (6 Nov). Gothenburg celebrates the royal founder of the city on the anniversary of his death (see p195).
St Martin's Day (10–11 Nov). Roast goose and "black soup" containing goose blood are served at parties for St Martin of Tours and Martin Luther.

DECEMBER

Nobel Day (10 Dec). The year's Nobel Prize laureates are honoured in a ceremony at Konserthuset (Concert Hall) and a banquet in Stadshuset (City Hall) attended by the King and Queen.
Lucia Celebrations (13 Dec). Sweden's chosen Lucia, with her girl attendants and "star boys", serves the Nobel laureates morning coffee with saffron buns and

performs traditional songs. In the evening a Lucia procession winds through the capital to celebrations and fireworks at Skansen. Similar Lucia processions take place throughout Sweden and, on a smaller scale, in many homes and schools.
Christmas Markets throughout Sweden (from early Dec). The markets at Skansen and Stortorget in Stockholm are particularly atmospheric.
Christmas (24–26 Dec). Filled with traditions, Christmas is the most important Swedish holiday. The main

Lucia, the "Queen of Light", with her attendants at Skansen

event is Christmas Eve when an abundant smörgåsbord is followed by gifts. Christmas Day often begins with a church service.
New Year (31 Dec–1 Jan). People go out on the town. Celebrations are televised from Skansen, including a traditional midnight reading of Tennyson's "Ring out wild bells..." Church bells peal and there are spectacular fireworks displays.

Northern Lights over Jokkmokk on a cold winter night

JANUARY

Hindersmässan (end Jan). Market in Örebro dating back to medieval times.
Ice Globe Theatre, Jukkasjärvi (mid Jan). Shakespeare season opens at the theatre in ice (see p272).

FEBRUARY

Jokkmokks Winter Market (first weekend in Feb). Colourful festival with traditional market, Sami reindeer sledding and races.
Gothenburg Boat Show (early Feb). New boats on show at the Swedish Exhibition Centre in Gothenburg.
Vikingarännet (as soon as the ice holds). Long-distance ski race over 80 km (50 miles) on Lake Mälaren from Uppsala to Stockholm.
Globen Gala (2nd half of Feb). Athletes converge on Globen arena for this top indoor competition.

Frozen Riddarfjärden in Stockholm as a winter park

PUBLIC HOLIDAYS

New Year's Day (1 Jan)
Epiphany (6 Jan)
Good Friday (Mar/Apr)
Easter Monday (Mar/Apr)
Ascension Day (6th Thu after Easter)
Labour Day (1 May)
Whit Monday (May/Jun)
Midsummer (Jun)
Christmas Day (25 Dec)
Boxing Day (26 Dec)

THE HISTORY OF SWEDEN

DESCRIBED IN THE 4TH CENTURY BC *as a land of frozen seas and midnight sun, this northerly nation of reindeer herders also produced the fearsome Viking traders of the 9th century. By the 17th century, Sweden, in its Age of Greatness, ruled supreme over the Baltic region. Vanquished by Russia in 1809, the country adopted a more peaceful role and today is heavily engaged in world affairs.*

In the last 100,000 years, Sweden has been covered by thick inland ice on at least three occasions. As the ice retreated northwards for the last time in approximately 12,000 BC, nomadic reindeer hunters moved in to use the newly revealed land, but it was not until 6500 BC that Sweden was entirely free of ice.

Rune stone, 9th century

Farming was gradually adopted in southern Sweden from 4000 BC, while hunting continued to remain prevalent in the inland areas of Norrland for a long time to come. The first examples of domestic pottery date from this period and burial mounds appeared in the southern provinces.

Finds from the Bronze Age (1800–500 BC) bear witness to increased contact with the outside world. A chieftain society based on power and social alliances began to develop. Magnificent bronze objects, huge burial mounds and cairns with grave goods as well as rock carvings date from this period *(see p212)*.

The transition to the Iron Age in 500 BC saw the first written accounts about Scandinavia. In the 4th century BC the Greek explorer and trader, Phytheas of Massilia, described the journey to "Thule", with its frozen seas and midnight sun. In his *Germania* (AD 98), the Roman Tacitus refers to the *"sviones"* as a powerful people with strong men, weapons and fleets.

With the growth of the Roman Empire, links with the Continent increased and numerous finds show evidence of trade with Rome via the many German tribes in the area north of the Rhine. The fall of Rome and the subsequent period of population migrations saw the rise of small kingdoms across Europe. In Sweden there was a kingdom centred on Uppsala where large *kungshögar* (King's Mounds) can still be seen today *(see p129)*.

From 800 until Christianity reached Sweden in the mid-11th century, the Vikings took the world by storm. As traders, settlers and plunderers, they set sail in search of land, slaves and treasure. They carried out raids throughout Europe, sailed as far as Baghdad and even reached America. Christian monks wrote of attacks on rich monasteries and towns. But the Vikings were more than wild barbarians. They were also hard-working farmers, traders, experienced sailors, craftsmen and shipbuilders.

TIMELINE

c. 12,000 BC Thick ice covers the country. As the ice retreats, reindeer herders gradually move into the southernmost coastal area

1500 BC Regional provinces build barrows and cairns to powerful men and women

500 BC Early Iron Age; a worsening climate and a decline in agriculture

Viking ship c. 980

12 000 BC	4000 BC	2000 BC	AD	500	1000

4000 BC Farming is gradually adopted in the south of the land

3700 BC Burials take place in chambered mounds, creating the first monuments in the Swedish countryside

1800 BC Bronze objects start to be made in Sweden along continental lines

AD 98 Tacitus refers to the *sviones* in his writings

800 The Viking period begins and the trading centre of Birka in Lake Mälaren is founded

◁ *Gustav Vasa* **(1523–60), painting by Cornelius Arendtz**

CHRISTIANITY AND THE BIRTH OF A KINGDOM

During the 11th and 12th centuries several families from different provinces battled for power over the central part of what is known today as Sweden. The country was more like a federation of self-governing provinces, a number of which, for a limited time, had influence over those around them.

Little is known of the kings and chieftains in the early Middle Ages other than brief mentions in sagas. In the 11th century, King Olof Skötkonung (d. 1020) was converted to Christianity and was baptized in 1008, along with his sons Anund Jakob (d. 1050) and Edmund the Old (d. 1060).

Birger Jarl's seal

Thereafter power passed to the Stenkil family, which had strong links with Västergötland where the Christian church had gained the most influence.

The church and the gradual transition to Christianity underway in the 12th century were vital to the growing power of the king. The priests brought with them an administrative tradition, a civil service and a rational system for regulating property. The church also reinforced the strength of the king ideologically through the idea that his power was derived from God.

Once the Stenkil dynasty came to an end around 1120, the royal houses of Västergötland (Erik) and Östergötland (Sverker) battled for supremacy. Both families died out in the first half of the 13th century at the time when the power of the *riksjarl* (earl) was at its height. The *riksjarl* was the king's most important statesman and the position gained greater influence through Birger Magnusson, known as Birger Jarl, who became *riksjarl* in 1248 under King Erik Eriksson. Until his death in 1266, Birger Jarl was the de facto wielder of power in Sweden, which by then had developed into a medieval kingdom similar to those elsewhere in Europe.

THE HANSEATIC LEAGUE AND THE BJÄLBO DYNASTY'S POWER STRUGGLE

The 13th century saw the founding of many of the medieval towns still standing today. Documents show that Stockholm existed as a town in 1252, four years after Birger Jarl became *riksjarl*. In 1289 it was described as the largest town in Sweden, but it was not yet a capital city. Its importance lay in its role as a trading centre, particularly for the German Hanseatic League, during the 14th century. The Hanseatic League had previously established a base in Visby on Gotland, which was one of its most important centres. In some places, the Hansa influence was so great that the king had to prevent Germans from holding more than half of the leading positions in the town.

Through Birger Jarl's son, Valdemar, elected king in 1250, power passed to

King Olof Skötkonung's baptism at Husaby well in Västergötland, 1008

TIMELINE

1080 Pagan revolt replaces the Christian, Inge the Elder, by the Svea family, who choose Blot-Sven as king	**1143** Alvastra monastery in Östergötland is founded by Cistercians		*Birger Jarl*	**1248** Birger Jarl is *riksjarl*, the king's foremost statesman

1100		**1150**		**1200**		**1250**

| **1008** Olof Skötkonung is baptized a Christian in Västergötland | **1101** The meeting of the three kings in Kungahälla sets the borders of the Nordic countries | **1130** Östergötland chief Sverker the Elder elected king | **1222** The last of the Sverker dynasty, Johan Sverkersson, dies and is succeeded by Erik Eriksson | **1250** Erik Eriksson is succeeded by Valdemar Birgersson, son of Birger Jarl and first of the Folkung dynasty |

the Bjälbo dynasty. Valdemar was replaced after a revolt by his brother Magnus Ladulås who was elected king in 1275. During Magnus's reign, Swedish legislation was reformed and the Ordinance of Alsnö of 1280 granted the nobility and church far-reaching privileges and freedom from taxation.

The king's nickname, Ladulås (literally "lock barn"), is said to derive from his ban on nobles from helping themselves to sustenance from peasants' barns when travelling.

On Magnus' death in 1290, his son Birger was still a minor and Sweden was ruled by a regency. Once the king reached his majority in 1303, a power struggle broke out between Birger and his brothers, Dukes Erik and Valdemar. Sweden was divided between the brothers until in 1317 Birger invited Erik and Valdemar to a banquet at Nyköping Castle and had them both imprisoned and left to die. Soon, Birger himself was forced to flee the country after a revolt and Magnus Eriksson, the three year-old son of Duke Erik, was elected king of Sweden in 1319.

Magnus's rule was characterized by severe domestic opposition and financial problems. Sweden also suffered the Black Death in 1350 in which one-third of the population died. The crisis led to the Swedish nobles in 1363 appealing to the Duke of Mecklenburg, whose son Albrecht was hailed king of Sweden the following year.

THE KALMAR UNION

Albrecht of Mecklenburg came to the throne with the support of the nobility, who reacted with a revolt when he subsequently sought to wield his own power. The nobles were backed by Queen Margareta of Denmark-Norway and Albrecht was defeated at

Beheading of 100 members of the Swedish nobility in the Stockholm Bloodbath, 1520

Fallköping in 1389, after which Denmark, Norway and Sweden came under the rule of Denmark. At a meeting in Kalmar in 1397, Margareta's nephew, Erik of Pomerania, was crowned king of Denmark, Norway and Sweden, thus establishing the Kalmar Union, which lasted until 1523.

The unification period was characterized by conflict in Sweden. Under Erik of Pomerania there was great dissatisfaction with newly-introduced taxes. A peasant revolt, known as the Engelbrekt revolt after its legendary leader, led to Erik being deposed in 1439. The Kalmar Union was unable to control the Council of State or the castles, and Sweden lacked a recognized supreme authority. Subsequent Danish kings were recognized as rulers in Sweden only for a few years and in between the country was controlled by representatives of the nobility.

At the Battle of Brunkeberg in Stockholm in 1471, the Danish King Christian I sought to enforce his power in Sweden, but was defeated by the viceroy, Sten Sture the Elder. A new Danish crusade under Christian II in 1520 culminated in the notorious Stockholm Bloodbath in which 100 Swedish nobles were executed.

1275 Magnus Ladulås elected king of Sweden at Mora Stones	**1349–50** Black Death rampages through Sweden	**1364** Albrecht of Mecklenburg elected king of Sweden	*Queen Margareta*	**1434** Engelbrekt leads revolt over the taxes and burdens imposed by the Kalmar Union	
1300		**1350**	**1400**		**1450**
1280 Ordinance of Alsnö grants freedom from taxation to the nobility		**1350** Magnus Eriksson's law applies throughout the land, although cities have their own laws	**1397** The Kalmar Union unites the Nordic countries under Queen Margareta	**1471** Sten Sture the Elder defeats Danish King Christian I at Brunkeberg	**1520** Swedish nobles executed in the Stockholm Bloodbath

Gustav Vasa making his ceremonial entry into Stockholm, Midsummer Day, 1523

THE VASA ERA

Among the nobles fortunate to avoid execution in the Stockholm Bloodbath was the young Gustav Eriksson. At the end of 1520 Gustav organized an army to oust the Danish King Christian from Sweden. Gustav was successful and on 6 June 1523 – later to become Sweden's National Day – he was named king. On Midsummer Day the new monarch, Gustav Vasa, made his ceremonial entry into war-torn Stockholm.

When Gustav Vasa took the throne, he discovered a nation in financial crisis. He called on parliament to pass a controversial law transferring the property of the church to the state, which then became the country's most important source of economic power. Another important result of this policy was the gradual separation from Catholicism and the adoption of the Lutheran State Church, which was to remain tied to the state until 2000.

During his reign, Gustav Vasa implemented tough economic policies in order to concentrate central power in Stockholm. This effective dictatorship also resulted in the Swedish parliament's decision in 1544 to make the monarchy hereditary.

Descendants of Gustav Vasa oversaw the rise of Sweden into one of Europe's great powers. During the reign of Gustav's eldest son Erik XIV (r. 1561–69), there were wars against Denmark, Lübeck and Poland. His brothers dethroned him. Erik died in prison, possibly by eating pea soup poisoned by his brother Johan III. During the reign of Karl IX, the third son, Sweden waged war against Denmark and Russia.

Portrait of Erik XIV (1561)

GUSTAV II ADOLF AND KRISTINA

When the next king, Gustav II Adolf, came to power in 1611, Sweden was involved in wars against Russia, Poland and Denmark. This reign came to be as remarkable as that of his grandfather and under his rule Sweden steadily increased its influence over the Baltic region. It was also in the 17th

TIMELINE

Vasa coat of arms

1523 Gustav Vasa is chosen as king and marches into Stockholm	**1542** Nils Dacke leads a peasants revolt in Småland	**1560** Gustav Vasa dies	**1568** Erik XIV imprisoned by his brothers at Gripsholms Slott	**1611** Gustav II Adolf becomes king
			1577 Erik XIV dies, probably poisoned	
1525		**1550**	**1575**	**1600**
1527 Reformation parliament confiscates church property	**1544** Hereditary monarchy established for Gustav Vasa's descendants	**1561** Eric XIV is crowned king and his brothers' powers curbed	**1570** Nordic Seven Years War ends	**1587** Johan III's son Sigismund chosen as king of Poland
			1569 Johan III crowned in Stockholm	**1612** Axel Oxenstierna made State Chancellor

century that Stockholm started to develop into the country's political and administrative centre. In 1630 Gustav II Adolf, with his influential chancellor Axel Oxenstierna, decided to intervene in the Thirty Years War *(see p36)*, first on the side of the Protestants, then in an alliance with France. Sweden had some military successes during the war, but paid a heavy price for winning the bloody battle at Lützen in 1632, as the king was killed in action.

Gustav II Adolf's only child, Kristina, came to the throne at the age of six. During her reign (1633–54), life at court was influenced by the world of science and philosophy. Kristina's reluctance to marry resulted in her cousin, Karl Gustav, becoming Crown Prince. Kristina abdicated and left for Rome, where she converted to Catholicism, a sensation at the time.

Young Karl XII with the widowed queen on his arm leaving the burning Tre Kronor Palace, 1697

Queen Kristina corresponding with leading scientists and philosophers of the time

THE CAROLIAN ERA

Karl X Gustav (1654–60) was the first of three Karls to reign. At the height of Sweden's era as a great power, he defeated Denmark by leading his army across the frozen waters of the Great Belt *(see p36)*, thus gaining Sweden's

southernmost provinces. Karl XI (1660–97) secured the border and divided the land more evenly between crown, nobility and peasants.

While the body of Karl XI lay in state at Tre Kronor in 1697, a fire broke out which destroyed most of the building. The new monarch was the teenage Karl XII (1697–1718). He faced awesome problems when Denmark, Poland and Russia formed an alliance in 1700 with the aim of crushing the power of Sweden. Karl XII set off to battle.

Denmark and Poland were soon forced to plead for peace, but Russia was a harder nut to crack. A bold push towards Moscow was unsuccessful and the Swedish army suffered a devastating defeat at Poltava in Ukraine in 1709. This marked the beginning of the end of Sweden's Age of Greatness.

Karl XII, possibly the most written about and controversial Swedish monarch, returned to Sweden in 1715 after an absence of 15 years. His plans to regain Sweden's position of dominance never came to fruition and he was killed in Norway in 1718. Sweden was in crisis. Crop failures and epidemics had wiped out one third of the population and the state's finances were drained.

1617 Death penalty introduced for conversion to Catholicism

1632 Gustav II Adolf killed at Battle of Lützen

1633 Six-year-old Kristina becomes queen

1654 Kristina abdicates; Karl X Gustav is crowned

1655 Kristina converts to Catholicism and is ceremonially greeted in Rome

1697 Tre Kronor castle destroyed by fire; 15-year-old Karl XII crowned

1625	1650	1675	1700

1618 Thirty Years War starts in Germany

Gustav II Adolf

1648 Peace of Westphalia gives Sweden new territories

1658 Sweden acquires new territory, including Skåne, under Peace of Roskilde

1680 Karl XI starts the era of Carolian autocracy and limits powers of the nobility

1709 Swedish army defeated by Peter the Great at Poltava

1718 Karl XII dies during siege of Fredriksten, Norway

Sweden's Age of Greatness

For more than a century (1611–1721) Sweden was the dominant power in northern Europe, and the Baltic was effectively a Swedish inland sea. The country was at its most powerful after the Peace of Roskilde in 1658, when Sweden acquired seven new provinces. Outside today's frontiers, the Swedish Empire covered Finland, large parts of the Baltic states, and important areas of northern Germany. Over 111 years as a great power Sweden spent 72 of them at war, but the period also marked great cultural development and more efficient state administration. Treasures were brought back as trophies and grand palaces were built.

SWEDISH EMPIRE

☐ *Sweden's empire after the Peace of Roskilde, 1658*

The Tre Kronor Castle
Built as a defensive tower in the 1180s, the Tre Kronor castle was the seat of Swedish monarchs from the 1520s and became the administrative centre of the Swedish Empire. Named after the three crowns on the spire, it burned down in 1697.

The columns of troops
ride out over the shifting ice
towards Danish Lolland.

THE THIRTY YEARS WAR

A major European war raged from 1618–48, largely on German soil. Sweden entered the fray in 1630 and joined forces with France in 1631 against the Austrian Habsburgs. The Swedish army had been reorganized and rearmed by Gustav II Adolf and immediately had successes at the battles of Breitenfeld (1630) and Lützen (1632), where the king was killed in action.

Later the Swedes pressed into southern Germany and also captured Prague (1648). Rich cultural treasures were brought home from the war. In 1648 the Peace of Westphalia gave Sweden several important possessions in northern Germany.

The death of Gustav II Adolf at the Battle of Lützen in 1632

Stockholm in 1640
The city's transformation from a small medieval town into a capital city can be seen in the network of straight streets, similar to the present layout.

Karl XI's Triumphs
The ceiling painting in Karl XI's gallery at the Royal Palace (see p56) by the French artist Jacques Foucquet (1693) shows in allegoric form the king's victories at Halmstad, Lund and Landskrona.

Field Marshal Count Carl Gustav Wrangel *(see p127)*

Karl X Gustav himself leads the Swedish army of 17,000 men.

The Powerful Nobility
The nobility were very influential in the Empire era and many successful soldiers were ennobled. The Banér family coat of arms from 1651 is adorned by three helmets and barons' crowns.

Karl X Gustav
Portrait of Karl X Gustav (r. 1654–60) as a general. It was in this role that he became known throughout Europe during the final phase of the Thirty Years War.

CROSSING THE GREAT BELT
When Denmark declared war on Sweden in autumn 1657, the Swedish army was in Poland. Marching west, it captured the Danish mainland, but without the navy was unable to continue to Copenhagen. However, unusually severe weather froze the sea, making it possible for the soldiers to cross the ice of the Great Belt, and the Danes had to surrender.

Karl XII's Pocket Watch
The warrior king's watch-case dates from 1700. It shows the state coat of arms, as well as those of the 49 provinces that belonged to Sweden at that time.

Karl XII's Last Journey
After he was hit by a fatal bullet at Fredrikshald in Norway (1718), the king's body was taken first to Swedish territory then on to Uddevalla for embalming. Painting by Gustav Cederström (1878).

Gustav III with the white armband he wore when mounting his *coup d'etat* in 1772

THE AGE OF LIBERTY AND THE GUSTAVIAN ERA

A new constitution came into force in 1719 which transferred power from the monarch to parliament. As a result, Sweden developed a system of parliamentary democracy similar to that of Britain at the time.

The "Age of Liberty" coincided with the Enlightenment, with dramatic advances in culture, science and industry. The botanist Carl von Linné became one of the most famous Swedes of his time. Another was the scientist, philosopher and author Emanuel Swedenborg, who is thought to have influenced both Balzac and Baudelaire. The production of textiles expanded in Stockholm, and Sweden's first hospital was constructed on Kungsholmen.

Changes in the balance of power around 1770 gave the new king, Gustav III, an opportunity to strike in an attempt to regain his monarchical powers. On 19 August 1772 Gustav accompanied the guards' parade to the Royal Palace where, in front of his life-guards, he declared his intention to mount a *coup d'etat*. The guards and other military units in Stockholm swore allegiance to the king, who tied a white handkerchief round his arm as a badge and rode out into the city to be acclaimed by his people. Absolute power had been restored.

Gustav III was influenced by the Age of Enlightenment and by French culture, which had a great effect on Swedish life *(see pp40–41)*. Over the years opposition grew to the king's powers, largely because of his costly war against Russia. In 1792 he was murdered by a nobleman during a masked ball at the Opera House.

Gustav III was succeeded by his son, Gustav IV Adolf. During his reign Sweden was dragged into the Napoleonic wars. After a war against Russia in 1808–9, Sweden lost Finland, which at the time accounted for one-third of Swedish territory. The king was deposed and went into exile.

THE ERA OF KARL JOHAN AND BOURGEOIS LIBERALISM

By the early 19th century the absolute powers of the monarch had been removed for all time, and the privileges

Napoleon's former marshal, Jean-Baptiste Bernadotte, as King Karl XIV Johan surrounded by his family

TIMELINE

1719 New constitution transfers power from the king to parliament	**1741** Carl von Linné appointed professor at Uppsala	**1754** Royal family moves into Royal Palace	**1780s** Immigrants given religious freedom	**1790** Sweden def Russia at the Battl of Svenskund **1792** Gustav III is murdered
1720	**1740**	**1760**	**1780**	**1800**
1738 Parliamentary power is established in the Age of Liberty as the "Hat" party wins elections	*Carl von Linné*	**1772** Gustav III crowned and mounts coup d'etat giving the king absolute power	**1786** Swedish Academy founded **1778** National costume decreed. Death penalty removed for some crimes	

Newspaper readers outside the *Aftonbladet* office in 1841

of the aristocracy were undermined even more in 1809 with a new constitution that divided power between the king, the government and parliament.

With a new class structure and the effect of the French Revolution, a new middle class emerged which also wanted to be more influential. Altercations between middle-class liberals and the conservatives prevailed. One of the best-known newspapers founded at this time was the liberal mouthpiece, *Aftonbladet*.

Difficulties in finding a suitable new monarch led to the choice of one of Napoleon's marshals, Jean-Baptiste Bernadotte, who took on the Swedish name of Karl Johan. Founder of the present royal dynasty, Karl XIV Johan continued to speak French and never fully learned Swedish. His French wife, Desirée, found Stockholm a cultural backwater after Paris.

In 1813 a Swedish army, with Karl XIV Johan at its head, became involved in the final battle against Napoleon. The Battle of Leipzig ended in defeat for France, but more significantly for Sweden,

Swedes heading for a new life in North America

Denmark had to hand over Norway to Sweden. The Norwegians were reluctant to unite with Sweden, but after a display of military power in Norway, a union between the two countries was agreed which lasted from 1814 to 1905.

A long era of peace began, and with it came a dramatic increase in population, which grew by 1 million to 3.5 million by 1850. Many Swedes were driven into poverty because of the shortage of work. Mass emigration followed. From the 1850s to the 1930s about 1.5 million people left Sweden, mostly for North America.

SOCIAL MOVEMENTS AND INDUSTRIALIZATION

As Sweden was transformed from an agricultural society into an industrialized country, the problems posed by the population surplus were gradually tackled. Its industrial revolution started around 1850, gathering momentum in the late 19th century, and the textile, timber and iron industries provided the main sources of employment. Here the early and fast development of a coherent railway network played an important role.

Social movements sprang up in the 19th century which still play an important role in Swedish life. One of the first was the temperance movement, which emerged from a background of alcohol abuse – in the 1820s annual consumption of spirits was 46 litres (80 pints) per person.

1809 Sweden loses Finland; Gustav IV Adolf deposed

1810 Parliament chooses Jean-Baptiste Bernadotte as Crown Prince

1842 Elementary schools established

1869 Emigration to North America increases due to crop failures

1876 L M Ericsson starts manufacture of telephones

August Strindberg

1905 Parliament dissolves union with Norway

| 1820 | 1840 | 1860 | 1880 | 1900 |

1818 Karl XIV Johan is crowned King of Sweden and Norway

1814 Sweden gains Norway in peace treaty with Denmark

1856 Sweden's first railway opens

1850 Sweden has 3.5 million inhabitants; 93,000 live in Stockholm

1879 August Strindberg's novel *The Red Room* is published

1908 Royal Dramatic Theatre opens in Stockholm

The Era of Gustav III

GUSTAV III (r. 1771–92) is one of the most colourful figures in Swedish history. The king's great interest in art, literature and the theatre made the late 18th century a golden age for Swedish culture, and several academies were founded at this time. After a bloodless revolution in 1772, Gustav III ruled with absolute power and initiated a wide-ranging programme of reform. But his attacks on the privileges of the nobility and his adventurous and costly foreign policy made him powerful enemies. In 1792 he was murdered during a masked ball at Stockholm's Opera House.

The Swedish Academy
The academy was founded by Gustav III in 1786 to preserve the Swedish language. Members received a token depicting the king's head at every meeting.

Gustav III's Coronation 1772
The coronation of the all-powerful monarch in Stockholm's cathedral was a magnificent ceremony, portrayed here by C G Pilo (1782). Every detail was overseen by Gustav himself, who used his flair for the dramatic in politics as well.

A courtier entertains by reading aloud.

Gustav III studies architectural designs.

COURT LIFE AT DROTTNINGHOLM

Hilleström's painting (1779) gives an insight into court life at Drottningholm, where the king resided between June and November. In what is now the Blue Salon, Gustav III and Queen Sofia Magdalena socialized with their inner circle. Behaviour was modelled on the French court and etiquette was even stricter at Drottningholm than at Versailles.

The Battle of Svensksund
Gustav III was not known as a successful warrior king, but in 1790 he led the Swedish fleet to its greatest victory ever, when it defeated Russia in a major maritime battle in the Gulf of Finland.

Life in the Inns
Stockholm abounded with inns, frequently visited by the city's 70,000 inhabitants. J T Sergel's sketch shows a convivial dinner party.

Murder at the Masked Ball

In 1792 Gustav III fell victim to a conspiracy at the Opera House. He was surrounded by masked men and shot by Captain Anckarström on the crowded stage. He died of his wounds 14 days later.

Gustav III's Mask and Cocked Hat

Despite his mask, Gustav III was easy to recognize since he was wearing the badges of two orders of chivalry. The drama intrigued the whole of Europe and inspired Verdi's opera Un Ballo in Maschera.

Flogging of the King's Murderer

Among the conspirators, only Anckarström was condemned to death. Before he was taken to his execution in Södermalm, he was flogged on three successive days on the square in front of Riddarhuset.

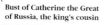

Queen Sofia Magdalena does her needlework.

Bust of Catherine the Great of Russia, the king's cousin

GUSTAVIAN STYLE

The mid-18th century saw the emergence of Neo-Classicism, with the focus on antiquities and Greek

ideals. Gustav III embraced this trend with great enthusiasm and supported the country's talented artists and authors. He established his own Museum of Antiquities *(see p57)* with marble sculptures which he brought home from Italy. In handicrafts, the sweeping lines of Rococo elegance were replaced by the stricter forms of what has become known as Gustavian Style. Rooms at the Royal Palace were renovated with decoration and furnishings adapted to suit this style.

Chair designed in Gustavian style

Swedish Court Costume

In 1778, Gustav III introduced a court costume, based on French lines, for daily wear at court, in order to restrain fashion excesses.

UNIVERSAL SUFFRAGE

Sweden's population reached 5 million around 1900, despite mass emigration to America. Many people moved to the towns to work in industry, and by the early 20th century Stockholm's population was about 300,000, a fourfold increase since the year 1800.

Increasing social awareness and the rise of the Social Democrat and Liberal parties in the early 20th century gave impetus to the demands for universal suffrage. Authors such as August Strindberg became involved. A political battle ensued which was not resolved until 1921, when universal suffrage was introduced for both sexes.

Another question which was hotly debated in the 19th century was the role of the king and the extent of his powers. In his "courtyard speech" at the Royal Palace in 1914, King Gustav V called for military rearmament. This led to a constitutional crisis and the resignation of the Liberal government. After the 1917 election, the king had to accept a government which contained repub-

Branting and Gustav V in conversation, 1909

lican-friendly Social Democrats, including the future prime minister, Hjalmar Branting. By then it was parliament, not the king, that decided what sort of government Sweden should have.

THE GROWTH OF THE WELFARE STATE

In 1936 the Social Democrats and Farmers' Party formed a coalition which developed what was to become known as the welfare state. The Social Democrat prime minister, Per Albin Hansson (1885–1946), defined the welfare state as a socially conscious society with financial security for all. Reforms introduced under this policy included unemployment benefit, paid holidays and childcare. As a result, poverty in Sweden virtually disappeared during the 1930s and 1940s.

The right of everyone to good housing was also part of welfare state policy. Under the principle of "work-home-centre" a new Stockholm suburb, Vällingby, was built in the early 1950s. The idea was to transform the dormitory suburbs into thriving communities where people would both live and work. The concept was unsuccessful. It soon became apparent that the people who lived there still worked somewhere else, and vice versa. The great shortage of housing in the 1960s led to the "million" programme, which involved the building of a million homes in a very short time. These areas soon became known as the "new slums" despite high standards of construction.

Calls for democratic reforms in June 1917 led to riots like this one outside the parliament building in Stockholm

TIMELINE

1920		1940	
1921 Universal suffrage for men and women	**1932** Suicide of industrial magnate Ivar Krueger is followed by stockmarket crash	**1940** Swedish-German agreement on transit of German military personnel	**1958** Women can be ordained as priests
			1955 Obligatory national health insurance
Selma Lagerlöf, winner of the Nobel Prize for Literature, 1909	**1930** Rise of Functionalist style in architecture, stimulated by the Stockholm Exhibition	**1939** Sweden's coalition government declares neutrality in World War II	**1952** Stockholm's first underground railway is inaugurated
			1950 First public TV broadcast in Sweden

THE WAR YEARS

Sweden declared its neutrality during both World Wars I and II. Its policy of continuing to trade with nations involved in the conflict during World War I provoked a number of countries into imposing a trade blockade on Sweden. The situation became so serious that hunger riots broke out in some towns.

World War II proved an even more difficult balancing exercise for Swedish neutrality, largely because its Nordic neighbours were at war. Through a combination of luck and skill, Sweden remained outside the conflict, but the concessions it had to make were strongly criticized both nationally and internationally.

Neutrality stamp issued in 1942

THE POST-WAR ERA

Although the Social Democrats dominated government from the 1930s to the 1970s, the socialist and non-socialist power blocs in Swedish politics have remained fairly evenly matched since World War II.

The policy of non-alignment has not proved an obstacle to Swedish involvement on the international scene, including the United Nations. The country has offered asylum to hundreds of thousands of refugees from wars and political oppression. Prime Minister Olof Palme (1927–86), probably the best-known Swedish politician abroad, was deeply involved in questions of democracy and disarmament, as well as the problems of the Third World. He was renowned for condemning undemocratic acts by right-wing and left-wing dictators. Palme's assassination on the streets of Stockholm in 1986 sent shock waves across the world. The murder has still not been solved.

Important changes took place during the closing decades of the 20th century. These included a new constitution in 1974 which removed the monarch's political powers. In 1995 Sweden joined the European Union after a referendum approved entry by a narrow majority. The start of the new millennium marked a change in the role of the church in Sweden, which severed its connections with the state after more than 400 years.

Sveavägen, the site of Palme's murder, 1986

As Sweden enters the third millennium, the country shows signs of economic downturn, even though most people still lead a good, socially secure life. Rapid technical developments and globalization have given Sweden new job opportunities and new inhabitants, as well as a leading international role in information technology.

The centre of Vällingby, which attracted attention among city planners worldwide in the 1950s

---

1967 Driving on the right introduced

1974 The monarch loses all political powers

1980 New constitution gives women the right of succession to the throne

2000 Öresund Bridge opens between Denmark and Sweden

1986 Prime Minister Olof Palme murdered in Stockholm

2003 Foreign Minister Anna Lindh murdered in Stockholm

1980

2000

1964 Art exhibition at Moderna Museet shows works by Andy Warhol, Roy Lichtenstein and Claes Oldenburg

1974 ABBA pop group wins Eurovision Song Contest

1973 Gustav VI Adolf dies and is succeeded by his grandson, Carl XVI Gustaf

1995 Sweden joins European Union

Crown Princess Victoria

2000 Swedish church separates from the state

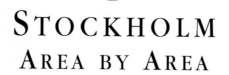

STOCKHOLM
AREA BY AREA

Stockholm at a Glance

STOCKHOLM HAS around 100 museums covering every conceivable subject, as well as buildings of historic and architectural interest, such as Stadhuset (City Hall). The museum collections range from the treasures and antiquities of Kungliga Slottet (the Royal Palace) to the latest in contemporary art at Moderna Museet and the spectacular *Vasa* warship at Vasamuseet. Open spaces abound, and it is even possible to swim in the heart of the city.

Hallwylska Palatset
Thanks to a methodical countess and her impeccable ta this lavishly decorated 1890s' palac has become a mag nificent museum with 67,000 exhib displayed in their original setting.

Stadshuset
This stunning building opened in 1923 is the seat of the capital's government and a symbol of Stockholm. It is also the venue for the annual Nobel Prize festivities.

VASASTADEN

CITY

KUNGS-HOLMEN

0 metres   500
0 yards   500

Swimming in the City
During the summer, swimmers bathe in the clean, warm water (about 20 °C/68 °F) in the city centre. Långholmen (see p102) has sandy beaches and smooth rocks – an ideal setting for a dip.

GA
ST.

Kungliga Slottet
In addition to its own attractions, the Royal Palace has four specialis museums: the Treasury, featuring Erik XIV's orb (1561), the Royal Armoury, Gustav III's Museum of Antiquities, and Tre Kronor Museur

Nordiska Museet

This enormous building, opened in 1907, houses many different artifacts illustrating Swedish life and customs, including this coat of Count Axel von Fersen (1780s).

Nationalmuseum

The National Museum of Fine Arts, Sweden's largest art gallery, has superb collections of 17th- and 18th-century Swedish paintings, as well as handicrafts, 18th-century French and 17th-century Dutch art. Rubens's Bacchanal on Andros *dates from the 1630s.*

ÖSTERMALM

Skansen

The world's first open-air museum, founded in 1891, shows the Sweden of bygone days with farms and manor houses, urban scenes and craftspeople at work. Nordic fauna and flora are also on display.

DJURGÅRDEN

SKEPPS-
HOLMEN

Moderna Museet

Paradise (1966) by Tinguely/de Saint Phalle marks the way to Moderna Museet, which houses remarkable collections of international and Swedish modern art.

ER-
LM

Vasamuseet

A fatal capsizal in 1628 and a successful salvage operation 333 years later gave Stockholm its most popular museum. The warship Vasa *is 95 per cent intact after painstaking renovation.*

GAMLA STAN

RELICS OF STOCKHOLM'S early history as a town in the 13th century can still be found on Stadsholmen, the largest island in Gamla Stan (Old Town). The island is a huge area of historical heritage, with the many sights just a few metres apart.

The Royal Palace is the symbol of Sweden's era as a great power in the 17th and early 18th centuries (*see pp36–7*), and its magnificent state rooms, apartments and artifacts are well matched to the Roman Baroque-style exterior. The historic buildings standing majestically

Anchor point on a palace façade

around Slottsbacken underline Stockholm's role as a capital city.

This area has a special atmosphere with much to offer: from the bustling streets of souvenir shops, bookstores and antique shops to elegant palaces, churches and museums. Many medieval cellars are now restaurants and cafés, while the narrow cobbled streets recall a bygone era.

Bridges lead to Riddarholmen, with its 17th-century palaces and royal crypt, and to Helgeandsholmen for the newer splendours of Riksdagshuset (the Parliament building).

SIGHTS AT A GLANCE

Palaces and Museums
Kungliga
  Myntkabinettet **3**
Livrustkammaren **2**
Medeltidsmuseet **16**
Postmuseum **10**
The Royal Palace (Kungliga Slottet) pp54–7 **1**

Public Buildings
Riddarhuset **14**
Riksdagshuset **15**

Historic Buildings
Tessinska Palatset **4**
Wrangelska Palatset **12**

Streets and Squares
Evert Taubes Terrass **13**
Mårten Trotzigs Gränd **8**
Stortorget **6**
Västerlånggatan **9**

Churches
Riddarholms-
  kyrkan **11**
Storkyrkan **5**
Tyska Kyrkan **7**

KEY

▨	Street-by-Street map *See pp50–51*
🚢	Ferry landing point
Ⓣ	Tunnelbana station
🚌	Bus stop
P	Parking

◁ **Prästgatan in Gamla Stan, with its yellow ochre plastering typical of the 18th century**

Street-by-Street: Slottsbacken

SLOTTSBACKEN IS MUCH MORE than just a steep hill linking Skeppsbron and the highest part of Gamla Stan (Old Town). It also provides the background for ceremonial processions and the daily changing-of-the-guard, and is the route for visiting heads of state and foreign ambassadors when they have an audience with the king at the Royal Palace. Alongside Slottsbacken the palace displays its most attractive façade, with the entrance to the Treasury (Skattkammaren), State Room (Rikssalen) and Palace Church (Slottskyrkan). Architect Nicodemus Tessin the Younger's ambition to make Stockholm a leading European city in architectural terms was realized in 1799 with the addition of the Obelisk.

The Olaus Petri statue by Storkyrkan stands in front of a tablet telling the cathedral's history since 1264.

Outer Courtyard

Axel Oxenstiernas Palats (1653) is, for Stockholm, an unusual example of the style known as Roman Mannerism. For 30 years, Axel Oxenstierna (1583–1654) himself was a dominant figure in Swedish politics *(see p35)*.

TRÅNGSUND

The Obelisk by Louis Jean Desprez was erected in 1799 to thank the citizens for supporting Gustav III's Russian war in 1788–90.

Stock Exchange *(see p54)*

STOR-TORGET

★ **Storkyrkan**
An impressive cathedral with a late Gothic interior, it is full of treasures from many different eras ⑤

Stortorget
This square is the heart of the "city between the bridges", with a well dating from 1778. It was the scene of the Stockholm Bloodbath in 1520 ⑥

STAR SIGHTS

★ **Storkyrkan**

★ **Livrustkammaren**

★ **The Royal Palace**

★ Livrustkammaren
Sweden's oldest museum displays royal weaponry, clothing and carriages from over five centuries. The picture shows Gustav II Adolf's stallion Streiff, from the battle of Lützen in 1632 ❷

LOCATOR MAP
See Street Finder map 3

★ The Royal Palace
The southern façade has a triumphal central arch with four niches for statues, created by French artists in the 18th century ❶

Gustav III's statue was sculpted by J T Sergel in 1799 in memory of the "gallant king" who was murdered in 1792.

Kungs-trädgården

↓ Slussen

Köpmantorget with statue of St George Slaying the Dragon (1912).

Kungliga Myntkabinettet
In a 16th-century setting, the Royal Coin Cabinet has the world's largest stamped coin, from 1644 ❸

Tessinska Palatset
Built by and for Nicodemus Tessin the Younger, architect of the Royal Palace, in 1694–7, this palace has been the residence of the Governor of Stockholm County since 1968 ❹

Finska Kyrkan, Slotts-backen's oldest building, dates from the 1640s. Originally a royal ball-games court for the palace, since 1725 it has been the religious centre for the Finnish community.

0 metres   100
0 yards   100

KEY

– – – Suggested route

The Royal Palace ❶

See pp54–7.

Livrust-kammaren ❷

Slottsbacken 3. **Map** 3 C2.
📞 08-519 555 44. 🚇 *Gamla Stan.*
🚌 *2, 43, 55, 76.* 🕐 *Jun–Aug:*
10am–5pm daily; Sep–May: 11am–
5pm Tue–Sun (Thu also 5–8pm).
🔒 ♿ 🚫 ♿ 📷
🌐 *www.livrustkammaren.se*

S WEDEN'S OLDEST museum, Livrustkammaren (the Royal Armoury) was founded in 1633 and is full of *objets d'art* and everyday items used by the Royal Family over the past five centuries. The oldest exhibit is Gustav Vasa's crested helmet dating from 1548. The museum also houses a variety of royal items which illustrate events in Swedish history. Among them are Gustav II Adolf's stuffed stallion, Streiff, which he rode at the Battle of Lützen in 1632; Gustav III's costume from the notorious masked ball at which he was murdered in 1792; and Karl XII's blue uniform with the still muddy boots he was wearing when he died at the siege of Fredrikshald in Norway in 1718.

Coronation ceremonies are illustrated by costumes such as those worn by King Adolf Fredrik and Queen Lovisa Ulrika in 1751. The king's attire alone was adorned with some 2 kg (4 lb) of silver. The coronation carriage, originally built in the 17th century, was modernized for this event. Its renovation in the 1970s took eight years and cost 700,000 kronor. The cellar vault, once used for firewood, is skilfully lit, providing an imaginative setting for the exhibits.

Sweden's first coin, struck in about AD 995

The coronation carriage of King Adolf Fredrik and Queen Lovisa Ulrika in Livrustkammaren

Kungliga Myntkabinettet ❸

Slottsbacken 6. **Map** 3 C3.
📞 08-519 553 00. 🚇 *Gamla Stan.*
🚌 *2, 43, 55, 76.* 🕐 *10am– 4pm*
daily. 📷 *by appointment.* ♿
♿ 🍴 🛒 📷
🌐 *www.myntkabinettet.se*

T HE ROYAL COIN CABINET is a museum highlighting the history of money from the 10th century to the present day – from the little cowrie shell via the drachma and denarius to the current cash card. The museum also gives an insight into the art of medal design over the past 600 years and shows both traditional portrait medals and modern examples such as those that have been awarded to Nobel laureates. Visitors can also see the first Swedish coin, struck in the late 10th century by King Olof Skötkonung. Other rarities include Queen Kristina's coin from 1644, weighing 19.7 kg (43 lb) and reckoned to be the world's heaviest coin. From the island of Yap in Micronesia the museum has acquired the world's largest means of payment, a so-called "rai-stone" which greets visitors in the foyer.

The many sections in the museum include "The World's Money", "State Finance" and "Saving in a Piggy Bank and Bank". "Summa Summarum" is a section designed for children and illustrates the use of money in play and real life.

The elegant Baroque garden in Tessinska Palatset's courtyard

Tessinska Palatset ❹

Slottsbacken 4. **Map** 3 C3.
🚇 *Gamla Stan.* 🚌 *2, 43, 55, 76.*
⬤ *to the public.*

T HE TESSIN PALACE at Slottsbacken is considered to be the most beautiful private residence north of Paris. It is the best-preserved palace from Sweden's era as a great power in the 17th century and was designed by and for Tessin the Younger (1654–1728), the nation's most renowned architect *(see p24).*

Completed in 1697, the building is located on a narrow site which widens out towards a courtyard with a delightful Baroque garden. The relatively discreet façade with its beautiful porch was inspired by the exterior design of Roman palaces. The decor and garden were influenced by Tessin's time in Paris and Versailles.

Tessin, who became a count and state councillor, spent large sums on the building's ornamentation. Sculptures and paintings were provided by the same French masters whose work had graced the Royal Palace. Later, however, his son, Carl Gustaf, had to sell the palace for financial reasons.

The building was acquired by the City of Stockholm as a residence for its governor in 1773. In 1968 it became the residence of the governor of the County of Stockholm.

Storkyrkan ❺

Trångsund 1. **Map** 3 B3. 📞 08-723 30 16. 🚇 Gamla Stan. 🚌 2, 43, 55, 76. 🕐 May–Aug: 9am–6pm daily; Sep–Apr: 9am–4pm daily. ✝ 11am Sat & Sun. Eng: Jul–Aug: 11am Fri. ✝ Eng: Jul–Aug: 1pm, 4pm Mon–Fri, 2pm Sat, noon Sun. 🅿️ ♿ 🚻

Sᴛᴏᴄᴋʜᴏʟᴍ's 700-year-old cathedral is of great national religious importance. It was from here that the Swedish reformer Olaus Petri (1493–1552) spread his Lutheran message around the kingdom. It is also used for royal ceremonies.

Originally, a small village church was built on this site in the 13th century, probably by the city's founder Birger Jarl. It was replaced in 1306 by a much bigger basilica, St Nicholas, which was altered over the centuries.

The Gothic character of the interior, acquired in the 15th century, was revealed in 1908 when, during restoration work, plaster was removed from the pillars, exposing the characteristic red tiling. The late Baroque period provided the so-called "royal chairs" and the pulpit, while the façade was adapted to bring it into keeping with the rest of the area around the Royal Palace. The 66-m (216-ft) high

Storkyrkan's façade in Italian Baroque style, seen from Slottsbacken

tower, added in 1743, has four bells, the largest of which weighs about 6 tons.

The cathedral houses some priceless artistic treasures, including *St George and the Dragon*, regarded as one of the finest late Gothic works of art in Northern Europe. The sculpture, situated to the left of the altar, was carved from oak and elk horn by Lübeck sculptor Bernt Notke. Unveiled in 1489, it commemorates Sten Sture the Elder's victory over the Danes in 1471 (*see p33*).

The Last Judgment (1696) is a massive Baroque painting by David Klöcker von Ehrenstrahl. The 3.7-m (12-ft) high bronze candelabra before the altar, likely to be German, has adorned the cathedral for some 600 years. One of the cathedral's most prized treasures is the silver altar, which gave the interior a completely new appearance in the 1650s. It was a gift from the diplomat Johan Adler Salvius.

The pews nearest to the chancel, the "royal chairs", were designed by Nicodemus Tessin the Younger in 1684 to be used by royalty on special occasions. In 1705, the pulpit was installed

The sculpture *St George and the Dragon* by Bernt Notke (1489) in Storkyrkan

above the grave of Olaus Petri.

On 20 April 1535, a light phenomenon was observed over Stockholm – six rings with sparkling solar halos. *The Parhelion Painting*, recalling the event, hangs in Storkyrkan and is thought to be the oldest portrayal of the capital. It shows the modest skyline dominated by the cathedral, at that time still the basilica of St Nicholas.

Storkyrkan's silver altar (detail)

The Royal Palace (Kungliga Slottet) ❶

Royal sceptre

DEFFENSIVE INSTALLATIONS or castles have stood on the island of Stadsholmen ever since the 11th century. The Tre Kronor (Three Crowns) fortress was completed in the mid-13th century, but became a royal residence only during the following century. The Vasa kings turned the fortress into a Renaissance palace which burned to the ground in 1697. In its place the architect Nicodemus Tessin the Younger created a new palace in Baroque style with an Italianate exterior and a French interior toned down to suit Swedish tastes. The palace's 608 rooms were decorated by Europe's foremost artists and craftsmen. Adolf Fredrik was the first king to move into the palace, in 1754. It is no longer the king's private residence, but remains one of the city's leading sights.

★ Changing the Guard
Stockholm's most popular tourist event is the daily changing of the guard at midday in the Outer Courtyard.

Entrance to the State Apartments

The Western Staircase
Tessin was especially proud of the two staircases, made from Swedish marble and porphyry. On the western staircase stands a bust of the gifted architect.

★ The Hall of State
This opulent hall has an atmosphere of ceremonial splendour and forms an ideal setting for Queen Kristina's silver throne, probably the palace's most famous treasure.

The Guest Apartments

Entrance to Treasury and Royal Chapel

A ROYAL WORKPLACE

The king and queen have their offices at the palace, where they hold audiences with visiting dignitaries, and official ceremonies. They travel around the country attending special events, official openings and anniversaries, and they make regular State visits abroad. The king is well known for his interest in the environment while the queen is heavily involved with her work for children, especially the disabled.

King Carl XVI Gustaf and Queen Silvia

The Royal Chapel
This delightful little church has a rich interior decorated by many different artists. The pulpit is the work of J P Bouchardon.

Gustav III's State Bedchamber

Sergel's bust of Gustav III (1779) stands in the room where the king died after being shot at the Opera House. The 1770s decor is by J E Rehn.

The Bernadotte Apartments are situated on the floor below Karl XI's Gallery.

Tre Kronor Museum entrance from Lejonbacken (see p57).

★ Karl XI's Gallery

One of the most magnificent rooms in the palace, this fine example of Swedish Late Baroque is used for banquets hosted by the king and queen. In the cabinet is this priceless salt-cellar dating from 1627–8.

Carl Hårleman played an important role in the design of the palace. His bust adorns this niche.

Logården is the terrace between the palace's east wings.

Livrustkammaren (see p52)

Gustav III's Museum of Antiquities

The museum's collection includes antique statues brought home by Gustav III from his journey to Rome.

Exploring the Royal Palace

THE PUBLIC AREAS of the Royal Palace allow visitors to walk through grand rooms of sumptuous furnishings and priceless works of art and craftsmanship. The Hall of State and the Royal Chapel are both characterized by their magnificent lavish decor and Gustav III's Museum of Antiquities contains ancient marble sculptures from the king's journey to Italy. The palace also houses the Treasury with the State regalia; the new Tre Kronor Museum, which depicts the palace before the 1697 fire; and the Livrustkammaren *(see p52)*.

The Pillar Hall in the Bernadotte Apartments with original decor

Karl XI's Gallery, the finest example of the Late Baroque period in Sweden

THE STATE APARTMENTS

THE ROYAL FAMILY has lived at Drottningholm Palace *(see pp106–9)* since 1982, but official functions still take place in the State Apartments, including banquets hosted by the king during visits by foreign heads of state. Other official dinners are held here, as well as the annual festivities in December to honour the Nobel laureates.

The dinners are served in Karl XI's Gallery, the finest example of Swedish Late Baroque, modelled on the Hall of Mirrors at Versailles. Each window is matched with a niche on the inner wall where some of the palace's priceless works of arts and crafts are exhibited. Most remarkable is the salt-cellar made from ivory and gilded silver designed by the Flemish painter Rubens (1577–1640). The room known as "The

King Karl XIV Johan's egg cup

White Sea" serves as a drawing room. Gustav III's State Bedchamber, where the king died after being shot at the Opera House in 1792 *(see pp40–41)*, is the height of Gustavian elegance. Along with Queen Sofia Magdalena's State Bedchamber, it was designed by the architect Jean Eric Rehn. The lintels on the doors to the Don Quixote Room, named after the theme of its tapestries, were made by François Boucher and are among the most treasured pieces.

THE GUEST APARTMENTS

AN IMPOSING part of the palace, these apartments are where visiting heads of state stay. The beautiful rooms include the Meleager Salon, where official gifts and decorations are exchanged, and a large bedroom with a sculpted and gilded bed. Other impressive rooms are the Inner Salon, whose decor was inspired by the excavations in Pompeii, and the Margareta Room, named after the present king's grandmother, which displays some pictures painted by her.

The apartments contain remarkable works of craftsmanship by such 18th-century masters as Georg Haupt, Ephraim Ståhle and Jean-Baptiste Masreliez.

THE BERNADOTTE APARTMENTS

THIS MAGNIFICENT suite has earned its name from the gallery displaying portraits of the Bernadotte dynasty. The apartments have some notable ceiling paintings and mid-18th-century chandeliers, and are used for many a ceremonial occasion. The elegant Pillar Hall is the venue for investitures, and the East Octagonal Cabinet with probably the palace's best Rococo decor, is where the king receives foreign ambassadors. Along with the western cabinet, its interior has remained just as it was planned by Carl Hårleman more than 250 years ago.

Oscar II's very masculine Writing Room, dating from the 1870s, also looks much as it did in his day. However, the palace was kept up to date with the latest technical advances: electricity was installed in 1883, and the telephone only one year later.

THE HALL OF STATE

ROCOCO AND Classicism were brought together in perfect harmony by the architects Nicodemus Tessin the Younger and Carl Hårleman when they designed the two-storey Hall of State.

The Hall provides a worthy framework for Queen Kristina's silver throne, a gift for the coronation in 1650 and one of the most valuable treasures in the palace. The throne was given to the queen by Magnus Gabriel de la Gardie and was made in Augsburg by the goldsmith

Abraham Drentwett. The canopy was added 100 years later for the coronation of King Adolf Fredrik and was designed by Jean Eric Rehn.

The room is lavishly decorated. The throne is flanked by colossal sculptures of Karl XIV Johan and Gustav II Adolf, while those on the cornice symbolize Peace, Strength, Religion and Justice.

Until 1975 the Hall of State was the scene of the ceremonial opening of the Swedish Parliament (Riksdagen), which included a march past of the royal bodyguard in full regalia. It is now used for official occasions and, like the Royal Chapel, is a venue for summer concerts.

The Hall of State, the most important ceremonial room in the palace

THE ROYAL CHAPEL

I T TOOK 50 YEARS to build the Royal Palace, and a lot of effort went into the interior decoration of the Royal Chapel. The work was carried out largely by Carl Härleman under the supervision of Tessin. As with the Hall of State, the co-operation between the two produced a magnificent result, enhanced by the contributions of several foreign artists.

A number of remarkable artifacts have been added over the centuries. The most recent was a group of six 17th-century-style bronze crowns, as well as two crystal crowns, given by the Court to King Carl XVI Gustaf and Queen Silvia to mark their marriage in 1976.

It also has some rare relics of the original Tre Kronor

fortress: new benches that had been ordered by Tessin. They had been rescued during the palace fire in 1697 and preserved, but not put in the chapel until the 19th century. The benches were made by Georg Haupt, grandfather of the Georg Haupt who was to create some of the palace's most prized furnishings (*see p80*).

GUSTAV III'S MUSEUM OF ANTIQUITIES

O PENED IN 1794 in memory of the murdered king, the Museum of Antiquities initially housed more than 200 exhibits, mainly acquired during Gustav's Italian journey in 1783–4 and then supplemented with more purchases at a later date.

In 1866 the museum's collection was moved to the city's National Museum (*see pp80–81*). During the 1950s the main gallery was renovated, followed by the smaller galleries 30 years later, which enabled the collection to be returned to its original setting.

The most prized exhibits are in the main gallery, the best known being the sculpture of Endymion, the eternally sleeping young shepherd and lover of the Moon Goddess Selene. The 18th-century sculptor Johan Tobias Sergel is represented by *The Priestess*, ranked as the collection's second most important piece. She is flanked by two large candelabras.

THE TREASURY

A T THE BOTTOM of 56 well-worn steps, below the Hall of State on the south side of the palace, is the entrance to the Treasury (Skattkammaren) where the State regalia, the most potent symbols of the monarchy, are kept. Occasionally, for an important event, King Erik XIV's crown, sceptre, orb and the keys of the kingdom are taken out of their showcase and placed beside the uncrowned King

Erik XIV's crown, made by Cornelis ver Weiden in Stockholm in 1561

Carl XVI Gustaf. The 1-m (3-ft) high silver baptismal font, which took the French silversmith Jean François Cousinet 11 years to make, is over 200 years old and is still used for royal baptisms. Hanging in the Treasury is the only undamaged tapestry among six dating from the 1560s, salvaged from the 1697 fire.

TRE KRONOR MUSEUM

T HE NEWEST attraction at the Royal Palace is the Tre Kronor (Three Crowns) Museum, which is housed in the oldest parts of the ruined Tre Kronor fortress, preserved under the north side of the palace. About half of a massive 12th-century defensive wall and brick vaults from the 16th and 17th centuries provide a dramatic setting for the museum which illustrates the palace's history over almost 1,000 years.

Two models of the Tre Kronor fortress show changes made during the second half of the 17th century and how it looked by the time of the fire. Among items rescued from the ashes are a schnapps glass, amber pots and bowls made from mountain crystal.

A glass bowl in the Tre Kronor Museum, saved from the 1697 fire

The imposing Stock Exchange on the north side of Stortorget

Stortorget ❻

Map 3 B3. 🚇 *Gamla Stan.* 🚌 *2, 3, 43, 53, 55,, 76.* **Nobelmuseet** 🕿 *08-23 25 06.* ⏰ *mid-May–mid-Sep: 10am–5pm Wed–Mon, 10am–8pm Tue; mid-Sep–mid-May: 11am–5pm Wed–Sun, 11am–8pm Tue.* ♿ 🏪 ♿ 🍴 Ⓦ *www.nobel.se/nobelmuseum*

IT WAS NOT until 1778, when the Stock Exchange (Börsen) was completed, that Stortorget ("the big square") in the heart of the Old Town, acquired a more uniform appearance. Its northern side had previously been taken up by several buildings that served as a town hall. Since the early Middle Ages the square had been a natural meeting point with a well and marketplace, lined with wooden stalls on market days.

A pillory belonging to the jail, which was once on nearby Kåkbrinken, used to stand on the square. It is now in the Town Hall on Kungsholmen.

The medieval layout is clear on Stortorget's west side, where the red Schantzska Huset (No. 20) and the narrow Seyfridtska Huset were built around 1650. The Schantzska Huset remains unchanged and has a lovely limestone porch adorned with figures of recumbent Roman warriors. The artist Johan Wendelstam was responsible for most of the notable porches in the Old Town. The 17th-century gable on Grilska Huset (No. 3) is also worth a closer study. Today there are cafés and restaurants in some of the vaulted cellars.

The decision to construct the Stock Exchange was taken in 1667, but the many wars delayed the start of the building by 100 years. The architect was the young and talented Erik Palmstedt (1741–1803), who also created the decorative cover for the old well. Trading on the floor of the Stock Exchange ceased in 1990. In 2001 the **Nobelmuseet** was opened here to mark the centenary of the Prize *(see p69)*. The exhibition explores the work and ideas of more than 700 creative minds by means of short films and original artifacts. On the upper floor, the Swedish Academy holds its ceremonial gatherings, a tradition maintained since Gustav III gave his inauguration speech here in 1786.

Tyska Kyrkan ❼

Svartmangatan 16. **Map** 3 B3. 🕿 *08-411 11 88.* 🚇 *Gamla Stan.* 🚌 *3, 43, 46, 53, 55, 59, 76.* ⏰ *May–Sep: noon–4pm daily; Oct–Apr: noon–4pm Sat & Sun.* ✝ *11am Sun, German.* 📷 *by arrangement in Swedish & German.* ♿

THE GERMAN CHURCH is an impressive reminder of the almost total influence that Germany had over Stockholm during the 18th century. The Hanseatic League trading organization was in control of the Baltic and its ports, which explains why the basic layout of Gamla Stan resembled that of Lübeck. Germany's political influence was only broken after the Stockholm Bloodbath and Gustav Vasa's accession to the throne in 1523 *(see p34)*, but its cultural and mercantile influence remained strong as German merchants and craftsmen settled in the city.

The church's congregation, which today has some 2,000 members, was founded in 1571. The present twin-aisle church was built in 1638–42, as an extension of a smaller church which the parish had used since 1576.

In German Late Renaissance and Baroque style, the interior has a royal gallery, added in 1672 for German members of

The royal gallery in the 17th-century Tyska Kyrkan

THE STOCKHOLM BLOODBATH

Detail of a painting of the Bloodbath (1524)

Stortorget is intimately linked with the Stockholm Bloodbath of November 1520. The Danish king, Christian II, besieged the Swedish Regent, Sten Sture the Younger, until he capitulated and the Swedes chose Christian as their king. The Dane promised an amnesty and ordered a three-day feast at Tre Kronor Fortress. Near the end of the festivities, the revellers were suddenly shut in and arrested for heresy. The next day more than 80 noblemen and Stockholm citizens were beheaded in the square.

the royal household. The pulpit (1660) in ebony and alabaster is unique in Sweden and the altar, from the 1640s, is covered with beautiful paintings surrounded by sculptures of the apostles and evangelists.

The sculptures on the south porch by Jobst Hennen date from 1643 and show Jesus, Moses and three figures portraying Faith, Hope and Love.

Mårten Trotzigs Gränd, the narrowest street in the city

Mårten Trotzigs Gränd ❽

Map 3 C4. 🚇 *Gamla Stan.* 🚌 *3, 43, 46, 53, 55, 59, 76.*

AT ONLY 90 CM (3 ft) wide, Mårten Trotzigs Gränd is the city's narrowest street. Climbing up the 36 steps gives a good impression of how the various parts of the Old Town differ in height and how tightly the houses are packed together.

Mårten Trotzigs Gränd is named after a German merchant called Traubzich who owned two houses here at the end of the 16th century. After being fenced off at both ends for 100 years, the street was reopened in 1945.

Västerlånggatan ❾

Map 3 B3. 🚇 *Gamla Stan.* 🚌 *3, 43, 46, 53, 55, 59, 76.*

ONCE A MAIN ROAD outside the city proper, built along parts of the original town wall, Västerlånggatan now runs through the heart

of the Old Town, and is usually thronging with people – tourists and locals – shopping or strolling. Starting at Mynttorget in the north, by the Chancery Office (Kanslihuset) and Lejonbacken, the lively and atmospheric street finishes at Järntorget in the south, where the export of iron was once controlled. On Järntorget is Bancohuset, which served as the headquarters of the State Bank from 1680 to 1906.

The building at No. 7 has been used by the Swedish Parliament since the mid-1990s. Its late 19th-century façade has a distinctive southern European influence.

No. 27 was built by and for Erik Palmstedt, who also designed the Stock Exchange and the well at Stortorget. No. 29 is a truly venerable building, dating from the early 15th century. The original pointed Gothic arches were revealed during restoration in the 1940s.

No. 33 is a good example of how new materials and techniques in the late 19th century made it possible to fit large shop windows into old houses. The cast-iron columns which can be seen in many other places also date from this period.

No. 68, Von der Lindeska House, has a majestic 17th-century façade and a beautiful porch with sculptures of Neptune and Mercury.

Postmuseum ❿

Lilla Nygatan 6. **Map** 3 B3.
📞 08-781 17 55. 🚇 *Gamla Stan.*
🚌 *3, 53.* 🕐 *11am–4pm Tue–Sun, Sep–Apr also Wed 4pm–7pm.*
📷 *by arrangement.* ♿ 🍴 📷
🌐 *www.posten.se/museum*

AN ATTRACTION in itself, the Postmuseum building takes up a whole area bought by the Swedish Post Office in 1720. About 100 years later

Västerlånggatan, Gamla Stan's most popular shopping street

the majestic-looking Post Office was built, incorporating parts of the 17th-century buildings already there. Stockholm's only Post Office until 1869, it was turned into the Postal Museum in 1906.

Letters have been sent in Sweden, in an organized way, since 1636, and the museum's permanent exhibits include a portrayal of early "peasant postmen" fighting the Åland Sea in their boat *Simpan*. Also on display is the first post bus which ran in northern Sweden in the early 1920s and a stagecoach used in eastern Sweden.

Mauritian stamp in the Postmuseum

The collection includes Sweden's first stamp-printing press and no less than four million stamps among which are the first Swedish stamps, produced in 1855. Also on show is "Penny Black", the world's first stamp dating from 1840, and some stamps issued by Mauritius in 1847.

There is a philatelic library holding 51,000 volumes and stamp collections, as well as computers and multimedia equipment for research. A special exhibition for children is on display in the basement.

Riddarholms-kyrkan ⓫

Birger Jarls Torg. **Map** 3 A3. 📞 08-402 61 30. 🅣 *Gamla Stan.* 🚌 *3, 53.* ⏰ *May–Aug: 10am–4pm daily; Sep: noon–3pm Sat & Sun.* 🎫 *Eng: 1pm.* 📷 🚫 ♿

Tʜɪs ᴄʜᴜʀᴄʜ ᴏɴ the island of Riddarholmen is best known as a place for royal burials. Its interior is full of ornate sarcophagi and worn gravestones, and in front of the altar are the tombs of the medieval kings Karl Knutsson and Magnus Ladulås.

Built on the site of the late 13th-century Greyfriars abbey, founded by Magnus Ladulås, the majestic brick church was gradually enlarged over the centuries. After a serious fire in 1835, it acquired its present lattice-work cast-iron tower.

Inside, the church is surrounded by splendid burial vaults dating back to the 16th century. The coffins rest on a lower level with space for a memorial above. The most recent was built in 1858–60 for the Bernadotte dynasty.

The vaults contain the remains of all the Swedish monarchs from Gustav II Adolf in the 17th century to the present day with two exceptions: Queen Kristina was buried at St Peter's in Rome in 1689 and Gustav VI Adolf, who was interred at Haga in 1973 *(see p96)*. The most magnificent sarcopha-gus is that of the 19th-century king, Karl XIV Johan, which had to be towed here by sledge from his porphyry workshops in northern Sweden.

Riddarholmskyrkan and the external burial vault by Tessin and Hårleman

Wrangelska Palatset, a royal residence after the Tre Kronor fire of 1697

Particularly moving are the graves of royal children, including the many small tin coffins that surround the last resting place of Gustav II Adolf and his queen, Maria Eleonora.

Wrangelska Palatset ⓬

Birger Jarls Torg 16. **Map** 3 A3. 🅣 *Gamla Stan.* 🚌 *3, 53.* ⬤ *to the public.*

Oɴʟʏ ᴛᴡᴏ ᴘᴀʀᴛs of Gustav Vasa's fortifications from 1530 remain – Birger Jarl's Tower and the southernmost tower of what became the Wrangel Palace. Built as a residence for the nobleman Lars Sparre in 1652–70, it was remodelled a few decades later by Carl Gustaf Wrangel. A field marshal in the Thirty Years War, Wrangel chose Nicodemus Tessin the Elder as his architect. The result was Stockholm's largest privately-owned palace.

In 1697 the royal family moved into the palace after the Tre Kronor fortress *(see p54)* was ravaged by fire. It became known as the King's House, and it was here in the same year that the 15-year-old Karl XII took the oath of office after the death of his father. Gustav III was born here in 1746 and in 1792 his assassin was incarcerated in the dungeons. The Court of Appeal now uses this building, as well as Rosenhane Palace

(Birger Jarls Torg 10) and Hessenstein House (Birger Jarls Torg 2), built in 1630 by Bengt Bengtsson Oxenstierna.

Evert Taubes Terrass ⓭

Norra Riddarholmshamnen. **Map** 3 A3. 🅣 *Gamla Stan.* 🚌 *3, 53.*

A sᴛᴀᴛᴜᴇ of Evert Taube, the much-loved troub-adour and ballad writer, stands on the terrace below Wrangelska Palatset looking out over the waters of Riddarfjärden.

In an ideal position, given the poet's close links to the sea, the bronze sculpture was created by Willy Gordon in 1990. Close by stands Christer Berg's granite sculpture *Solbåten* (Sun Boat), un-veiled in 1966. Inspired by the shape of a shell, from some angles it also resembles a sail.

Evert Taube (1890–1976)

Riddarhuset ⓮

Riddarhustorget 10. **Map** 3 A3. 📞 08-723 39 90. 🅣 *Gamla Stan.* 🚌 *3, 53.* ⏰ *11:30am–12:30pm Mon–Fri.* 📷 🚶 *by appointment.* 🌐 *www.riddarhuset.se*

Oғᴛᴇɴ ʀᴇɢᴀʀᴅᴇᴅ as one of Stockholm's most beauti-ful buildings, Riddarhuset (House of Knights) stands on Riddarhustorget, the city's centre until the 19th century. Built in 1641–7 on the initiative of the State Chancellor, Riddarhuset provided the knights with a base for meetings and events. The building is a supreme example of Dutch Baroque design by the architects Simon and Jean de la Vallée, Heinrich Wilhelm and Justus Vingboons.

Over the entrance on the northern façade is the knights' motto *Arte et Marte* (Art and War) with Minerva, Goddess of Art and Science, and Mars, God of War.

The sculptures on the vaulted roof symbolize the knightly virtues. On the south side is *Nobilitas* (Nobility) holding a small Minerva and spear. She is flanked by *Studium* (Diligence) and *Valor* (Bravery). Facing the north is the male equivalent, *Honor*, flanked by *Prudentia* (Prudence) and *Fortitudo* (Strength).

Inside, a magnificent double staircase leads up to the Knights' Room. This has a painted ceiling by David Klöcker Ehrenstrahl (1628–98) and Riddarhuset's foremost treasure, a sculpted ebony chair, 1623. The walls are covered with coats of arms.

Riddarhuset, built in the 17th century in imposing Dutch Baroque style

Riksdagshuset ⓯

Riksgatan 3 A. **Map** 3 B2. 08-786 40 00. Kungsträdgården. 3, 43, 53, 62. tours & meetings in the Chamber. daily in summer; weekends in winter; ring for details. www.riksdagen.se

THE PARLIAMENT building (Riksdagshuset) and State Bank (Riksbank) on Helgeandsholmen were inaugurated in 1905 and 1906 respectively. In the 1970s and 1980s the

two buildings were combined and restored and a modern extension built to house a new, single debating chamber. The chamber is truly Nordic in its decoration with benches of Swedish birch and wall-panelling in Finnish birch carved in Norway. A large tapestry, *Memory of a Landscape* (1983), by Elisabeth Hasselberg-Olsson, covers 54 sq m (581 sq ft) of wall and took 3,500 hours to make. Parliamentary debates can be watched from the public gallery.

The original two-chamber Parliament is used for meetings of the majority party. The former Upper House has three paintings by Otte Sköld (1894–1958); the other chamber contains works by Axel Törneman and Georg Pauli. Between the chambers is a 45-m (148-ft) long hall with an elegant display of coats of arms. The Finance Committee meets in the oak-panelled library surrounded by old prints and *Jugendstil* (Art Nouveau-style) lamps. Facing the Norrbro entrance is the original 1905 stairwell with columns, floor, steps and balusters in various marbles. The

present entrance was the State Bank's main hall until 1976 and contains paintings from the Parliamentary collection.

Medeltids-museet ⓰

Strömparterren, Norrbro. **Map** 3 B2. 08-508 317 90. Kungsträdgården. 43, 62. Jul & Aug: 11am–4pm Thu–Tue, 11am–6pm Wed; Sep–Jun: 11am–4pm Tue–Sun, (also 4–6pm Wed). www.medeltidsmuseet.stockholm.se

THIS FASCINATING museum of medieval Stockholm is built around some of the capital's archaeological remains, mainly parts of the city wall that date from the 1530s. They were discovered in 1978–80. Completely underground, the museum includes finds evoking Stockholm's early history. Among them is the 22-m (72-ft) long Riddarholm ship, dating from the 1520s, which was found off Riddarholmen in 1930.

Medieval stone head of Birger Jarl at Medeltidsmuseet

The museum provides a good picture of Stockholm's early days. From the entrance, a 350-year-old tunnel leads into a reconstructed medieval world. There is a pillory in the square and gallows with the tools of the executioner's trade. The harbour has been recreated, with a quayside, jetties, boathouses and warehouses. As was the custom, a spruce wreath hangs outside the wine cellar to show that supplies of wine and beer have arrived from the Continent.

The new Parliament building, with the older building behind

CITY

THE AREA KNOWN AS CITY today was where, in the mid-18th century, the first stone-built houses and palaces outside Gamla Stan started to appear for the burghers and nobility. After World War II, the run-down buildings around Hötorget were demolished to form what is now Sergels Torg; many homes were replaced by rather dreary office blocks.

In recent years, though, the area has livened up and become the true heart and commercial centre of Stock-

Street light near Kungliga Operan

holm. A hub for public transport and banking, City is the place for the best department stores and shopping malls, exclusive boutiques and nightspots. The centre also has some beautiful parks and pleasant squares which serve as popular meeting places. The unique landscape surrounding Stockholm permeates even City, offering sudden unexpected glimpses of water complete with bustling boat life and a string of anglers along the embankments.

SIGHTS AT A GLANCE

Museums
Armémuseum ⑭
Dansmuseet ⑤
Hallwylska Palatset ⑱
Medelhavsmuseet ⑥
Musikmuseet ⑮
Strindbergsmuseet
  Blå Tornet ⑪

Churches
Adolf Fredriks
  Kyrka ⑫
Jacobs Kyrka ③
Klara Kyrka ⑧

Squares
Kungsträdgården ②

Public Buildings
Arvfurstens Palats ⑦
Hovstallet ⑯
Kungliga Biblioteket ⑬
Nordiska Kompaniet ①

Theatres and Musical Stages
Konserthuset ⑩
Kulturhuset och
  Stadsteatern ⑨
Kungliga Dramatiska
  Teatern ⑰
Kungliga Operan ④

KEY

	Street-by-Street map
---	See pp64–5
🅃	Tunnelbana station
🚋	Tram stop
🚌	Bus stop
🅿	Parking

0 metres   500
0 yards   500

◁ **Sagerska Palatset, official residence of the prime minister, between Rosenbad (left) and Arvfurstens Palats**

Street-by-Street: Around Kungsträdgården

WITH A HISTORY GOING back to the 15th century, the King's Garden (Kungsträdgården) has long been the city's most popular meeting place and recreational centre. Both visitors and Stockholmers gather here for summer concerts and festivals, or just to enjoy a stroll under the lime trees. Around the park is a wealth of shops, including the upmarket department store Nordiska Kompaniet, boutiques, churches, museums and restaurants. A short walk takes you to Gustav Adolfs Torg, flanked by the Royal Opera House and other stately buildings, including the Swedish Foreign Office.

Les Ballets Suédois
donneront leur spectacle d'ouverture le
20 Novembre au
Théâtre des Champs-Élysées

CONTRE TOUS LES ACADÉMISMES

VIVE LA VIE

Dansmuseet
Anything connected with dance, such as costumes, stage-set sketches and posters for the famous Les Ballets Suédois, can be seen here **5**

★ **Medelhavsmuseet**
This museum near Gustav Adolfs Torg has vast collections from prehistoric cultures around the Mediterranean **6**

Gustav II Adolf's equestrian statue, designed by L'Archevêques, was unveiled in 1796.

FREDSGATAN

REGERINGSGATAN

Sagerska Palatset

STRÖMGATAN

GUSTAV ADOLFS TORG

STRÖMGATAN

NORRBRO

NORRSTRÖM

Opera-källaren *(see p294)*

SOPHIA·ALBERTINA
ÆDIFICAVIT·

Arvfurstens Palats
The Swedish Foreign Office is based in this palace, built for Gustav III's sister Sofia Albertina in 1794 **7**

★ **Kungliga Operan**
Built in 1898 with a magnificently ornate auditorium, the Royal Opera House replaced an earlier one from the time of Gustav III **4**

KEY

- - - Suggested route

**Queen Kris-
tina's summer
house** by the
cobble-stoned
Lantmäteri-
backen.

Sergels
Torg

HAMNGATAN

VÄSTRA TRÄDGÅRDSGATAN

KUNGSTRÄDGÅRDSGATAN

Statue of
Karl XIII

Molin's
fountain

The NK clock,
part of the city
skyline.

LOCATOR MAP
See Street Finder maps 1 & 2

Nordiska Kompaniet
*Designed by Ferdinand
Boberg in 1915, the granite
palace houses Sweden's most
exclusive department store* ❶

Kungsträdgården
*The king's kitchen garden
was sited here in the 15th
century. Today it is one of
the most popular recreation
centres in the city, both in
summer and winter* ❷

0 metres 100
0 yards 100

Karl XII's statue
*by Molin was built
1868 to mark the
200th anniversary of
the king's death.*

Jacobs Kyrka
*Started in 1580, the
church was consec-
rated in 1643. Its
stone porches are
beautifully crafted* ❸

STAR SIGHTS

★ **Medelhavsmuseet**

★ **Kungliga Operan**

Nordiska Kompaniet ❶

Hamngatan 18–20. **Map** 2 D4. 📞 08-762 80 00. 🚇 *T-centralen.* 🚌 *2, 47, 55, 62, 69, 76.* 🕐 *10am–7pm Mon–Fri, 10am–6pm Sat, 10am–5pm Sun.*

DESIGNED BY Ferdinand Boberg, the granite palace on Hamngatan houses the department store Nordiska Kompaniet (NK). Opened in 1915, NK was – and still is – aimed at an exclusive clientele. It made its name as a showcase for Swedish arts and crafts, writing design history when the textiles department, Textilkammaren, opened in 1937. The manager was the textile artist Astrid Sampe who commissioned leading contemporary artists and designers to supply work. Olle Baertling, Arne Jacobsen, Alvar Aalto and Viola Gråsten all contributed patterns. Sampe also introduced new fabric printing techniques.

Today at NK you can find almost everything from perfume, clothing and sporting equipment to glass, silver and porcelain, but above all, the store is, as its founder Josef Sachs once described it, a commercial and cultural theatre.

Kungsträdgården ❷

Map 3 B1. 🚇 *Kungsträdgården.* 🚌 *2, 47, 55, 62, 65, 69, 76.*

THE "KING'S GARDEN" is a popular meeting place for Stockholmers where there is something for everyone going on all year round. This open urban space is bordered by treelined promenades, with a modern fountain in the middle. At the Strömgatan end there is a square named after Karl XII with J P Molin's statue of the warrior king, unveiled in 1868, at its centre. In Kungsträdgården itself there is a statue of Karl XIII (1809–18) by Erik Göthe. During the summer, the park is the venue for food festivals, concerts, dancing and street theatre. In winter, the skating rink attracts children and grown-ups alike. Also to be seen is Molin's fountain, made from gypsum in 1866 and cast in bronze. It is the city's oldest park, starting as the royal kitchen garden in the 15th century. During Erik XIV's reign in the 16th century, it was transformed into a formal Renaissance garden. Queen Kristina built a stone summer house here in the 17th century, which stands at Västra Trädgårdsgatan 2, by the cobblestoned Lantmäteribacken.

Molin's fountain

Jacobs Kyrka ❸

Jakobs Torg 5. **Map** 3 B1. 📞 08-723 30 38. 🚇 *Kungsträdgården.* 🚌 *2, 55, 62, 65, 76.* 🕐 *11am–3pm daily, Thu also 5.30–6.30pm.* ✝️ *12.10pm Mon–Fri, 11am Sun. In Eng 6pm Sun.* **Concerts** *3pm Sat.* 📷 *by appointment.* ♿

IN MEDIEVAL TIMES there was a small chapel where Kungsträdgården now lies. Dedicated to St Jacob, the patron saint of wayfarers, the chapel and another modest-sized church were pulled down by King Gustav Vasa in the 16th century. His son, Johan III, wanted to provide two new churches in Norra Malmen, as the area was then called, and work to build the churches of St Jacob and St Klara (*see p68*) started in 1580. St Jacob's was consecrated first, in 1643. It has been restored several times since then, in some cases rather clumsily. However, several valuable items have been preserved, including a baptismal font from 1634 and some church silver, as well as porches by the stonemasons Henrik Blom and Hans Hebel.

The organ's façade was created by the architect Carl Hårleman and the large painting on the west wall of the southern nave is by Fredrik Westin, Sweden's most distinguished historical painter of the early 19th century.

Altar in Jacobs Kyrka, dating in part from the 17th century

Kungliga Operan ❹

Gustav Adolfs Torg. **Map** 3 B1. 📞 08-791 43 00. 🚇 *Kungsträdgården.* 🚌 *43, 62, 65.* **Ticket Office** 🕐 *12–6pm Mon–Fri, 12–3pm Sat.* 📷 *by appointment.* ♿ 🖥️ 📷 🌐 *www.operan.se*

OPERA HAS BEEN staged in Sweden since 18 January 1773, when a performance took place at Bollhuset at Slottsbacken. Kungliga Operan (The Royal Opera House) on Gustav Adolfs Torg was inaugurated on 30 September 1782, but by the late 19th century it had become a fire hazard. The architect Axel Anderberg was commissioned to design a new opera house which was

View of Kungsträdgården, towards Hamngatan

The splendid golden foyer at Kungliga Operan

given to the State in 1898 by a consortium founded by the financier K A Wallenberg.

The colouring of the building in late-Renaissance style is in keeping with the Royal Palace and Parliament building, and some details of the architecture are common to all three. The beautiful staircase with ceiling paintings by Axel Jungstedt was inspired by the Paris Opera. The same artist's portrait of Oscar II hangs in the 28-m (92-ft) long golden foyer, where Carl Larsson was responsible for the decorative paintings. The wings at either side of the stage have been retained, as has the width of the proscenium arch (11.4 m/37 ft). Also saved was J T Sergel's group of angels, holding the national coat of arms, above the stage. An angel in Vicke Andrén's ceiling painting is holding a sketch of the Opera House.

Gold ceiling in Kungliga Operan

Dansmuseet **❺**

Gustav Adolfs Torg 22–24. **Map** 3 B1.
📞 08-441 76 50. 🚇 Kungsträd-gården. 🚌 43, 62, 65.
🕐 11am–4pm Tue–Fri, noon–4pm Sat & Sun. 📷 ♿ 🖥 🎞 📁
🌐 www.dansmuseet.se

IN 1999 THE Dance Museum moved into new premises on Gustav Adolfs Torg, in a former bank building opposite the Norrbro bridge. The museum was originally established in Paris in 1953 by the Swedish aristocrat Rolf de Maré (1888–1964). He was a noted art collector and founder of the renowned avant-garde company Les Ballets Suédois. The collection features all aspects of dance – costumes and masks, scenery sketches, art and posters, books and documents – and includes an archive on popular dance. Apart from the exhibition hall, there is also a data bank – the Rolf de Maré Study Centre – which contains video facilities, a library and archives. The museum shop stocks Sweden's largest collection of dance videos for sale.

Medelhavs-museet **❻**

Fredsgatan 2. **Map** 3 B1.
📞 08-519 553 80. 🚇 Kungsträd-gården. 🚌 43, 62, 65. 🕐 11am–8pm Tue, 11am–4pm Wed–Fri, noon–5pm Sat & Sun. 📷 ♿ 🖥 🎞 📁
🌐 www.medelhavsmuseet.se

GODS AND PEOPLE from pre-historic cultures around the Mediterranean rub shoulders in Medelhavsmuseet (the Museum of Mediterranean and Near East Antiquities). Its many treasures include a large group of terracotta figures discovered by archaeologists on Cyprus in the 1930s. There is an extensive display covering ancient Egypt, with bronze weapons, tools and some remarkable mummies. Greek and Islamic culture, Roman and Etruscan art are all represented and complemented by temporary exhibitions.

Medelhavsmuseet is housed in a former bank, built in the 17th century for Gustav Horn, a general in the Thirty Years War. The stairwell, dating from 1905, and the peristyles and colonnade around the upper part of the hall are worth a visit in themselves.

Arvfurstens Palats **❼**

Gustav Adolfs Torg 1. **Map** 3 B1.
🚇 Kungsträdgården. 🚌 43, 62, 65.
⬤ to the public.

OPPOSITE THE Royal Opera House, on the other side of Gustav Adolfs Torg, stands Arvfurstens Palats (Prince's Palace), built for Gustav III's sister Sofia Albertina and completed in 1794. She commissioned the architect Erik Palmstedt to carry out the work. He was a pupil of Carl Fredrik Adelcrantz, designer of the original opera house.

The palace and its decor are shining examples of the Gustavian style, thanks to the contributions of artists and craftsmen such as Louis Masreliez and Georg Haupt and their pupils Gustaf Adolf Ditzinger, J T Sergel and Gottlieb Iwersson. In 1906 the building was taken over by the Swedish Foreign Office.

Nearby is the elegant Sager-ska Palatset (1894) in French Renaissance style, which is used by the prime minister as an official residence.

Arvfurstens Palats (1794), now the Swedish Foreign Office

Edvin Öhrström's obelisk in Sergels Torg, with Kulturhuset to the left

Klara Kyrka �8

Klara Östra Kyrkogata. **Map** 1 C4.
🕿 08-723 30 31. 🚇 T-centralen.
🚌 47, 52, 59, 65. ◷ 10am–5pm
daily. **Concert** 6pm Sat. 🕆 8am Thu,
11am Sun, 2pm Sun (Swahili). ♿ ⓩ

THE CONVENT OF St Klara
stood on the site of the
present church and cemetery
until 1527, when it was pulled
down on the orders of Gustav
Vasa. Later, his son Johan III
commissioned a new church,
completed in 1590.

The church was ravaged by
fire in 1751. Its reconstruction
was planned by two of the
period's most outstanding
architects, Carl Härleman and
later Carl Fredrik Adelcrantz.
The pulpit was made in 1753
to Härleman's design, and J T
Sergel (see p81) created the
angelic figures in the northern
gallery. A pair of identical
angels adorns the exquisite
chancel, based on the
sculptor's gypsum originals.

In the 1880s, the 116-m
(380-ft) tower was added. The
20th-century church artist, Olle
Hjortzberg, created the paintings in the vault in 1904.

Interior of Klara Kyrka with
decoration by Olle Hjortzberg

Kulturhuset and Stadsteatern ⓽

Sergels Torg 3. **Map** 1 C4. **Kulturhuset**
🕿 08-508 315 08. **Stadsteatern**
🕿 08-506 202 00. 🚇 T-centralen.
🚌 47, 52, 59, 69. ◷ 11am–6pm
Tue–Fri, 11am–4pm Sat–Sun.
📷 some areas. ♿ 🍴 ▣ ▣
🌐 www.kulturhuset.stockholm.se

THE DISTINCTIVE GLASS façade
of Kulturhuset (Cultural
Centre) fronts the southern
side of Sergels Torg. The
winning entry in a Nordic
architectural competition,
Kulturhuset has become a
symbol of Swedish Modern-
ism. It was designed by Peter
Celsing and opened in 1974.
Refurbished to meet the
needs of the new millennium,
the complex contains three
galleries which mount
regularly changing exhib-
itions. In the auditorium, a
varied programme of music,
dance, drama and lectures is
presented. The centre known
as "Kilen" stages an art form
which is a cross between
drama, stand-up comedy,
installation art and dance.

In the Children's Room,
youngsters can read books,
draw pictures, listen to stories
or watch films. "Lava" focuses
on youth culture nationwide.
There is a library for fans of
strip cartoons and reading
rooms providing international
newspapers and magazines.

Among the shops here is
Designtorget, selling items of
Swedish design, and an art
bookshop, Konst-ig. There are
two cafés: Café Panorama
serves snacks, and Café Access
is for surfing the Internet.

Kulturhuset also houses
Stadsteatern (City Theatre),
whose main auditorium
opened in 1990. This part of
the building was formerly
occupied by Parliament while
its chamber on Helgeandsholmen was being rebuilt (see
p61). The theatre was
designed by architects Lars
Fahlsten and Per Ahrbom and
contains six stages of varying
size and style under one roof.

Konserthuset ⓾

Hötorget. **Map** 1 C4.
🕿 08-786 02 00. 🚇 Hötorget. 🚌 1,
52, 56. **Ticket Office** ◷ 11am–6pm
Mon–Fri, 11am–3pm Sat, and 2 hours
before a concert. 🎫 ♿ ▣ ▣
🌐 www.konserthuset.se

A NORDIC VERSION of a Greek
temple, Konserthuset
(the Concert Hall) is a masterpiece of the architect Ivar
Tengbom (1878–1968) and is

CITY'S TRANSFORMATION

During the 20th century Stockholm's population grew from
250,000 to more than 1.6 million. By the 1920s it was obvious that the old heart of the city
would not meet the future needs
of business, public administration
and the growth in traffic. In 1951
a controversial 30-year ongoing
programme to transform the
lower Norrmalm city centre was
launched. Slums on 335 of the 600
sites were pulled down and 78
new buildings were built. Two-
thirds of the area's buildings were
added during this period.

The first steps towards a
new Hötorg City, 1958

The *Orpheus* sculpture group by
Carl Milles at Konserthuset

THE NOBEL PRIZES

Alfred Nobel (1833–96) was an outstanding chemist and
inventor. He left his fortune to endow the
prestigious Nobel Prizes – consisting of a
monetary award and a medal – which
have been presented every December
since 1901. The ceremony takes
place in Konserthuset, where
prizes are awarded for physics,
chemistry, physiology or medicine,
and literature. Since 1969 the Bank
of Sweden has given a prize for
economic sciences in Nobel's memory. The Nobel Peace Prize is presented in Oslo on the same day. In 1901
each prize was worth 150,000 kr; in
2003 the figure was 10 million kr.

The Nobel Medal,
awarded annually

an outstanding example of the
1920s' Neo-Classical style.
Tengbom's tradition has been
carried on by his son Anders
(b. 1911), who was in charge
of its renovation in 1970–71,
and his grandson Svante
(b. 1942), who had a similar
task in 1993–6.

Constructed in 1923–6, the
main hall has undergone major
reconstruction and modern-
ization to overcome acoustical
problems. Its interior is very
simple in contrast to the
Grünewald Hall, by the artist
Isaac Grünewald (1889–1946),
which is in the more lavish
style of an Italian Renaissance
palace. The four marble statues
in the main foyer are by Carl
Milles, creator of the *Orpheus*
sculpture group outside.

The Concert Hall is the
home of the Swedish Royal
Philharmonic Orchestra,
which gives some 70 concerts
every year, and international
star soloists perform regularly.
It is also the venue for the
Nobel Prize presentations.

Strindbergsmuseet
Blå Tornet ⓫

Drottninggatan 85. **Map** 1 C3.
📞 08-411 53 54. 🚇 *Rådmansgatan.*
🚌 *52, 65.* ⏰ *noon–7pm Tue,
noon–4pm Wed–Sun; Jun–Aug:
noon–4pm Tue–Sun.* 📷 *2.30pm Thu,
1pm Sat & Sun.* 🔌 📷
🌐 *www.strindbergsmuseet.se*

THE WORLD-FAMOUS dramatist
August Strindberg (1849–
1912) lived at 24 different

addresses in Stockholm over
the years. He moved to the last
of these in 1908, and gave it
the name Blå Tornet (the Blue
Tower). By then he had gained
international recognition.

The apartment, now the
Strindbergsmuseet, was newly
built with central heating, toilet
and lift, but lacked a kitchen.
Instead he relied on Falkner's
Pension, in the same building,
for food and other services.
On his last few birthdays the
great man would stand on his
balcony and watch his
admirers stage a torchlight
procession in his honour.

Opened in 1973, the
museum shows the author's
home with his bedroom and
dining room and his study as it
was on his death, as well as
3,000 books, photographic
archives, press cuttings and
posters. In the adjoining
premises, a permanent
exhibition portrays Strindberg
as author, theatrical director,
artist and photographer. Temporary exhibitions and other
activities are often held here.

Strindberg's desk and writing
materials in his study

Adolf Fredriks
Kyrka ⓬

Holländargatan 14. **Map** 1 C3.
📞 08-20 70 76. 🚇 *Hötorget.* 🚌
52. ⏰ *1–7pm Mon, 10am–4pm
Tue–Sat, 10am–4pm Sun.*
Concert *12.15 Tue.* ✝ *7pm Mon,
12.15pm Wed & Thu, 11am Sun.*
📷 *by appointment.* 🔌 📷 📷

KING ADOLF FREDRIK laid the
foundation stone of this
church in 1768 on the site of
an earlier chapel dedicated to
St Olof. Designed by Carl
Fredrik Adelcrantz, in Neo-
Classical style with traces of
Rococo, the church has been
built in the shape of a
Greek cross and has
a central dome.

The interior has
undergone a
number of
changes, but both
the altar and pulpit
have remained
intact. The
sculptor Johan
Tobias Sergel
created the
altarpiece and
the memorial
to the French
philosopher
Descartes who
died in Stockholm in 1650.
The paintings in the dome
were added in 1899–1900 by
Julius Kronberg. More recent
acquisitions include altar silver-
ware by Sigurd Persson.

The cemetery is the resting
place of the assassinated
Prime Minister Olof Palme
(1927–86). J T Sergel is also
buried here.

Memorial to
Descartes

Armémuseum, with the dome of Hedvig Eleonora Kyrka in the background

Kungliga Biblioteket ⑬

Humlegården. **Map** 2 D3.
📞 08-463 40 00. 🅣 Östermalmstorg. 🚌 1, 2, 55, 56, 91, 96.
🕓 9am–8pm Mon–Thu, 9am–7pm Fri, 10am–5pm Sat; mid-Jun–mid-Aug: 9am–6pm Mon–Thu, 9am–5pm Fri, 11am–3pm Sat. 🎫 by appointment. ♿ 🖪 🆆 www.kb.se

THIS IS SWEDEN'S national library and an autonomous Government department in its own right. Ever since 1661, when there were only nine printing presses in Sweden, copies of every piece of printed matter have had to be lodged with Kungliga Biblioteket (Royal Library). Since 1993 this requirement has also applied to electronic documents. As there are now some 3,000 printers and publishers in Sweden the volume of material is expanding rapidly. The stock of books is increasing at the rate of 35,000 volumes a year.

The imposing original building, dating from 1865–78, had to be expanded in the 1920s, and again in the 1990s.

The library is in a beautiful setting in Humlegården, created by Gustav II Adolf in 1619 to grow hops for the royal household. Ever since the 18th century, the park has been a favourite recreation area for Stockholmers.

The 13th-century "Devil's Bible" in Kungliga Biblioteket

Armémuseum ⑭

Riddargatan 13. **Map** 2 E4.
📞 08-788 95 60. 🅣 Östermalmstorg. 🚌 62. 🕓 11am–8pm Tue, 11am–4pm Wed–Sun. 🎫 ♿ 🖪 🆆 www.armemuseum.org

THE OLD ARMOURY on Artillerigården has been the home of the Armémuseum (Royal Army Museum) since 1879. During the 1990s, the 250-year-old building and its displays underwent extensive renovation to create one of the capital's best-planned and most interesting museums.

Dramatic life-size settings have been made to portray Sweden's history of war and defence, showing not only what happened in battle but how the lives of the women and children at home were affected. Diaries, intelligence manuals, rifles, flags and even cutlery add a note of reality.

Processions for royal visits start from the museum and during the summer guardsmen march from here to the Royal Palace at 11.45am daily for the changing of the guard.

Musikmuseet ⑮

Sibyllegatan 2. **Map** 2 E4.
📞 08-519 554 90. 🅣 Östermalmstorg. 🚌 47, 62, 69, 76. 🕓 11am–4pm Tue–Fri, noon– 4pm Sat–Sun. 🎫 ♿ 🖪 🆆 www.stockholm.music.museum.se

AFTER BEING HOUSED on nine different sites, the Museum of Music finally moved into this former royal bakery in 1979. It is the capital's oldest preserved industrial building, right in the city centre. Bread was baked here for military personnel in Stockholm from 1640 right up to 1958. Today the museum's collection includes about 6,000 instruments, and it also holds Sweden's national musical archive. With 20,000 manuscripts, it is a gold mine for anyone interested in Swedish folk music. The archive is open to visitors by appointment. There is a regular programme of temporary exhibitions.

A so-called *hummel* instrument once owned by the troubadour C M Bellman

Hovstallet ⑯

Väpnargatan 1. **Map** 2 E4. 📞 08-402 61 06. 🅣 Östermalmstorg. 🚌 47, 62, 69, 76. 🕓 for guided tours. 🕓 May–Jun. 🎫 2pm Sat & Sun; Jul–Aug: 2pm Mon–Fri. ♿

THE ROYAL MEWS looks after transport for the Royal Family and Royal Household. It maintains about 40 carriages, a dozen cars, carriage horses, and a few horses used for riding. The royal horses are Swedish half-breeds.

There are many treasures among the carriages, such as the glass-panelled State Coach known as a "Berliner". It was built in Sweden at the Adolf Freyschuss carriage works and made its debut at Oscar II's silver jubilee in 1897. It is still used today on ceremonial occasions.

Incoming foreign ambassadors travel to the Royal Palace for their formal audience with the monarch in Karl XV's coupé. Open carriages from the mid-19th century drawn by two horses are normally used for processions.

INGMAR BERGMAN

The playwright and producer Ingmar Bergman was born at Östermalm in 1918. His long series of masterly films have

made him world-famous, but he started his career in the theatre. From 1963–6 he was Director of Kungliga Dramatiska Teatern, where he is still a guest producer. His break-through as a film producer came with *Smiles of the Summer Night* (1955), and *The Seventh Seal* (1957) was a cinematic milestone. *Fanny and Alexander* (1982) was his last major film, since when he has written screenplays and published his autobiography, *Magic Lantern*.

Ingmar Bergman at a press conference, 1998

The Hallwylska Palatset courtyard, seen through the gateway arch

Kungliga Dramatiska Teatern ⑰

Nybroplan. **Map** 2 E4. 📞 *08-667 06 80.* 🚇 *Östermalmstorg.* 🚌 *47, 62, 69, 76.* **Ticket Office** 🕐 *noon–7pm Tue–Sat, noon–5pm Sun (except Jun–Aug).* 📷 🚫 ♿ 🍴 🌐 *www.dramaten.se*

WHEN PLANS WERE drawn up in the early 20th century to build the present Kungliga Dramatiska Teatern (Royal Dramatic Theatre) at Nybroplan, the State refused to give financial aid, so it was funded by lotteries instead. The results exceeded all expectations, giving the architect Fredrik Lilljekvist generous resources which he used to the full.

The new theatre, known as Dramaten, took six years to build and opened in 1908. The design was lavish, both in the choice of materials and in the contributions by leading Swedish artists.

The Jugendstil façade, inspired by Viennese archi-

tecture, is in expensive white marble. Christian Ericsson created the powerful relief frieze, Carl Milles the centre section and John Börjesson the bronze statues *Poetry* and *Drama*. These are complemented in the foyer by *Tragedy* and *Comedy* by Börjesson and Theodor Lundberg respectively.

The ceiling in the foyer is by Carl Larsson, while the upper lobby's back wall was painted by Oscar Björk, and the auditorium's ceiling and stage lintel by Julius Kronberg. Gustav Cederström provided the central painting in the marble foyer.

When Gustav III founded the Royal Dramatic Theatre in 1788 it performed in a building on Slottsbacken. The colour scheme there – blue, white and gold – was chosen for the new venue, but was changed to "theatre red" in the 1930s.

The original colours were reinstated in 1988.

Kungliga Dramatiska Teatern's Jugendstil façade in white marble

Hallwylska Palatset ⑱

Hamngatan 4. **Map** 2 D4. 📞 *08-519 555 99.* 🚇 *Östermalmstorg.* 🚌 *46, 47, 55, 62, 69, 76.* 🚗 *noon–3pm every hour Tue–Sun, also 6pm Wed, 1pm Sun (Eng). 26 Jun–15 Aug: 11am–4pm daily every hour, also 6pm Wed, in Eng 1pm daily.* 📷 🚫 📷 🌐 *www.hallwylskamuseet.se*

THE IMPRESSIVE façade of Hamngatan 4 is nothing in comparison with what is concealed behind the heavy gates. The Hallwyl Palace was built from 1892–7 as a residence for the immensely wealthy Count and Countess Walther and Wilhelmina von Hallwyl. When the Countess died in 1930 the State was left a fantastic gift: an unbelievably ornate palace whose chatelaine had amassed a priceless collection of *objets d'art* over many decades. Eight years later the doors opened on a new museum with 67,000 catalogued items.

Wilhelmina left nothing to chance. The architect Isak Gustav Clason (1856–1930) had no worries about cost and nor did the decorative painter and artistic adviser Julius Kronberg. Every detail had to be perfect. A typical example is the billiards room which has gilt-leather wallpaper and walnut panelling, with billiard balls sculpted into the marble fireplace.

The paintings in the gallery, mostly 16th- and 17th-century Flemish, were bought over a period of only two years.

BLASIEHOLMEN & SKEPPSHOLMEN

OPPOSITE THE Royal Palace on the eastern side of the Norrström channel lies Blasieholmen, a natural springboard to the islands of Skeppsholmen and Kastellholmen.

Several elegant palaces were built at Blasieholmen during Sweden's era as a great power in the 17th and early 18th centuries. But the area's present appearance was acquired in the period between the mid-19th century, when buildings such as Nationalmuseum were erected, and just before World War I. In the early 1900s, stately residences such as Bååtska Palatset became overshadowed by smart hotels, opulent bank build-

Porthole in wooden boat

ings and entertainment venues. Blasieholmen is also the place for auction houses, art galleries, antiques shops and second-hand bookshops. And the quayside is the departure point for sightseeing and archipelago boats.

Skeppsholmen is reached by a wrought-iron bridge with old wooden boats moored next to it. In the middle of the 17th century the island became the base for the Swedish Navy and many of its old buildings were designed as barracks and stores. Today they house some of the city's major museums and cultural institutions, juxtaposed with the avant-garde construction of the Moderna Museet.

SIGHTS AT A GLANCE

Museums
Arkitekturmuseet ❸
Moderna Museet pp78–9 ❷
Nationalmuseum pp80–81 ❼
Östasiatiska Museet ❶

Islands and Squares
Blasieholmstorg ❾
Kastellholmen ❻
Raoul Wallenbergs Torg ⓬

Synagogues
Synagogan ❿

Hotels and Restaurants
af Chapman ❹
Berns' Salonger ⓫
Grand Hôtel ❽

Concert Halls
Nybrokajen 11 ⓭

Public Buildings
Kungliga
   Konsthögskolan ❺

KEY

▭	Street-by-Street map *See pp74–5*
🚌	Bus stop
⛴	Ferry landing point
Ⓣ	Tunnelbana station
🅿	Parking

0 metres   250
0 yards   250

◁ **Skeppsholmsbron, linking Blasieholmen and Skeppsholmen, with the ship** *af Chapman* **in the background**

Street-by-Street: Skeppsholmen

Skeppsholmen has long since lost its importance as a naval base and has been transformed into a centre for culture. Many of the naval buildings have been restored and traditional wooden boats are moored here, but pride of place now goes to the exciting Moderna Museet. The island is ideal for a full-day visit, with its location between the waters of Strömmen and Nybroviken acting as a breathing space in the centre of Stockholm. The attractive buildings, the richly wooded English-style park and the view towards Skeppsbron and Strandvägen also make Skeppsholmen a pleasant place for those who would just prefer to have a quiet stroll.

Teater Galeasen is Stockholm's avant-garde theatre for new Swedish and international drama.

Blasie-holmen

Skepps-holmsbron (bridge)

★ **Östasiatiska Museet**
This belt plaquette in Ordos style from the 1st or 2nd century BC is part of a remarkable collection of arts and crafts from China, Japan, Korea and India, from the Stone Age to the 19th century ❶

Skeppsholmen Church (1824–42) in well-preserved Empire style.

Salute battery (see p76)

Admiralty House

Paradise (1963), a sculpture group by Jean Tinguely and Niki de Saint Phalle for Montreal's World Exposition, has stood outside the site of the Moderna Museet since 1972.

Youth Hostel

Swedish Society of Crafts & Design

af Chapman
Built in 1888, the full-rigged former freighter and school ship has served as a popular youth hostel since 1949. Skeppsholmen Church (left) and the Admiralty House (1647–50, rebuilt 1844–6) are in the background ❹

Kungliga Konsthögskolan
The first part of the Royal College of Fine Arts was completed in the 1770s, but it acquired its present appearance in the mid-1990s. This cast-iron boar stands at the entrance ❺

Loading crane
built in 1751 –
the oldest of its
type in Sweden.

The festival area on the quayside
below the Moderna Museet is the
venue for the popular International
Jazz & Blues Festival, which takes
place for a week in July each year.

LOCATOR MAP
See Street Finder map 4

Arkitekturmuseet
*The Museum of Architecture
highlights thousands of years
of building, with a collection
of models showing master-
pieces worldwide, including
this model of the Stockholm
City Library by Asplund* **3**

★ Moderna Museet
*Designed by Rafael
Moneo, the museum
was opened in 1998
when Stockholm was
Cultural Capital of
Europe. It has an
exciting collection of
modern art, and fine
views across the water* **2**

Monument commem-
orating the battle
at Svensksund in 1790
(see p40)

Kastell-
holmen

KEY

– – –   Suggested route

Långa Raden is used by the
State Board of Culture, and also
for exhibitions and as homes.
The buildings, dating from about
1700, originally accommodated
King Karl XII's bodyguard.

STAR SIGHTS

★ **Moderna Museet**

★ **Östasiatiska Museet**

0 metres   100

0 yards   100

Arkitekturmuseet, housed in the Neo-Classical former naval drill hall

Östasiatiska Museet ❶

Tyghusplan. **Map** 4 D2. ☎ 08-519 557 70. Ⓣ Kungsträdgården. 🚌 65. 🚢 Djurgårdsfärja. ◯ noon– 8pm Tue, noon–5pm Wed–Sun. 🎧 2pm Sun in Eng by appointment. 🚫 ♿ ▯ W www.ostasiatiska.se

IT IS NOT UNUSUAL for Western capitals to have a museum devoted to art and archaeology from China, Japan, Korea and India. But it is not every Museum of Far Eastern Antiquities that, like Östasiatiska Museet, can claim one of the world's foremost collections of Chinese art outside Asia.

On a visit to the Yellow River valley in China in the early 1920s, the Swedish geologist Johan Gunnar Andersson discovered hitherto unknown dwellings and graves containing objects dating from the New Stone Age.

He was allowed to take a selection of items back to Sweden, and these formed the basis for the museum, founded in 1926. A key figure in its development was the then Crown Prince, later to become King Gustav VI Adolf,

who was both interested in and knowledgeable about archaeology. Later, he bequeathed to the museum his own large collection of ancient Chinese arts and crafts.

The museum has been on Skeppsholmen since 1963, when it was moved into a restored house which had been built in 1699–1700 as a depot for Karl XII's bodyguard.

Moderna Museet ❷

See pp78– 9.

Arkitektur-museet ❸

Exercisplan. **Map** 4 E3. ☎ 08-587 270 00. Ⓣ Kungsträdgården. 🚌 65. 🚢 Djurgårdsfärja. ◯ 10am–8pm Tue–Wed, 10am– 6pm Thu–Sun. 🎧 2pm Sat & Sun (in Eng: summer only). 🚫 ♿ 🍴 ▭ ▯ W www.arkitekturmuseet.se

THE SWEDISH Museum of Architecture shares an entrance hall and restaurant with the new Moderna Museet. It has also reclaimed

its earlier home, a one-time naval drill hall.

In the permanent exhibition, more than 100 architectural models guide visitors through the history of Swedish building. They include the oldest and simplest of wooden houses to the highly sophisticated construction techniques and innovative styles of the present day.

It is fascinating to move from an almost 2,000-year-old longhouse to a modern supermarket, interspersed with examples of architecture in Gothenburg from the 17th century to the 1930s and the new Årsta bridge situated to the south of Stockholm.

Models of historic architectural works worldwide, from 2000 BC up to the present day, are also on show.

The museum offers an ambitious programme – albeit only in Swedish – alongside the permanent and temporary exhibitions, including lectures, study days, city walks, guided tours, school visits and family events on Sunday afternoons, which involve model-building.

THE SKEPPSHOLMEN CANNONS

A salute battery of four 57-mm rapid-fire cannons is sited on Skeppsholmen and is still in use. Salutes are fired to mark national and royal special occasions at 12 noon on weekdays and 1pm at weekends: 28 January – the King's name day; 30 April – the King's birthday; 6 June – Sweden's National Day; 14 July – Crown Princess Victoria's birthday; 8 August – the Queen's name day; 23 December – the Queen's birthday.

The salute battery on Skeppsholmen

Chinese Bodhisattva in limestone (c.530), Östasiatiska Museet

af Chapman ❹

Västra Brobänken. **Map** 4 D3.
📞 08-463 22 66. 🚇 *Kungsträdgården.* 🚌 *65.* ⛴ *Djurgårdsfärja.* 🍴
💤 See **Where to Stay** p281.

THE SAILING SHIP *af Chapman* is one of Sweden's
most attractive and unusual
youth hostels. The ship has
136 beds, and there are a
further 152 beds in the hostel
building facing the gangway.

Visitors staying in more
conventional accommodation
can still go on board and
enjoy *af Chapman*'s special
atmosphere. The three-masted
ship was built in 1888 at the
English port of Whitehaven
and used as a freight vessel.
She came to Sweden in 1915
and saw service as a sail
training ship until 1934. The
City of Stockholm bought the
vessel after World War II and
she has been berthed here
since 1949. She is named after
Fredrik Henrik af Chapman,
a master shipbuilder who was
born in Gothenburg in 1721.

Kungliga Konst-
högskolan ❺

Flaggmansvägen 1. **Map** 4 E3. 📞 08-
614 40 00. 🚇 *Kungsträdgården.* 🚌
65. ⛴ *Djurgårdsfärja.* 🔲 *to the
public for special events.* ♿ 💤

A STROLL AROUND Skepps-
holmen provides an
opportunity to have a closer
look at the beautifully
restored 18th-century naval
barracks which now houses
Kungliga Konsthögskolan (the
Royal College of Fine Arts). At
the entrance there are two
statues depicting a lion and a
boar. "In like a lion and out
like a pig" is an old saying
among the lecturers and the
200 or so students at this
college, still rich in tradition.

The college started out in
1735 as an academy for
painting and sculpture for the
decorators working on Tessin's
new Royal Palace. Gustav III
granted it a royal charter in
1773. Before it moved here in
1995, the college was located
on Fredsgatan as part of
Konstakademien, although
since 1978 it had been run

independently with departments for painting, sculpture,
graphics, computing and
video, as well as offering
courses for architects.

The college is not normally
open to the public, apart from
an "open house" once a year.
Then visitors can enjoy the
beautiful interiors, especially
the vaulted 18th-century cellars.

**The medieval-style castle on
Kastellholmen, built in 1846–8**

Kastellholmen ❻

Map 4 F4. 🚇 *Kungsträdgården.*
🚌 *65.* ⛴ *Djurgårdsfärja.*

RIGHT IN THE middle of
Stockholm, Kastellholmen
is a typical archipelago island
with granite rocks and steep
cliffs. From Skeppsholmen it is
reached by a bridge built in
1880. Every morning since
1640 a sailor has hoisted the
three-tailed Swedish war flag
at the castle. Whenever a
visiting naval vessel arrives,
the battery's four cannons

fire a welcoming salute from
the castle terrace.

The charming brick pavilion
by the bridge was built in 1882
for the Royal Skating Club,
which used the water between
the two islands when it froze.

Nationalmuseum ❼

See pp80–81.

Grand Hôtel ❽

Södra Blasieholmshamnen 8. **Map** 3
C1. 📞 08-679 35 00. 🚇 *Kungsträdgården.* 🚌 *2, 55, 62, 65, 76.*
See **Where to Stay** p281 and **Where
to Eat** p294.

OSCAR II'S head chef, Régis
Cadier, founded the
Grand Hôtel, Sweden's only
five-star hotel, in 1874. Since
1901, the hotel has accommodated the Nobel Prize
winners each year.

Traditional Swedish
delicacies are served in an
abundant *smörgåsbord* in the
elegant Grands Veranda.
There is also a stylish gourmet
restaurant, Franska Matsalen.
The Cadier Bar is named after
the hotel's founder.

The hotel has 19 banquet-
ing and conference suites, the
best known of which is the
lofty *Vinterträdgården*
(Winter Garden) which can
accommodate 800 people.
The *Spegelsalen* (Hall of
Mirrors) is a copy of the hall at
Versailles and was where the
Nobel Prize banquet was held
until 1929, when it became
too big and was moved to
City Hall (see p100).

Grand Hôtel on Blasieholmen, Sweden's only five-star hotel

Moderna Museet ❷

THE MUSEUM OF Modern Art is an airy building, designed by the Catalan architect Rafael Moneo in 1998. The museum has a top-class collection of international and Swedish modern art, as well as photography and film. Built partly underground, the complex includes a cinema and auditorium; the photographic library is the most comprehensive collection of its type in northern Europe and there is also a collection of video art and art documentaries. A wide choice of books on art, photography, film and architecture can be found in the bookshop and the Restaurant MM Mat has attractive views over the water.

Breakfast Outdoors (1962)
This sculpture group by Picasso, executed in sandblasted concrete by Carl Nesjar, stands in the museum garden near the entrance

To Arkitekturmuseet

Main entrance to both Moderna Museet and Arkitekturmuseet (see p76).

Bookshop

KEY

- ☐ Museum's own collections
- ☐ Temporary exhibitions
- ☐ Non-exhibition space

Entrance level

Restaurant MM Mat

Photographic library

Auditorium

★ Monogram
This work by Robert Rauschenberg (c.1956) includes an angora goat with painted nose and ears, a white car tyre and a collage with fragments of the word DADA. A self-portrait?

Cinema

Middle level

★ The Dying Dandy (1918)
The cosmopolitan artist Nils Dardel (1888–1943) produced this Expressionistic painting when he was about to marry. It can be interpreted as a farewell to his misspent youth.

RAFAEL MONEO

Rafael Moneo (b. 1937) is one of the leading contemporary architects. As a young architect, Moneo took part in the project to build the Sydney Opera House. His flair for adapting building design to sensitive surroundings was recognized in 1989 when his was chosen out of 211 entries as the winner of the competition to design the new Moderna Museet.

Moderna Museet's northern façade

GALLERY GUIDE

*The large room on the entrance
level is used for temporary
exhibitions. Three rooms on
the same level have an alternat-
ing selection of collections
from the eras 1900–45, 1946–
70 and 1971 to the present
day. The middle level has an
auditorium, cinema and
photographic library. Another
entrance is at the lowest level.*

★ **The Child's Brain** (1914)
*The surrealist Giorgio de
Chirico gave his work the
title* The Ghost, *but in the
irrational spirit of the movement Louis Aragon renamed
it in a pamphlet about the
artist's 1927 retrospective.*

STAR FEATURES

★ **The Dying Dandy
by Dardel**

★ **Monogram
by Rauschenberg**

★ **The Child's Brain
by de Chirico**

Blasieholmstorg ⑨

Map 3 C1. 🚇 *Kungsträdgården.*
🚌 *2, 55, 62, 65, 76.*

TWO OF THE city's oldest
palaces are located in this
square, flanked by two bronze
horses. The palace at No. 8
was built in the mid-17th
century by Field Marshal
Gustaf Horn. It was rebuilt
100 years later, when it
acquired the character of an
18th-century French palace.
Foreign ambassadors and
ministers lodged here when
they visited the
capital, so it
became known
as the Ministers'
Palace. Later it
became a base for
overseas admin-
istration and soon
earned its present
name of Utrikes-
ministerhotellet
(Foreign Ministry
Hotel). Parts of the
building are now used as
offices by the Musical Academy
and the Swedish Institute.

**Bronze horse on
Blasieholmstorg**

Bååtska Palatset stands
nearby at No. 6. Its exterior
dates from 1669 and was
designed by Tessin the Elder.
In 1876–7 it was partly rebuilt
by F W Scholander for the
Freemasons, who still have
their lodge here.

Another interesting complex
of buildings can be found on
the square at No. 10. The
façade which faces on to
Nybrokajen, along the water's
edge, is an attractive example
of the Neo-Renaissance style
of the 1870s and 1880s.

Synagogan ⑩

Warendorffsgatan 3. **Map** 3 C1.
📞 08-87 858 00. 🚇 *Kungsträdgården.* 🚌 *2, 55, 62, 65, 76.*
🕙 *all year 9.15am Sat; Jun–Aug:
6.30pm Fri; Hebrew and partly
English.* 🎧 *summer and by
appointment.* ♿

IT TOOK MOST of the 1860s
to build the Conservative
Jewish community's syna-
gogue on land reclaimed from
the sea. When it was inaugurated in 1870, the building
was standing on 1,300 piles

**Monument to the victims of the
Holocaust during World War II**

which had been driven down
to a depth of 15 m (50 ft). It
is built in what the architect,
F W Scholander, called
"ancient Eastern style". The
synagogue can be
visited on guided
tours during the
summer. Alongside
is the congre-
gation's assembly
room and library.
Outside is a
monument erected
in 1998 in memory
of 8,000 victims
of the Holocaust whose
relations had been rescued
and taken to Sweden during
World War II.

There is also an Orthodox
synagogue in the city centre,
reached through the Jewish
Centre (Judiska Centret) on
Nybrogatan at No. 19.

Berns' Salonger ⑪

Berzelii Park. **Map** 2 D4. 📞 08-566
322 00. 🚇 *Kungsträdgården,
Östermalmstorg.* 🚌 *2, 47, 55, 62,
65, 69, 76.* ♿ **Where to Eat** *p294.*

THIS HAS BEEN one of Stockholm's most legendary
restaurants and entertainment
venues since 1863. Both
salons, with their stately
galleries, magnificent crystal
chandeliers and elegant
mirrors, were restored to their
original splendour by the
British designer and restaur-
ateur Terence Conran to mark
the new millennium.

The new-look Berns' is one
of Stockholm's biggest
restaurants, with seating for
400 diners. The gallery level,
with its beautifully decorated
dining rooms, was made
famous by August Strindberg's
novel *The Red Room* (1879).

Nationalmuseum ❼

THE NATIONAL MUSEUM is a landmark on the southern side of Blasieholmen. The location by the Strömmen channel inspired the 19th-century German architect August Stüler to design a building in the Venetian and Florentine Renaissance styles.

Completed in 1866, the museum houses Sweden's largest art collection, with some 16,000 classic paintings and sculptures. Drawings and graphics from the 15th century up to the early 20th century bring the total up to 500,000. The applied art and design section has works spanning five centuries, including a 500-year-old tapestry, porcelain and examples of work by master furniture-makers, such as Georg Haupt. Space is also devoted to the development of modern Swedish design *(see pp22-3)*, 1900–2000.

The Love Lesson (1716–17)
Antoine Watteau's speciality was the so-called fêtes galantes, depicting young couples in playful mood.

★ The Conspiracy of the Batavians under Claudius Civilis (1661–2)
Originally intended for Amsterdam, Rembrandt depicts the Batavians' conspiracy against the Romans, symbolizing the Dutch liberation campaign against Spain.

Level 2

Chest of Drawers (1780)
This impressive piece of furniture was created by Georg Haupt, who was one of the foremost Swedish cabinet-makers of the 18th century.

Atrium through levels 1 and 2

Gravure gallery

Entrance

David and Bathsheba (1490)
This tapestry from Brussels is created in the decorative medieval style, with pomegranates, faces and hands forming an exquisite work.

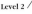

STAR FEATURES

★ **The Lady with the Veil by Roslin**

★ **The Conspiracy of the Batavians by Rembrandt**

Entry for wheelchairs

★ **The Lady with the Veil**
Alexander Roslin's elegant portrait (1769) is often considered to be a glamorized symbol of 18th-century Sweden.

VISITORS' CHECKLIST

Södra Blasieholmshamnen.
Map 4 D2. 08-519 543 00.
Kungsträdgården. 65; or 2, 55, 62, 76 to Karl XII's Torg.
11am–8pm Tue & Thu (Jun–Aug to 5pm Thu); 11am–5pm Wed, Fri–Sun.
24, 25 & 31 Dec, 1 Jan, some other hols. in Eng.
W www.nationalmuseum.se

The Upper Staircase
At the back is Carl Larsson's monumental mural The Entry of King Gustav Vasa of Sweden in Stockholm 1523. *On the opposite wall is his* Midwinter Sacrifice.

The Faun (1774)
Johan Tobias Sergel was the foremost sculptor of the Gustavian era. This piece is regarded as his most triumphant work.

Level 1

Auditorium

Entrance level

KEY

☐ Painting and sculpture

☐ Applied art and design

☐ Temporary exhibitions

☐ Non-exhibition space

☐ No admission

GALLERY GUIDE

Level 2 is devoted to painting and sculpture. The accent is on Swedish 18th- to early 20th-century art, but the 17th-century Dutch and Flemish, and 18th-century French schools are also represented. Exhibits may change. Level 1 shows mainly Swedish applied art and design, particularly furniture, porcelain, silver and glass from the 15th century up to modern Swedish design. To the left of the main entrance is the Gravure Gallery with temporary exhibitions of graphics etc.

Raoul Wallenbergs Torg 12

Map 2 E4. Östermalmstorg.
2, 47, 55, 62, 65, 69, 76.

THIS SQUARE IS dedicated to Raoul Wallenberg (1912–unknown), who during World War II worked as a diplomat at the Swedish Embassy in Budapest. By using Swedish "protective passports" and safe houses throughout the city he helped a large number of Hungarian Jews to escape deportation to the Nazi concentration camps.

In 1945, when Budapest was liberated, Wallenberg was imprisoned by the Soviet Union and according to Russian sources he died in Moscow's Lubianka prison in 1947. His fate has never been satisfactorily explained despite strenuous efforts by the Swedes to seek the truth.

The small square adjoins Berzelii Park and Nybroplan and faces the Nybrokajen waterfront. The definitive design of the square has been hotly debated because it is set in an architecturally sensitive area, but great efforts have been made to ensure that it remains a worthy memorial to Raoul Wallenberg.

Nybrokajen 11 13

Nybrokajen 11. **Map** 3 C1. 08-407 16 00. Kungsträdgården, Östermalmstorg. 47, 62, 69, 76.
Djurgårdsfärja. for concerts (phone for details). W www.nybrokajen11.rikskonserter.se

CONSTRUCTED IN the 1870s, this building facing the waters of Nybroviken once housed the Musical Academy. Its concert hall, opened in 1878, was the first in the country, and was used to present the inaugural Nobel Prize in 1901. Designed in Neo-Renaissance style with cast-iron pillars, the hall has a royal box and galleries, and can seat up to 600 people.

It is run by the state musical organization, Rikskonserter, and is a popular venue for chamber and choral concerts, jazz and folk music.

MALMARNA & FURTHER AFIELD

Old tram at Djurgården

As STOCKHOLM grew, the heart of the city, Gamla Stan, became cramped and building spread out to the surrounding areas, known as "Malmarna" (the "ore hills"). Parts of these now make up present-day Stockholm.

Södermalm came into the ownership of the city in 1436. Much of Stockholm's old charm can still be found in the areas around Fjällgatan, Mosebacke and Maria-berget. To the north, the Norrmalm area expanded rapidly and became known as Stockholm's northern suburb in the 17th century. The once-rural Östermalm was transformed in

the late 19th century into an affluent residential area with grand, wide boulevards, contrasting with the 1930s Functionalist style of the adjoining Gärdet district.

To the west is Kungsholmen, the centre for local government, with distinguished buildings such as Stadshuset (the City Hall) and Rådhuset (the Law Court). Nationalstadsparken (the National City Park), a green area of ecological and cultural interest surrounding the city and reaching into its central districts, offers lovely walking routes and many of the city's foremost museums.

SIGHTS AT A GLANCE

KEY

	Stockholm City Centre
	Motorway
	Major road
	Minor road

Historiska Museet ❶

THE MUSEUM OF NATIONAL ANTIQUITIES, Historiska Museet, was opened in 1943. It was designed by Bengt Romare and Georg Sherman. Bror Marklund (1907–77) was responsible for the decoration around the entrance and the richly detailed bronze gateways depicting events in early Swedish history. The museum originally made its name with its exhibits from the Viking era, as well as its outstanding collections from the early Middle Ages. Contemporary church textiles are also on show. Many of Historiska Museet's gold treasures have been gathered together to form one of Stockholm's most remarkable sights, Guldrummet (the Gold Room).

Upper floor

Exhibitions showing the mass migrations and the Wendic era.

Bronze Age Find
This Bronze Age artifact, thought to be a percussion instrument, was discovered in a bog in southern Sweden in 1847.

Courtyard

★ The Alunda Elk
This 21-cm (8-inch) stone axe, discovered in 1920 at Alunda in central Sweden, resembles an elk's head. It is a ceremonial axe, probably made in Finland or Karelia in around 2000 BC.

Ground floor

Rosen- gården

The Bäckaskog Woman
The 155-cm (5-ft) tall Bäcka- skog woman lived around 5000 BC. She died at the age of 40–50 and was buried sitting in a cramped pit.

STAR FEATURES

★ **The Alunda Elk**

★ **Maria from Viklau**

★ **The Gold Room**

The Viking Era
This eventful era is reflected in a department whose exhibits include a Viking sword with artistic embellish- ments, and ornaments in the shape of Nordic animals.

The Skog Tapestry
This once hung in the wooden church at Skog in northern Sweden. It is one of the museum's oldest textile treasures.

Baroque Hall

Stairs descending to the Gold Room

Main entrance

★ **Maria from Viklau**
This Madonna figure without child is the best-preserved example from Sweden's early medieval period. The colourful wooden sculpture is richly gilded.

VISITORS' CHECKLIST

Narvavägen 13–17. **Map** 2 F4.
☎ 08-519 556 00. 🚌 44, 56.
Ⓣ Karlaplan. 🕐 mid-Sep–mid-May: 11am–5pm Tue–Sun, also 5–8pm Thur; mid-May–mid-Sep: 11am–5pm daily.
● 24, 25 & 31 Dec and some holidays.
Ⓦ www.historiska.se

GALLERY GUIDE
The exhibitions are divided chronologically on two floors with the prehistoric section on the ground floor and the Middle Ages on the upper floor, where there is also a Baroque Hall. In the basement, reached by a staircase from the entrance hall, is the Gold Room with stunning gold and silver objects.

KEY

- ☐ Prehistoric Era
- ☐ Middle Ages and Baroque
- ☐ Temporary exhibitions
- ☐ Non-exhibition space

★ **THE GOLD ROOM**

Since the early 1990s the museum's many priceless gold artifacts have been on show in Guldrummet (the Gold Room), a 700-sq m (7,500-sq ft) underground vault built with 250 tons of reinforced concrete to ensure security. The room is in two circular sections. The inner section houses the main collection, with 50 kg (110 lb) of gold treasures and 250 kg (550 lb) of silver from the Bronze Age to the Middle Ages.

The Elisabeth Reliquary was originally a drinking goblet which was mounted with gold and precious stones in the 11th century. In about 1230 a silver cover was added to enclose the skull of St Elisabeth. Sweden seized it in Wurzburg in 1631, as a trophy in the Thirty Years War.

The Gold Collars were found between 1827 and 1864; the three-ringed collar in a stone quarry in eastern Sweden, the five-ringed in a ditch on the island of Öland, and the seven-ringed hanging on a spike in a barn.

The underground Gold Room in Historiska Museet

Strandvägen with its stately houses and boats along the quayside

Strandvägen ❷

Map 4 E1. 🚌 *47, 69, 76.*
🚇 *Östermalmstorg, Karlaplan.* 🚊 *7.*

IN THE EARLY 1900s Stockholm's 10 richest citizens – seven of whom were wholesale merchants – lived in palatial new houses along Strandvägen. Before 1897, when a major exhibition was held just across the water on Djurgården, this muddy, hilly stretch known as Ladugårdslands Strandgata aspired to becoming "a street, the like of which will not be found anywhere else in Europe". It was a long process. Even after all the grand buildings had been completed, the wooden quay erected in the 1860s was something of an eyesore. It was still used up to the 1940s by boats bringing firewood from the archipelago islands.

Nevertheless, the renamed Strandvägen, with its three rows of lime trees, soon became the elegant boulevard envisaged and, then as now, it was a popular place for a stroll, to admire the elegant façades, watch the boats and to see and be seen.

The financiers behind this and other housing projects in the early 1900s were wealthy and could call on the best architects, including I G Clason (1856–1930). Clason was influenced by Italian and French Renaissance styles for his work on No. 19–21 (Thaveniuska Huset) and No. 29–35 (Bünszowska Huset), where he designed gateways made of ships' timbers. No. 55 (Von Rosenska Palatset) is also by Clason.

Junibacken ❸

Galärvarvsvägen. **Map** 4 F1.
📞 *08-587 230 00.* 🚌 *44, 47.* 🚊 *7.*
⛴ *Djurgårdsfärja.* ⏱ *10am–5pm Tue–Fri, 9am–6pm Sat & Sun; July: 9am–7pm daily.* 🅿 ♿ 🍴 🚻 🛍
Ⓦ *www.junibacken.se*

THEY ARE ALL HERE – Pippi Longstocking, Mardie, Karlsson on the Roof, Emil, Nils Karlsson Pyssling, Ronja the robber's daughter, the Lionheart Brothers and many more favourite characters

A colourful scene from one of Astrid Lindgren's stories

from Astrid Lindgren's children's books. In accordance with the popular novelist's wishes, visitors can also meet the creations of other Swedish children's authors. When she heard about Staffan Götesam's project for a children's cultural centre she was adamant it should not be just an Astrid Lindgren museum.

Nevertheless Junibacken is still something of a tribute to the much-loved author. It was officially opened by the Royal Family in the summer of 1996 and has become one of the city's most popular tourist attractions. A mini-train takes visitors from a mock-up of the station at Vimmerby (the author's home town) to meet some of her characters, finishing with a visit to Pippi's home in Villekulla Cottage, where children can play in the different rooms.

There is also a well-stocked children's bookshop and a restaurant.

WOODEN BOATS ALONG STRANDVÄGEN

Until the 1940s sailing vessels used to carry firewood from Roslagen on the Baltic coast to the quayside at Strandvägen. This trade had lost its importance by the 1950s, and boating enthusiasts started buying up these old vessels. Some were renovated and sailed to the Caribbean, others became illegal drinking or gambling clubs on Strandvägen. New harbour regulations led to the formation of two associations to administer the boats. The wooden boats moored here today are owned by people who want to preserve a piece of cultural heritage. Every boat has a sign describing its history.

Old wooden boats along the Strandvägen quay

ASTRID LINDGREN AND PIPPI LONGSTOCKING

Astrid Lindgren has written around 100 children's books which have been translated into 74 languages, making her one of the world's most-read children's authors. Publishers turned down her first book about Pippi Longstocking, but she went on to win a children's book competition two years later, in 1945. Her headstrong and tough character Pippi soon won the hearts of children worldwide.

Born on 14 November 1907 in Vimmerby in southern Sweden, Astrid stopped writing books at 85, but her characters live on at Junibacken.

Astrid Lindgren (1907–2002)

Nordiska Museet ❹

See pp88–9.

Biologiska Museet ❺

Lejonslätten. 📞 08-442 82 15. 🚌 44, 47. 🚋 7. ⏰ Apr–Oct: 11am–4pm daily; Nov–Mar: noon–3 pm Tue–Sun. 📷 by appointment. 🎫♿🅿 W www.biologiskamuseet.com

THE NATIONAL ROMANTIC influences of the late 19th century inspired the architect Agi Lindegren when he was commissioned to design Biologiska Museet (Museum of Biology) in the 1890s. He based his plans on the simple lines of the medieval Norwegian stave churches.

The man behind the museum was the zoologist, hunter and conservationist Gustaf Kolthoff (1845–1913). In 1892, he persuaded the industrialist C F Liljevalch – who later financed the nearby art gallery – to form a company with the aim "to develop and maintain a biological museum to include all the Scandinavian mammals and birds as stuffed specimens in natural surroundings". Within a few months of opening in autumn 1893, Gustaf Kolthoff had delivered a couple of thousand stuffed animals, as well as birds' nests, young and eggs, to the museum. Many of the creatures are

shown against a diorama background, with about 300 species of Scandinavian birds and land mammals in their respective biotypes. Kolthoff's friend, the artist Bruno Liljefors, was responsible for the paintings.

Since 1970 the Museum of Biology has belonged to the Skansen Foundation. During the 1990s it underwent extensive renovation and was reopened on 13 November 1993 – exactly 100 years after its original inauguration.

Vasamuseet ❻

See pp90–91.

Gröna Lund ❼

Lilla Allmänna Gränd 9. 📞 08-587 501 00. 🚌 44, 47. 🚋 7. ⛴ Djurgårdsfärja. ⏰ mid-Apr–mid-Sep: opening hours vary. 🎫♿🅿 📷 W www.gronalund.com

A TAVERN CALLED Gröna Lund (Green Grove) existed on this site in the 18th century, and it was one of the haunts

Gröna Lund funfair seen from Kastellholmen

of the renowned troubadour Carl Michael Bellman *(see p93).*

Jakob Schultheis used the tavern's name for the modest-sized funfair which he opened here in 1883 with a two-level horse-drawn roundabout as the main attraction. Today Gröna Lund is Sweden's oldest amusement park.

The 130-day season, starting on 1 May, is short but hectic. Gröna Lund draws about 10,000 visitors a day to its attractions, which include a thrilling roller-coaster, ferris wheel and haunted house. The latest addition to the park's attractions is the free-fall "Power Tower", an 80-m (262-ft) high tower from which visitors drop at a frightening speed.

The park also has restaurants and cafés, three stages, a cabaret restaurant, a theatre and beautiful gardens.

Nearby is Liljevalchs Konsthall, a gallery featuring collections of Swedish, Nordic and international art. It also holds temporary exhibitions, including the annual Spring Salon.

Biologiska Museet's wooden façade, inspired by Nordic medieval design

Nordiska Museet ④

Resembling an extravagant Renaissance
castle, Nordiska Museet portrays everyday
life in Sweden from the 1520s to the present
day. It was created by Artur Hazelius
(1833–1901), who was also the founder of
Skansen *(see p92)*. In 1872, he started to
collect objects which would remind future
generations of the old Nordic farming culture.

The present museum, designed by Isak
Gustav Clason, was opened in 1907. Today it
has more than 1.5 million exhibits, with everything from luxury clothing and priceless
jewellery to everyday items, furniture and
children's toys, and replicas of period homes.

Doll's Houses
*The doll's houses show typical homes
from the 17th century to
modern times. This
example illustrates
one from 1860.*

Level 3

Corridor to
staircase

Level 2
(Main Hall)

Ground
floor

**State Bedchamber from
Ulvsunda Castle**
*At the end of the 17th century, the
lord of the manor at Ulvsunda
accommodated prominent guests
in this prestigious bedchamber.*

Star Features

★ **Table Settings**

★ **Strindberg Collection**

★ **Main Hall**

Gallery Guide
*The museum has four floors.
From the entrance, stairs lead
up to the temporary exhibitions
in the Main Hall on Level 2. On
the ground level is a section
covering the Sami People and
Culture. Floor 3 has the
Strindberg Collection, Doll's
Houses, Table Settings, Traditions
and the Fashion and Textile
Galleries. On the fourth floor
are sections on Folk Art,
Interiors, Swedish Homes and
Small Objects.*

Obelisk with the
inscription: "The day
may dawn when not
even all our gold is
enough to form a pic-
ture of a bygone era."

**Equestrian statue
of Karl X Gustav**

Main
entrance

★ **Table Settings**
*In the mid-17th century
table settings were a
feast for the eyes. A
swan is the centrepiece
at this meal.*

The Proposal
This painting, in the Interiors section, is by Knut Ekwall (1843–1912) and depicts a town flat in the 1880s. The room is heavily decorated with objets d'art, *ornaments and textiles.*

VISITORS' CHECKLIST

Djurgårdsvägen 6–16. **Map** 4 F2.
08-519 560 00. 44, 47.
7. Djurgårdsfärja. 10am–
4pm Mon–Fri, 10am–5pm Sat &
Sun; Jun–Aug: 10am–5pm daily.
some holidays. Eng.
w www.nordiskamuseet.se

Bridal Crown
It used to be a tradition of the church to lend a crown like this to brides as a symbol of innocence.

Level 4

Children's Playworld

★ Strindberg Collection
This picture, Snowstorm at Sea *(1894), by the writer August Strindberg (see p69), is among the museum's collection of 16 of his paintings.*

KEY

☐	Folk art
☐	Small Objects 1700–1900
☐	Swedish Homes, Interiors
☐	Table Settings, Traditions
☐	Strindberg Collection
☐	Fashion Gallery
☐	Doll's Houses
☐	Textile Gallery
☐	The Sami People
☐	Temporary exhibitions
☐	Non-exhibition space

Entrance with access for pushchairs, prams and wheelchairs

★ Main Hall
As visitors enter this huge hall, they are greeted by a monumental statue of King Gustav Vasa. It was made in painted and gilded oak by Carl Milles in 1924.

Vasamuseet ⑥

AFTER A MAIDEN VOYAGE of just 1,300 m (1,422 yd) in calm weather, the warship *Vasa* capsized in Stockholm's harbour on 10 August 1628. About 50 people went down with what was supposed to be the pride of the navy, only 100 m (109 yd) off the southern tip of Djurgården. Guns were all that were salvaged from the vessel in the 17th century and it was not until 1956 that a marine archaeologist's persistent search led to the rediscovery of *Vasa*. A complex operation began to salvage the wreck, followed by a 17-year conservation programme. The city's most popular museum opened in 1990, less than a nautical mile from the scene of the disaster.

Gun-port Lion
More than 200 carved ornaments and 500 sculpted figures decorate Vasa.

★ Lion Figurehead
King Gustav II Adolf, who commissioned Vasa, *was known as the Lion of the North. So a springing lion was the obvious choice for the figurehead. It is 4 m (13 ft) long and weighs 450 kg (990 lb).*

To the restaurant

Museum shop

Information desk

Entrance

Emperor Titus
Carvings of 20 Roman emperors stand on parade on Vasa.

Bronze Cannon
More than 50 of Vasa's *64 original cannons were salvaged in the 17th century. Three 11-kg (24-lb) bronze cannons are on display in the museum.*

★ Stern
Vasa's *stern was badly damaged, but has been painstakingly restored to reveal the ship's magnificent ornamentation.*

The main mast
was originally 52 m (170 ft) high.

Exit to Museifartygen

Gun Ports
Vasa *carried more heavy cannons on its two gun-decks than earlier ships of the same size. This contributed to its capsizing.*

Reconstruction of the upper gun deck

Main film auditorium

Gun Deck
Visitors cannot board the ship, but there is a full-size replica of the upper gun deck with carved wooden dummies of sailors, which gives a good idea of conditions on board.

THE SALVAGE OPERATION

The marine archaeologist Anders Franzén had been looking for *Vasa* for many years. On 25 August 1956 his patience was rewarded when he brought up a piece of blackened oak on his plumb line. From the autumn of 1957, it took divers two years to clear space beneath the hull for the lifting cables. The first lift using six cables was a success, after which *Vasa* was raised in 16 stages into shallow water. Plugs were inserted into holes left by rusted iron bolts, then the final lift began and on 4 May 1961 *Vasa* was towed into dry dock.

Vasa in dry dock after being salvaged in 1961

STAR FEATURES

★ **Lion Figurehead**

★ **Stern**

Hornborgastugan, a 19th-century timber cottage at Skansen

Skansen ❽

Djurgårdsslätten 49. ☎ 08-442 80 00.
🚌 44, 47. 🚋 7. 🚢 Djurgårdsfärja.
🕐 daily Oct–Apr: 10am–4pm; May:
10am–8pm; Jun–Aug: 10am–10pm;
Sep: 10am–5pm. 🏠 Jun–Aug.
🔴 24 Dec. 🅿 ♿ 🚻 🍴 🔊
Seglora Kyrka 🏛 call for details.
🌐 www.skansen.se

T HE WORLD'S FIRST open-air
museum, Skansen was
established in 1891 to
show an increasingly
industrialized society
how people once
lived. It comprises
around 150 houses
and farm buildings
from all over
Sweden. But it is
not just a museum,
Skansen also plays an
important role in nurturing the
country's folklore and
traditions. Sweden's National
Day, Walpurgis Night, Midsummer, Christmas and New
Year's Eve celebrations take
place here *(see pp26–9)*.

In the Town Quarter,
complete with 19th-century
wooden town houses, glassblowers, bookbinders and
other craftspeople demons-
trate their skills. The 300-year-
old Älvros farmhouse, from
the Härjedalen region,
represents rural life with an
intriguing collection of everyday tools. At the other end of
the scale, Skogaholms
Herrgård *(see p18)*, a Carolian
manor from 1680, shows how
the wealthy lived. The shingle-
roofed Seglora Church (1729)
is popular for weddings.

Nordic animals such as elk,
wolves and bears, can be
seen in the zoo, and exotic
snakes in the aquarium.

**Brown bear
at Skansen**

Waldemarsudde ❾

Prins Eugens Väg 6.
☎ 08-545 837 00. 🚌 47. 🚋 7.
🕐 11am–5pm Tue–Sun, 11am–8pm
Thu. 🅿 ♿ 🚻 🍴 🔊 🛍
🌐 www.waldemarsudde.com

P RINCE EUGEN'S Waldemar-
sudde, which passed into
State ownership after his death
in 1947, is one of Sweden's
most visited art galleries.
The prince was trained as a
military officer, but
became a successful
artist and was one
of the leading land-
scape painters of
his generation. He
produced mon-
umental paintings
for several of the city's
important buildings,
including Kungliga Operan,
Kungliga Dramatiska Teatern

and Rådhuset. Among his
own works hanging in
Waldemarsudde, his former
palace, are three of his most
prized paintings: *Spring*
(1891), *The Old Castle* (1893)
and *The Cloud* (1896).

Together with works by his
contemporaries, the gallery
holds an impressive collection
of early 20th-century Swedish
art. Oscar Björck, Carl Fredrik
Hill, Richard Bergh, Nils
Kreuger, Eugène Jansson,
Bruno Liljefors and Anders
Zorn are all featured.

Prince Eugen was a
generous patron to the next
generation – the group known
as "The Young Ones" – so
works by younger artists,
including Isaac Grünewald,
Einar Jolin, Sigrid Hjertén and
Leander Engström are also in
the collection. Sculptors of the
same era are well represented,
particularly Per Hasselberg,
whose works can be seen in
both the gallery and the park.

Prince Eugen and his
architect, Ferdinand Boberg,
drew up the sketches for the
palace, completed in 1905.
The same architect was called
in later to design the gallery,
which was finished in 1913.
This now includes parts of the
collection of some 2,000
works, as well as the Prince's
own paintings.

The guest apartments remain
largely unchanged, and the

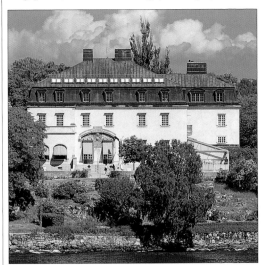

Prince Eugen's Waldemarsudde, seen from the water

Hornsgatan (1902) by Eugène Jansson, in Thielska Galleriet

two upper floors with the Prince's studio at the top are used for temporary exhibitions. The buildings are surrounded by beautiful gardens.

Thielska Galleriet ❿

Sjötullsbacken 6–8.
☎ 08-662 58 84. 🚌 69.
🕐 noon–4pm Mon–Sat, 1–4pm Sun.
♿ by appointment. 📷 📠

WHEN THE magnificent apartments of the banker Ernest Thiel (1860–1947) on Strandvägen started to overflow with his comprehensive collection of Nordic art from the late 19th and early 20th centuries, he commissioned the architect Ferdinand Boberg to design a dignified villa on Djurgården.

However, during World War I Thiel lost most of his fortune. His collection was bought by the State, which opened Thielska Galleriet in his villa in 1926.

Thiel was regarded as something of a rebel in the banking world. He was particularly fond of works by painters belonging to the Artists' Union, which had been formed in 1886 to counter the influence of the traditionalist Konstakademien (Royal Academy of the Arts).

There are paintings by all the major Swedish artists who formed an artists' colony at Grèz-sur-Loing, south of Paris, including Carl Larsson, Bruno Liljefors, Karl Nordström and August Strindberg.

In additon, the gallery features works by Eugène Jansson, Anders Zorn and Prince Eugen, as well as wooden figures by Axel Petersson and sculptures by Christian Eriksson. Thiel also acquired pieces by foreign artists, not least his good friend Edvard Munch.

Etnografiska Museet ⓫

Djurgårdsbrunnsvägen 34.
☎ 08-519 550 00. 🚌 69. 🕐 11am–5pm daily. 📷 ♿ 🚻 🛍 📠 🍴
🌐 www.etnografiska.se

THE NATIONAL MUSEUM of Ethnography is a showcase for the collections brought home to Sweden by enterprising travellers and scientists from the 18th century to the present day. All are arranged in imaginative displays designed to provide a better understanding of the unknown or unfamiliar from around the world.

Another aspect of the museum's work is to reflect the multicultural influences on Sweden brought about by the large-scale immigration into the country during the late 20th century.

The explorer Sven Hedin (1865–1952), who was the last Swede to be ennobled (in 1902), contributed many exhibits to the museum, including Buddha figures and Chinese costumes, as well as Mongolian temple tents donated by leaders of the Kalmuck people in western China to King Gustav V.

Another section of interest shows masks and totem poles from western Canada.

A Japanese tea house was opened in 1990, which is a work of art in itself. Here, visitors to the museum can take part in traditional tea ceremonies during the summer.

Religious mask from British Columbia

The museum runs an extensive educational programme. It has published an international magazine, *Ethnos*, every year since 1936 and maintains a comprehensive reference library.

The "Babajan" restaurant offers a taste of foods from all over the world, and provides an impressive list of beers from far and near.

AN IMMORTAL TROUBADOUR

Carl Michael Bellman (1740–95) was a much-loved troubadour. Gustav III gave him a job as secretary of a lottery, but he was best known around Stockholm's many taverns – particularly on Djurgården. His works about the drunken watchmaker Jean Fredman and his contemporaries (*Fredman's Epistles* and *Fredman's Songs*) have never lost their popularity and form part of Sweden's musical heritage. A bust of Bellman was unveiled on Djurgården in 1829 in the presence of Queen Desideria.

Bust of Bellman by J N Byström (1829)

Kaknästornet with the buildings of Sjöhistoriska Museet, Tekniska Museet and Folkens Museum Etnografiska in the foreground

Tekniska Museet ⑫

Museivägen 7. ☎ 08-450 56 00. 🚌 69. ◯ 10am–5pm Mon–Tue, Thu–Fri, 10am–8pm Wed, 11am–5pm Sat & Sun. 🎫 by appointment. 📷 ♿ 🛗 🍴 🛍 🆆 www.tekniskamuseet.se

Tʜᴇ ᴍᴜsᴇᴜᴍ ᴏꜰ Science and Technology contains a wealth of exhibits connected with Sweden's technical and industrial history. It also houses the science centre, Teknorama, with hands-on experiments designed for children and young people.

The machinery hall features the country's oldest preserved steam engine. Built in 1832, it was used in a coal mine in southern Sweden. The locomotive "Lotta" is here, along with the classic model T-Ford and early Swedish cars from Volvo, Scania and Saab. Swinging from above is Sweden's first commercial aircraft, built in 1924. There is another rarity – the scientist Emanuel Swedenborg's model of a "flying machine" (1716).

The museum also has sections on electric power, computing, technology in the home, and the Swedish forestry, mining, iron and steel industries.

Tekniska Museet's machinery hall with historic aircraft

Sjöhistoriska Museet ⑬

Djurgårdsbrunnsvägen 24. ☎ 08-519 549 00. 🚌 69. ◯ 10am–5pm Tue–Sun; spring and autumn also 10am–8.30pm Tue. 🎫 📷 ♿ 🛍 🆆 www.sjohistoriska.nu

Tʜᴇ ɴᴀᴛɪᴏɴᴀʟ ᴍᴀʀɪᴛɪᴍᴇ Museum focuses on shipping, shipbuilding and naval defence. It is housed in an attractive building, designed by the architect Ragnar Östberg in 1938, in a beautiful location by the calm waters of Djurgårds-brunnsviken.

There are some 100,000 exhibits, including more than 1,500 model ships. The oldest Swedish model is a reproduction of the "Cathedral ship" from the early 1600s. The model collection comprises every conceivable type of ship from small coasters and Viking longboats to oil tankers, coal vessels, dinghies, full-riggers and submarines. A series of models on a scale of 1:200 shows the development of ships in Scandinavia since the Iron Age.

Life-size settings provide a good idea of life on board the various ships. Among them are the exquisite original cabin and elegant stern from the royal schooner *Amphion*. Designed by the leading shipbuilder F H af Chapman and built at the Djurgården shipyard, *Amphion* was Gustav III's flagship in the

Figurehead, about 1850

1788–90 war with Russia. Contrasting with this is the cramped forecastle from the schooner *Hoppet*, where four crew members ate, slept and spent their time off watch.

The museum has some notable examples of ship decoration from the late 17th century. They include part of the national coat of arms recovered by divers in the 1920s from the stern of the *Riksäpplet*, which sank at Dalarö in 1676. A large relief portrayal of Karl XI on horseback from the stern of *Carolus XI* – an 82-cannon ship launched from the shipyard in 1678 – is also on show. It is thought that the relief was removed some years later when the ship was renamed *Sverige*. There are many fine figureheads in the collection, including one depicting Amphion, the son of Zeus, playing his lyre, which adorned the schooner of the same name.

Linked to the museum is the Swedish Marine Archaeology Archive, containing an extensive collection of maritime documents and photographs. There is a special children's section with a workshop which is open on Sundays and in school holidays.

On the gable facing Djurgårdsbrunnsviken is *The Sailor*, a monument to the victims of naval warfare by Nils Sjögren.

Kaknästornet ⑭

Ladugårdsgärdet. ☎ 08-667 21 05. 🚌 69. ◯ May–Aug: 9am–10pm daily; Sep–Apr: 10am– 9pm daily. 🎫 by appointment. 📷 ♿ 🍴 🛍 🛗

Aɴᴄʜᴏʀᴇᴅ ʙʏ 72 steel poles, driven 8 m (26 ft) into the rock, the 34-storey Kaknästornet soars to a height of 155 m (508 ft). The tower, designed by the architects Bengt Lindroos and Hans Borgström, was opened in 1967. It was erected as a centre for the country's television and radio broadcasting and also contains technical equipment to conduct conferences by satellite between European cities. Five dishes to the left of the tower – the largest of which has a diameter of 13 m (43 ft) – relay signals to and from satellites. The main hall containing the transmitters and receivers has been blasted out of the rock below the dishes.

The observation points on levels 30 and 31 provide a spectacular view of the city, and the restaurant on the 28th floor has panoramic windows. It is reached by two lifts, travelling at 18 km/h (11 mph). There is a tourist information office at the entrance, selling souvenirs, maps and the Stockholm Card (*see p321*). Decorative features include a wall relief by Walter Bengtsson, which was inspired by the tower's daunting technology.

Tessinparken & Nedre Gärdet ⓮

Map 3 F2. 🚇 *Karlaplan, Gärdet.* 🚌 *1, 4, 62, 72.*

THREE GENERATIONS of the Tessin family of architects (*see p24*) have given their name to this park which opened at Lower Gärdet in 1931. Tessinparken runs from north to south and is attractively designed with lawns, play areas, paths and ponds. The adjoining houses, built

Millesgården, home of the sculptor Carl Milles in the early 20th century

between 1932 and 1937, have their own gardens and blend in such a way that they give the impression of being part of the park itself.

The earliest houses, nearest to Valhallavägen, still show signs of 1920s Classicism, although Gärdet's real hallmark is Functionalism (*see p24*). The lower white houses along Askrikegatan, marking the northern boundary of the park, are Functionalist in style and noticeably different from other buildings in Gärdet. Some 60 different architects were involved in designing the Gärdet development, including Sture Frölén.

A granite statue of a woman with a suitcase, *Housewife's Holiday*, stands in the part of Tessin Park adjoining Valhallavägen. It was made by Olof Thorwald Ohlsson in the 1970s. At the other end of the park is a colourful concrete statue, *The Egg*, by Egon Möller-Nielsen.

Functionalist style, Tessinparken

Millesgården ⓰

Herserudsvägen 32, Lidingö.
🚇 *Ropsten, then bus 203 or 207, or train to Torsvik.* 📞 *08-446 75 90.*
🕐 *mid-May-Aug: 10am–5pm daily; Sep-mid-May: noon–5pm Thur–Sun.*
✉ *by appointment.* ♿ ⬛ 🍴 🛍
🌐 *www.millesgarden.se*

CARL MILLES (1875–1955) was one of the 20th century's greatest Swedish sculptors and the best known internationally. From 1931 he lived for 20 years in the USA, where he became a prolific monumental sculptor with works such as the *Meeting of the Waters* fountain in St Louis and the *Resurrection* fountain in the National Memorial Park outside Washington DC. In Stockholm visitors can see 15 of his public works, including the *Orpheus* fountain in front of Konserthuset (*see p69*).

In 1906 Milles purchased land on the island of Lidingö on which he built a house, completed in 1908. He lived here with his wife until 1931, and also after his return from the USA. In 1936 he and his wife donated the property to the people of Sweden. Millesgården extends over a series of terraces filled with sculptures and includes Milles' studios with originals and replicas of his work. There is a magnificent garden – a work of art in itself – and a fine view over the water.

Tessinparken, surrounded by Functionalist-style housing dating from the late 1930s

Running track at Stadion, 1912

Stadion ⑰

Lidingövägen 1–3. **Map** 2 E2.
📞 08-508 260 00. 🚇 Stadion.
🚌 4, 55, 72, 73. 📅 mid-Apr–mid-Oct. 🎫 during events. ♿ 🛍

A NEW MAIN ARENA was built
for the 1912 Olympic
Games in Stockholm, the
towers of which have become
a familiar landmark on the
capital's skyline. The architect
of Stadion, Torben Grut
(1871–1945), followed the
National Romantic influences
of the day. The complex is
richly decorated. The clock
tower has two
figures by Carl
Fagerberg, *Ask
and Embla*, the
counterparts of
Adam and Eve in
Nordic mythology.
There are also busts of
Victor Balck, the man
behind the 1912
Olympics, and
P H Ling, the
father of Swedish
gymnastics.

Four notable sculptures
were added in the 1930s. The
painter and gymnast Bruno
Liljefors created *Play* at the
main entrance, Carl Eldh
made *The Runners*, and Carl
Fagerberg provided *Relay
Runners* and *The Shot-Putter*.

Stadion has continued to be
an important venue for
athletics events. The European Athletics Championships
were held here in 1958, and
an international athletics gala
is staged every summer. In
1990 it hosted the World
Equestrian Championships.

The arena is also the venue
for ice hockey and bandy (a
type of hockey) champion-
ship events.

Naturhistoriska Riksmuseet ⑱

5 km (3 miles) N of city centre along
road 264. 📞 08-519 540 00.
🚇 Universitetet. 🚌 40, 540.
📅 10am–7pm Tue–Sun; Jun–Jul: also
10am–7pm Mon. 🎫 by appointment.
🎫 ♿ 🛍 📷 🍴 **W** www.nrm.se

C OMPLETED IN 1916, the vast
Naturhistoriska Riks-
museet (Natural History
Museum) was designed by
Axel Anderberg and decorated by Carl Fagerberg. The
museum is a venerable
institution, founded in
1739 by Carl von
Linné *(see p128)* as
part of Vetenskaps-
akademien (the
Academy of
Science). It is one
of the 10 largest
museums of its
kind in the world.
Over the centuries,
the number of
exhibits has risen
to 17 million.

During the 1990s it was
modernized and there are
both permanent and
temporary exhibitions on a
wide range of themes from
dinosaurs and sea creatures to
the "Marvels of the Human
Body". The hugely popular
Cosmonova opened at the
same time. Both a planet-

**Polar bear, Natur-
historiska Riksmuseet**

arium and an IMAX cinema,
its screen is 25 times the size
of a conventional one. The
Vega Monument was erected
in front of the museum in 1930
to mark the 50th anniversary
of explorer Adolf Erik
Nordenskiöld's return from
the first voyage through the
Northeast Passage in his ship
Vega. Designed by Ivar Johnsson, it is an obelisk in granite
topped with a copper ship.

Hagaparken ⑲

4 km (2.5 miles) N of city centre, along
E4. 🚌 515. **Haga Parkmuseum**
📞 08-27 42 52. 📅 Jun–Aug:
11am–5pm Tue–Sun. **Gustav III's
Paviljong** 📞 08-402 61 30. 📅 every
hour Jun–Aug: noon–3pm Tue–Sun.
Fjärils- & Fågelhuset 📞 08-730 39
81. 📅 Apr–Sep: 10am–4pm Tue–Fri,
11am–5.30pm Sat & Sun; Oct–Apr:
10am–3pm Tue–Fri, 11am–4pm Sat &
Sun. ● 24, 25 & 31 Dec. 🛍 🍴 in
Koppartälten and Fjärils- & Fågelhuset
and Café Vasaslätten.

K ING GUSTAV VASA decided to
create a royal park in the
popular Haga area in the mid-
18th century. The king's
vision was realized by the
architect of the moment,
Fredrik Magnus Piper. The
result was an English-style
park with some very unusual
buildings, including the
Chinese Pagoda and the
Roman battle tent,
Koppartälten. A royal palace
inspired by Versailles in
France was also planned, but
construction came to a halt
after the king's death and it
remained unfinished.

Gustav III's Pavilion, a
Gustavian masterpiece
designed by Olof
Tempelman, with an
interior by Louis
Masreliéz, is the park's
greatest architectural
attraction, while
Fjärils- & Fågelhuset

Hagaparken's Roman battle tent, designed by Louis Jean Desprez (1790)

has exotic butterflies and birds flying freely around a tropical greenhouse.

Haga Slott, built in 1802–04 for Gustav IV Adolf, was the childhood home of the present monarch, Carl XVI Gustaf, and his sisters. Now it is used for government receptions and to accommodate visiting heads of state.

Hagaparken is very popular with Stockholmers, who come all year round. The park is part of Ekoparken, an oasis of nature and culture close to the city centre *(see box)*.

Exotic butterflies in the greenhouses at Hagaparken

Ulriksdal ⑳

7 km (4 miles) N of Stockholm.
📞 08-402 61 30. 🚌 503. **Palace**
🕐 *Jun–Aug: noon–4pm Tue–Sun.*
📷 *Jun–Aug: noon, 1pm, 2pm & 3pm.* **Orangery** 🕐 *Jun–Aug: noon–4pm Tue–Sun.* 🚫 ♿ 🅿️ 🚻 ♿ 🛍️ 🅆 www.royalcourt.se

SITUATED ON a headland in the bay of Edsviken, Ulriksdal's attractive buildings and leafy surroundings are well worth a visit. At the entrance to the grounds is one of Stockholm's best-known restaurants, Ulriksdals Wärdshus *(see p296)*.

The original palace was built in the 1640s and designed by Hans Jakob Kristler in German/Dutch Renaissance style. The owner, Marshal of the Realm Jakob de la Gardie, named the palace Jakobsdal. It was bought in 1669 by the Dowager Queen Hedvig Eleonora. Fifteen years later, she donated the palace to her grandson Ulrik as a christening gift, and it was renamed Ulriksdal.

Around this time the architect Tessin the Elder *(see p24)* suggested some rebuilding

Ulriksdal with its magnificent 18th-century Baroque exterior

work, but only a few of his proposals saw the light of day. However, the stucco work by Carlo Carove in the southern wing can be seen. In the 18th century the palace acquired its Baroque exterior.

After being a popular place for festivities in the time of Gustav III (1746–92), it began to lose its glamour. Interest was revived under Karl XV (1826–72), and furnishings and handicrafts many hundreds of years old are on show in his rooms.

The park was laid out in the mid-17th century. It has 300-year-old lime trees, as well as one of Europe's most northerly beechwoods. Carl Milles's two sculptures of wild boars stand by the pool in front of the palace. A stream is crossed by a footbridge, which is supported by Per Lundgren's *Moors Dragging the Nets*.

More art can be seen in the orangery, designed by Tessin the Elder in the 1660s and rebuilt in 1705. It now houses a sculpture museum.

The palace chapel, a popular place for weddings, was designed by F W Scholander and built in 1865 in Dutch Neo-Renaissance style. The riding school, built in 1671, was converted into a theatre by Carl Hårleman and C F Adelcrantz in the 1750s. Performances are staged in the theatre every summer.

EKOPARKEN – THE NATIONAL CITY PARK

Ekoparken – the world's first National City Park – was established by the Swedish Parliament in 1995. Its creation has enabled the capital to safeguard the ecology of its "green lung", a 27-sq km (10.5-sq miles) area for recreation and outdoor activities.

The park threads through Stockholm's central districts, including Skeppsholmen and the southern part of Djurgården, and continues northwest to northern Djurgården, Hagaparken, Brunnsviken and Ulriksdal. It also encompasses the tiny islands of Fjäderholmarna *(see p110)*. Much of the park was a royal hunting ground as early as the 16th century, scattered with beautiful palaces and other sights.

Haga Forum, at the southern entrance to Hagaparken, provides plenty of information about Ekoparken.

There are also boat tours on Brunnsviken, with stops at some of the sights. For further details, telephone 08-587 140 40.

Breeding herons at Isbladskärret, part of Ekoparken's rich bird-life

Karlbergs Slott, a palace dating from the 1630s – now one of Sweden's military academies

Vin- & Sprithisto-riska Museet ㉑

Dalagatan 100. **Map** 1 A1.
📞 08-744 70 70. 🚇 Odenplan.
🚌 65, 69. 🕐 10am–7pm Tue,
10am–4pm Wed–Fri, noon–4pm Sat
& Sun. ♿ 📷 🛒 ♨ 🎧 🍴
🌐 www.vinosprithistoriska.se

SWEDISH PUNSCH and schnapps
are the themes of Vin- &
Sprithistoriska (Wine and
Spirits Historical Museum),
located in a former wine
warehouse. The building was
designed by
Cyrillus Johansson
and completed in
1923, but as the
trade of wine in
barrels decreased,
the warehouse
began to be used
for other pur-
poses until
1967, when the first exhibition
was staged.

**Schnapps label, Vin- &
Sprithistoriska Museet**

Today's museum dates from
1989. It shows how a wine
shop would have looked
around 1900. From the same
era is a typical southern
Swedish distillery in which
potatoes were used to make
schnapps. There is also a
collection of spices added to
schnapps and liqueurs, and
50,000 labels are on show.

Visitors can listen to some
200 "schnapps songs" via a
computer, which also has the
texts of 2,000 drinking songs.

Karlbergs Slott ㉒

Karlsbergs Slottsväg. 📞 08-562 813
01. 🚌 42, 72 to Karlberg station,
then 15-min walk. 📷 groups only, by
appointment.

ADMIRAL KARL Karlsson
Gyllenhielm started to
build Karlbergs Slott in the
1630s, during the Thirty Years
War. From 1670 the palace
was extended and rebuilt by
Magnus Gabriel de la Gardie,
with Jean de la Vallée as his
architect. When Karlberg became royal property in 1688,
it was one of
Sweden's most
majestic palaces.
It was where the
"hero King" Karl
XII (1682–1718)
grew up, and it
was here that he
lay in state after
his death at the
Battle of Fredrikshald *(see
p35)*. In 1792 the architect
C C Gjörwell converted the
property into the Royal
War Academy, which later
became the Karlberg
Military School, and since
1999 it has been the site
for one of the country's
military academies.

The interior decorations
include Carl Carove's
magnificent stucco-work
which can be seen in the
grand hall. The palace
church has been
renovated several times,
but the 17th-century lanterns
are original. De la Gardie's
wood-panelled "rarities room"
is now the sacristy, but once
it housed his collection
of valuables.

Judiska Museet ㉓

Hälsingegatan 2. **Map** 1 A2. 📞 08-
31 01 43. 🚇 Odenplan. 🚌 2, 4,
47, 72. 🕐 noon–4pm Mon–Fri &
Sun. 📷 in English by appointment.
📷 ♿ 🛒 🍴

IN 1774 AARON ISAAC became
the first Jewish immigrant
to settle in Stockholm and
practise his religion. Today,
half of Sweden's Jewish
population of around 18,000
live in the Stockholm area.
Judiska Museet depicts the
history of the Swedish Jews
from Isaac's time to the
present day. It focuses on
Judaism as a religion, its inte-
gration into Swedish society
and the Holocaust. A

**An eight-stemmed *chanuki*
(candlestick) at Judiska Museet**

comprehensive collection of
pictures and other items
provide an insight into Jewish
life in Sweden with its
traditions and customs. The
beautiful *Torah* (the five
books of Moses), the bridal
canopy, and the collection of
eight-stemmed *chanukis*
(candlesticks) are just some of
the museum's treasured
spiritual artifacts.

**The old observatory (1748–53) at
the top of the Observatory hill**

Observatorie-museet ㉔

Drottninggatan 120. **Map** 1 B2.
📞 08-545 483 90. 🚇 *Odenplan.*
🚌 52. *Oct–Mar: 6pm Tue includes
telescope observation if sky is clear; in
Eng by appointment.* 🅿 🛈 🛗
🌐 www.observatoriet.kva.se

A NUMBER OF institutions
connected with science
and education can be found
on and around the hill of
Brunkeberg. The oldest is the
former observatory designed
by Carl Hårleman for the
Royal Scientific Academy and
opened in 1753. In 1931,
astronomical research was
moved to Saltsjöbaden in the
Stockholm archipelago and
replaced by Observatorie-
museet (the Observatory
Museum). Here visitors can
see the observation room with
its instruments, the two median
rooms, the weather room and
the instrument workshop.
There is a splendid view of
Stockholm from the museum's
dome and in good weather it
is possible to view the stars.
The grove which surrounds
the old observatory began to
take shape in the 18th century.
It is an idyllic enclosed area,
first opened to the public in

GUNNAR ASPLUND

Gunnar Asplund (1885–1940) was a dominant figure among
Swedish and internationally renowned architects in the
1930s. His first major commission was the chapel at the
Skogskyrkogården Cemetery, designed in National Romantic
style. His last work was Heliga
Korsets Kapell, the cemetery's crematorium (1935–40). Regarded as a
masterpiece in the Functionalist
style, it has earned a place on the
UNESCO World Heritage list (*see
p105*). Asplund designed Stadsbiblioteket (City Library, 1920–28).
He pioneered the Functionalist
style as chief architect for the
Stockholm Exhibition in 1930.

**Stockholm Exhibition, by
Gunnar Asplund, 1930**

the 20th century. On top of
Brunkeberg is Sigrid Fridman's
statue *The Centaur*.
A park stretches down to
Sveavägen, where a pond is
fed by a stream running
down the hillside. The statue
Dancing Youth is by Ivar
Johnsson. At the southern
entrance of the park is Nils
Möllerberg's sculpture *Youth*.

Stadsbiblioteket ㉕

Sveavägen 73. **Map** 1 B2.
📞 08-508 311 00. 🚇 *Rådmansgatan.* 🚌 2, 4, 42, 52, 53, 72.
🕙 *10am–8.30pm Mon–Thu,
10am–6pm Fri, noon–4pm Sat & Sun;
Jun–Aug: 11am–7pm Mon–Thu,
11am–5pm Fri.* ♿ 🛈 🛗

G UNNAR ASPLUND'S master-
piece, Stadsbiblioteket
(City Library), is one of the
capital's most architecturally
important buildings. Asplund,

the champion of the Functionalist style prevalent in the
1930s, designed a public library which was dominated by
Classical ideals. It was opened
in 1928.
Internally, the furnishings
and many of the light fittings
were designed by Asplund
himself. The work of Swedish
artists is well represented: in
the entrance hall are Ivar
Johnsson's stucco reliefs with
themes from Homer's *Iliad*;
the sparkling mural painting
in the children's section, *John
Blund*, is by Nils Dardel; and
the depiction of the stars in
the heavens by Ulf Munthe.
The door lintels, door handles
and drinking fountains are by
Nils Sjögren. Hilding Linnquist
was responsible for the giant-
sized tapestry, and also for
four mural paintings using
ancient fresco techniques.
The library lends more than
a million books every year.

Stadsbiblioteket, in Neo-Classical style, designed by Gunnar Asplund

Stadshuset **26**

ROBABLY SWEDEN'S BIGGEST architectural project of the 20th century, the City Hall was completed in 1923 and has become a symbol of Stockholm. It was designed by Ragnar Östberg (1866–1945), the leading architect of the Swedish National Romantic style, and displays influences of both the Nordic Gothic and Northern Italian schools. Several leading Swedish artists contributed to the rich interior design. The building contains the Council Chamber and 250 offices for city administrative staff. The annual Nobel Prize festivities take place in the Blue Hall.

Engel-brekt

★ **The Golden Room**
The Byzantine-inspired wall mosaics by Einar Forseth (1892–1988) have 19 million fragments gold leaf. The theme of the north wall is Queen of Lake Mälaren.

Norra Trapptornet, crowned by a sun.

Stairway to the gallery

★ **The Blue Hall**
The banqueting room is made from handmade bricks. The name is from the initial plan to paint the bricks blue, but the architect changed his mind.

★ **The Prince's Gallery**
A fresco, The City on the Water, *in the Prince's Gallery, was painted by Prince Eugen (see p92), who donated it to the City Hall.*

Three Crowns
Sweden's heraldic symbol, Tre Kronor, dating from the 14th century, tops the 106-m (348-ft) tower.

Courtyard

VISITORS' CHECKLIST

Hantverkargatan 1. **Map** 1 B5.
 08-508 290 58. Råd-
huset. 3, 62. for guided
tours. 1 Jan, 24–26 & 31
Dec, and during special events.
 Swedish & English. Jun–
Aug: 10am, 11am, noon, 2pm
and 3pm daily; Sep–May: 10am
& noon daily.
Tornmuseet May– Sep:
10am–4.30pm daily.
 www.stockholm.se/
stadshuset

The Council Chamber
Stockholm's 101 councillors meet in this magnificent chamber, which contains furnishings designed by Carl Malmsten.

Engelbrekt the Freedom Fighter
by Christian Eriksson (1858–1935).

Marriage room

The Dance
The steps leading to Riddarfjärden are flanked by two statues by Carl Eldh. Dansen is the figure of a woman, Sången (The Song) of a man.

STAR FEATURES

★ **The Golden Room**

★ **The Blue Hall**

★ **The Prince's Gallery**

Västerbron bridge, opened in 1935, linking Kungsholmen with Södermalm across Lake Mälaren

Västerbron ②

🚌 4, 40, 74.

A S STOCKHOLM expanded and car-use increased in the 1920s, it became necessary to build an additional bridge between the northern and southern shores of Lake Mälaren. German experts dominated the architectural competition launched in 1930, but their plans were implemented by Swedish architects and engineers and Västerbron bridge was completed in 1935.

The attractive design blends well with the landscape. The bridge is built in two spans of 168 m (551 ft) and 204 m (669 ft) with a vertical clearance of 26 m (85 ft). There are footpaths and cycle lanes on each side and a walk to the centre of Västerbron is rewarded with a magnificent view of central Stockholm.

Exercise yard in the former royal prison on Långholmen

Långholmen ②

🚇 Hornstull, then 3 min walk.
🚌 66. 🅿

B ELOW THE MAJESTIC Väster- bron bridge is the island of Långholmen, which is linked to Södermalm by two

bridges. Långholmen is best known for the various prisons which have been located here since 1724. During the 20th century it was the site of the largest prison in Sweden, housing 620 inmates. The prison closed in 1975, since when the island has become a popular recreational area.

The prison buildings have been demolished, but the former royal jail dating from 1835 remains. The one-time cells now form both a hotel and a prison museum. There is also a youth hostel and an excellent restaurant, as well as a museum to the poet C M Bellman *(see p93)* with a café in the gardens which run down towards Riddarfjärden.

Långholmen's park has an open-air theatre, and offers excellent swimming both from the beaches and the rocks.

Stockholms Stadsmuseum ②

Ryssgården. **Map** 3 B5.
☎ 08-508 316 00. 🚇 Slussen. 🚌
2, 3, 43, 53, 55, 76. ⏱ 11am–5pm
Tue–Sun (Sep–May: also 5–9pm Thu;
Jun–Aug: also 5–7pm Thu). 🎫 🚫
📷 ♿ 🏬 🛍
🌐 www.stadsmuseum.stockholm.se

H EMMED IN between the traffic roundabouts of Slussen and the steep hill up to Mosebacke Torg is Stock- holms Stadsmuseum (City Museum). It is housed in a late-17th-century building originally designed by Tessin the Elder as Södra Stadshuset (Southern City Hall). After a fire, it was completed by Tessin the Younger in 1685. It

has been used for various purposes over the centuries, including law courts and dungeons, schools and city- hall cellars, theatres and churches, until in the 1930s it became the city museum.

The museum documents the history of Stockholm. The city's main stages of develop- ment are described in a slide- show and a series of four per- manent exhibitions. The first starts with the Stockholm Bloodbath of 1520 *(see p58)* and continues through the 17th century. The eventful 18th century is illustrated with exhibits that include the Lohe Treasure – 20 kg (44 lb) of silver discovered in Gamla Stan in 1937. The other sections depict industrial- ization in the 19th century and the tremendous growth in the 20th century with the emergence of a new city centre and new suburbs.

The library has a large picture archive and a reference room where visitors can find out virtually anything they want to know about Stock- holm. There are children's ac- tivities, concerts and lectures.

The 18th-century Lohe Treasure at Stockholms Stadsmuseum

Katarinahissen 30

Stadsgården. **Map** 3 C5.
Ⓣ Slussen. 🚌 2, 3, 43, 53, 55, 76.
⚪ 7.30am–10pm Mon–Sat,
10am–10pm Sun. 🚹 ♿ ❄

Katarinahissen is the oldest of Stockholm's "high-rise" attractions. The 38-m (125-ft) high lift was opened to the public in March 1883 and is still a prominent silhouette on the Söder skyline. The first Swedish neon sign was erected here in 1909 – a legendary advertisement for Stomatol toothpaste. Since the 1930s, the sign has been placed on a nearby rooftop.

The original lift was driven by steam, but it switched to electricity in 1915.

In the 1930s it was replaced by a new lift when the Cooperative Association (KF) built its large office complex at Slussen. In its first year of operation, the lift was used

by more than a million passengers, but its record year was 1945, when it carried a total of 1.8 million people between Slussen and Mosebacke Torg.

**Stomatol sign,
Katarinahissen**

At the top there is a bar and a gourmet restaurant, Gondolen. The views from here are spectacular.

Katarina Kyrka (1695) after its extensive restoration due to a devastating fire in 1990

Katarina Kyrka 31

Högbergsgatan 13. 📞 08-743 68 40.
Ⓣ Slussen, Medborgarplatsen.
🚌 2, 3, 53, 76.
⚪ Apr–Sep: 11am–5pm Mon–Fri,
10am–5pm Sat & Sun. 🎵 Jun–Aug:
12.30pm; other times by appointment.
🎵 12.30pm Tue & Thu (organ
music), noon Wed. ♿ 🖼 ⬛

The buildings surrounding the hilltop on Katarinaberget date partly from the 18th century, although there have been churches on the site since the late 14th century. The most impressive of all the buildings is the 17th-century Katarina Kyrka,

designed by one of the era's greatest architects, Jean de la Vallée (1620–96). King Karl X Gustaf was also deeply involved in the project, and specified that the church should have a central nave with the altar and pulpit positioned right in the middle. Construction began in 1656 and the church was finally completed in 1695. In 1723 it was badly damaged by fire, along with large parts of the surrounding area, but it was restored over the next couple of decades.

Major restoration was carried out in the 20th century, and a new copper roof was added in 1988. Then two years later, on the night of 16 May 1990, there was another fire and the interior and virtually all its fittings were destroyed. Only the outer walls survived.

The architectural practice of Ove Hidemark was commissioned to design a new church which, as far as possible, was to be a faithful reconstruction of the original.

In order to carry out such a detailed reconstruction, the architects resorted to the use of 17th-century building techniques. Experts and craftsmen skilfully joined heavy timbering on to the central dome in the traditional way, and the church's central arch was rebuilt with bricks specially made in 17th-century style.

In 1995, Katarina Kyrka was reconsecrated and, in the eyes of many people, looked more beautiful than ever. The altar was sited exactly where it was originally planned.

The reconstruction cost 270 million kronor, of which 145 million kronor was covered by insurance. The remainder was raised through public donations.

Katarinahissen with Stockholms Stadsmuseum in the background

Fjällgatan ❷

Street light

Pᴇʀ ᴀɴᴅᴇʀs ꜰᴏɢᴇʟsᴛʀöᴍ (1917–98), probably Söder's best-known author, wrote: "Fjällgatan must be the city's most beautiful street. It's an old-fashioned narrow street which runs along the hilltop with well-maintained cobblestones ... and with street lights jutting out from the houses. Then the street opens up and gives a fantastic view of the city and the water..." This area offers an experience of the authentic Söder and its unique atmosphere.

The Heights of Söder
With its 300-year-old houses and terraced gardens, the Söder hilltop stands like a giant stage-set behind Stadsgården harbour.

Fjällgatan
Most of the houses were built along this picturesque street after a devastating fire in 1723. No. 34 is said to be the area's oldest.

Viewpoint with magnificent vista across the city.

Café

| 0 metres | 100 |
| 0 yards | 100 |

FJÄLLGATAN

STIGBERGSGATAN

Katarina Vägen

Stigberget

Norwegian Church

Mamsell Josabeth's Steps
were named after Josabeth Sjöbert (1812–82), a local painter.

Tjärhovsplan

Söder Cottages
Typical well-preserved cottages can be found along Stigbergsgatan. One of them is No. 17, the house of the block-maker Olof Krok during the 1730s.

Sista Styverns Trappor
This alley of steps was once known as Mikaelsgränd after a 17th-century executioner. Later it was named after the inn on the harbour, Sista Styvern ("The Last Penny").

Kᴇʏ

- - - Suggested route

Vita Bergen 🗉

Södermalm. 🚌 2, 3, 55, 66, 76.

Today famous for its popular open-air theatre performances, this park is also an opportunity to see houses originally built for workers at Söder's harbours and factories. They were simple homes, often with a small garden and surrounded by a fence. In 1736 the building of new wooden houses was forbidden because of the fire risk, but slum districts, as this was then, were exempted.

Around 1900, when Sofia Kyrka was built, the area was turned into a leafy hillside park with allotment-garden cottages to the east. The park has a bronze statue, *Elsa Borg*, by Astri Bergman Taube (1972), wife of the great troubadour Evert Taube (see p60).

Globen 🗈

3 km (2 miles) S of Stockholm.
🗉 Globen. 🛈 08-725 10 00.
⭘ during events. ⭙ by appt. 🖔
🖪 🗐 🗆 W www.globen.se

In 1989 Stockholm acquired a new symbol in the shape of the indoor arena Globen. The spherical building has given the southern part of the city a radically new silhouette.

Globen offers a wide programme, ranging from international sports events to top artists and famous personalities such as Nelson Mandela.

Designed by Berg Architects, it has a circumference of 690 m (2,260 ft) and a height of 85 m (279 ft). There are 13-sq m (140-sq ft) viewing screens.

The silhouette of Globen arena dominating the surrounding area

Chapel of the Holy Cross by Gunnar Asplund at Skogskyrkogården

Skogskyrko-gården 🗉

6 km (3.5 miles) S of Stockholm.
🛈 08-508 301 93. 🗉 Skogskyrko-gården. ⭘ May–Sep: 5pm Mon.
🖔 🗆

Nature and architecture have combined to give the Skogskyrkogården Cemetery a place on the UNESCO World Heritage list. The cemetery is the creation of architects Gunnar Asplund (see p99) and Sigurd Lewerentz, winners of a design competition for the site in 1914. It is set amid pinewoods which provide a sombre framework for the various chapels and crematorium, all of which are important examples of Sweden's National Romantic and Functionalist styles.

Asplund's first work, Skogs-kapellet (Woodland Chapel),

Epitaph to Gunnar Asplund

featuring a steep shingled roof, was opened at the same time as the cemetery in 1920. It was decorated by Carl Milles and contains an an altar painting by Gunnar Torhamn. This was followed five years later by Uppståndelsekapellet (the Resurrection Chapel), designed by Lewerentz.

In 1940 Asplund's last masterpiece, Skogskrematoriet (Woodland Crematorium), was completed, along with its three chapels representing Faith, Hope and the Holy Cross. John Lundqvist's *The Resurrection* stands in the pillared hall of Heliga Korsets Kapell, the largest of the chapels, where there is also a mural painted by Sven Erixson. Adjoining the chapel is Asplund's black granite cross. The Hill of Meditation lies to the west. Skogskyrko-gården is the final resting place of Greta Garbo.

GRETA GARBO

The legendary Greta Garbo, one of the 20th century's outstanding film stars, was born in 1905 in a humble part of Södermalm. At the age of 17 she joined the theatre academy of Dramaten and made her film debut in *Peter the Tramp*. Her breakthrough came in 1924 in Mauritz Stiller's film of Selma Lagerlöf's book *The Atonement of Gösta Berling*. The following year she moved to Hollywood, where she soon became the reigning star. Garbo appeared in 24 films, including *Anna Karenina* (1935) and *Camille* (1936). She never married and lived a solitary life until her death in 1990. Her ashes were interred at the Skogskyrkogården Cemetery in 1999.

Garbo in *As You Desire Me* (1932)

Drottningholm ㊱

THE UNIQUE BAROQUE and Rococo environment of Drottningholm – its palace, theatre, park and Chinese Pavilion – have been perfectly preserved. This royal palace emerged in its present form towards the end of the 17th century, and was one of the most lavish buildings of its era. Contemporary Italian and French architecture inspired Tessin the Elder (1615–81) in his design, which was also intended to glorify royal power. The project was completed by Tessin the Younger, while architects such as Carl Hårleman and Jean Eric Rehn finished the interiors. The Royal Family uses parts of the palace as their private residence. Drottningholm was designated a UNESCO World Heritage Site in 1991.

Baroque Garden
The bronze statue of Hercules (1680s) by the Dutch Renaissance sculptor Adrian de Vries adorns the parterre in the palace's Baroque Gardens.

Upper South Bodyguard Room
This ante-room to the State Room, used for ceremonial occasions, was decorated with stucco works by Giovanni and Carlo Carove, and ceiling paintings by Johan Sylvius.

Apartments of the Royal Family

STAR FEATURES

★ Staircase

★ Queen Lovisa Ulrika's Library

★ Queen Hedvig Eleonora's State Bedroom

Writing Table by Georg Haupt
Standing in the Queen's Room is this masterpiece (1770) commissioned by King Adolf Fredrik as a gift to Queen Lovisa Ulrika. Textiles for the walls and furnishings date from the 1970s.

★ **Queen Lovisa Ulrika's Library**
The Queen commissioned Jean Eric Rehn (1717–93) to decorate this splendid library, which illustrates her influence on art and science in Sweden in the 18th century.

VISITORS' CHECKLIST

10 km (6 miles) W of Stockholm. 🚇 Brommaplan, then bus 177, 301, 323. 🚢 May–Sep. **Palace** 📞 08-402 62 80. 🕐 May–Aug: 10am– 4.30pm daily; Sep: noon–3.30pm daily; Oct–Apr: noon–3.30pm Sat & Sun. ● public hols. 🎫 ♿ 📷 📹 **Chinese Pavilion** 🕐 May–Sep. 🎫 ♿ 🚻 **Theatre Museum** 🕐 May–Sep. 🎫 ♿ 📹 **W** www.royalcourt.se

The Palace Church in the northern cupola was completed by Hårleman in the 1720s.

Entrance

★ **Staircase**
Trompe-l'oeil paintings by Johan Sylvius adorn the walls, giving the impression that the already spacious interior stretches further into the palace.

★ **Queen Hedvig Eleonora's State Bedroom**
Morning receptions ("levées") were held in this lavish Baroque room designed by Tessin the Elder. It took about 15 years for Sweden's foremost artists and craftsmen to decorate the room, which was completed in 1683.

Exploring Drottningholm

THE PALACE OF DROTTNINGHOLM IS complemented by the Court Theatre (Slottsteatern), the world's oldest theatre still in active use, the Theatre Museum (Teatermuseum) and the elegant Chinese Pavilion (Kina Slott). The complex is situated on the shores of Lake Mälaren, surrounded by Baroque and Rococo gardens, and lush English-style parkland. In summer there are jousting tournaments, the theatre stages opera and ballet, and the church is used for High Mass and concerts.

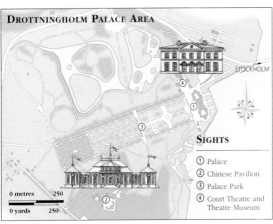

DROTTNINGHOLM PALACE AREA

STOCKHOLM

0 metres   250
0 yards   250

SIGHTS

① Palace
② Chinese Pavilion
③ Palace Park
④ Court Theatre and Theatre Museum

Karl XI's gallery at Drottningholm, featuring the victory at Lund, 1667

THE PALACE APARTMENTS

THE FIRST THING that meets the eye on entering the apartments is a Baroque corridor with a view that frames part of the gardens in all their splendour. The central part of the palace is dominated by the staircase, crowned by a lantern with ceiling paintings by Ehrenstrahl. There are examples of Baroque stucco work by Giovanni and Carlo Carove. Marble statues of the nine muses and their protector, Apollo, are placed at the corners of the balustrades.

The Green Salon is reached from the lower vestibule via the Lower Northern Bodyguard Room. This is the beginning of the main ceremonial suite, which continues with Karl X's Gallery where paintings illustrate his major military exploit, the crossing of the iced-over Store Bælt (Great Belt) by the Swedish army in

Medallion symbolizing life and death

1658. Queen Hedvig Eleonora (1636–1715) held audiences in the Ehrenstrahl Salon, named after the artist whose paintings dominate the walls. More prominent guests were received in the State Bedroom which later in Queen Lovisa Ulrika's time was in fact used for sleeping. Her Meissen porcelain can be seen in the Blue Cabinet; the Library has her collection of more than 2,000 books. Behind the Upper Northern Bodyguard Room, with a ceiling by Johan Sylvius, is a Gustavian drawing room with a bureau by Johan Niklas Eckstein. In 1777, following Gustav III's assumption of power, the Blue Salon was decorated in the Neo-Classical style.

The Chinese Salon was used as a private bedroom by King Adolf Fredrik. It is directly above the Queen's State Bedroom and there is a hidden staircase linking the two floors. The "bureau"

opposite the tiled stove is also a sofa bed. The Oscar Room was refurbished by Oscar I (1799–1859) and is adorned by a tapestry dating from the 1630s. After the General's Room, Karl XI's Gallery commemorating the victory at Lund (1667), and the Golden Salon, comes the Queen's Salon. Just as the adjoining State Room has portraits of all the European monarchs, the portraits in the Queen's Salon are of European queens. This floor finishes with the Upper South Bodyguard Room, an ante-room to the State Room and lavishly decorated by the Carove stucco artists and the ceiling painter Johan Sylvius.

THE CHINESE PAVILION

ON HER 33RD birthday in 1753 Queen Lovisa Ulrika was given a Chinese pavilion by her husband, King Adolf Fredrik. It had been manufactured in Stockholm and the previous night it was shipped to Drottningholm and assembled a short distance from the palace. It had to be taken down after 10 years because rot had set in, and was

The Chinese Pavilion, an extravaganza in blue and gold

replaced by the Chinese Pavilion (Kina Slott) which is still one of the major attractions at Drottningholm. The polished-tile building was designed by D F Adelcrantz (1716–96).

At this time there was great European interest in all things Chinese. In 1733 the newly formed East India Company made its first journey to China. After Lovisa Ulrika's death in 1782 this interest waned, but it was rekindled in the 1840s. The Chinese Pavilion is a mixture of what was considered 250 years ago to be typical Chinese style along with artifacts from China and Japan. Efforts have been made to restore the interior to its original state with the help of a 1777 inventory.

Four smaller pavilions belong to the building. In the northeastern pavilion the king had his lathe and a carpenter's bench. Alongside is the Confidencen pavilion, where meals were taken if he wished to be left undisturbed. The food was prepared in the basement, the floor opened and the dining table hauled up. The adjoining Turkish-style "watch tent" was built as a barracks for Gustav III's dragoons. It now houses a museum about the estate.

Tiled stove in a cabinet in the Chinese Pavilion

THE PALACE PARK

THE PALACE'S three gardens are each of a completely different character but still combine to provide a unified whole. The symmetrical formal garden started to take shape in 1640. The garden was designed to stimulate all senses with sights, sounds and smells. It starts by the palace terrace with its "embroidery" parterre and continues as far as the Hercules statue. The water parterre is situated on slightly higher ground and is broken up with waterfalls and topiaries. The sculptures, mainly carved by the Flemish

sculptor Adrian de Vries (1560–1626) were war trophies from Prague in 1648 and from Fredriksborg Castle in Denmark in 1659.

The avenues of chestnut trees were laid out when the Chinese Pavilion was completed, as well as the Rococo-inspired garden area – a cross between the formal main garden and the freer composition of the English park. The English park has natural paths and a stream with small islands, along with trees and bushes at "natural" irregular intervals. Gustav III is reputed to have been responsible for its design and also planned several buildings. Not all his plans were realized, but he added four statues which he had bought during his travels in Italy.

The first 300 of a total of 846 lime trees were planted in the avenues flanking the Baroque garden as early as 1684.

THE COURT THEATRE AND THEATRE MUSEUM

THE DESIGNER OF the Chinese Pavilion, Carl Fredrik Adelcrantz, was also responsible for the Drottningholm Court Theatre (Slottsteatern), which dates from 1766. The theatre was commissioned by Queen

Court Theatre stage machinery dating from 1766

The magnificent 18th-century stage in the Drottningholm Court Theatre

Lovisa Ulrika, but Adelcrantz did not have the same resources as the architects of the palace itself. This simple wooden building with a plaster façade is now the world's oldest theatre still preserved in its original condition. The interior and fittings are masterpieces of simple functionality. The pilasters, for example, are made from gypsum and the supports from papier mâché. The scenery, with its wooden hand-driven machinery, is still in working order.

After Gustav III's death in 1792 the theatre fell into disuse until the 1920s, when the machinery ropes were replaced, electric lighting was installed, and the original wings were refurbished.

The scenery is adapted to 18th-century plays. It can be changed in just a few seconds with the help of up to 30 scene-shifters. The sound effects are simple but authentic: a wooden box filled with stones creates realistic thunder, a wooden cylinder covered in tent cloth produces a howling wind. Every summer there are about 30 performances, mainly opera and ballet from the 18th century. The theatre is open daily for visitors to the palace.

A Theatre Museum and shop are housed in Duke Carl's pavilion, built in the 1780s. The museum focuses on 18th-century theatre, with decoration sketches, paintings, scenery models and costumes. A *Commedia dell'arte* room contains paintings by Pehr Hilleström and sketches for Gustav III's dramatic productions by Louis Jean Desprez.

The Stockholm Archipelago ③⑦

E XTENDING 80 KM (50 MILES) EAST from the sheltered
waters of Stockholm to the open sea, the archipelago
encompasses tens of thousands of islands of all shapes
and sizes, some inhabited, others not. Many of the inner
archipelago's larger islands, such as Värmdö, Ingarö and
Ljusterö, are linked to the mainland by bridges and car
ferries, making them in parts little more than city suburbs.
But the majority of the archipelago islands, with their
traditional wooden houses, cosy hotels and youth
hostels, and summer sailing regattas, can be reached by
an extensive network of scheduled ferries departing from
Stockholm, Vaxholm, Stavsnäs and Dalarö.

Huvudskär in Stockholm's outer archipelago

ARCHIPELAGO HIGHLIGHTS

① Fjäderholmarna
② Vaxholm
③ Grinda
④ Finnhamn
⑤ Möja
⑥ Sandhamn
⑦ Utö

🦌 Fjäderholmarna

6 km (4 miles) E of Stockholm. 🚌 53.
🚢 May–Sep from Nybrokajen and
Slussen. **Baltic Aquarium** 🛈 08-718
40 55. 🕐 May–mid-Sep. 📞 phone
to book: 08-715 80 65. ♿ 🅿️ 🍴 🛍️

With the inclusion of the
Fjäderholmarna islands in
Ekoparken (see p97), the city's
"green lung" has acquired a
small part of the archipelago.
The main island, Stora
Fjäderholmen, is only 25
minutes by boat from
Nybrokajen or Slussen.

There was an inn here as
long ago as the 17th century,
conveniently sited for
islanders on their way to the
city to sell their wares. Today
there is an attractive harbour,
restaurants, an art gallery and
museums devoted to boating
and angling, as well as the
Baltic Aquarium. Local handicrafts include
metalwork,
weaving, wood-
carving and glass-
making. The
other three
islands have a
rich birdlife and
one, Libertas, has
Sweden's last
remaining
gas-powered
lighthouse.

🏛️ Vaxholm

25 km (16 miles) NE of Stockholm.
🛈 08-541 314 80. 🚌 670. 🚢 from
Strömkajen and Nybrokajen. **Vaxholm
Fortress** and **Vaxholm Fortress
Museum** 🛈 08-541 721 56/57. 🕐
mid-Jun–Sep: 11.30am–5.30pm daily.

The archipelago's main community, Vaxholm, is easily
reached by boat from
Stockholm on a delightful
one-hour journey through the
archipelago. Vaxholm Fortress,
on the nearby island of
Vaxholmen, guards this busy
port. First fortified in 1548 by
Gustav Vasa, the more recent
19th-century citadel houses a
military museum.

Two of Stockholm's best-
known architects have left
their mark on Vaxholm. The
law courts were given their
present appearance in 1925
by Cyrillus Johansson, and

**Vaxholm Fortress, strategically
sited on the approach to Vaxholm**

the hotel on the headland, by
Erik Lallerstedt (1899), has
Jugendstil ornamentation.

The wooden buildings and
shops around the square and
along Hamngatan provide a
pleasant stroll.

🦌 Grinda

30 km (19 miles) E of Stockholm.
🛈 08-542 490 72. 🚌 670 from
Östra station to Vaxholm, then boat.
🚢 from Strömkajen and Nybrokajen.
🅿️ 🍴 (summer only).

Grinda is a leafy island,
typical of the inner archipelago, about one and a half
hours by boat from the city. It
has some excellent beaches
and rocks for swimming, as
well as good fishing. The
architect Ernst Stenhammar,
who designed the Grand
Hôtel in Stockholm (see p77),
built a large Jugendstil villa
here, which is now a pub and

**The Fjäderholmarna islands, a popular summer
excursion just 25 minutes by boat from the city**

Sandhamn, the yachting centre in Stockholm's outer archipelago

restaurant with guest rooms. There are chalets to rent, a campsite and a youth hostel in a former barracks. Boats and bicycles can be hired.

🏝 Finnhamn

40 km (25 miles) NE of Stockholm. 🛈 08-542 462 12. 🚢 from Strömkajen and Nybrokajen. 🚻 🍴 🏕
Finnish ships used to moor at Finnhamn on their way to and from Stockholm. This attractive group of islands lies two and a half hours by boat from Stockholm at the point where the softer scenery of the inner archipelago gives way to the harsher landscape of the outer islands. As on Grinda, the main island has a wooden villa designed by Ernst Stenhammar (1912). Today it is the largest youth hostel in the archipelago. There is a restaurant, chalets to rent and a campsite. Smaller islands nearby are accessible by rowing boat.

🏝 Möja

50 km (31 miles) E of Stockholm. 🛈 08-571 640 53. 🚌 670 to Vaxholm, then boat. 🚢 from Strömkajen and Nybrokajen. 🚻 🍴 🏕
Fishing and strawberry-growing were the mainstays of this idyllic corner of the archipelago. Now there are few Möja strawberry growers and only one professional fisherman among the island's 300 inhabitants. Instead, picturesque harbours attract the sailing fraternity in particular. Nature reserves on and around Möja shelter a rich abundance of wildlife. Services on the island are good in the summer, with cottages, boats and kayaks for hire, and guest houses.

🏝 Sandhamn

50 km (31 miles) E of Stockholm. 🛈 08-571 530 00. 🚌 433, 434 from Slussen to Stavsnäs, then boat. 🚢 from Strömkajen and Nybrokajen. 🚻 🍴 🏕
Over the past 200 years Sandhamn has been a meeting point for sailors. The Royal Swedish Yacht Club is based in Seglarrestaurangen (Sailors' Restaurant), and every year the world's yachting elite arrive to take part in the Round Gotland Race.

Sandhamn is a pretty village with narrow alleys and houses adorned with decorative carvings. There are shops, crafts centres and a swimming pool. About 100 people live here permanently. The Customs House, built in 1752, is a listed heritage building and former home of poet and artist Elias Sehlstedt (1808–74).

Camping is not permitted, but hotel, bed-and-breakfast and chalet accommodation are available and there are great sandy beaches.

VISITORS' CHECKLIST

🚉 SL traffic information in Eng, 08-600 10 00. 🚢 Strömma Kanalbolaget, 08-587 140 00; Vaxholmsbolaget, 08-679 58 30. 🎭 Vaxholm: Archipelago fair (mid-Aug). 🚩 Sandhamn: Round Gotland Yacht Race (1st week in Jul), Sandhamn Regatta (3rd week in July), Vaxholm: Archipelago Boat Day (1st Wed in Jun). 🌐 www.stockholmtown.com

🏝 Utö

50 km (31 miles) SE of Stockholm. 🛈 08-501 574 10. 🚢 in summer, from Strömkajen. 🚻 🍴 🌐 www.utoturistbyra.se
No other island in the archipelago has as rich a history as Utö, which was inhabited before the Viking era. In the 12th century the islanders started to mine iron ore, and this activity continued until 1879. Their story is told in the Mining Museum adjoining the hotel. Today's holiday homes along Lurgatan were built as miners' cottages in the 18th century. A windmill, built in 1791, provides an unrivalled view of the island.

Utö is one of the best seaside resorts in the Stockholm area, and is ideal for a weekend or full-day excursion.

Hotel, youth hostel, camping, chalet and bed-and-breakfast accommodation are available. Bicycles, rowing boats and canoes can be hired. The bakery is renowned for its delicious "Utölimpa" bread.

EXCURSIONS BY STEAMBOAT

Traditional steamboats are a familiar feature on the waters around Stockholm. Both in the archipelago and on Lake Mälaren visitors can still enjoy the tranquil atmosphere of a steamboat voyage. One of the veterans, *SS Blidösund*, built in 1911, is operated by voluntary organizations and serves mostly the northern archipelago. Some routes, for example Stockholm–Mariefred, are operated partly or completely by steamers. Most of the other passenger boats from the early 20th century have been fitted with oil-fired engines, but still provide a nostalgic journey back in time.

SS Blidösund, one of the oldest in Stockholm's fleet of steamboats

STOCKHOLM STREET FINDER

KEY TO STREET FINDER

▨	Major sight	🅿	Car park
▨	Place of interest	ℹ	Tourist information office
▨	Other building	✚	Hospital
🚆	Train station	👮	Police station
Ⓣ	Tunnelbana station	✝	Church
🚌	Main bus stop	✡	Synagogue
🚍	Long-distance bus station	⊠	Post office
⛴	Ferry boarding point	☼	Viewpoint
🚊	Tram stop	—	Railway line

One-way street

Pedestrian street

SCALE OF MAP PAGES 1–2

0 metres   250
0 yards   250

SCALE OF MAP PAGES 3–4

0 metres   250
0 yards   250

Nybroviken

Ferry to Djurgården & Skeppsholmen

STRANDVÄGEN

DJUR GÅRDEN

Ladugårdslands-viken

Junibacken

Nordiska museet

ASIE- OLMEN

Museiparken

National-museum

Galär-parken

MUSEIKAJEN

Vasa-museet

2

Skeppsholms-bron

Öst-asiatiska museet

NORRA BRANAN

SLUPSKJULSVÄGEN

ÖSTRA BROBÄNKEN

Tyghus-plan

Batteri-parken

SKEPPS-HOLMEN

Moderna museet

Skeppsholms-kyrkan

SVENSKSUNDSVÄGEN

af Chapman

VÄSTRA BROBÄNKEN

Amiralitets-parken

Exercis-plan

Arkitektur-museet

FLAGGMANSV.

Långa raden

SVENSKSUNDSVÄGEN

Svensksundsparken

LÅNGA RADEN

Holm-amiralens Torg

GRÖNA GÅNGEN

LÅNGA GÅNGEN

Strömmen

Konst-högskolan

SÖDRA BROBÄNKEN

ÖSTRA BROBÄNKEN

Kastellholms-bron

KASTELL-BACKEN

Kastellholmen

KASTELLHOLMSKAJEN

ÖRLOGSVÄGEN

Kastell-parken

Ferry to Skeppsholmen & Djurgården

Saltsjön

GÅRDSLEDEN

STADSGÅRDSHAMNEN

KATARINAVÄGEN

STADSGÅRDSHAMNEN

SWEDEN
AREA BY AREA

Sweden at a Glance

Sweden is a long country, traditionally divided into Norrland, Svealand and Götaland. In Norrland the landscape is characterized by its proximity to the Arctic, with mountains in the west, rivers running east towards the coast, and an interior of forest or marshland. With the exception of the larger towns along the coast, the area is sparsely populated. In Svealand the countryside is hilly, with lakes and rivers interspersed with farmland. Island archipelagos lie offshore. The population is concentrated in Mälardalen, centring on Stockholm. Götaland, comprising the southern part of the country, offers the most variation with differing landscapes and a high urban and rural population.

The Mountains of Härjedalen *a haven for outdoor activities in b summer and winter (see pp260–6)*

The Fryken Lakes *in Värmland are edged by superb manor houses such as Rottneros, whose park overlooking Mellanfryken contains an outstanding collection of statues, including Carl Milles' Nike (see p232).*

Fiskebäckskil, *with its red fishermen's huts and white wooden houses, is typical of the coastal villages of Bohuslän (see p215).*

Götaplatsen, *Gothenburg's finest square, features Carl Milles' statue* Poseidon *with Konstmuseet in the background (see p200).*

Österlen, *on the southwestern coast of Skåne, is characterized by rolling agricultural land and the half-timbered farmhouses typical of the area (see p183).*

WESTE
SVEALA
(See pp22

WESTERN
GÖTALAND
(See pp206–2

GOTHENBURG
(See pp190–205)

K A T T E G A T T

SOUTH
GÖTALA
(See pp17

◁ **Skäckerfjällen**, a nature reserve in western Jämtland, forming a backdrop to Lake Anjan

NORTHERN
NORRLAND
(See pp262–75)

The Ice Hotel *in Jukkasjärvi is an extraordinary creation built entirely of ice and
snow. It melts in the spring sunshine each
year and is recreated in October* (see p272).

Uppsala*, the seat of
Sweden's archbishop,
has a High Gothic
cathedral founded in
1455 – although parts
of it date from the
13th century – and
the oldest university
in the Nordic coun-
tries, established in
1477* (see pp128–9).

UTHERN
•RRLAND
pp246–61)

GULF OF BOTHNIA

TERN
ALAND
122–39)   ***STOCKHOLM***
(See pp44–117)

BALTIC SEA

Visby*, "the town of roses and ruins", with its medieval
perimeter wall and half-timbered houses, is a UNESCO World
Heritage Site* (see pp164–7).

TERN
ALAND
140–57)   ***GOTLAND***
(See p158–69)

The Kingdom of Crystal
*is the part of Småland
known for its glass-
ware, both artistic
and practical. The
plate,* Amber, *was
designed by Göran
Wärf at Kosta
Glasbruk in 2003*
(see pp152–3).

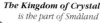

| 0 kilometres | 200 |
| 0 miles | 100 |

EASTERN SVEALAND

THE WATERWAYS *of Lake Mälaren and the vast archipelago extending to the Baltic both divide and unite the provinces of Uppland, Södermanland and Västmanland. This is a land of verdant islands and glittering bays, splendid castles and little wooden towns, and a cultural heritage that predates the Vikings. With Stockholm at the centre, the region is home to one-third of Sweden's population.*

This area was the cradle of ancient Svea, as can be seen in the rock carvings, burial mounds and standing stones in the shapes of ships that dot the landscape. It was from the town of Birka on Lake Mälaren and from Roslagen in Uppland that the Vikings headed east on plundering raids and trading missions around Europe and beyond *(see p31)*. The centre of the ancient pagan Æsir cult in Uppsala held out against Christianity until the 12th century. Many beautiful, small medieval churches testify to the fact that Christianity finally dominated. They are richly decorated with paintings depicting biblical scenes for the benefit of the local congregations. Uppsala itself became a cathedral city and the seat of the archbishop in 1258.

The many castles and fortresses which guard the waterways are an eye-catching sight. Several of these date back to the Middle Ages, but the most important, such as Skokloster, are the result of the great wealth which flooded into the country after Sweden's victories in the various European wars of the 17th century *(see pp35–7)*. Shipping brought further prosperity to the region, with centres such as Arboga lying on the iron route between Bergslagen, Stockholm and the Uppland harbours. There are well-preserved ironworks in all three provinces, including Engelsbergs Bruk, a UNESCO World Heritage Site.

The extensive archipelago straddles the coasts of Uppland and Södermanland, and Lake Mälaren itself is so full of islands that the archipelago appears to continue uninterrupted.

All the architectural sights and natural attractions of Eastern Svealand are best enjoyed at a slow pace by bicycle or boat, or on foot.

The flat skerries of the outer archipelago

◁ Gripsholms Slott at Mariefred on Lake Mälaren, established by Gustav Vasa in 1540

Exploring Eastern Svealand

T HIS, THE HEARTLAND OF SWEDEN, offers as many
tempting treats as the most well-stocked Swedish
smörgåsbord. Whether travelling by car, bus, train,
bicycle or on foot, visitors will enjoy frequent
glimpses of lakes and bays, as water is a constant
presence. This makes travelling by boat an
unbeatable way of discovering Eastern Svealand's
history and culture and enjoying the area's natural
beauty. There are hundreds of canoe trails, and
canoes and boats can be hired all over the region.
For walkers, Sörmlandsleden, Upplandsleden
and Bruksleden in Västmanland offer more than
1,500 km (940 miles) of stunning trails.

**Botanist Carl von Linné's Hammarby
outside Uppsala** *(see p129)*

**Julita Gård, a Södermanland estate and
open-air museum**

SIGHTS AT A GLANCE

Map labels: Ludvika, NORBERG, FAGERSTA **㉕**, KOPPARBERG **㉖**, Filip-stad, GRYTHYTTAN **㉗**, VÄSTMANLAND, NORA **㉘**, KÖPING **㉒**, ARBOGA **㉑**, ESKILSTUNA **⑲**, MÄLARDALENS SLOTT **⑱**, VÄST **㉓**, Örebro, HJÄLMAREN, Kumla, JULITA GÅRD **⑳**, FLEN **⑮**, KATRINEHOLM, SÖDERMANLAND

KEY

═══	Motorway
▬▬	Major road
═══	Minor road
─►	Train line
- -	Ferry route

One of the traditional steamers of the archipelago and Lake Mälaren

Ceiling fresco by Albertus Pictor, Härkeberga Church *(see p130)*

GETTING AROUND

Destinations on both sides of Lake Mälaren can be reached quickly via the major motorways. Travelling north–south, the E4 is a good road, although Stockholm can be a bottleneck at times. The minor roads tend to offer motorists a more pleasurable experience. The railway network serves many locations, but in Roslagen in Uppland and the more remote areas the main option is the bus. Summer offers the opportunity to take to the water, with good connections to the archipelago on high-speed ferries or traditional steamers.

SEE ALSO

• **Where to Stay** p283

• **Where to Eat** pp296–7

Österbybruk's English gardens with estate offices and clock tower

Österbybruk ❶

Uppland. 🏛 *2,100.* 🚊 *1 Jun–31 Aug: Ånghammaren 0295-214 92.* 🚌 *823 from Uppsala.* 📧 🚻 **Vallonsmedjan** ⭕ *Jun–Aug: 11am–5pm Sat & Sun.* 📷 *by appointment, 0295-200 72.* **Liljeforsateljén** ⭕ *May–mid-Jun, mid-Aug–Sep: noon–4pm Sat & Sun; mid-Jun–mid-Aug: noon–5pm daily.* 🎪 *Hurdy-Gurdy Festival (weekend before Midsummer), Fire Festival (2nd weekend Aug).*

IRON PLAYED a key role in the region and nowhere is this more apparent than at Österbybruk. It is the area's oldest ironworks, dating back to the 15th century, but things only really took off when Dutchman Louis de Geer bought the foundry in 1643. With the help of migrant Walloon blacksmiths, he developed the iron industry so crucial to Sweden's position as a great power.

As the world's only fully preserved Walloon forge, the 15th-century **Vallonsmedjan** uses puppets, sound and light to recreate life in the hammer mills. Around it are charming 18th- and 19th-century streets.

The 18th-century manor house was home to wildlife painter Bruno Liljefors in the early 20th century. In summer, his popular animal paintings are exhibited in **Liljeforsateljén** in the gardens.

Dannemora Gruva was the mine on which local ironworking was built. Gaping opencast pits such as Storrymningen are relics of an industry that has gone on here since the Middle Ages. Above the mine is the building in which

Mårten Triewald built Sweden's first steam engine in 1726.

🚋 **Dannemora Gruva**
2 km (1 mile) west of Österbybruk. 📞 *0295-214 92.* ⭕ *Jun–Sep: daily.* 📷 📧

Forsmarks Bruk ❷

Uppland. 🚌 *from Uppsala.* 🚊 *next to Brukscaféet, Jun–Aug: 0173-500 15.* 📷 *mid-Jun–mid-Aug: 10am, noon, 2pm Mon–Fri, noon, 2pm Sat & Sun.* 📧 🚻 📷 🛏 ♿

THE HISTORIC ironworks of Forsmarks Bruk retains its well-preserved streets with their beautiful, whitewashed rows of houses and a manor house built in 1767–74. The manor is set in extensive English-style gardens.

The nuclear power station of **Forsmarks Kärnkraftverk** lies on the coast, 3 km (2 miles) from the ironworks. It provides one-seventh of Sweden's electricity. Guided tours include such features as the vast biotest lake where the environmental impact of the cooling water is studied.

Louis de Geer's Walloon ironworks empire also included the impressively preserved **Lövstabruk**.

🏛 **Forsmarks Kärnkraftverk**
3 km (2 miles) north of Forsmark. 🚊 *0173-812 68.* ⭕ *Mon–Fri.* 📷 *mid-May–mid-Aug: tours from Forsmarks Bruk; other times by appointment.* ♿

🚋 **Lövstabruk**
16 km (10 miles) north from Forsmark. 🚊 *summer: 0173-500 15.* ⭕ *summer: daily (manor).* 📷 ♿ 📧 🚻

Öregrund ❸

Uppland. 🏛 *1,600.* 🚌 *639 from Stockholm.* 🚊 *Jun–Aug: Harbour Office 0173–305 55; all year round: Östhammar Tourist Office, Rådhusgatan 6, Östhammar, 0173–178 50.* 🖼 🎪 *Fishing Festival (1st Sat in Jul), Roslagsloppet speedboat race (3rd weekend in Aug).* 🌐 *www.onab.net/turism*

THE TWIN TOWNS of Öregrund and Östhammar are closely linked geographically and historically. At the end of the 15th century, the citizens of Östhammar founded Öregrund in order to obtain a better harbour. Seafaring and iron-exporting became vital to the town. In 1719, Öregrund was burned by the Russians, but the wooden buildings were rebuilt according to a town plan from 1744. The Town Hall is from 1829. At the end of the 19th century, the sleepy area became a seaside resort and continues to attract visitors to this day.

The Öregrund and Östhammar region is home to many well-preserved old ironworking communities, including **Harg** and **Gimo**. Built in 1763–70, Gimo Manor was the first in Sweden to be designed in Gustavian style by Jean Eric Rehn.

Outside Gimo lies **Skäfthammars Kyrka**, a medieval church particularly renowned for its lectern, which was built for the Gimo smiths.

⛪ **Skäfthammars Kyrka**
Gimo, 16 km (10 miles) southeast of Östhammar. 🚊 *0173-419 94.* ⭕ *call for info.*

Öregrund Church's shingle-clad, free-standing bell tower (1719)

Albert Engström's studio on the granite cliffs outside Grisslehamn

Grisslehamn ❹

Uppland. 👥 4,700. 🚌 🛈 Inner Harbour 0175-331 02. 🔼 🗺️ Postrodden boat race to Åland (Jun).

THE CHOPPY Åland Sea constantly batters the red granite cliffs of northern Väddö at Grisslehamn. This is the closest point in Sweden to Finland and the reason for the town's existence. Today's ferry crossing to Eckerö takes only two hours, but things were much tougher in the 17th and 18th centuries when this was the main link with the eastern outposts of the Swedish empire. Until 1876, the post was rowed across the water by local fishermen in open boats. To commemorate the "post rowers", a race is held across the Åland Sea every year in similar boats.

Today, apart from those making the ferry crossing, the sleepy fishing port of Grisslehamn attracts Väddö's many holidaymakers. Delicious fresh fish can be bought from the red sheds on the harbourside.

In 1900, painter and writer Albert Engström (d. 1940) moved to Grisslehamn. He became much loved for his priceless characters such as the tramp, Kolingen, and the Roslagen figure, Österman. Engström's studio on the coast is now a museum. On the harbour is the **Albert Engströmsmuseet**, a reconstruction of his home containing Engström's art and memorabilia.

🏛 **Albert Engströmsmuseet**
Next to ferry terminal. 📞 0175-331 02.
◯ May–Sep. 🗺️ 📷

Norrtälje ❺

Uppland. 👥 16,400. 🚌 640 from Stockholm. 🛈 Danskes Gränd 4, 0176-719 90. 🔼 🗺️ Norrtälje Jazz Festival (late Jun/early Jul).
Ⓦ www.norrtalje.se

AN IDYLLIC town, built of wood, Norrtälje is the natural hub of Roslagen, the area which covers large parts of the Uppland coast. Norrtälje received its town charter from Gustav II Adolf in 1622, when an important armaments factory was established here. In the second half of the 19th century, the town became a seaside resort, not least due to the health-giving properties of the mud found in Norrtälje Bay.

Thousands of summer residents from Stockholm still head for Norrtälje. The town centre and the buildings along the Norrtäljeån river retain their 18th-century features. The church was built in 1726 and the Town Hall dates from 1792. Attractions include **Roslagsmuseet** in the old armaments factory, focusing on seafaring and coastal life. **Pythagoras** is an unusual museum in a former diesel engine factory and one of Sweden's best preserved industrial relics.

Viking ship in Norrtälje

🏛 **Roslagsmuseet**
Hantverkargatan 23. 📞 0176-576 30.
◯ Mon–Fri; May–Aug: also Sat. 🗺️ ♿
🏛 **Pythagoras**
Verkstadsgatan 6. 📞 0176-100 50.
◯ mid-Jun–mid-Aug: Mon–Fri. 🗺️ 📷

Skokloster ❻

Uppland. 📞 018-38 60 77. 🚉 SL train from Stockholm to Bålsta, then bus 894. 🚌 from Stockholm and Uppsala. ◯ 30 min before first tour. 📷 Apr–Oct: 1pm Mon–Fri (Sep: also 3pm), noon, 1pm, 2pm, 3pm Sat & Sun; May–Aug: noon, 1pm, 2pm, 3pm daily (mid-Jun–mid-Aug also 4pm). Eng tours 10 min past the hour except Apr & Oct Mon–Fri. 🗺️ 🅿️ 🍽 🛈 📷 Skokloster Pageant (last week in Jul).

ONE OF THE BEST preserved Baroque castles in Europe, Skokloster, on Lake Mälaren, contains a unique collection of furniture, art, weapons, textiles and books. Construction was started in 1654 for army commander Carl Gustav Wrangel, who accumulated incredible treasures during the Thirty Years War (1618–48). This magnificent building was a way for Wrangel to show off his success, but he only ever lived here for a few weeks. Time seems to have stood still at the castle: the Banquet Hall, for example, remains incomplete, with all the tools lying where the craftsmen left them. The most sumptuous rooms are the armoury and library.

Next to the castle is the **Skokloster Motormuseum** with its fine collection of veteran cars and aeroplanes.

🏛 **Skokloster Motormuseum**
📞 018-38 61 86. ◯ Apr–Sep: daily.
🗺️ ♿

The Baroque Skokloster Castle, beautifully situated on Lake Mälaren

Uppsala ❼

THE CITY OF LEARNING on the idyllic Fyrisån river long remained a small town despite becoming the seat of the archbishop in 1258, having the first university in Scandinavia in 1477 and being the venue for parliaments and coronations. Scientists such as Carl von Linné and Anders Celsius gained the university worldwide glory, but as late as 1800 the town had only 4,000 inhabitants. It wasn't until 20th-century industrialization and the expansion in education that Uppsala grew into Sweden's fourth largest city. The Gothic cathedral, castle, historic university buildings, botanical gardens and ancient Gamla (Old) Uppsala make this one of Sweden's foremost sights.

The cathedral's twin spires, restored in the 19th century

🔒 Domkyrkan

Domkyrkoplan 2. 📞 018-18 72 01.
🕐 daily. 📷 🔒 🔲 daily.
Skattkammaren 🕐 daily. 📷
The first sight on approaching Uppsala is the 119-m (390-ft) high twin spires of the largest cathedral in the Nordic region. The building, with its impressive, colonnaded Gothic nave, was consecrated in 1435. Many monarchs have been crowned here and kings Gustav Vasa and Johann III, as well as botanist Carl von Linné and theosophist Emanuel Swedenborg (1688–1772), are buried here. The High Altar contains the remains of St Erik, patron saint of Sweden, in a golden shrine.
The cathedral treasury, Skattkammaren, in the north tower has a superb collection of textiles and silver.

🏛 Gustavianum

Akademigatan 3. 📞 018-471 75 71.
🕐 Tue–Sun. 🔵 public holidays.
📷 Sat & Sun (also Eng). 📷
Sweden's oldest university building takes its name from Gustav II Adolf who, in 1620, donated a number of medieval buildings from which this one was created. The unusual dome was built in 1662 for Olof Rudbeck's Theatrum Anatomicum. This is an amphitheatre with standing room for 200 spectators – students and paying members of the public – who would gather here to watch dissections of executed criminals. The room which visitors see today is largely a faithful reconstruction.
The Gustavianum mounts exhibitions connected with the work of the university since its foundation in 1477. One of the gems on show is the Augsburg Art Cabinet from the early 17th century. It is a kind of universal museum showing the world view of the time in miniature. Various archaeological collections from Egypt and the Classical world are also on display.

🏛 Universitetshuset

St Olofsgatan/Övre Slottsgatan.
📞 018-471 57 30. 🕐 Mon–Fri and for events. 🔒
The university's imposing main building was constructed in 1887 in Neo-Renaissance style. It contains an attractive audit-orium and is home to part of the university's art collection.

🏛 Carolina Rediviva

Dag Hammarskjölds Väg 1. 📞 018-471 39 00. 🕐 Mon–Sat (mid-May–mid-Sep also Sun). 🔵 public holidays. 📷 mid-May–mid-Sep. 🔒
In 1841, the 200-year-old university library moved into this specially designed build-ing which houses 5 million printed books and 4 km (2 miles) of shelving holding handwritten manuscripts. Rarities include the Silver Bible from the 6th century and Olaus Magnus's *Carta Marina* (1539).

🏛 Uppsala Slott

Slottsbacken. 📞 727 24 85. 🕐 for guided tours. 📷 phone for info.
Konstmuseet 🕐 Tue–Sun. 🔲 🍴
Standing on a glacial ridge, this Vasa castle competes with the cathedral for domination of the city. Established as a fortress in 1549, it was added to several times, but never finished. A disastrous city fire in 1702 destroyed much of the castle and restoration work was started by Carl Härleman. The castle now houses Uppsala's art museum and the governor's residence.

CARL VON LINNÉ

"God created, Linné organized," goes the saying about the Swedish king of plants. It is thanks to Linné's ground-breaking *Systema Naturae*, first published in 1735, that the

world has the familiar system of binomial nomenclature, giving all plants and animals two Latin names. In 1741, Linné, also known as Linnaeus, became prof-essor of medicine at Uppsala and his spirit has suffused the city ever since. At his country house in Hammarby, Linné tutored students. It was not unknown for him to greet them dressed only in his nightshirt, for the morning's nature walk. According to Linné "nature does not wait for powder and wigs".

Bust of Carl von Linné, 1707–78

Burial mounds next to Gamla Uppsala church and Disagården

VISITORS' CHECKLIST

Uppland. 124,000. 25 km (16 miles) south of the centre. Kungsgatan. Fyristorg 8, 018-727 48 00. Vaksala market (Sat). Walpurgis Night celebrations (30 Apr), Fyris Festival (early Jun), Culture Night (2nd Sat in Sep). W www.uppsalatourism.se

Botaniska Trädgården

Villavägen 8. 018-471 28 38. daily. public holidays. greenhouse.

The botanical gardens have had an educational function since the end of the 18th century. They hold more than 130,000 plants, many exotic, in a beautiful setting that includes several greenhouses, one of which is tropical. The first garden was established on the banks of the Fyrisån river by Olof Rudbeck in 1655. In 1741, Carl von Linné took it over and made it one of the leading gardens of its time. Lovingly restored, it is now known as the Linné garden. After a donation from Gustav III in the late 18th century, teaching was switched to the castle garden, where the Linneanum, housing the orangery, opened in 1807.

Gamla Uppsala

Route 290 or E4, 5 km north of the centre. **Disagården** 018-16 91 00. mid-May–Aug: daily. Sun.

Gamla Uppsala is like a time capsule. Royal burial mounds rise up from the plain as they have done for 1,500 years. This was a centre for worshipping the Norse gods long into the 11th century, with a temple which, according to Adam of Bremen's description from 1070, was clad entirely in gold and contained images of Odin, Thor and Frey. Every nine years, a bloody festival was celebrated with men, stallions and dogs sacrificed in the trees around the temple. In the early 12th century, the heathen temple gave way to a Christian church, then a cathedral. But in 1273, the

seat of the diocese moved to Uppsala and the cathedral became a parish church of which only small parts remain. Nearby is Disagården, an open-air museum focusing on the life of local farmers in the 19th century.

Linné's Hammarby

13 km (8 miles) southeast of Uppsala. 018-32 60 94. May–Sep: **Gardens** daily. **Museum** Tue–Sun. Whitsun, Midsummer's Eve.

Linné bought Hammarby farm in 1758, because he thought the air in Uppsala was bad for his health. The estate was his rural retreat, where he was able to cultivate plants that could not tolerate the moist soil in the botanical gardens. The farm is now owned by the state and run by Uppsala University.

UPPSALA CITY CENTRE

Botaniska Trädgården ⑥
Carolina Rediviva ④
Domkyrkan ①
Gustavianum ②
Universitetshuset ③
Uppsala Slott/ Konstmuseet ⑤

KEY

🚆 Railway station
🚌 Bus terminus
🅿 Parking
✝ Church
ℹ Tourist information

0 metres 300
0 yards 300

Steninge Slott near Sigtuna, one of the best examples of a 17th-century Carolian country house

Sigtuna ❽

Uppland. 🚶 *7,700.* 🚍 🚆 to Märsta
C, then bus. 🚌 🚏 ℹ *Stora Gatan
33, 08-594 806 50.* 📅 *Medieval
Festival (Sat & Sun after Midsummer),
Sigtuna Meeting (last Sat & Sun in
Aug).* 🌐 *www.sigtuna.se*

SWEDEN'S SECOND OLDEST town
after Birka was founded in
980 and soon became a centre
of Christianity. Ruins of three
of the original seven churches
in medieval Sigtuna, St Per,
St Lars and St Olof, still
remain. The attractive main
street, Stora Gatan, is lined
with colourful wooden
buildings and follows the
original route. Still in use today
is the 13th-century church of
St Maria, with its medieval
paintings. It is the oldest brick-
built church in Mälardalen.

Sigtuna has Sweden's smallest town hall, built in 1744,
and Lundströmska Gården, an
early 20th-century home
furnished in the style of the
period. There are around 150
11th-century rune stones in
the surrounding region.

The area is also well-
endowed with stately homes.
These include Skokloster *(see
p127)* and the royal palace of
Rosersberg, with some of
Europe's best-kept interiors
from the period 1795–1825.

East of Sigtuna is **Steninge
Slott**, architect Tessin the
Younger's Italianate Baroque
masterpiece built in the 1690s.
The attractive gardens contain
a monument to Count Axel
von Fersen, renowned not
least for his romance with the
French queen Marie
Antoinette, and a cultural
centre and art gallery.

🏛 **Rosersbergs Slott**
15 km (9 miles) from Sigtuna. 📞 *08-
590 350 39.* ◯ *Mid-May–Aug: daily
for guided tours.* 🚫

🏛 **Steninge Slott**
7 km (4 miles) east of Sigtuna. 📞 *08-
592 595 00.* **Palace** ◯ *May–Aug daily.*
Cultural Centre ◯ *daily.* 🚫 🍴

Enköping ❾

Uppland. 🚶 *19,200.* 🚆 🚌 🚍 ℹ
Kungsgatan 42, 0171-250 40.
🌐 *www.enkoping.se*

THIS CENTRALLY located
town on Lake Mälaren
calls itself Sweden's "nearest
town". Another
name is
"Horseradish
Town" from the vegetable
production which made the
town known in the 19th
century. And Enköping
remains a city of greenery
with its inviting parks.

Enköping was granted a
town charter in 1300. It was
a spiritual centre with three
churches and a mon-
astery. Of these, only
the largely remodelled
Vårfrukyrkan remains.

Northeast of the
town, the medieval church of
Härkeberga is a real gem. At
the end of the 15th century, its
star chamber was decorated
by the master painter Albertus
Pictor with colourful
representations of biblical
stories *(see p125).*

🔒 **Härkeberga Kyrka**
10 km (6 miles) northeast of Enköping
◯ *Mar–Sep daily.*

*Triumphal
cross, Härke-
berga Kyrka*

Birka ❿

Uppland. 🚢 *from Stockholm and
Södertälje during summer season.*
Birkamuseet 📞 *08-560 514 45.*
◯ *May–Sep: 10am–5pm daily.* 🚫

THE TRADING POST of Birka
on the island of Björkö in
Lake Mälaren was established
in the 8th century and is
thought to be the oldest town
in Scandinavia. The founder
was the Svea king, who
had his royal residence on
nearby Adelsö.
About 100 years
later, Birka is
described by a
writer as having "many
rich merchants and an
abundance of all types of
goods and a great deal of
money and valuables". It
was thought to have had
1,000 inhabitants, including
craftsmen of every kind,
whose products
attracted merchants
from distant countries.
The town was planned
on uncomplicated
lines. People lived in modest
houses which stood in rows
overlooking the long jetties.
At these lay the ships which
took the Vikings out on
trading missions and war
expeditions. In 830 the arrival
of a monk named Ansgar
marked the start of Sweden's
conversion to Christianity. But
Birka's moment of greatness
soon passed. In the 10th

Iron Age burial ground at Birka on the island of Björkö in Lake Mälaren

century, the town was abandoned in favour of Sigtuna,
on the nearby mainland.

Today, Björkö is a green
island with meadows and
juniper-covered slopes. It has
a fascinating museum and
ongoing archaeological digs.
The museum shows how
Birka would have looked in
its heyday, along with some
of the finds. Visitors can also
share in the day's discoveries
when digs are in progress.

In summer, services are
held in the Ansgar Chapel.
There is a harbour, restaurant,
and good places to swim.

**Testing the laws of nature at
Tom Tits Experiment, Södertälje**

Södertälje ⑪

Södermanland. 👥 63,300. 🚢 🚉 �
🛈 Saltsjögatan 2, 08-550 227 00.
📅 Broloppet race (3rd Sat in Aug).
🌐 www.sodertaljeturism.com

GOOD COMMUNICATIONS are
the key to the economic
success of Södertälje, one of
Sweden's oldest towns. In the
9th century, a rise in land
levels rendered the sound
between the Baltic Sea and
Lake Mälaren unnavigable and
so Tälje became a reloading
point. The small town flourished in the Middle Ages but
fires, war and plague almost
eradicated it in the 17th and
18th centuries. Fortunes
improved with the construction of the canal in 1819, and
with the arrival of the railway
in 1860 industrialization took
off. The town grew quickly.
Today, major companies such
as vehicle-maker Scania and
pharmaceuticals giant
AstraZeneca form the basis of
a booming commercial life.

Södertälje's history is the
focus of **Torekällbergets
Museum**, an open-air
museum with animals, historic
buildings and a craft quarter.
Marcus Wallenberg-hallen

Neat wooden houses lining the harbour canal in Trosa

contains a large collection of
veteran vehicles from Scania's
100-year production history.

At **Tom Tits Experiment**,
inquisitive children are free to
discover for themselves how
the laws of nature work
through experiments with
sound, light, air and water.

🏛 **Torekällbergets Museum**
📞 08-550 214 22. 📅 Tue–Sun. 🖥 🍴
🏛 **Marcus Wallenberg-hallen**
📞 08-553 825 00. 📅 Mon–Fri. 🚫
public holidays.
🏛 **Tom Tits Experiment**
Storgatan 33. 📞 08-522 525 00. 📅
daily. 🚫 24/12–1/1. 📷 🖥 🍴 🎁 ♿

Ytterjärna ⑫

Södermanland. 🚉 to Järna, then bus.
🛈 Kulturhuset, 08-554 302 00.
📅 May–Aug: 9am–4pm daily,
Sep–Apr: 9am–4pm Mon–Fri.
🚫 public holidays. 📷 ♿ 🖥 🍴

SINCE THE 1960s, Ytterjärna
has become the centre for
Swedish anthroposophists,
followers of the teachings of
Austrian philosopher Rudolf
Steiner (1861–1925).
Anthroposophists focus on the
development of the whole
human being, particularly in
the fields of art, music,
farming and medicine. There
are a number of Steiner
organizations here,
including schools, the
Vidarkliniken hospital,
biodynamic farms and
market gardens. The
Kulturhuset is renow-
ned as a centre for art,
music and theatre, and
for the building's
audacious design by
architect Erik Asmussen,
with its intertwined
dialogue of colour and
shape inside and out.

Trosa ⑬

Södermanland. 👥 4,200. 🚉 to
Vagnhärad or Södertälje, then bus.
🛈 Torget 1, 0156-522 22. ⛴
📅 Trosa Market (2nd Sat in Jul).
📅 Dance at the harbour (Wed in
Jul–1st week in Aug).

KNOWN AS THE END of the
World, idyllic Trosa is
something of a geographical
dead end if you are not
venturing into the wonderful
Trosa archipelago beyond.
Like so many coastal towns, it
was burned to the ground by
the Russians in 1719, although
the church dating from 1711
was spared. Pretty groups of
red wooden buildings can be
found mainly in Kåkstan,
where Garvaregården is an
arts and crafts museum. The
main square, with its miniature town hall and market, is
a focal point for the town.

Nearby, **Tullgarns Slott**
was the favourite summer
residence of Gustav V
(1858–1950). The beautiful
18th-century palace has
magnificent interiors and
English-style gardens.

♣ **Tullgarns Slott**
On E4, 10 km (6 miles) north of Trosa.
📞 08-551 720 11. 📅 mid-May–Aug:
daily, Sep: Sat & Sun. 📷 📷

**Kulturhuset by Erik Asmussen, in the
anthroposophists' Ytterjärna**

Nyköpingshus, site of the fatal Nyköping Banquet in 1317

Nyköping ⓮

Södermanland. ⓰ 27,200. ⓐ ⓑ ⓒ
ⓘ Stadshuset, Stora Torget, 0155-24
82 00. ⓓ ⓔ Nyköping Banquet
(Tue–Sun in Jul). ⓦ www.nykoping.se

SÖDERMANLAND'S county town
is probably best-known for
the notorious Nyköping
Banquet in 1317. King Birger
invited the Dukes Erik and
Valdemar to a banquet at
which the disputes between
the brothers were to be
resolved. Instead, Birger had
the dukes thrown into
Nyköpinghus's dungeon,
where they were left to die.
The story is retold in summer
in a colourful pageant at the
castle. A fire in 1665 destroyed
the original castle and only
the tower remains. In the
adjoining county governor's
residence, the **Sörmlands
Museum** contains a lively mix
of historical exhibitions.
A pleasant way to see the
sights in the summer is to take
the Tuffis tourist train which
departs from Stora Torget. On
the coast north of the town,
Nynäs Slott is also worth a visit.

🏛 Sörmlands Museum
Nyköpingshus. ⓒ 0155-24 57 00.
⏰ mid-May–mid-Aug: daily, other
times: Tue–Sun. ⓐ ⓑ ⓘ

Flen ⓯

Södermanland. ⓰ 6,200. ⓐ ⓑ ⓘ
Sveavägen 1, 0157-190 23; Malm-
köping (summer) 0157-194 44. ⓐ
Malma Market (last Sat & Sun in Jul).
ⓔ Flen Festival (2nd weekend in Jun).

ONE OF THE YOUNGEST towns
in Sweden, Flen only
gained its town charter in
1949. It is the surrounding area

with the same name which
offers the attractions.

ENVIRONS: On Lake
Valdemaren, just east of the
town, lies Stenhammar's
beautiful castle, renowned as
the residence of Prince
Vilhelm in the early 1900s.
The castle is now used by
Carl XVI Gustav and is not
open to the public. Northeast
of Flen is the prime minister's
summer residence, **Harpsund**,
where the gardens are open
to visitors. The old
regimental town of
Malmköping has
Malmahed, a
former military
site, now a
museum and
nature centre.
There are
several military
museums, as well
as **Museispårvägen**,
displaying veteran trams and
other public transport vehicles.
Visitors can enjoy a short tram
ride through the countryside.

🏛 Museispårvägen
Malmköping, 17 km (11 miles) north
of Flen, road 55. ⓒ 0157-204 30.
⏰ 2nd Sat May–1st Sun Sep: Sat,
Sun & public holidays, 4th week
Jun–1st week Aug: daily. ⓓ

**Volvo taxi (1950),
Museispårvägen**

Mariefred ⓰

Södermanland. ⓰ 4,700. ⓐ ⓑ
ⓘ Rådhuset, 0159-297 90. ⓐ
ⓔ Steam Day (1st Sat & Sun in Jun),
Medieval Festival (3rd Sat & Sun in
Jul). ⓦ www.strangnas.se

THE TOWN OF Mariefred
should ideally be
approached from the water to
get the best view of the
splendid **Gripsholms Slott**.
The first fortress on this site
was built in the 1380s by the
Lord High Chancellor, Bo
Jonsson Grip, who gave the
castle its name. Work on the
present building, initiated by
Gustav Vasa, started in 1537,
but extensive alterations were
made by Gustav III in the late
18th century. It was during
this period that the National
Portrait Gallery was set up. It
now contains 4,000 portraits,
representing the celebrities of
the past 500 years.
Gripsholms Slott has a
number of well-preserved
interiors from various
periods, with
highlights including
Gustav III's theatre
and the White
Salon. The town
of Mariefred,
which grew up
in the shadow of
the castle, derives
its name from a
medieval Carthusian
monastery. An inn has stood
on the site of the monastery
since the early 17th century.
The peaceful old streets of
Mariefred with their delightful
wooden buildings are a
pleasure to stroll around. Art
enthusiasts should head for
Grafikens Hus on a hill
leading up to the former royal
farm, where stables and

Mariefred Town Hall (1784), site of the town's tourist office

◁ **Strömsholms Slott, the centre of Sweden's equestrian sport** (see p136) haylofts have been converted into attractive galleries.

One of the best ways to visit Mariefred is by boat. The 1903 steamer *S/S Mariefred* plies the three-and-a-half-hour voyage from Stockholm. There is a Railway Museum in the town and **ÖSlJ**, the Östra Södermanlands Järnväg museum society, operates narrow-gauge steam trains from the harbour on a 20-minute trip to Läggesta.

♣ Gripsholms Slott

1 km (half a mile) south of the centre.
☎ 0159-101 94. ⬤ *mid-May–mid-Sep: daily; other times: Sat & Sun.*
⬤ *21 Dec–1 Jan.* 🖼 🚻 ▢ 🏠

⛪ ÖSlJ

500 m (546 yd) west of the centre.
☎ 0159-210 00. ⬤ *1 May–Sep: Sat & Sun; Midsummer–1st week in Aug also Mon–Fri.* 🖼 ▢

Bedchamber of Duke Karl (Karl IX, 1550–1611), Gripsholms Slott

Strängnäs ⓱

Södermanland. 🏙 15,000. 🚉 🚌
🛈 *Grassagården, 0152-296 94 (summer), otherwise 0159-297 90.*
🎪 *Strängnäs market (2nd Sat in Oct).*
🌐 *www.strangnas.se*

AS KEEPER OF THE KEYS of the Kingdom, Strängnäs was an important centre in the Middle Ages. It was mentioned as an episcopal see as early as 1120 and is dominated by the imposing tower of its Gothic cathedral, **Domkyrkan**, completed in 1280. It was here that Gustav Vasa was chosen as king on 6 June 1523, the date which was to become Sweden's National Day. Quaint wooden buildings surround the cathedral. To its east is Roggeborgen, the bishop's palace from the 1480s.

Strängnäs Municipality includes the largest island in

Red-painted, 18th-century wooden buildings in central Strängnäs

Lake Mälaren, **Selaön**. There are more rune stones here than in any other part of Södermanland, indicating that this was an ancient cultural centre. Selaön is also the location of the former summer residence of the Strängnäs bishops, Tynnelsö Slott, which was transformed by Karl IX in the 17th century into a Renaissance palace.

The newly renovated Mälsåkers Palace dating from the 17th century is another of Selaön's attractions.

🏛 Domkyrkan

Stora Torget. ☎ 0152-245 00. ⬤ *daily.*
🖼 *by appointment.* ✝ *Wed & Sun.*

Mälardalen's Castles ⓲

See pp136–7.

Eskilstuna ⓳

Södermanland. 🏙 80,000. 🚉 🚌
🛈 *Rademachergatan 50, 016-10 70 00 (also Torshälla).*
🌐 *www. maranadsforing.eskilstuna.se*

THE TOWN IS NAMED after St Eskil, the Englishman who became Svealand's first Christian bishop and built his

A panda, one of many exotic animals at Eskilstuna's Parken Zoo

church on the riverbank along Eskilstunaån at the end of the 10th century. During Sweden's Age of Greatness in the 17th century, Eskilstuna flourished after Karl X Gustav gave master smith Reinhold Rademacher a 20-year monopoly on the manufacture of items such as cannons, knives and scissors. Rademachergatan still has a few forges kept as they were in the 1650s, where visitors can try their hand at being a blacksmith.

Today's modern industrial town and centre of learning features more than 200 items of public art, including Carl Milles's *Hand of God* (see p95) in Stadsparken.

Parken Zoo is one of Sweden's leading zoos, as well as a popular amusement park with a heated outdoor pool. The entrance is guarded by the Phantom, whose Skull Cave is a magnet for youngsters and comic fans alike.

ENVIRONS: North of Eskilstuna is **Torshälla**, a small town of cobbled streets and well-kept wooden houses. The magnificent 12th-century church dominates the old quarter. Northeast of Torshälla is **Sunbyholms Slott** *(see p136)* from where a 10-minute walk leads to **Sigurdsristningen**, Sweden's finest rock carving.

🐾 Parken Zoo

1 km (half a mile) west of the centre. ☎ 016-100 100. **Zoo**
⬤ *Easter week, May–mid-Sep: daily; mid-Sep–Oct: Sat & Sun.*
Amusement Park ⬤ *May: Sat & Sun; Jun–mid-Aug: daily; mid-Aug–mid-Sep: Fri–Sun.* 🖼 🛒
♿ ▢ 🍴 🏠

A Tour of Mälardalen's Castles ⑱

THERE ARE MORE THAN 100 sturdy castles, opulent palaces and ravishing country houses around Lake Mälaren. Often strategically located near Iron Age and Viking settlements, they highlight the significance of this extensive waterway. Wik's 15th-century castle and the Vasa kings' solid, 16th-century fortress of Gripsholm show how long the need for defences lasted. From the mid-17th century, the grand palaces of Sweden's Age of Greatness, such as Skokloster, predominated, as manifestations of their owners' wealth and power. Many have excellent museums.

Engsö
The medieval castle was rewor in French Rococo style in the 17 It has many beautiful interiors f various periods and a major collection. The castle grounds a nature reserve full of wild

Tidö ⑥
Lord Chancellor Axel Oxenstierna's country house, built in 1642, is a fine example of a Baroque manor. It is noted for its handsome state apartment and 43 inlaid wooden doors. A museum displays 30,000 antique toys.

Grönsöö ④
The grand manor from the early 17th century stands guard high above Lake Mälaren. It is still occupied by the von Ehrenheim family, and its grounds represent 400 years of garden history.

Strömsholm ⑦
Equestrianism dates from the 16th century at Strömsholm, with its beautiful pastureland and bridle paths. The palace was built in the 1670s in Carolian Baroque style.

KEY

▬ Suggested route

═ Other roads

♠ Other castles open to the public

TIPS FOR DRIVERS

This tour, taking in the ten suggested palaces, involves a trip of more than 500 km (300 miles), lasting three days, despite the generally good roads. An option is to select a group of palaces close to each other. For more information, see
W *www.malarslott.nu*
C *Mälarslott, 016-48 06 80.*

Gripsholm ⑧
Gustav Vasa's brick Renaissance castle *(see p134)*, started in 1540, is a symbol of Swedish independence. Visitors have access to 60 rooms from various periods, the highlight of which is Gustav III's theatre, and the National Portrait Gallery.

0 kilometres

0 miles

Wik ③

This 15th-century castle is Sveland's best-preserved late-medieval fortress. With its solid walls and moat, Wik was considered impregnable. It was remodelled in 1656–60. Today, Wik is a hotel and conference centre.

Skokloster ②

Field Marshal Carl Gustaf Wrangel's 17th-century showpiece contains treasures from his campaigns, as well as exceptional collections of art, furniture, weapons and books. It also has a motor museum *(see p127)*.

Steninge ①

Built in the 1690s, the palace was designed by Nicodemus Tessin the Younger in the style of an Italian villa *(see p130)*.

Drottningholm ⑩

This royal palace, built in the 17th century, was one of the most lavish undertakings in Sweden. With its theatre, gardens and Chinese Pavilion, Drottningholm is a UNESCO World Heritage Site *(see pp106–9)*.

Sturehof ⑨

This stylish 18th-century country house in Botkyrka was designed by C F Adelcrantz for Gustav III's finance minister, Johan Liljekrantz, who owned the renowned Marieberg porcelain factory. The building houses a collection of the factory's famously stunning tiled stoves.

Julita Gård ⑳

Södermanland. **(** 0150-48 75 00. 🚆 🚌 Mälarbanan to Eskilstuna, then bus 404, 405. ◑ May–Sep daily.

THIS EXTENSIVE Södermanland estate on Lake Öljaren is said to be the world's largest open-air museum. It was created in the first half of the 20th century by the romantic Lieutenant Arthur Bäckström and in 1941 was donated to Stockholm's Nordiska Museet. Julita is a working estate farm with parks and gardens, and an 18th-century manor house built on the site of a medieval Cistercian monastery.

The estate has a collection of buildings reflecting rural life in Södermanland. Threatened national species of cow, pig, sheep, hen and duck are cared for at the Swedish agricultural museum. There is also a dairy museum. Children are welcome to pop into the house of the much-loved children's literary character, Pettson, and his cat Findus.

Julita Gård's buildings representing rural life in Södermanland

Arboga ㉑

Västmanland. 👥 11,000 ✈ 🚆 🚌 🚢 🚹 🖼 Medieval Festival (Aug).

RED-PAINTED iron warehouses, Ladbron quay and the railway line recall Arboga's great age as the chief shipping port for iron from Bergslagen. Fahlströmska Gården is a typical 16th-century warehouse with a huge loft.

Arboga was an important town in medieval times and the site of Sweden's first parliament in 1435. Churches from the period include the hospital chapel on Stortorget, which has been preserved as a town hall. The 14th-century **Heliga Trefaldighets Kyrka** on Järntorget has a splendid Baroque pulpit by Burchardt Precht.

Anundshögen, the 7th-century burial mound of King Bröt-Anund, with a stone ship in the foreground

Köping ㉒

Västmanland. 🏛 18,100. 🚃 🚌 🚆
Barnhemsgatan 2, 0221-256 55.
🎭 Köpingsyran Festival (28–30 May).

THE PORT OF KÖPING on Lake
Mälaren has been a vital
link for transporting products
to and from the mines and
forests of Bergslagen since
medieval times. The city
burned down in 1889, but
buildings to the west of the
river were saved, including
the 17th-century **Nyströmska
Gården**, a joiner's yard where
it is possible to see how the
town's special tilt-top table
was made. Other attractions
include the motor museum,
**Bil och Teknikhistoriska
Samlingarna**.

East of Köping is the 11th-
century church of Munktorp.

🏛 **Bil och Teknikhistoriska
Samlingarna**
Glasgatan 19. 📞 0221-206 00. 🕐
May–Sep: daily. Pre-booked groups all
year round. 🏛 Midsummer. 🎫🖥🔲

Västerås ㉓

Västmanland. 🏛 104,000. 🚃 🚌
🚶 🏛 Stora Gatan 40, 021-10 38 30.
🎭 Arosfestivalen (16–19 Jun), Power
meet (9–11 Jul).

STRATEGICALLY SITUATED at the
point where the Svartån
river runs into Lake Mälaren,
the county town of Västerås
has been an important trading
centre since Viking times.
Construction of the castle and
cathedral began in the 13th
century and in 1527 Parliament was convened here.
The cathedral, **Domkyrkan**,
contains the sarcophagus of
Erik XIV (r.1561–69), the
unfortunate king who was
allegedly poisoned by his

brother Johan III, by pea
soup laced with arsenic.

Around the cathedral lies
the town's old centre of
learning, where Johannes
Rudbeckius opened Sweden's
first upper secondary school
in 1623.

In the 17th and 18th
centuries Västerås became a
major port for the Bergslagen
region. Today it is an industrial centre and headquarters
of the engineering giant Asea-
Brown-Boveri (ABB).

To the east of the town lies
the 7th-century Anundshögen
mound where Bröt-Anund,
the king who settled Bergslagen, is said to be buried.
Standing stones in the shapes
of ships 50 m (164 ft) long can
be seen around the mound.
The area was an important
Viking meeting place.

Northwest of the town is
Skultuna Messingsbruk,
Europe's oldest active brass-
works, founded in 1607 and
renowned for its cannons and
stylish candlesticks.

ℹ️ **Domkyrkan**
Västra Kyrkogatan 6. 📞 021-81 46
11. 🕐 daily. 🎫
🏛 **Skultuna Messingsbruk**
16 km (10 miles) NW of Västerås.
📞 021-783 01. 🕐 Tue–Sun
10am–4pm. 🎫 tel for info. 🖥🔲

Sala ㉔

Västmanland. 🏛 12,100. 🚃 🚌
ℹ️ Norrbygatan 12, 0224-552 02.
🎭 Autumn market (last Fri & Sat in
Sep). 🖥 www.sala.se/turism

DURING THE 16th century,
the silver mine in Sala
was one of the richest in the
world; 200,000 kg (440,000
lb) were mined up to 1570,
providing valuable funds for
the state coffers. The former

Silvergruvan mine is open to
the public down to a level of
60 m (200 ft). There are beautiful walks around the old pits
and canals, and silver treasure
hunts are organized in the
mine for children.

Aguélimuseet showcases
the work of Sala's own artist,
Orientalist Ivan Aguéli (1869–
1917), and other Modernists.

🏛 **Silvergruvan**
Drottning Christinas Väg. 📞 0224-
131 45. 🕐 Sat–Sun noon–4pm,
call to book other times. 🎫🎫🖥
🔲 🔢
🏛 **Aguélimuseet**
Norra Esplanaden 7. 📞 0224-138 20.
🕐 Wed–Sat 11am–4pm. 🎫🎫🔲

Hauling plant at the Sala silver
mine, in use until 1908

Fagersta ㉕

Västmanland. 🏛 11,000. 🚃
ℹ️ Norbergsvag 19, 0223-131 00.
🎭 Spring Festival (21–23 May),
Autumn Festival (27–28 Aug).

IRON-WORKING has shaped
Fagersta since the outset. In
Dunshammer, just south of
the town, Iron Age blast
furnaces show how iron used
to be extracted from bog ore.
Today Fagersta is home to
metal-manufacturing and
stainless steel industries.

At the UNESCO World
Heritage Site of **Engelsbergs
Bruk**, the historic blast
furnace and ironworks have
been preserved in working

order and give a remarkable impression of how the site operated between the 17th and 19th centuries.

Oljeön, the world's oldest preserved oil refinery (1875–1902), lies 1.5 km (1 mile) from the ironworks.

Running through Fagersta is the 200-year-old Strömsholm canal from Lake Mälaren to Smedjebacken in Dalarna. It was a vital transport link for the Bergslagen foundries. Twenty-six locks, six of them in Fagersta, raise boats a total of 100 m (330 ft). Passenger ferries operate on the canal.

🏛 Engelsbergs Bruk
15 km (10 miles) E of Fagersta.
📞 0223-131 00. ⏰ 2nd week in May–Midsummer: Sat & Sun; 4th week in Jun–mid-Aug: daily; 3rd week in Aug–Sep: Sat & Sun. 🚗 ♿ 📷 🅿

The mansion at the Engelsberg ironworks, dating from the 1740s

Kopparberg ㉖

Västmanland. 🚶 3,300. 🚌 to Örebro, then bus. 🛈 Gruvstugutorget, 0580-805 55. 🎣 Gold panning competitions (1st weekend in Jul). 🌐 www.ljusnarsberg.se

THE DISCOVERY of copper in the early 17th century attracted miners from Falun, who brought with them the name of their old mine and called the place Nya Kopparberget (New Copper Hill). The 2.5-km (2-mile) path, Kopparstigen, provides a good view of the many mine buildings. Along the

way is **Kopparbergs Miljömuseer**, a complex including a goldsmiths' museum, postal museum and 1880s photography studio. The 17th-century courthouse and unusually large and impressive wooden church from 1635 are also worth looking at.

🏛 Kopparbergs Miljömuseer
Gruvstugutorget. 📞 0580-805 55. ⏰ Jun–Aug: daily. ♿

Grythyttan ㉗

Västmanland. 🚶 900. 📞 0591-340 60. 🚌 to Örebro, then bus. 🍴

A LOCAL VEIN of silver brought prosperity and town status to Grythyttan in 1649, but when the silver ran out 33 years later, the town charter was withdrawn. In recent years, Grythyttan has awakened from its long slumber and reinvented itself as a gastronomic centre.

It all started when the inn, built in 1640, was given a new lease of life in the 1970s, thanks to inspired innkeeper Carl Jan Granqvist. Now, in addition to Grythyttan's wooden houses and red-painted church, there is a catering college centred on **Måltidens Hus i Norden**. It occupies Sweden's spectacular pavilion built for EXPO 1992 in Seville. A varied range of activities offers something for everyone interested in food and cooking, alongside exhibitions and a cookery book museum.

South of Grythyttan lies **Loka Brunn**, a classic

Kopparberg's old mining community, now an idyllic wooden village

Grythyttan's inn with its beautifully renovated 17th-century interior

Swedish spa founded in the 1720s. The site has state-of-the-art facilities, but the old spa, with its gardens and spring, has been preserved in the Swedish spa museum. You can sample the spring water and view the restored bathhouse, pharmacy, clinic and royal kitchen built in 1761.

🏛 Måltidens Hus i Norden
Sörälgsvägen 4. 📞 0591-340 60. ⏰ end of Jun–mid-Aug: daily; other times: Mon–Fri. 🚗 ♿ exhibition. 🅿 ♿ 🍴
🏛 Loka Brunn
15 km (9 miles) S of Grythyttan. 📞 0591-631 00. ⏰ daily. ♿ 🚗 museum. 🅿 🍴 📷 ♿

Nora ㉘

Västmanland. 🚶 6,400. 🚌 to Örebro, then bus. 🛈 Station House on Norasjön side, 0587-811 20. 🎣 Nora Western Festival (1st weekend in Jun), Nora Festival (2nd week in Jun), Noramarken fair (4th weekend in Aug).

THIS IDYLLIC wooden town is an ideal place to stroll around, with its cobbled streets and charming shops, many in 18th-century buildings. **Göthlinska Gården** (1793) is an interesting museum furnished in the style of a middle-class family home from around 1900.

The highlight of the Nora mining area's monuments is **Pershyttan**, 3 km (2 miles) west of the centre, where the charcoal blast furnace dates from 1856. In summer, a steam train operates from Nora on the Nora Bergslags Veteranjärnväg, Sweden's first normal-gauge railway. Nora's train sheds house historic steam trains, diesel engines and carriages.

EASTERN GÖTALAND

THE THREE PROVINCES OF *Östergötland, Småland and Öland, which make up Eastern Götaland, each retain their own distinctive character. Östergötland is the agricultural heart of Sweden, Småland is the centre of glassmaking and Öland attracts sun-seekers and nature lovers. They are all popular tourist areas typified by their little red cottages and historical sights, quiet lakes and great coastlines.*

In north Östergötland, the major towns of Norrköping and Linköping are almost part of Greater Stockholm. Once beyond the steep hills of Kolmården, which form the northern border, flat agricultural land extends as far as the eye can see. Besides being the granary of Sweden, this is historical soil – it was here that the royal Folkung dynasty had its roots and it was here that Birgitta Gudmarsson (St Bridget) advised the political and religious leaders of the 14th century.

The hills north of Gränna and the ruins of Brahehus castle mark the beginning of Småland. For a long time Småland formed the border with Denmark and it was from this region that Nils Dacke led a peasants' revolt in the 16th century. The land is poorer and stonier than Östergötland with small farms and crofters. Mass emigration drained the area of thousands of people during the famine of the 19th century.

However, Småland has had its success stories: it is the ideal location for one of its major industries, glassworking, which relies on timber and water. The landscape has also been immortalized in the books of Astrid Lindgren, who was born in the province and turned the place where she grew up into a playground for her popular children's characters, Emil and Pippi Longstocking.

The region's archipelago is a favourite with boat-lovers, stretching south from the Sankta Annas islands in Östergötland through the Kalmarsund between Småland and Öland. Thanks to Ölandsbron bridge, the long narrow island of Öland is easily accessible. Holiday-makers are drawn to its sandy beaches, while botanists head for the Alvar plain and ornithologists for Ottenby bird station.

The crew of a sailing boat preparing to pass through the lock at Berg on the Göta Canal

◁ **The ruins of Brahehus castle with views over Lake Vättern and the island of Visingö**

Exploring Eastern Götaland

This is too big an area to explore in just a few days, but by leaving the major roads and heading cross-country it is possible to have a taste of the different provinces. In the north, the tourist route between Väderstad and Alvastra is a quiet road which leads to several of Östergötland's main sights. Cycling is the perfect way to get around, and cruising in comfort on the Göta Canal *(see pp146–7)* offers an unforgettable experience. For a tour of the Kingdom of Crystal *(see p152)* a car is almost essential, but otherwise Småland has countless canoeing routes, lakes for swimming and sights along small forested roads ideally explored by bike.

The mythical Omberg on Lake Vättern seen from Brahehus castle *(see p150)*

Key

▬	Motorway
▬	Major road
═	Minor road
⊶	Railway line
- -	Ferry route

Getting Around

The main artery for traffic in this part of the country is the E4 which passes west of Växjö, via the cities of Norrköping, Linköping and Jönköping, on its way south towards Helsingborg. The E22 runs along the coast, leaving the E4 at Norrköping and continuing via Västervik and Kalmar to Malmö. The larger towns, both on the coast and inland, can be reached by train, but local buses or a car will be needed to visit places in the countryside. There are domestic flights to all major cities.

See Also

- **Where to Stay** pp283–4
- **Where to Eat** pp297–8

Örebro

MEDEVI BRUNN

MOT
VADST

7 OMB

TRAN

8
GRÄNNA

Gothenburg

9 JÖNKÖPING

EKS

VETLA

GISLAVED

VÄRNAMO

SMÅL

Bolmen

11 VÄX

LJUNGBY

Helsing-
borg

Alvastra Monastery, founded by French Cistercians in 1143

Grazing land on Öland with some of the island's 400 preserved windmills in the background

SIGHTS AT A GLANCE

Lion on the prowl in the Safari Park at Kolmårdens Djurpark

Kolmårdens Djurpark ❶

Östergötland. Junction from E4, 12 km (7 miles) N of Norrköping. 🚉
🚌 ℹ️ 011-24 90 00. ⭕ May–Jun, 2nd–last week in Aug: 10am–5pm daily; Jul–first week in Aug: 9am–6pm daily; Sep: 10am–5pm Sat–Sun.
♿🚻⏸🅿🅰♿🛗
🆆 www.kolmarden.com

I N 1962 THE IDEA was mooted to turn Kolmården's forests into a recreational area and zoo. Three years later the park opened, but this is no ordinary zoo. The animal enclosures are large and attractively landscaped.

There is a drive-through Safari Park which brings visitors close to the creatures of the savannah who live here alongside Nordic species such as brown bears and wolves.

A Dolphinarium offers spectacular shows with trained dolphins. Snakes and crocodiles inhabit the outdoor Tropicarium, while the Aparium is designed so that the apes can be viewed indoors and out.

There is a cable-car ride around the park providing a bird's-eye view of the grounds.

Norrköping ❷

Östergötland. E4. 🏰 8,300. 🚉
🚌 ℹ️ Dalsgatan 9, 011-15 50 00.
🐎 Norrköping International Horse Show (4th week in May), National Day Festival (first week in Jun).
🆆 www.destination.norrkoping.se

I N THE 17TH CENTURY the skills of entrepreneur Louis de Geer, combined with water power from the Motala Ström

river system, transformed Norrköping into Sweden's first industrial town. Norrköping and neighbouring Linköping make up Sweden's fourth largest urban region.

Although Norrköping is an industrial town, the mix of old and new buildings, parks and trams make it an attractive place to visit. On a small island in Motala Ström sits **Arbetets Museum** (Museum of Labour), in an old spinning mill known as Strykjärnet (the Iron).

ENVIRONS: The area has a long history of habitation – around 1,650 carvings, some dating back to 1000 BC, can be seen at **Himmelstalund** on the edge of town.

About 10 km (6 miles) south of Norrköping on the E4 is the 17th-century **Löfstad Slott** with its beautiful English-style park. The castle remains as it was in 1926 on the death of the owner, Emelie Piper.

🏛 **Arbetets Museum**
Laxholmen. ☎ 011-18 98 00.
⭕ daily. ♿🚻♿ public holidays.
🏛 **Löfstad Slott**
10 km (6 miles) S of Norrköping.
☎ 011-33 50 67. ⭕ Jun–Aug: daily; May: Sat, Sun, public holidays; Apr, Sep, Oct: Sun; Nov–Mar: phone for info. ♿🚻⏸

Strykjärnet (the Iron) in Norrköping, housing Arbetets Museum

Linköping ❸

Östergötland. E4. 🏰 94,000. 🚉
🚌 ✈ ℹ️ Klostergatan 68, 013-20 68 35. 🐎 Ekenäs Castle Tournament (Whitsun), Summer Festival (2nd week in Jul), Handicraft Festival and Folk Festival (4th week in Aug).
🆆 www.linkoping.se

T HE COUNTY capital and cathedral city of Linköping lies in the middle of the Östgöta plain. First populated 3,000 years ago, it is now Sweden's fifth largest city, and is known for its university and high-tech industry.

Construction of the **Domkyrkan** (Cathedral) started in the mid-13th century. The interior contains superb medieval stone carvings. The Renaissance altarpiece is by the Dutch painter M J Van Heemskerck (1498–1574).

The old town open-air museum, **Gamla Linköping**, is a collection of 80 buildings from the city and surrounding area. This charming setting, complete with picturesque wooden buildings, cobbled streets and gardens, is a window on a past way of life.

Malmen, site of Sweden's first military flying school (1911), is now home to the **Flygvapenmuseum** (Swedish Air Force Museum). Exhibits include examples of Swedish military aircraft and other items from aviation history.

ENVIRONS: Kaga Kyrka, one of the region's best-preserved medieval churches, is located on the Svartån river south of Linköping. Dating from the 12th century, its walls are decorated with frescoes.

On Erlången lake, 10 km (6 miles) southeast of the centre lies the castle of **Sturefors**, renowned for its 18th-century interiors and beautiful grounds. The castle is a private residence, but parts of the grounds are open to the public.

🏠 **Domkyrkan**
St Persgatan. ☎ 013-20 50 50, 20 50 57. ⭕ daily. 🅿 phone for info.
♿🛗
🏛 **Gamla Linköping**
2 km (3 miles) west of the centre.
☎ 013-12 11 10. ⭕ daily.
🅿🅰⏸

🏛 Flygvapenmuseum

4 km (3 miles) west of the centre.
📞 013-28 35 67. ☐ Sep–May:
Tue–Sun; Jun–Aug: daily. ♿
✉ phone for details. ☐ ☐

Göta Canal ❹

See pp146–7.

Medevi Brunn ❺

Östergötland. Road 50. 🚊 🚌
ℹ 0141-911 00. ♫ Grötlunken
marching band processions (Jun/Jul).

I N THE 17TH-CENTURY the
scientist and doctor Urban
Hjärne analyzed water from
the Medevi spring and
declared it to be "superior to
other medication". Thus
began the transformation of
Medevi Brunn into a health
spa. Today, the season at
Medevi starts at Midsummer
and lasts for six weeks, during
which time the traditional
brass sextet Brunnsorkester
performs daily concerts.

South of Medevi, on the
edge of Lake Vättern, lies
Övralid, the former home of
poet and Nobel laureate
Verner von Heidenstam
(1859–1940). Designed by
Heidenstam himself, the
house has stunning views
across the lake.

🏛 Övralid

10 km (6 miles) N of Motala, Road 50.
📞 0141-22 05 56, 22 00 36.
☐ 15 May–31 Aug: daily. ♿
✉ 10am–5pm on the hour. ☐

**Medevi Brunn, the first health spa
in the Nordic countries**

Vadstena Slott, built in 1545 for protection against the Danes

Vadstena ❻

Östergötland. Road 50. 🚶 5,700.
🚊 🚌 ℹ Castle, 0143-315 71.
🎭 St Bridget Festival (3rd week in
May), Vadstena Academy Opera
performances (Jul).

S ITUATED ON Lake Vättern,
Vadstena is dominated by
the abbey, which dates back
to the 14th century and St
Bridget, and the mid-16th-cen-
tury castle of the Vasa kings.
Cobbled streets, wooden
buildings and glorious gardens
add to the town's character.

The stately **Vadstena Slott**
was built in 1545 as a fortress
against the Danes and is
surrounded by a moat. As well
as being a museum, the castle
also houses the county record
office and hosts opera, theatre
performances and concerts.

The abbey area encompasses
the original abbey, Vadstena
Kloster, established in 1384

and dissolved after the
Reformation in 1595, and
Vadstena Klosterkyrka
(1430). This abbey church
houses the relics of St Bridget
and a life-like wooden
sculpture of the saint. It is also
the site of the recently founded
convent Pax Mariae, home to
around ten Brigittine nuns.

ENVIRONS: Less than 20 km
(12 miles) south of Vadstena
towards Skänninge is **Bjälbo
Kyrka**, a late-12th-century
church. Bjälbo is said to be
the birthplace of the founder
of Stockholm, Birger Jarl.

🏛 Vadstena Slott

100 m (110 yd) SW of the centre.
📞 0143-315 71. ☐ First 2 weeks in
May, mid-Sep–Apr: Mon–Fri; mid-
May–mid-Sep daily. ✉ Jun–Aug.
☐ ♿
🔒 Vadstena Klosterkyrka
☐ daily. 📞 0143-315 70, 0143-298
50. ✝ Sun. ✉ Jun–Aug. ♿

ST BRIDGET, SWEDEN'S PATRON SAINT

At the age of only 13, Bridget (c.1303–73) was married to
local dignitary Ulf Gudmarsson. She became lady of the
manor of Ulvåsa in Östergötland and the mother of eight
children. Even as a child, she had religious visions and as
an adult made pilgrimages to Santiago de Compostela in
Spain in 1341–2, Rome in 1349
and Jerusalem in 1372–3.
Some of her visions also had
political themes and Bridget
became influential in the political arena. In 1370 she gained
the Pope's permission to found
a monastic order, the Brigittine
Order. The first nuns were
ordained in 1384. Bridget died
on returning to Rome following
her pilgrimage to Jerusalem. Her
remains were taken to Vadstena
in 1374. Canonized in 1391,
Bridget is the patron saint of
Sweden, and in 1999 became
the patron saint of Europe.

**Sculpture of St Bridget in
Vadstena Klosterkyrka**

Göta Canal ❹

OPENED IN 1832, the Göta Canal provided a vital link for transporting timber and iron between Stockholm and Gothenburg. But it was another 100 years before leisure traffic took off on the waterway. Today in summer, the canal bustles with small craft and passenger boats and it is possible to cruise the entire length on the classic *M/S Diana* (1931), *Wilhelm Tham* (1912) and *Juno* (1874). Other boats take passengers along shorter stretches and there are numerous special packages available, such as combining cycling holidays with canal trips. There are guest marinas offering services along the entire length of the canal. Motala is regarded as the "capital" of the canal, and the man behind its construction, Baltzar von Platen (1766–1830), is buried here.

Building the Canal
Karl XIV Johan inspects construction near Berg in Östergötland with Crown Prince Oscar. Baltzar von Platen is standing bareheaded to the left of the king.

Sjötorp on Lake Vänern marks the end point of the canal in Västergötland.

Karlsborgs Fästning *(see p221),* towers above the canal.

Lock-keeper
The majority of lock gates along the stretch of canal which lies in Västergötland are still worked by hand by friendly and patient lock-keepers.

KEY

▦	Motorway
▬	Other road
⋊⋉	Canal

Borensberg
The long-established Göta Hotell is an idyllic summer spot on the canal. Built in 1894, it offers food and accommodation to passers-by.

Bergs Slussar

The staircase of seven locks at Berg raises boats a total of 18 m (59 ft). The spectacle of opening the lock gates always attracts an audience.

VISITORS' CHECKLIST

Östergötland and Västergötland.
🛈 AB Göta Kanalbolag in Motala,
0141-20 20 50. 🚍 🚆 🛥
🖭 *Nostalgic Canal Race (early Jul),
Göta Kanalrännet Skating Race
(early Jan), Sweden Action Games
(mid-Jun).* 🖳 www.gotakanal.se

From the lake

of Roxen voyagers can spot the distant Ulvåsa Slott, where St Bridget *(see p145)* was once lady of the manor.

Canal Boats

From May to August traditional white boats such as M/S Juno ply the canal. Built in 1874, Juno is one of the oldest boats afloat with sleeping accommodation still in use.

Mem is the first lock in the canal system on the journey west.

Climbing From the Baltic to Lake Vänern

"The Blue Band of Sweden" as the Göta Canal is known, is the high point of Swedish engineering history. It took 58,000 men, mainly soldiers, and 22 years to build a waterway across Sweden from the Baltic Sea to join the already completed Trollhättan Canal *(see p217)*, and provide a route through to the Kattegatt. The problem was not simply digging the canal, but coping with a difference in height of around 92 m (301 ft). Completing this mammoth project took more than just spades and advantage was taken of the latest technological innovations – dredgers, hoists, cranes, pile drivers, mortar mills and optical instruments. Most of the machinery was imported from England, but as the project grew, and with it the need for mechanical equipment, Baltzar von Platen eventually took the initiative to set up a factory in Motala where the mechanical equipment could be made or modified. The canal has 58 locks between Mem on the Baltic and Sjötorp on Lake Vänern.

From Mem the canal begins its climb to reach the highest point between Lakes Vättern and Vänern

View over Lake Vättern from Hjässan, the highest point of Omberg

Omberg ❼

Östergötland. 20 km (12 miles) S of Vadstena. 🚍 ℹ *Naturum, Stocklycke, 0144-332 45.* ◷ *May– Aug: 11am– 5pm daily; Apr, Sep & Oct: noon–4pm daily.* ✍ 🏠 🆆 *www.e.lst.se/omberg*

RISING MOUNTAIN-LIKE from the wide Östgöta plains is Omberg. Its highest point is 175 m (574 ft) above Lake Vättern. It is the legendary home of Queen Omma, whose name means "steam" and indeed the fog that often surrounds the hill gives it a mythical quality. Orchid marshes, beech woodlands and ancient forest flourish on the limestone-rich rock. Walking trails cross the area. To the south lies author Ellen Key's home, **Strand**, and the nature reserves of Bokskogen and Stora Lund. On the plains southeast of Omberg is the ruin of **Alvastra Kloster** where St Bridget *(see p145)* once stayed.

To the east, Omberg slopes down to Lake **Tåkern**, barely 1 m (3 ft) deep and favoured by flocks of geese and cranes in spring and autumn. The **Rökstenen** at Röks Kyrka is a large 9th-century runestone.

🏛 **Strand**
1 km (half a mile) W of Ödeshög. 📞 *0144-330 30.* ◷ *15 Apr–Midsummer, mid-Aug–mid-Sep: Tue–Sun.* ✍

Gränna ❽

Småland. E4. 🚶 *2,600.* 🚍 ℹ *Brahegatan 38, 0390-410 10.* 🎭 *Andrée Festival (2nd week in Jul), County Festival (3rd week in Jul).* 🆆 *www.grm.se/turistinfo*

GRÄNNA WAS AT its height in the 17th century in the days of Count Per Brahe, who founded the town and whose plan is still evident today. On the square in the centre of town, **Grenna Museum** has fascinating tales to tell of the tragic expedition to the North Pole headed by the town's famous son Salomon August Andrée in the hot-air balloon *Örnen.* Inspired by Andrée, Gränna has become a centre for balloon flights. The town is also known for its *polkagris* (peppermint rock), an ideal souvenir. The red and white sweet originated in 1859 when widow Amalia Eriksson started a rock factory in the town.

Along the beautiful stretch of the E4 beside Lake Vättern, just north of Gränna, lies the ruined **Brahehus** castle, built for Count Per Brahe in the 1640s. On a clear day Brahehus offers magnificent views over Vättern towards Västergötland on the other side of the lake and **Visingsö**. This flat island can be reached by boat from Gränna. It is the largest island in Lake Vättern, 14 km (9 miles) long and 3 km (2 miles) wide with a population of 800. In the 12th and 13th

Polka-gris

centuries the island was the seat of Sweden's first kings, including Magnus Ladulås. Per Brahe built the castle, Visingsborgs Slott, now a ruin, and a church on the island in the 17th century. The boat trip from Gränna takes about 25 minutes and the service is frequent in the summer months.

🏛 **Grenna Museum**
Brahegatan 38–40. 📞 *0390-410 15.* ◷ *daily.* ● *24, 25, 31 Dec, 1 Jan.* ✍ 🏠 📷 ♿

Jönköping ❾

Småland. E4. 🚶 *81,400.* 🚍 🚌 ⚓ ℹ *Railway station, 036-10 50 50.* 🎭 *Jönköping Market (end of May), Kalajs Carnival (May/Jun).* 🆆 *www.jonkoping.se*

KING MAGNUS Ladulås granted Jönköping its charter in 1284, by which time the town was already an important trading centre. For a long time Småland formed Sweden's southern border with Denmark, but when the Danes invaded in 1612 the people set fire to their town and fled to Visingsö.

In the 19th century Jönköping became synonymous with matchstick production; the Lundström brothers opened their first factory here in the 1840s. In the old part of town, **Tändsticksmuseet** (the Match Museum) is set in a former match factory (1848). The historic Västra Storgatan 37 houses **Viktor Rydbergs**

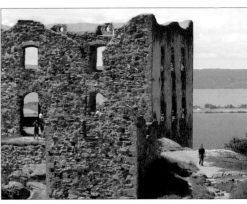

The ruins of Brahehus Castle on Lake Vättern looking towards Visingsö

◁ **Kapelludden on the east of Öland, and the 13th-century ruins of St Bridget's chapel**

Museum. Local history comes under the spotlight at **Jönköpings Läns Museum**. The museum also has a display of work by the local artist John Bauer *(see p21)*, as well as contemporary art.

ENVIRONS: Just outside Jönköping, **Hakarps Kyrka** is famous for its paintings by Edvard Orm. **Taberg**, a hill south of Jönköping, is known as "the Alps of Småland". It has a café at its peak, 343 m (1,125 ft) above sea level. The countryside is stunning, with extensive views over Lake Vättern. Sights include a mine and an industrial museum and there are hiking trails and overnight accommodation.

🏛 Tändsticksmuseet
Tändsticksgränd 27. 📞 *036-10 55 43.* ⭕ *daily.* ⬤ *public holidays & eves of public holidays.* 🔲

🏛 Jönköpings Läns Museum
Dag Hammarskjölds Plats 2. 📞 *036-30 18 00.* ⭕ *Tue–Sun.* 🔲

Eksjö ❿

Småland. Road 32/33. 🚶 *16,000.* 🚉🚌ℹ️ *Norra Storgatan 29, 0381-361 70.* 🏁 *Ränneslättsloppet Motocross Race (4th week in Oct), Hussar Festival (last Sun in Jun).* 🌐 *www.eksjo.se*

THE SMALL TOWN of Eksjö, in the highlands of southern Sweden, is the country's most genuine wooden town. It has a long military tradition. This was border country until the 17th century and Eksjö was burned down by its own people in conjunction with a Danish retreat. In the 1560s Erik XIV drew up a new town plan for Eksjö, which largely remains today. Gamla Stan (the Old Town) escaped the fire and its buildings remain intact and have been sympathetically renovated.

ENVIRONS: About 13 km (8 miles) east of Eksjö, the **Skurugata** nature reserve encompasses an impressive canyon in porphyritic rock, 800 m (2,625 ft) long and 35 m (115 ft) deep. From Eksjö to the neighbouring town of Nässjö is just over 20 km (12

miles). Nässjö owes its existence to the coming of the railway in the 1860s. At that time the village had 57 inhabitants; today it has nearly 30,000 and the railway companies Statens Järnvägar and Banverket are still the main employers. Sights in Nässjö include **Järnvägsmuseum** (the Railway Museum) and Hembygdsparken with its collection of 18th-and 19th-century buildings.

🏛 Järnvägsmuseum
Brogatan 10, Nässjö. 📞 *0380-722 07.* ⭕ *15 Jun–13 Aug: Wed, Sat–Sun.*

Växjö ⓫

Småland. Road 25/30. 🚶 *52,000.* 🚉🚌🚲ℹ️ *Norra Järnvägsgatan 3, 0470-414 10.* 🏁 *Karl-Oskar Festival (first week in Aug), Children's Festival (early June).* 🌐 *www.vaxjo.se*

A BISHOPRIC as early as the 12th century, Växjö was granted its town charter by King Magnus Erikson in 1342. For some time the town lay on the border with Denmark and it was from here that Nils Dacke led his peasant revolt against the Danes in the 16th century. Devastating fires, the most recent in 1843, destroyed the town, which has since been rebuilt. The cathedral dates originally from the end of the 12th century, but has

The twin steeples of Växjö's 12th-century cathedral

been remodelled over the centuries. It contains an altar-piece in glass and wood made in 2002 by the glass artist Bertil Vallien.

Smålands Museum, with Sveriges Glasmuseum (Glass Museum), depicts the history of the county of Kronoberg and the development of the glassworks. Next to it is **Utvandrarnas Hus**, which focuses on the mass emigration in the 19th century.

🏛 Smålands Museum
Södra Järnvägsgatan 2. 📞 *0470-70 42 00.* ⭕ *Jun–Aug: daily; Sep–May: Tue–Sun.* ⬤ *public holidays.*

🏛 Utvandrarnas Hus
Vilhelm Mobergs Gata 4. 📞 *0470-201 20.* ⭕ *Sep–Apr: Tue–Sat; May–Aug: daily.* 🔲

EMIGRATION TO AMERICA

Disillusioned by poverty, religious intolerance and political discontent, many Swedes in the late 1860s dreamed of a better life in North America. Famine in Sweden, combined with the end of the Civil War in the fast expanding USA, prompted around 100,000 Swedes to emigrate in 1868–71, the majority from southern Sweden, particularly the barren lands of Småland. Another major wave followed in the 1880s when 350,000 people left Sweden.

Nobel Prize-winner Vilhelm Moberg's epic trilogy *The Emigrants* describes the tough life Swedish emigrants faced in their new land.

Emigration to the USA tailed off with the Depression of the 1930s, but by then 1.2 million Swedes had already left their homeland.

***Emigrants on the Way to Gothenburg**, Geskel Saloman (1821–1902)*

A Tour through the Kingdom of Crystal ⑫

Växjö, "GATEWAY TO THE KINGDOM OF CRYSTAL", is an ideal starting point for a tour of at least nine of the famous glassworks set in the beautiful countryside between Växjö and Nybro. Access to timber and water accounts for the concentration of glassworks in this area of Småland, where forest, lakes and waterways dominate the landscape. The glassworks are mostly only 20–30 km (12–20 miles) apart, and many have shops offering discounted items and displays of the designers' latest creations.

Kosta ③
The oldest glassworks, Kosta (1742), like Boda and Åfors, has attracted some of Sweden's foremost contemporary designers. Shown here is the entrance to the original office.

Bergdala ①
Bergdala's signature is blue-edged glass, but designers are pushing the boundaries when it comes to colour and shape. The temperature of the smelting oven is a constant 1,150° C (2,102° F).

Strömbergshyttan ②
Studioglas was established in 1987 by three master glassblowers, who work with young designers to create groundbreaking works of art.

KEY

■ Suggested route

═ Other roads

TIPS FOR DRIVERS

Length: Växjö–Nybro, road 25, approx. 85 km (53 miles). Well signposted.

Places to eat: Many glassworks have a café/restaurant and some of the larger ones serve herring dishes at special herring evenings.

Åfors ④
The trio Bertil Vallien, Ulrica Hydman-Vallien and Gunnel Sahlin work for the glassworks in Fina Stugan, one of the most exciting galleries in the area. Glass eggs are by Ulrica Hydman-Vallien.

0 kilometres 10

0 miles 5

Orrefors ⑧

The glassworks was founded in 1898 and has become the flagship of Swedish glass-making, producing functional, decorative items and *objets d'art*. The work of Orrefors over the years is on show in its museum.

Crystal bowl by Simon Gate (1883–1945)

Målerås ⑨

The employees bought this glassworks from Kosta in 1981. It is famous for its crystal animal reliefs by glass artist and master etcher Mats Jonasson.

Pukeberg ⑦

The glassworks was founded in 1871. Extensive production in this beautiful old setting has mainly been focused on lighting and domestic glassware using traditional methods.

Johansfors ⑤

This glassworks is known as the Eden of the Kingdom of Crystal, symbolized by Christopher Ramsey's *Astrakhan Apple*. Glass-blowing is demonstrated daily and there is a museum.

Boda ⑥

Skilled designers at Boda have made Swedish glass world famous over the years. Kjell Engman is taking this tradition further, here with a piece made in 2003.

Vimmerby ⑬

Småland. Road 33/34. 🚶 *8,000.* 🚌
🚆 ✈ ℹ *Västra Tullportsgatan 3,
0492-310 10.* 🎭 *Stora Tabberaset
local festival (first weekend in Aug),
Holiday Race (2nd week in Jul).*

THE SMALL TOWN of Vimmerby began as a marketplace on the "King's Road" between Stockholm and Kalmar. It was strategically important and constantly fought over by the Danes, who burned it to the ground on many occasions. Few old buildings remain, but along Storgatan there is the austere Neo-Classical-style Rådhuset (Town Hall) from the 1820s. Like the houses of Tenngjutar-gården and Grankvistgården, it is one of Vimmerby's historical monuments.

For many years Vimmerby has been associated with Astrid Lindgren *(see p87),* who was born in Näs and set many of her popular children's books in this area. All her beloved characters can be encountered in **Astrid Lindgrens Värld** (Astrid Lindgren's World). The park also includes the Astrid Lindgren Centre with an exhibition about the author.

ENVIRONS: Norra Kvill National Park, 20 km (12 miles) northwest of Vimmerby, is an area of virgin forest in the highlands of Småland containing pine trees over 350 years old. The park slopes down to a small lake, Stora Idegölen, with waterlilies and bogbean.

🎢 **Astrid Lindgrens Värld**
Fabriksgatan. 📞 *0492-798 00.*
⏰ *15 May– end of Aug: daily.* 💳 🔲
♿ 🚻 🛍 🍴 🌐 *www.alv.se*

**Miniature house in Astrid
Lindgrens Värld, Vimmerby**

Picturesque red cottages on Båtsmansgränd in Västervik

Västervik ⑭

Småland. E22. 👥 *21,000.* 🚗 🚌 ✈
🛈 Strömsholmen, 0490-889 00.
🎭 *Song Festival (first week in Jul).*
W www.vastervik.se/turist

STRATEGICALLY SITED at the mouth of Gamlebyviken Bay, Västervik was the subject of frequent Danish attacks, despite protection from the once mighty fortress of Stegeholm. The last attack in 1677 destroyed the town. Rebuilt, it became a major seafaring centre. The area known as Gamla Norr contains the oldest preserved houses in Västervik, including Aspagården and the former poor-house, Cederflychtska Huset. **Kulbackens Museum** outlines the history of the town. Part of the museum is in the open air with animals and traditional buildings. The railway line was closed in 1984, but train enthusiasts have reopened the 70-km (43-mile) stretch from Västervik to Hultfred, to preserve it as part of Sweden's industrial heritage.

The annual Folk Festival first took place in 1966 and has since grown to become a major event. It is held in the ruins of Stegeholm fortress.

Lunds By, just outside Västervik, is the oldest and best preserved village in the region, comprising eight small red cottages around a square. This charming place was chosen as a location to film Astrid Lindgren's book *The Bullerby Children*.

🏛 **Västerviks Museum**
Kulbacken. ☎ *0490-211 77.*
○ *May–Aug: daily; Sep–Apr: Mon–Fri.* 🔲 📷 🔲 🖶

Oskarshamn ⑮

Småland. E22. 👥 *17,100.* 🚗 🚌
🛈 *Hantverksgatan 18, 0491-881 88.*
🎭 *Oskarshamn Harbour Festival (mid-Jul).* W www.oskarshamn.se/turistbyra

KING OSKAR I gave his name to this town, previously known as Döderhultsvik, which gained its charter in 1856. It grew up around the harbour and today is still an important place with a lively seafaring industry. The old areas of Besväret and Fnyket have wooden 19th-century houses and are ideal for exploring on foot. There are great views over the water and the island Blå Jungfrun from Långa Soffan, an extra-ordinarily long 72-m (79-yd) bench built close to the harbour in 1867.

Oskarshamn has several museums. On show at **Döderhultarmuseet** are the original wooden figures by sculptor Axel Petersson, also known as "Döderhultarn", together with a description of his life in late-19th-century Småland. **Oskarshamns Sjöfartsmuseum** (Maritime Museum) has a superb collection of local maritime history.

An expressive carved wooden figure by "Döderhultarn" Axel Petersson (1865–1925)

ENVIRONS: Stensjö By is a cultural museum showing how a village looked in the 18th century, with meadows, arable land and animals. Just under 40 km (25 miles) west of Oskarshamn at Högsby there is the **Aboda Klint** nature reserve and a permanent exhibition about film star Greta Garbo, whose mother came from here. Children and adults enjoy the toy museum, **Nostalgia**, in Fågelfors, where visitors can see but not touch 2,000 toys from the past.

🏛 **Döderhultarmuseet**
Hantverksgatan 18. ☎ *0491-880 40.*
○ *Tue–Sun.* 📷 *pre-book.* 🔲 🔲
🖶 ♿

🏛 **Oskarshamns Sjöfartsmuseum**
Hantverksgatan 18. ☎ *0491-880 45.*
○ *Tue–Sun.* 📷 *pre-book.* 🔲 🔲
🖶 ♿

🏛 **Nostalgia**
Bruksgatan 43, Fågelfors, 40 km (25 miles) W of Oskarshamn. ☎ *070-304 18 63.* ○ *end Jun–first week in Sep: Tue–Sun.* 🖶

Blå Jungfrun ⑯

Småland. 20 km (12 miles) E of Oskarshamn. 🚢 *from Oskarshamn & Byxelkrok.* 🛈 *Oskarshamn Tourist Office, 0491-881 88.*

IN THE NORTHERN part of Kalmarsund, the sound separating the mainland from the island of Öland, the national park Blå Jungfrun (the Blue Maiden) encompasses an island about 800 m (875 yd) in diameter and the waters surrounding it. Blå Jungfrun's highest point is 86 m (282 ft) above sea level, making it easily visible from the mainland and from Öland.

According to legend, the island is the site of Blåkulla, home of the witches, and is the subject of many a dark tale. Carl von Linné *(see p24)* described it as "horrible". Others have found it romantic, including the poet Verner von Heidenstam, who was married here in 1896. The island is mainly bare pink granite, polished smooth by ice and

Medieval Kalmar Slott, a beautifully preserved castle rebuilt in Renaissance style in the 16th century

water, with deciduous forest in the south and a population of black guillemots. It is unlikely that it was inhabited, although a stone labyrinth was built here and there are caves. Boats run from Oskarshamn or Byxelkrok *(see p156)* to Blå Jungfrun, once a day, weather permitting. The journey takes 90 minutes from Oskarshamn with a three-and-a-half-hour stay on the island.

Kalmar ⑰

Småland. E22. 👥 *34,000.* 🚉 🚌 ⛴
🛈 *Ölandskajen 9, 0480-41 77 00.*
📅 *Kalmar Market (3rd week in Jul), Medieval Market in Salvestaden (3rd week in Jul).* 🌐 *www.kalmar.se*

FOUNDED IN THE 12th century, Kalmar's key position on Kalmarsund made it a flourishing trading post as well as a target for Danish attack. To prevent the latter, **Kalmar Slott** was built in 1200 and it was here in the castle that the Kalmar Union was formed in 1397, binding the Scandinavian kingdoms for 130 years *(see p33)*. In 1523 Gustav Vasa gained control of Kalmar and fortified the town.

Today, the magnificent Renaissance castle has been restored and contains furnished apartments and exhibitions. With its twisting streets and 17th and 18th-century buildings, the area around the castle, Gamla Stan (Old Town), is made for walking. Next to the castle is **Kalmar Konstmuseum** (Art Museum) showing Swedish art.

The Italian Baroque **Domkyrkan** (cathedral) on the island of Kvarnholmen dates from the second half of the 17th century and was

designed by Tessin the Elder *(see p24)*. In front of it is the square Stortorget, restored to its original austere appearance. Kvarnholmen is also home to **Kalmar Läns Museum** with the man-of-war *Kronan* and out on "Kattrumpan" **Kalmar Sjöfartsmuseum**, featuring 5,000 maritime exhibits.

ENVIRONS: Ölandsbron, the bridge across Kalmarsund, opened in 1972 and provided a major boost for tourism to Öland. The bridge is 6,072 m (19,921 ft) long, 13 m (43 ft) wide and a sight in its own right. Nearly 35 km (22 miles) north of Kalmar on the coast is the idyllic village of **Pataholm**, a shipbuilding and seafaring community dating from the Middle Ages, with well-preserved historic buildings and cobbled streets.

🏰 **Kalmar Slott**
Kungsgatan 1. ☎ *0480-45 14 90*
◻ *Apr–Sep: daily; other times: 2nd weekend in the month.* 🎫 🅿 ♿
🏛 **Kalmar Konstmuseum**
Slottsvägen 1D. ☎ *0480-42 62 82.*
◻ *daily.* ● *24, 25 & 31 Dec.*
🎫 *pre-book.* 🅿 ♿
🏛 **Kalmar Läns Museum**
Skeppsbrogatan 51. ☎ *0480-45 13 00.* ◻ *daily.* ● *24, 25 & 31Dec, 1 Jan, 1 May.* 🎫 *pre-book.* 🅿 ♿ 🖥

Färjestaden ⑱

Öland. Road 136. 👥 *4,500.* 🚌 🛈
Träffpunkt Öland, 0485-56 06 00.
📅 *Victoria Day (14 Jul).*

THE ÖLANDSBRON Bridge connects Färjestaden on Öland with the mainland. Since the bridge's arrival in the 1970s, Färjestaden has more or less become a suburb of Kalmar. The first

turning to the north in Färjestaden leads to **Ölands Djurpark**, a popular destination for families. The zoo has 200 species of animals, a water world and amusement park, circus and theatre performances.

Beijershamn, south of Färjestaden, is an interesting reed-covered birdwatching area with wetland and archipelago species. Not far from here is **Karlevistenen**, a remarkable 11th-century runestone dedicated to a hero named Sibbe the Wise.

Vickleby village street, on road 136 to the south, is the epitome of idyllic Öland. Next to the church is Capellagården School of Craft and Design, founded by furniture designer Carl Malmsten in the 1950s and currently a centre for various design-related courses. The school exhibits and sells students' work.

East of Färjestaden, in the forest, is the Iron Age fort of **Gråborg** with the medieval ruins of St Knut's chapel just outside it.

🦌 **Ölands Djurpark**
3 km (2 miles) N of Färjestaden.
☎ *0485-392 22, info 0485-308 73.*
◻ *mid-May–Sep: daily.* 🎫 ♿ 🅿

A gigantic clown at the entrance to Ölands Djurpark

Solliden, the king's summer residence, whose park is open to the public

Borgholm 🄆

Öland. Road 136. 🏛 *3,200.* 🚏
ℹ *Sandgatan 25, 0485-890 00.*
🎭 *Borgholm Festival 1 Jul, Victoria Day 14 Jul.*

IN SUMMER Borgholm town centre bustles with shoppers and boats fill the guest harbour. Borgholm became a seaside resort at the end of the 19th century and some of the older buildings still have their ornamented wooden verandas where gentlemen enjoyed their coffee and punsch at the beginning of the last century.

Dominating the town is **Borgholms Slottsruin**, a vast ruined medieval castle with an eventful past. There is a museum inside. Guides recount the history of the ruins and offer special tours for children in summer. Also in summer, the castle stage is a popular venue for concerts.

ENVIRONS: Just south of the centre lies **Sollidens Slott**, the summer residence of the Swedish royal family, completed in 1906. On 14 July each year, the birthday of Crown Princess Victoria is celebrated here with various events. Exhibitions are held in the pavilion and there is a palace gift shop.

Störlinge Kvarnrad, a row of seven windmills on the eastern coast road, is just a sample of the 400 windmills still standing on the island. There are around 150 km (93 miles) of beaches around Borgholm, two of the best being Köpingsvik and Böda.

🎻 **Borgholms Slottsruin**
1 km (half a mile) S of Borgholm.
🄲 *0485-123 33.* ⭕ *Apr–Sep: daily; Oct–Mar: by app.* ▢▢▢▢▢ 🅟
🏛 **Solliden**
1.5 km (1 mile) S of Borgholm.
🄲 *0485-153 56.* ⭕ *mid-May–mid-Sep: daily.* ▢▢▢▢▢

Byxelkrok 🄇

Öland. Road 136. 🏛 *200.* 🚏
ℹ *Tourist Information Skeftekärr, 0485-221 11.*

ALMOST AT THE northernmost end of Öland's west coast on Kalmarsund is the popular old fishing village of Byxelkrok. Boats to Blå Jungfrun *(see p154)* depart from here. About 5 km (3 miles) to the north is **Neptuni Åkrar**, an area of ridged stones resembling ploughed fields with several ancient monuments, including the Iron Age stone ship Forgalla-skeppet.

Löttorp, the largest town in northern Öland, is home to a paradise for car-mad children – **Lådbilslandet** (Boxcar Country), Glabo Gocart. Here youngsters can race round the 6-km (4-mile) course in

The island Blå Jungfrun *(see p154)* seen from Byxelkrok harbour

motorized vehicles, attend driving school or enjoy the playground.

Böda, 10 km (6 miles) north of Löttorp, has wonderful sandy beaches. It is also the site of **Skäftekärr Järnåldersby**, a reconstructed Iron Age village. Complete with goods, animals, houses and people, it provides a fascinating insight into Iron Age life. The village also has an arboretum featuring a collection of *Thuja occidentalis* planted in the late 19th century.

🚗 **Lådbilslandet**
40 km (25 miles) N of Borgholm.
🄲 *0485-203 35.* ⭕ *mid-Jun–mid Aug: daily.* ▢▢▢
🎻 **Skäftekärr Järnåldersby**
50 km (31 miles) N of Borgholm.
🄲 *0485-221 11.* ⭕ *2nd week in Jun–mid-Aug: daily. 1 May–first week in Jun, mid-Aug–first week in Oct: Fri–Sun; Wed & Thu: pre-book.* ▢ ▢▢▢

Ölands Museum 🄈

Öland. 20 km (12 miles) NE of Färjestaden. 🄲 ℹ *0485-56 10 22.* ⭕ *May–Aug: 10am–5.30pm daily.* ▢▢▢▢

HIMMELSBERGA, in the centre of the island, is home to Ölands Museum, an open-air museum of art and cultural history. It centres around a well-preserved linear village with 18th- and 19th-century farms. The interiors of the houses show how life was once lived, and pigs, chickens and sheep are kept in the grounds. A shop sells crafts and books about Öland. Next to the museum is a gallery showing work by local artists.

South of Himmelsberga, **Gärdslösa Kyrka** is one of the most interesting churches on Öland. It dates from the mid-13th century and has excellent limestone murals, a beautiful votive ship and a 17th-century pulpit.

The fort of **Ismantorps Borg** in Länglöt has been dated to the 5th century. Archaeological finds show that it was probably an important marketplace and cult site. It is encircled by a wall up to 6 m (19 ft) thick and 3 m (10 ft) high with nine gates.

Öland's best preserved row of windmills can be seen in Lerkaka, just to the south of Himmelsberga. The interesting **Lerkaka Linmuseum** shows how linen is made.

🏛 **Lerkaka Linmuseum**
25 km (16 miles) NE of Färjestaden.
📞 *0485-56 20 90.*
🕙 *Midsummer–mid-Aug: daily.*

Stora Alvaret 22

Öland. 🚌 🛈 *Ölands Turist, 0485-56 06 00.*

T HE EXTRAORDINARY limestone plain of Stora Alvaret dominates southern Öland. Here, the bedrock is around 400 million years old and is covered in a thin layer of soil that was used from prehistoric times as grazing land. In the year 2000 the area was declared a UNESCO World Heritage Site.

In spring the ground is covered in pasque flowers (*Pulsatilla pratensis*). The dominant species include meadow oat-grass (*Helictotrichon pratense*), sheep's fescue (*Festuca ovina*) and a moss species, *kalkbackmossa* (*Homalothecium lutescens*). Juniper bushes are common and lichen inches over bare rock.

The extreme climate has created almost desert-like conditions to which the flora and fauna have had to adapt. Mountain and Mediterranean plants grow here as well as a

unique species of rock-rose (*Helianthemum oelandicum*). The island is a resting place for cranes, but conditions on the plain are so harsh that only a few birds, such as the skylark and wheatear, have succeeded in adapting to the environment.

Eketorps Borg 23

Öland. 🚌 🛈 0485-66 20 00. 🕙 *May–Aug: daily; first three weekends in Sep.* ⬤ *Midsummer's Eve.* 🏰 *Iron Age Festival (first week in Aug).* 🌐 www.kalmarlansmuseum.se/eketorp

T HE ONLY ONE of Öland's ancient forts to have been completely excavated, Eketorps Borg was built in three stages. It originated in the 4th century to protect the population and was later converted into a fortified farming village with military functions, but was abandoned in the 7th century. It was thrust into use again at the end of the 12th century in the war between the royal houses of Erik and Sverker.

The fort has been partly reconstructed to show how people lived and worked in the Iron Age. In the museum the numerous artifacts uncovered on the site are on display, including jewellery and weapons.

Around 10 km (6 miles) north of Eketorp lies **Seby Gravfält** with no fewer than 285 visible ancient monuments in the form of different kinds of burial sites, mainly dating from the Iron Age.

Look out for hedgehogs, a threatened species

Långe Jan at Öland's Southern Cape, Sweden's tallest lighthouse

Öland's Southern Cape 24

Öland. 🚌 🛈 *Ottenby Naturum, 0485-66 12 00 (Easter–Oct: daily).* 🐦

I N THE MID-16TH CENTURY the area around Öland's southern cape became a royal hunting ground and even today descendants of the fallow deer introduced by Johan III in 1569 can be spotted. The northern boundary of his land is marked by Karl X's wall, built in the 1650s to prevent local people and their animals from entering the grounds. To the south, Sweden's oldest and tallest lighthouse, **Långe Jan**, stands to attention, 41.6 m (136 ft) high, and offers amazing views.

At the southernmost tip of the island is a nature reserve, Ottenby Naturum, and **Ottenby Fågelstation** (the bird station). Ornithologists come here to study migratory birds close up and conduct research. The station has several bird-related exhibitions and offers guided tours around the nature reserve.

🐦 **Ottenby Fågelstation**
Öland's Southern Cape. 📞 *0485-66 12 00.* 🕙 *Easter–Oct: daily.* 🐦 *Set guided bird tours Jul–first week in Aug.* ♿ 📷

The mighty walls of Eketorps Borg, a partly reconstructed Iron Age fort

GOTLAND

SWEDEN'S LARGEST ISLAND, *Gotland is a popular holiday destination, favoured for its mild climate, sandy beaches, distinctive landscape and beautiful walled town of Visby. It is known as the "Pearl of the Baltic". The island's strategic position made it an important trading centre especially in the Middle Ages. Gotland celebrates its heritage with enthusiasm in the annual Visby Medieval Week.*

In geological terms, Gotland is fairly old. It consists of layers of rocks which were deposited in a tropical sea during the Silurian period around 400 million years ago. Fossils can still be found washed up along the shore. At the northern and southernmost tips of the island, the limestone comes to the surface and plant life is sparse. In the centre of the island forest dominates. The high limestone cliffs with their large bird population are broken by sandy beaches beloved by sun-worshippers, and standing offshore are numerous extraordinary sea stacks, known as *raukar*.

The long, warm autumns and mild winters allow trees such as walnut and apricot to survive in sheltered spots. No less than 35 different orchids can be found on the island and the flower meadows which blossom at Midsummer are typical of Gotland. The island's fauna lacks the large mammals of the mainland. The odd fallow deer is probably an escapee from an enclosure, but there is a herd of *russ*, Gotland's little wild ponies, as well as foxes and wild rabbits.

A wealth of archaeological finds have been uncovered on the island, from the ship burials of the Bronze Age to the silver treasure of the Viking period. More than 90 medieval churches dot the landscape and the museums have numerous artifacts from the Hanseatic period and the Danish King Valdemar Atterdag's capture of Visby in 1361. Visby itself is a UNESCO World Heritage Site.

Gotlanders have their own dialect, *Gutamål*, and their own traditions. These are especially reflected in the games of the annual Gotland Olympics and in the Medieval Week in Visby *(see p27)*, a 21st-century recreation of the Middle Ages with tournaments, jesters and fair maidens.

Hoburgen in southern Gotland, a 35-m (115-ft) high limestone cliff containing red "Hoburg" marble

◁ Domkyrkan Sta Maria dating from 1225, the only one of Visby's ancient churches which is not in ruins

Exploring Gotland

A VISIT TO GOTLAND naturally begins in Visby, where the ferry terminal and airport are located. To experience this unusual part of Sweden it is best to strike out into the countryside and discover the exceptional landscape with its distinctive flora, long sandy beaches, curious limestone sea stacks and multitude of medieval churches. Hiring a bike and cycling round Gotland is a popular way of seeing the island. There are almost no hills and car-free country lanes constantly lead to new hideaways. There is plenty of bed-and-breakfast accommodation and the island has many good campsites for those with tents or caravans. Bookings should be made well in advance for the month of July.

A ruined medieval church towering above the Visby rooftops

SIGHTS AT A GLANCE

Bro Kyrka **6**
Bunge **2**
Fårö **1**
Fröjel Kyrka **11**
Gotska Sandön **15**
Hoburgen **14**
Karlsöarna **12**
Ljugarn **9**
Lojsta **10**
Lummelundagrottorna **5**
Petes **13**
Roma **8**
Slite **3**
Tingstäde **4**
Visby pp164–7 **7**

KEY

━━ Major road

══ Minor road

· · Ferry route

TINGSTÄDE **4**
LUMMELUNDA-GROTTORNA **5**
149
147
SLITE
148
6 **BRO KYRKA**
147
VISBY **7**
146
140
8 **ROMA**
GOTLAND
142
143
143
● **KLINTEHAMN**
LJUGARN **9**
11 **FRÖJEL KYRKA**
10 **LOJSTA**
12 **KARLSÖARNA**
141
144
● **HEMSE**
140
13 **PETES**
142
● **BURGSVIK**
0 kilometres
0 miles
14 **HOBURGEN**

SEE ALSO

Fårö ❶

Gotland. 🚶 600. 🚢 🛈 Mar–Sep: at
Fårö church 0498-22 40 22; Oct–Feb:
Visby Tourist Office, 0498-20 17 00.
🐑 Lamb festival (last Sat in Sep).

A SUMMER PARADISE for visitors
from the mainland and
further afield, Fårö appears
exotic even to a Gotlander
from the main island. Lying at
the northern tip of Gotland,
the little island of Fårö has a
language and traditions all of
its own. During the summer
car ferries shuttle back and
forth on the 15-minute trip
from Fårösund to Broa. At
other times of year the service
is more limited.

Sparse, low pine forest and
moorland with swamp and
marshland cover the island.
There are sheep everywhere.
Off the main road between
Broa and Fårö lighthouse
there are plenty of cattle grids,
which prevent the sheep
from straying.

Off the northwest coast are
the spectacular limestone
stacks, known as *raukar*, of
Langhammars and Diger-
huvud. The sand dune of
Ullahau is at the northern end
of the island, and Sudersand's
long sandy beach is popular
with holiday-makers. The
easternmost cape of
Holmudden is topped by the
30-m (98-ft) high lighthouse,
Fårö Fyr. Roughly in the centre
of the island, **Fårö Kyrka**
offers stunning views over the
inlet of Kyrkviken. The church
contains votive paintings
dating from 1618 and 1767,
depicting seal hunters
miraculously being rescued
from the sea.

🏛 Fårö Kyrka
5 km (3 miles) N of Broa. 📞 0498-22
10 74. ⊙ Jun–Aug: daily; Sep–May:
Sat & Sun. 🏛 🎫 by appointment.

Sheep grazing in front of a typical Gotland farmhouse, today a
tempting renovation project for incomers from the mainland

GETTING AROUND
The most common way to get to Gotland is by ferry or fast
catamaran, either from Nynäshamn or Oskarshamn. In
summer there are several crossings a day to Visby.
Another option is to arrive by air on one of the daily
flights from Stockholm, Norrköping or Nyköping. On
Gotland, the only means of public transport is the bus.
Services outside Visby are infrequent with perhaps just
one morning and one afternoon bus, making a car or a
bike a necessity for getting around. Bicycles can be hired
at the ferry terminal and elsewhere around the island.

of Gotland's many long sandy beaches attracting hundreds of
sands of visitors to the island every summer

"The coffee pot", an eroded
limestone stack on Fårö's coast

Bunge

Gotland. Road 148. 🏃 *900.* 🚌
🛈 *Fårösund, 0498-22 11 12.*
🎪 *Tournament (first week in Jul).*

The village of Bunge is renowned for its 14th-century church **Bunge Kyrka**, built in Gothic style. Its tower was constructed in the 13th century to defend an earlier church – holes from pikes and arrows in the north wall bear witness to past battles.

Inside are beautiful limestone paintings dating from around 1400, which are thought to depict the Teutonic Knights fighting the Vitalien brothers, pirates of Mecklenburg who occupied Gotland in the 1390s. In the chancel is a poor box in limestone signed by stonemason Lafrans Botvidarson. Like the font, it dates from the 13th century.

Next to the church is **Bungemuseet**, one of Sweden's largest rural museums. It was created in 1917 by Bunge schoolteacher Theodor Erlandsson, who wanted to show how the people of Gotland used to live. In the fields next to the school he gathered together cottages, buildings and cultural objects from different parts of Gotland covering the 17th, 18th and 19th centuries as well as four carved stones from the 8th century. The museum hosts many events in the summer, including medieval tournaments, markets and handicraft festivals. In Snäckersstugan cottage, with the date 1700 carved into the gable, visitors can enjoy a cup of coffee and attempt to make out the Gotland proverbs painted on the ceiling.

Just north of Bunge is the busy **Fårösund**, one of the larger towns in northern Gotland with around 1,000 inhabitants. For many years the area was dominated by the military and countless young men were drilled here in defence of the island. Since the coastal artillery unit was disbanded in 2000 with the loss of many jobs, the area risks going into decline.

8th-century picture stone, Bungemuseet

🛈 **Bunge Kyrka**
60 km (37 miles) N of Visby.
🕿 *0498-22 10 74 (Tue & Fri).* 🕐 *mid-May–May: daily.* ✝ *every other Sun.*

🏛 **Bungemuseet**
2 km (1 mile) E of Bunge. 🕿 *0498-22 10 18.* 🕐 *15 May–15 Aug: daily.* 📷 *ring for appointment.*

Slite ❸

Gotland. Road 147. 🏃 *1,600.* 🚌
⛴ 🛈 *Square, 0498-22 24 63 (May–Aug).* ⛳ *Golf round Gotland (2nd week in May).*

Occupying a stunning setting in a bay facing its own archipelago is the town of Slite. It is the second largest community in Gotland. Slite had a long and troubled history from the

Majestic limestone stack at Kyllaj, Slite Bay

Viking period onwards, and development only really took off in the late 19th century with an upturn in seafaring. Today the town is dominated by a cement factory.

In summer, the fine sandy beaches, harbour, tennis courts, stunning stone stacks and lime kiln attract holiday-makers. The islands offshore are perfect for short trips, including Enholmen with Karlsvärd fortress, which dates from 1853–6.

Environs: On the opposite side of the bay is Hellvi, with the delightful old harbour of **Kyllaj** complete with lime kilns. The quiet beach is in a beautiful setting overlooking weathered sea stacks. Strandridaregården, the 18th-century coastguard's house, now belongs to Bungemuseet.

Northwest of Slite is **Lärbro Kyrka**, a mid-13th century church with an 11th-century watch tower next to it. In the churchyard are buried 44 of the former prisoners of war who came from the German concentration camps to the hospital at Lärbro in 1945.

St Olofsholm, nearby, is dedicated to Olav the Holy who visited Gotland in 1029 to convert the island to Christianity. In medieval times it was a place of pilgrimage. This is also the site of Ytterholmen's large group of limestone stacks and a glorious pebble beach.

🛈 **Lärbro Kyrka**
10 km (6 miles) N of Slite. 🕿 *0498-22 51 25.* 🕐 *15 May–30 Sep: daily.* ✝ *every other Sun.*

Buildings at Bungemuseet with thatched roofs of Gotland sedge

Tingstäde 4

23 km (14 miles) N of Visby. 280.
Bunge Tourist Office, Fårösund (May–Aug) 0498-22 11 22.
Nature trail with lady's slipper in flower (early Jun).

Halfway between Visby and Fårösund on road 148 lies Tingstäde, a community best-known for its sea rescue radio station and its marsh. The church dating from the 13th and 14th centuries has one of the highest towers on the island.

Tingstäde marsh is, in fact, a shallow lake and popular, child-friendly bathing spot. Submerged in the centre of the lake is Bulverket, a 10th–11th-century fortress surrounded by a palisade of 1,500 stakes.

Lummelunda-grottorna 5

Road 149, 13 km (8 miles) N of Visby. 11 May–15 Sep: 0498-27 30 50, other times ring to book.
obligatory. Cave adventure must be pre-booked.

In 1948 two local school-boys discovered an opening in the ground in Martebo marsh and crawled in. They had chanced upon the entrance to a giant net-work of caves and passage-ways, now Gotland's main tourist attraction. Today the entrance is at Lummelundas Bruk. Exploration of the caves continues, but the part which is open for viewing provides a fantastic show of stalactites and stalagmites, magic mirrors of water and spine-tinglingly tight openings. The geological museum, Silurum, is located at the entrance.

Immediately to the south of the caves is **Krusmyntagården**, a herb garden designed in traditional monastic style with wonderful views over the sea.

Krusmyntagården

Road 149, 10 km (6 miles) N of Visby. 0498-29 69 00.
Jun–Aug: daily.

Bro Kyrka 6

Road 148, 11 km (7 miles) NE of Visby. 0498-27 27 55, 070-25 92 070. Apr–Oct: 8.30am–7pm daily. every other Sun.

Tradition has it that Bro Kyrka is built over a votive well and in medieval times it was a famous votive church, particularly among sailors. The building dates from the 13th and 14th centuries. Inside, the prayer chamber contains 5th-century picture stones.

About 1 km (half a mile) north of Bro Kyrka, on road 148, are two picture stones known as "Bro Stajnkällingar". According to legend, two elderly women were turned to stone for arguing on the way to the Christmas Mass.

From Bro, a turning leads to Fole church on road 147, and a short detour takes you to **Vatlings Gård**. The estate has Gotland's best-preserved medieval stone house outside Visby and is well worth a visit.

Vatlings Gård

Road 147, 18 km 18 km (11 miles) E of Visby.
daily. 0498-29 27 00.

Roma Kungsgård, built in 1733 using materials from Roma Kloster

Visby 7

See pp164–7.

Roma 8

18 km (11 miles) SE of Visby.
Roma Kungsgård: 0498-500 57, 501 23. Jun–Aug: daily.

Cistercian monks from Nydala monastery in Småland founded **Roma Kloster** in 1164. The monastery was built on the pattern of the French mother monastery and became a religious centre for the entire Baltic region. The three-aisle church in the Fontenay style was completed in the 13th century. The monastery was abandoned during the Reformation in 1530 and ended up in the ownership of the Danish crown as a royal manor under Visborg Castle.

When Gotland came under Swedish rule in 1645, the monastery was practically in ruins. The county governor used materials from the site to build his residence, **Roma Kungsgård**, in 1733. Only the church remained intact, and that was used as a stable. In 1822, Roma Kungsgård was rented to the crown and served as an army store.

The ruins of Roma monastery are a popular tourist attraction. Even today they bear witness to the monks' skill in construction techniques. The beautiful vaulted ceilings are reminiscent of Roman aqueducts.

In the summer, Romateatern performs Shakespearian plays on an open-air stage set among the ruins.

A painting on wood in Bro Kyrka showing Adam and Eve in paradise

Street-by-Street: Visby ❼

Sign for Gamla Apoteket

A TOWN OF ROSES and ruins, the walled city of Visby is a UNESCO World Heritage Site as well as a popular party town in summer, when it fills up with holiday-makers from the mainland. Its cobbled streets are lined with picturesque cottages, haunting medieval ruins and a multitude of cafés and bars. Away from the busy, more touristy parts of Strandgatan, Stora Torget and around the pleasure boat harbour, the evocative ambience recalls the town's medieval history *(see p167)*. This is also evident from the imposing town wall and its many towers, including Kruttornet (the Gunpowder Tower), which offers great views.

Konstmuseet
Visby Town Wall *by Hanna Pauli (1864–1940) is on display in the Museum of Art.*

★ Gotlands Fornsal
The Historical Museum is devoted to Gotland's past from ancient times to modern day. The Science Centre and Natural History Museum are in the same building.

Burmeisterska Huset
Hans Burmeister, a wealthy merchant from Lübeck, built this house in the 17th century. It is one of the best-preserved examples of its kind in Visby.

Visby town wall
has 19 towers and gates, including Kruttornet (Gunpowder Tower).

KEY

--- Suggested route

STAR SIGHTS

★ **Domkyrkan Sta Maria**

★ **Gotlands Fornsal**

0 metres

0 yards

Kapitelhusgården
*In this leafy medieval
courtyard setting, the
public can try their hand
at medieval crafts.
During the summer, it
can become busy,
especially during
Medieval Week.*

**iska
rden →**

St Drotten, the
sister church to
St Lars.

★ **Domkyrkan Sta Maria**
*Completed in 1225, the
cathedral was the church
of the German merchants.
It is the only one of
Visby's 17 medieval churches
which is not in ruins.*

St Lars, also known
as the church of Sta
Anna after the moth-
er of the Virgin Mary.

Söderport ▼

Around Stora Torget
*Entertainment focuses on the main
square, Stora Torget. Gutekällaren, with
a summer terrace on the square, is one
of the many restaurants and bars here.*

Ruins of Sta Karin (St Catherine's) Church
*Franciscan monks built the church and
monastery of Sta Karin in 1233. Dominicans
rebuilt it in the 14th century. But in 1525
was destroyed by an army from Lübeck.*

Exploring Visby

Within the walls, Visby is relatively small and all the sights are within easy walking distance. The main streets run north to south: Strandgatan with historic sights and nightlife spots, St Hansgatan with its many churches, and Adelsgatan, the shopping street leading from Söderport (South Gate) to Stora Torget, the main square. North of here are quieter residential streets and alleyways, making for a lovely stroll. Near Norderport (North Gate) it is possible to climb up on the ramparts and admire the magnificent wall.

Visby Town Centre

◻ Street-by-Street: Visby, see pp164–5

Medieval vaulted street in Visby, a UNESCO World Heritage Site

The Heart of the Town
The medieval inner town of Visby is shaped by its mighty town wall, almost 3.5 km (2 miles) in length. Construction of the wall began at the end of the 13th century. It was originally 5.5 m (18 ft) high and designed to protect against attack from the sea. On the inland side, the wall was surrounded by a deep moat. Within the ramparts, narrow cobbled streets are lined with tightly-packed houses, wealthy merchants' homes and the ruins of historic churches. UNESCO described the town as the "best fortified commercial city in northern Europe" and declared it a World Heritage Site in 1995.

Just outside the wall is Almedalen, the former site of the Hanseatic harbour. Today the area is a park. South of Almedalen is Visby marina, which throngs with boats, especially during Medieval Week in August.

▦ Around Stora Torget
At the heart of Visby lies Stora Torget (Big Square) from which the roads to the town gates radiate. This is still a focal point for visitors to Visby, despite the development of a modern town centre outside Österport, and there is a lively market here in summer. Several medieval houses surround the square, including the restaurants of Gutekällaren, with its characteristic stepped gable, and Munkkällaren, with its deep vaulted cellars and inner courtyard.

The ruins of the church of Sta Karin (St Catherine), dating from the 1230s, form a dramatic backdrop on the southern side of Stora Torget. In the cloisters there is a permanent exhibition on Visby's medieval churches. In the shadow of the ruins is Rosengård, a café where generations have ordered coffee and delicious pastries.

▥ Gotlands Fornsal
Strandgatan 14. 📞 0498-29 27 00.
🕓 15 May–14 Sep: daily; 15 Sep–14 May: Tue–Sun. 🎫 📷 🚻 🛈 ♿
Gotland's long history going back to prehistoric times has made this collection one of Sweden's richest regional museums. It is housed in a former royal distillery, built in the 1770s.

The Hall of Picture Stones contains an impressive array of carved stones from the 5th–11th centuries, some of which feature runic inscriptions. Next door, the Gravkammaren (Grave Room) shows burial customs from ancient times to the Vikings. Several skeletons are on display, including the 8,000-years-old Stenkyrkamannen (Stenkyrka Man). One of the most remarkable sights is the collection of Viking silver treasure – no fewer than 700 items have been recovered from sites around the island.

Church art is well represented. The museum holds the original, Gothic Öja Madonna (Öja church in southern Gotland has to make do with a copy). A large gallery displays medieval furniture, as well as collections from later periods including shops and toys.

Picture stones from the 5th–11th centuries in Gotlands Fornsal

Visby's medieval town wall, approximately 3.5 km (2 miles) long and up to 5.5 m (18 ft) high

Ruins of St Nicolai

St Nicolaigatan. *Visby Tourist Office 0498-20 17 00.*

The ruins of St Nicolai are all that remains of a Dominican monastery founded in Visby in 1228. The Black Friars expanded it and built a Gothic cathedral which they dedicated to the patron saint of sailors and merchants, St Nicholas. When the people of Lübeck stormed Visby in 1525 much of the cathedral was destroyed.

Between 1929 and 1990 a pageant, *Petrus de Dacia,* was performed here every summer. This Gotlander was a famous mystic and author, and prior of the Dominican monastery at the end of the 13th century. Today, musical and theatrical events are staged in the ruins and the Gotland Chamber Music Festival is held here each summer. The audience sit protected from wind and weather by the remaining part of the roof.

Ruins of Helge And

Helge Ands Plan. *Gotlands Länsmuseum 0498-29 27 00.*

Helgeandstiftelserna was a religious order founded during the early 13th century to take care of the poor and the sick. The ruin of Helge And (Church of the Holy Spirit) is one of Visby's most remarkable church ruins and dates from this period. The octagonal building has two floors opening onto a choir. Two large staircases lead up to the first floor. It was designed in this way to allow patients from the hospital to reach the church via a passage from the upper floor. Today the ruins are used for cultural events and are open to visitors during the summer.

Botaniska Trädgården

Kärleksporten. *0498-21 83 87.* *24 hrs daily. Nights in Medieval Week.*

Gotland's Botanical Garden was founded in 1856 by the Badande Wännerna (Society of the Bathing Friends), a gentlemen's club formed in 1814 to work for the benefit of the public. The society also established Gotland's first school and set up its first bank. To reach the garden, follow the promenade along the shore from the harbour and go through Kärleksporten (Gate of Love) in the north-west corner of the town wall.

Inside the gate, the lush park offers a spice-scented herb garden and a pretty rose garden (at its peak Jul–Aug). There are also many plants and trees exotic to the Nordic countries, such as walnut, mulberry and ginkgo. In its midst stand the ivy-clad ruins of St Olof's church and there is a water-lily pond and a small pavilion making an ideal resting place.

VISBY'S EARLY HISTORY

Archaeological finds, including Roman, Arabic and Russian coins, show that Gotland had a lively foreign trade already in Viking times. At the end of the 12th century, trade with Germany took off and the Hanseatic League was formed – a mercantile and political association between German merchants and towns around the North Sea and the Baltic. The League was centred on Visby and the town enjoyed a boom in the 13th century with people coming from all around to settle here. Towards the end of the century a trading-political power struggle on Gotland led to internal strife and the gradual decline of Visby. Poor harvests and the Black Death contributed to the decline, as did the introduction of large ships capable of travelling longer distances. In 1361 Visby was captured by Valdemar Atterdag and Gotland succumbed to Danish rule. Then in 1525 Visby was plundered by its rival Hanseatic town, Lübeck, and buildings were destroyed or abandoned.

Valdemar Atterdag pillaging Visby in 1361

The small community of Ljugarn with typical Gotland limestone houses close to the sea

Ljugarn **9**

40 km (25 miles) SW of Visby.
🚶 295. 🚌 🚆 Visby Tourist Office,
0498-20 17 00. 🏐 Beach volleyball
cup (3rd week in Jul).

THIS CHEERFUL resort was Gotland's first and makes a good centre for touring the southeast of the island. There was a harbour here long before Russian forces raided Ljugarn on their way to laying waste to the east coast of Sweden in 1714–18. By 1900, the small community, with its long sandy beach, limestone sea stacks and guesthouse, had become a popular bathing spot.

In Alskog, just outside Ljugarn, among fields of Bronze and Iron Age relics, is **Gotlands Djurpark**, a zoo of non-Nordic animals such as camels, zebras and kangaroos.

South of Ljugarn is the 13th–14th century **Lau Kyrka**. One of Gotland's largest churches, it has a triumphal crucifix from the 13th century. Northwest of Ljugarn, **Torsburgen** fortress was built in the 3rd or 4th century and is one of the largest of its kind in Scandinavia. It is protected by naturally steep slopes and a wall 7 m (23 ft) high and up to 24 m (79 ft) wide. To reach it, take the forest road from the 146 towards Östergarn, 2 km (1 mile) east of Kräklingbo church.

The idyllic **Katthammars-vik**, north of Ljugarn, was once a flourishing port and limeworks. In the early 1800s lime baron Axel Hägg bought Katthamra manor, which he

had rebuilt and decorated in Empire style. Today there is a hotel and youth hostel here, but the manor house itself is a private home.

🦌 **Gotlands Djurpark**
48 km (30 miles) SE of Visby. 📞 0498-49 35 00. 🕐 late May–Aug: daily. 🎫 🚻 🛍️

Lojsta **10**

15 km (9 miles) S of Visby.
🚶 120. 🚌 🚆 Visby Tourist Office,
0498-20 17 00. 🏇 Gotland pony
judging (4th week in Jul).

LIKE SO MANY of Gotland's churches, **Lojsta Kyrka** dates from the mid-13th century. The choir and the nave have ornamental paintings and the figures above the triumphal arch are by the master known as "Egypticus" in the mid-14th century.

On **Lojsta Hed**, an area of forest and heath north of the church, lives a herd of semi-wild Gotland ponies *(russ)*, the stubborn little horse native to the island. The animals are owned by local farmers and by Gotlands Läns Hushållningssällskap. Several annual events are organized, such as the release of the stallion in early June, and the high point of the year, the Gotland pony judging at the end of July.

About 2.5 km (2 miles) from Lojsta towards Etelhem is a large building with a sedge roof, **Lojstahallen**. This is an excellent reconstruction of a late-Iron Age hall building. Next to it is a medieval fortress, Lojsta Slott.

Fröjel Kyrka **11**

40 km (25 miles) S of Visby. 🚌
📞 0498-24 00 05, 070-51 71 38.
🕐 May–Aug: 8am–8pm daily; 1 Sep–15 Sep: 8am–7pm daily, other times ring. ✝️ every other Sun. 🎫 🛍️ 🚻 ♿

IN A STUNNING LOCATION, high up overlooking the sea, is the saddle-roof church of Fröjel Kyrka, built in the 12th and 13th centuries. Inside an impressive triumphal crucifix by the craftsman who created the rood screen of Öja church. The churchyard has an ancient maze which shows that the site was used long before the arrival of Christianity.

North of the church lies the magnificent **Gannarve Skeppssättning** (Gannarve Ship Barrow). This has been dated to the late Bronze Age (1000–300 BC) and is 30 m (98 ft) long and 5 m (16 ft) wide.

The splendid Gannarve Bronze Age stone ship barrow

Karlsöarna **12**

Gotland. **Stora Karlsö** ⛴️ from Klinte-hamn. 🚆 Visby Tourist Office, 0498-20 17 00. 🎫 🚻 🛍️ **Lilla Karlsö** ⛴️ from Djupvik. 🚆 0498-48 52 48, summer: 0498-24 11 39. 🎫

MANY MYTHS have been spun around Stora and Lilla Karlsö, the rocky islands 6.5 km (4 miles) off the west coast of Gotland.

Stora Karlsö covers 2.5 sq km (1 sq mile) and is a nature reserve with steep cliffs, caves such as "Stora Förvar",

Bird islands Lilla Karlsön (left) and Stora Karlsön seen from Gotland

moorland, leafy groves, and rare flowers and birds. Here, between the bare rocks in May and June, the orchids *Adam och Eva (Dactylorhiza sambucina)* and *Sankt Pers nycklar (Orchis mascula)* form carpets of blooms. Sea birds such as auks, gulls and eider duck can be seen. Razorbills lay their eggs among the stones on the beach, while guillemots prefer the shelves of the steep cliffs.

A guided tour takes a couple of hours and is included in the price of the boat crossing. There is also a museum in Norderhamn.

Like Stora Karlsö, **Lilla Karlsö** is also a nature reserve. The island has been grazed by sheep since the Bronze Age. It is home to guillemots, razorbills, cormorants and gulls. Eider duck, little terns, Sandwich terns and velvet scoters nest on the flat land. The Swedish Society for Nature Conservation organizes guided tours. There is a youth hostel on the island – book in advance.

Petes Museigård, typical 18th- and 19th-century Gotland houses

Petes ⑬

Gotland. 🏛 🛈 *Länsmuseet på Gotland, 0498-29 27 00.* ⏰ *Mid-Jun–Aug: 11am–5pm, daily.*

T O THE SOUTHWEST of Gotland, just before Hablingbo church on coastal road 140, there is a turning to the seaside community of Petes. Here, the well-preserved houses show Gotland's architecture from the 18th and 19th centuries.

For younger visitors, **Barnens Petes** displays classic toys such as stilts, hobby horses, hoops, wooden rifles and wooden dolls.

The unbroken sandy beaches of Gotska Sandön

Hoburgen ⑭

80 km (50 miles) S of Visby. 🚗

F AR TO THE SOUTH lies Hoburgen, a 35-m (115-ft) high steep cliff of fossil-rich limestone with seams of the local red Hoburgen marble. On the clifftop is a lighthouse built in 1846. From here it is 176 km (97 miles) to the northernmost lighthouse on the island of Fårö.

Below the lighthouse is Sweden's most famous sea stack, Hoburgsgubben (the Old Man of Hoburg), guarding the caves of Skattkammaren (the Treasure Chamber) and Sängkammaren (the Bed Chamber).

Hoburgen is a favourite spot for ornithologists who come to study the multitude of birds which swoop over Gotland's southernmost outpost all year round. In summer there is a restaurant nearby.

Profile of Hoburgsgubben, the "Old Man of Hoburg"

Gotska Sandön ⑮

🛈 *Visby Tourist Office, 0498-20 17 00; booking: 0498-24 04 50.* 🚢 *from Nynäshamn and Fårösund.*

J UST 40 KM (25 MILES) north of Fårö lies the most isolated island in the Baltic, Gotska Sandön. It is one of Sweden's national parks and features a unique landscape of deserted, constantly changing sandy beaches and dunes, pine forests and a rich flora. There are migratory birds, unusual beetles, but only one mammal, the hare. The island became a national park in 1909.

Gotska Sandön has been inhabited since the dawn of civilization, although the population has never been large. Colonies of grey seals led seal hunters to settle on the island and the dangerous waters offshore attracted wreck plunderers. In the 17th and 18th centuries sheep were grazed here and later crops were grown. As recently as the 1950s a few lighthouse keepers and their families (and one female teacher) lived here, but now the lighthouse is automated and the only permanent resident is a caretaker.

There is no harbour and regular boat traffic from Fårö or Nynäshamn is infrequent and dependent on the weather. It is possible to camp or stay in a shared sleeping hut or cottage. Accommodation must be booked before arrival.

SOUTHERN GÖTALAND

SWEDEN'S TWO SOUTHERNMOST PROVINCES, *Skåne and Blekinge, together form Southern Götaland, with the country's third largest city, Malmö, as the region's main town and gateway to Europe. The gentle, undulating landscape retains its Danish atmosphere from times past. Castles and medieval and Viking sites abound, and the historic naval port of Karlskrona is a* UNESCO *World Heritage Site.*

The province of Skåne has an undeserved reputation for being completely flat, but apart from the plain of Söderslätt the countryside is surprisingly hilly with the rocky ridges of Söderåsen, Linderödsåsen and Romeleåsen dividing the region. To the northwest, the area is bounded by the imposing Hallandsåsen ridge.

The province of Blekinge, crisscrossed by rivers and lakes, is known as the Garden of Sweden. It has its own island archipelago with sheltered harbours beloved by sailors. North, towards the border with Småland, the slightly wild forest landscape predominates.

Throughout Southern Götaland the Danish influence prior to 1645 *(see p35)* is still evident, not least in the architecture, which differs greatly from elsewhere in Sweden. A common sight in rural Skåne is the traditional, often half-timbered farmhouse with a thatched roof, built around a cobbled courtyard. Castles and manor houses, in many cases built by the Danish nobility, are a feature of the countryside. In the coastal communities, former fishing huts are today cherished by their summer residents.

Southern Götaland differs from the rest of Sweden in atmosphere, too. The people of Skåne are known for being relaxed and for loving good food – and in large quantities – something which has lent this part of the country its inn culture, which has its equivalent in the Danish *kroen* just across Öresund.

Having been sparring partners in the long-distant past, Sweden and Denmark have recently been linked by the Öresund Bridge from Malmö to Copenhagen. Both sides of the sound are now collaborating over the creation of a visionary new Swedish-Danish region, Örestad.

Ales Stenar, a stone ship on Skåne's south coast, thought to be a late Viking grave or cult site

◁ Traditional thatched-roof farmhouse in Östarp, built in 1811 and set around a courtyard

Exploring Southern Götaland

As well as arable fields and willow windbreaks, this southernmost part of Sweden has its share of gently rolling hills, forests and lakes. The region is ideal for cycling through the country from village to village, discovering manor houses and castles along the way, walking through nature reserves or along the Skåneleden trail, canoeing, fishing, swimming in the many small lakes and rivers, driving, or sailing along the coast and putting into shore at fishing harbours on tiny islands. Towns such as Lund and Malmö offer a wealth of history, best discovered on foot, Karlskrona is renowned for its naval port and maritime past, and Trelleborg has a reconstructed Viking fortress.

Spiral beech trees in Trollskogen forest, Torna Hällestad

```
0 kilometres        30

0 miles          20
```

**Statue of the founder of Karlskrona,
Karl XI, in front of Trefaldighetskyrkan**

**The 8-km (5-mile) long Öresund Bridge, completed in 2000,
linking Sweden with Denmark and Continental Europe**

KEY

━━ Motorway

━━ Major road

═ Minor road

┅┅ Railway line

- - Ferry route

GETTING AROUND

The E20 motorway across the Öresund Bridge from Continental Europe joins the E6, E22 and E65 south of Malmö and continues north to Helsingborg where it meets the E4 to Stockholm. The region has several airports and there are train connections to the large towns. Local commuter trains serve districts around the major cities. Ferries from Germany operate to Trelleborg and Ystad and there are frequent ferries from Denmark to Helsingborg.

SEE ALSO

• *Where to Stay* pp285–6

• *Where to Eat* pp298–9

Hovs Hallar, a nature reserve on the bay of Laholmsbukten

Bjärehalvön ●

Skåne. Road 105. 🚌 🚃 ⌧ ❶
*Båstad Tourist Office 0431-750 45,
Torekov Tourist Office 0431-36 31 80.*
🎻 *Båstad Chamber Music Festival (4th
week in Jun), Båstad tennis (Jun/Jul).*
w *www.bastad.se*

SEVERAL POPULAR resorts
surround the peninsula of
Bjärehalvön, between the bays
of Skälderviken and Laholmsbukten. The medieval town of
Båstad is now best known for
hosting the annual Swedish
Open tennis tournament, but it
also has beautiful old houses
and glorious beaches. Just
over 10 km (6 miles) to the
west is the old fishing village
of **Torekov**. Boat trips run
from Torekov to the nature
reserve **Hallands Väderö**, a
remnant of the Hallandsåsen
ridge now left 3 km (2 miles)
out to sea. Of special note is
the alder marsh.

On the northern cape of the
peninsula is **Hovs Hallar**, a
geologically interesting area
with dramatic rocks and caves.
The area is a nature reserve
popular with birdwatchers and
walkers. Hovs Hallar is the
westernmost end of the
Hallandsåsen ridge, which
forms the border between the
Bjärehalvön peninsula and
Halland *(see p207)*. With its
meadows and varied flora, the
ridge is ideal for walking.

West of Båstad along the
coast is **Norrvikens
Trädgårdar**, a paradise for
garden lovers created by
architect Rudolf Abelin in the
early 20th century. There are

**Fruit trees in blossom at
Norrvikens Trädgårdar gardens**

several different gardens,
including a Baroque garden
and a Japanese garden.

The town of **Ängelholm**,
nestling between the
Bjärehalvön and Kullahalvön
peninsulas at the end of the
bay of Skälderviken, has a
sandy beach 6 km (4 miles)
long. Historically, Ängelholm
was known for its pottery
industry and today clay
cuckoos, the town's symbol,
are made here.

❦ Norrvikens Trädgårdar
5 km (3 miles) W of Båstad.
【 *0431-36 90 40.* ◯ *May–Aug:
daily.* 🚽 🎁 ❶

Kullabygden ❷

Skåne. Road 111/112. 🚌 🚃 ❶ *Cen-
tralgatan 20, Höganäs, 042-33 77 74.*
🎻 *Music in Kullabygden (2nd week
in Jul), Kulla Market in Jonstorp (first
week in Jul).*

THE BEAUTIFUL Kullen Peninsula has been inhabited
since the Iron and Bronze
Ages. Today, the pretty
medieval fishing villages of
Arild, Mölle, Höganäs and
Viken have become popular
seaside resorts. Höganäs is
best known for its ceramics.

Just outside Arild lies
Brunnby Kyrka, parts of
which are 12th-century. The
church contains impressive
ceiling paintings. **Krapperups
Slott**, north of Höganäs, dates
from the mid-16th century; the
castle houses an art gallery
and museum.

♜ Krapperups Slott
7 km (4 miles) N of Höganäs. 【 *042-
34 41 90.* **Castle** ◯ *by appointment.*
Gallery & museum ◯ *late-Apr–May:
Fri–Sun; Jun–Jul: daily; Aug: Tue–Sun;
selected days in Dec.* 🎁 ❶ 🚽

Helsingborg ❸

Skåne. E4. 🏠 *88,000.* ⌧ 🚌 🚃 ⚓
❶ *Stortorget/Södra Storgatan 1, 042-
10 43 50.* 🎻 *Helsingborg Festival
(3rd week in Jul), Horse Festival (last
weekend in Jul).*
w *www.helsingborgsguiden.com*

KNOWN AS THE "Pearl of the
Sound", Helsingborg is a
lively town, spectacularly

TYCHO BRAHE

Astronomer Tycho Brahe was born in Skåne in 1546 into a
Danish noble family. At the age of 13 he was sent to
university in Copenhagen to study philosophy and went on
to study at several German universities. Inspired by an
eclipse of the sun in 1560, he took up astronomy. He
believed that the old methods of measurement to determine
the position of the planets were not sufficiently exact and
designed a new system. In 1572 he obser-
ved a new bright star in the constellation
Cassiopeia. His discoveries in astronomy
paved the way for a new view of the
universe. In recognition, the Danish
king granted Brahe the island of Ven,
where he had an observatory built
(see p175) which became the
finest in Europe. Following a
difference of opinion with the
Danish court, Brahe went into
exile and settled in Prague where
he died in Prague in 1601.

**Statue of Tycho Brahe in
St Ibbs Kyrka on Ven island**

ocated on the shores of the Öresund within sight of the Danish coast. The town's strategic position at the narrowest point of the sound ed to a stormy history, and he 34-m (111-ft) tower **Kärnan** is all that remains of ts 12th-century fortress. The prick tower of the town hall 1897) also features on the skyline. It was designed by architect Alfred Hellerström and contains glass paintings by Gustav Cederström, which are well worth a look.

Jacob Hansen's half-timbered house, built in 1641, is the oldest house in Helsingborg. The new **Dunkers Kultur-hus**, by Danish architect Kim Utzon, encompasses a museum, art gallery and theatre under one roof.

The open-air **Fredriksdal Friluftsmuseum** displays historical buildings from the region and has a botanical garden containing the wild plants of Skåne.

ENVIRONS: Ramlösa Brunn, 5 km (3 miles) southeast of Helsingborg, is known for its spring water, discovered in the late 19th century and now on offer in the Water Pavilion.

The castle of **Sofiero** was bequeathed to Helsingborg municipality by Gustav VI Adolf. The park is particularly famous for its Royal Gardens containing more than 300 varieties of rhododendron.

Tycho Brahe's underground observatory on the island of Ven

🏛 **Dunkers Kulturhus**
Kungsgatan 11. [042-10 74 00.
◯ Tue–Sun. ⬜🄿🄿🄿
🏛 **Fredriksdals Friluftsmuseum**
Hävertgatan 1. [042-10 45 00.
◯ daily. ⬜🄿🄿♿
♣ **Sofiero**
Sofierovägen, 5 km (3 miles) N of the centre. [042-13 74 00. **Parken**
◯ Apr–Sep: daily. ⬜ **Slottet**
◯ Jun–Aug: guided tours only. ⬜🄿

Klippan ❹

Skåne. Road 21. 👥 8,000. 🚉 🚌
🄸 Storgatan 46, 0435-282 00.
🏛 Åby Market (3rd Tue–Wed in Jun), Ljungbyhed old-time market (3rd Fri–Sat in Aug).

LOCATED ON the Söderåsen ridge, 30 km (19 miles) east of Helsingborg, Klippan is known for having Sweden's oldest operating paper mill, built in the 16th century.

There are many churches in the area worth a visit. Today only the sacristy remains of **Herrevadskloster**, a former Cistercian monastery founded in the 12th century. This has been restored and is used as a chapel. Art exhibitions are held here in the summer.

Söderåsen National Park offers leafy forests, dramatic screes, babbling brooks and breathtaking views from Kopparhatten and Hjortspränget. The Skåneleden trail runs through the park.

The 17th-century mansion **Vrams Gunnarstorp**, 10 km (6 miles) west of Klippan, is built in the Dutch Renaissance style. The stunning park with its acclaimed hornbeam avenue is open to the public.

🏰 **Kärnan**
Slottshagen. [042-10 59 91.
◯ Apr–Oct: daily. ⬜🄿

Helsingborg's recently renovated tower, Kärnan

🏛 **Herrevadskloster**
10 km (6 miles) E of Klippan, road 13.
[0435-44 19 90. **Museum** ◯
daily. 🄿 pre-book. 🍴⬜♿🏠

Landskrona ❺

Skåne. 👥 27,000. 🚉 🚌 🄸 Storgatan 36, 0418-47 30 00. 🄿 Vallåkraträffen Customized Car Festival (mid-Aug), Gardening Festival (Aug).

THE SHIPBUILDING town of Landskrona was granted its charter in the 15th century. In 1549, the Danish king Christian III built the Citadel as protection against the Swedes. This substantial fortress surrounded by a moat dominates the town. Most of the sights can be found in the area around it, including **Landskrona Museum**, with its local history collection, and Konsthallen (Art Gallery) surrounded by a sculpture park.

ENVIRONS: In the sound between Sweden and Denmark lies the island of **Ven**, where Tycho Brahe set up his underground observatory, Stjärneborg, in the 1580s. The Tycho Brahe Museum features multimedia shows about the observatory.

There is a ruined castle on Ven, Uraniborg, and at the highest point of the island stands the medieval church of St Ibb. Steep Backafallen is the place for the most spectacular views.

The island can be reached by regular ferries from Landskrona all year round and by fishing boat from Råå during the summer.

🏛 **Landskrona Museum**
Slottsgatan. [0418-47 31 20.
◯ noon–5pm daily. ● Easter Saturday, Saturday before Whitsun, Midsummer Eve, 24, 25 & 31 Dec.
🛥 **Ven**
In Öresund 7 km (4 miles) W of Landskrona. 🚢 from Landskrona. [0418-47 30 00, 0418-724 20. **Tycho Brahe Museum** ◯ 11 Apr–30 Sep: daily. 🄿 pre-book. ⬜🄿⬜♿🏠

Bosjökloster, originally an 11th-century Benedictine convent

Frostavallen 6

Skåne. 3 km (2 miles) N of Höör on road 21. 🚌 to Höör. 🚌 🛈 Höör Tourist Office, 0413-275 75.

THE BEAUTIFUL countryside around Höör in central Skåne offers something for everyone, from hiking, canoeing and swimming to fishing from the shore or by boat on Vaxsjön lake. The availability of restaurants, cafés, hotels, cottages and campsites makes Frostavallen ideal for a day trip or a longer stay. There are playgrounds and all kinds of leisure equipment are available for hire.

Nearby is **Skånes Djurpark**, a zoo specializing in Nordic animals, which makes a popular excursion for children. It has more than 1,000 wild and domesticated Nordic animals. Watch lynx being fed or enjoy a pony ride.

A very different kind of experience is offered at **Höörs Stenåldersby**, where visitors can see for themselves what life was like in a Stone Age village. Flint-knapping and bow-making can be tried.

🦌 **Skånes Djurpark**
Frostavallen. 🕻 0413-55 30 60. 🕐 daily. 🖼 🎫 🚻 🛒 summertime. ♿
🏛 **Höörs Stenåldersby**
Next to Skånes Djurpark. 🕻 0413-55 32 70. 🕐 Jul by appointment.

Bosjökloster 7

Skåne. Road 13. 🕻 0413-250 48. 🚌 🕐 May–Sep: 10am–6pm. 🎫 🖼 🛒 🍴 Park 🕐 May–Oct: 8am–8pm; other times: 10am–5pm. 🏹 Hunting and Fishing Festival (last weekend in Aug).

ON A PENINSULA between the lakes of Östra and Västra Ringsjön lies one of Sweden's most remarkable houses. Bosjökloster was built around 1080 as a convent and soon became one of the wealthiest in Skåne. Rich families paid a great deal to secure a place for their daughters, often donating goods and land. This all came to an end with the Danish Reformation in 1536 and its possessions were transferred into private ownership.

In 1875–9 Bosjökloster was reconstructed to a design by architect Helgo Zettervall and became the prime example of his skill for renovating Swedish manors and palaces.

In the early 20th century the property was bought by Count Philip Bonde and today it is owned by his grandson.

The family opened the house to the public in 1962 and is now it is one of the most popular stately homes in Skåne with parks and gardens, a restaurant, café, mini-zoo, boats for hire and fishing, too. The park features a 1,000-year-old oak tree. The oldest room in the house, Stensalen, is devoted to exhibitions of arts and crafts.

Östarp 8

Skåne. Near road 11. 🚌 **Kulturens Östarp** 🕻 046-804 07. 🕐 15 Apr–30 Sep: 11am–5pm Tue–Sun; 1 Oct–14 Apr: noon–5pm Tue–Sun. 🎫 🖼 🍴 🏹 Medieval Festival (2nd weekend in Jun). 🌐 www.kulturen.com

IN THE MIDDLE AGES the town of Östarp was owned by a monastery. But it fell to the crown during the Reformation in the 16th century and was subsequently destroyed to make way for a manor house, which itself burned down. All that remained of the town was Östarps Gamlegård, built in 1812. This farmhouse was bought in 1923 by Kulturen in Lund, and today forms the centrepiece of the open-air Kulturens Östarp. It is a living museum using horses rather than machinery to farm the land. There is an excellent inn.

The countryside around Östarp is dotted with castles and stately homes, and Lake Vombsjön is a paradise for birdwatchers and fishermen alike. On the eastern shore of the lake is **Övedskloster**, a beautiful 18th-century manor house set in an elegant park. The property has been owned by the Ramel family since 1753. The main house, "Stora huset", is one of the most stunning Rococo-style houses in Sweden. It was designed by Carl Hårleman (see p24) and completed in 1776. The park, modelled on Versailles, is open to the public in the summer. Surrounding the

The 18th-century windmill at Kulturens Östarp museum

Old buildings of Lund preserved by the open-air museum of Kulturen

estate is a village of fine half-timbered houses.

🏛 Övedskloster
Road 11 from Lund towards Sjöbo.
📞 046-630 63. 🕐 daily (park only).
🐎 Horse trials (early Sep).

Lund ⑨

Skåne. E 22. 👥 60,000. ✈ Sturup.
🚉 🚌 ℹ Kyrkogatan 11, 046-35 50
40. 🐎 Walpurgis Night (30 Apr
& 1 May), Cultural Evening (3rd Sat
in Sep).

FOUNDED BY King Sven Tveskägg more than 1,000 years ago, the university town of Lund was once Denmark's capital. In the Middle Ages it was a religious, political and cultural centre and site of a cathedral, **Lund Domkyrka**, which was consecrated in 1145. Over the centuries it has been rebuilt, most recently by Helgo Zettervall, 1860–80. Look out for the 14th-century astronomical clock and a sculpture in the crypt of the giant Finn supporting the cathedral's vaulting.

Lund University was established in 1666, in the grounds of the bishop's palace, Lundagård. A new main building was completed in 1882, and now the university is the second largest seat of learning in Sweden with around 40,000 students.

In the heart of the partly medieval city centre lies **Kulturen**, an open-air museum with perfectly preserved streets, cottages and town houses. Kulturen

also has extensive historical collections. The 14th-century chapel of Laurentiikapellet, in central Lund, is thought to have been the library of the monastery of St Laurence.

Of Lund's many museums, **Historiska Museet**, containing Domkyrkomuseet, is one of Sweden's largest museums of archaeology, and includes an exhibition devoted to the history of the cathedral. **Lunds Konsthall**, designed by Klas Anshelm and opened in 1957, displays contemporary art.

ENVIRONS: The spring flowers are magnificent at **Dalby Söderskog**, a national park 10 km (6 miles) southeast of Lund, where there is a forest of elm, ash and oak trees. **Gårdstånga Kyrka**, 10 km (6 miles) north of Lund, is a 12th-century Romanesque church. The impressive carvings inside were crafted by local woodcarver Jacob Kremberg in the 17th century.

🔒 Lunds Domkyrka
Kyrkogatan. 📞 046-35 87 00.
🕐 daily. 🎧 🚹 ♿

🏛 Kulturen
Tegnerplatsen. 📞 046-35 04 00.
🕐 May–Sep: daily; Oct–Apr:
Tue–Sun. 🎧 🎫 📷 🚹 ♿
🏛 Historiska Museet
Krafts Torg 1. 📞 046-222 79 44.
🕐 Tue–Fri. 🎧 🎫
🏛 Lunds Konsthall
Mårtenstorget 3. 📞 046-35 52 95.
🕐 Tue–Sun. 🎧 🎫 Thu & Sun. 📷 ♿

Skanör/Falsterbo ⑩

Skåne. Road 100. 👥 7,000. ✈
Sturup. 🚌 ℹ Östra Hamnplan 2,
040-42 54 54. 🐎 Falsterbo Horse
Show (first weekend in Jul),
Sandcastle Competition (last Sat in
Jul). 🌐 www.vellinge.se/turism

TODAY THE TWIN towns at the far end of Skåne's south-western cape are idyllic seaside resorts, but they owe their development to the lucrative herring industry in the Middle Ages.

Sights include the ruins of the 14th-century fort of **Falsterbohus**, **Falsterbo Museum** with its local history collection, and **Falsterbo Konsthall**, an art gallery in the old railway station. On the headland is **Falsterbo Lighthouse**, built in 1793. It is now a historical monument although it is still in working order. Skanör Town Hall dates from 1777 and the church is 13th-century.

Bärnstensmuseet, the Amber Museum in Höllviken, near the Viking earthworks of Kämpinge Vall, is worth visiting to see both the amber and archaeological finds.

Giant Finn in the cathedral

🏛 Bärnstensmuseet
Kämpinge, 10 km (6 miles) E of
Falsterbo. 🚌 📞 040-45 45 04.
🕐 Tue–Sun. 🎧 🎫

The low, single-storey houses in the small town of Skanör

Malmö ⓫

Sweden's gateway to Europe, Malmö is the country's third largest city. It was founded in the mid-13th century. Under Danish rule from 1397 to 1523, Malmö was an important town, but once it was returned to Sweden its position waned until an upturn in its fortunes at the end of the 18th century. Today, thanks largely to the Öresund Bridge and associated development, Malmö is once more in the spotlight. The city has a lively, distinctly European atmosphere and has become a centre for contemporary art and design. The old town is centred on Stortorget with its historic Town Hall and governor's residence.

Stortorget with Residenset (left) and Rådhuset (right)

🏛 Rådhuset
Stortorget. ● to the public.
📷 by special arrangement, phone 040-34 12 00.
The centre of Malmö is the square Stortorget, laid out in the 1530s by the town's mayor Jörgen Kock. Stortorget is dominated by Rådhuset, the town hall, originally built in Renaissance Dutch style in 1546. Only the cellar remains of the medieval building, which had a stepped roof and served both as a prison and an inn. In the 1860s architect Helgo Zettervall carried out extensive renovation work, giving the town hall a completely new look. A number of changes were, in fact, made in the cellars, too (including the removal of the prisoners). The inn is still standing today and is one of the most popular bars in Malmö.

🏛 Jörgen Kocks Hus
Stortorget. ● to the public.
Stortorget also contains Jörgen Kocks Hus, a large six-storey building with a stepped gable roof, constructed in 1525. Jörgen Kock, appointed mint-master for Denmark in 1518, moved the work of the mint

to his house in Malmö. Four years later he was elected mayor of the city and became one of the most powerful men in Malmö. He was involved in the rebellion over the Danish succession and was captured and sentenced to death, but escaped and was reinstated as mayor of Malmö in 1540.

🏛 Residenset
Stortorget. ● to the public.
In the mid-18th century the two buildings Kungshuset and Gyllenpalmska Huset were combined to form the new governor's residence. Around 100 years later the building was given a new façade by architect F W Scholander, to which Helgo Zettervall adapted his extensive redesign of the town hall. Today the building is the home of the county governor.

🏛 St Petri Kyrka
Göran Olsgatan 1. 📞 040-35 90 56.
🕐 daily. ⬆ 📷 by appointment, phone 040-35 90 49 to book. ♿
In a street behind Stortorget is Malmö's cathedral, St Petri Kyrka. Built in the early 12th century, the church was modelled on St Mary's in

Lübeck and is made from red brick. The high tower, constructed in the late 19th century after two 15th-century towers collapsed, is a prominent landmark on the Malmö skyline. Originally the church contained beautiful limestone paintings, but these were removed during renovation in the mid-19th century. Only the paintings in Krämarkapellet (the Tradesman's Chapel) are preserved in their medieval state.

The cathedral is full of treasures from the 16th and 17th centuries when Malmö's prosperity was at its height. The magnificent 15-m (49-ft) high altar in Renaissance style is beautifully ornamented, painted and gilded. The pulpit dating from 1599 is in sandstone and black limestone. Later additions include the organ front, a masterpiece created to a design approved by Gustav III in 1785. The original medieval organ is said to be the oldest working organ in the world and is now in Malmö Museum.

🏛 Vagnmuseum
Drottningtorget. 📞 040-34 44 59.
🕐 Jun–Aug: Fri & Sun; Sep–May: Fri.
📷 by appointment.
In Drottningtorget square, Vagnmuseum (the Carriage Museum) is housed in the 19th-century hussars' riding school. The museum contains a superior collection of horse-drawn carriages, from the elegant to the everyday, fire engines and bicycles.

Vagnmuseum is part of Malmö Museer and is covered by the joint entrance ticket.

The hussars' riding school containing the Vagnmuseum

Rooseum art gallery occupying an old power station

🏛 Rooseum

Gasverksgatan 22. ☎ 040-12 17 16. ⬤ Wed–Sun. ⬤ some public holidays. 🌐 free admission Fri. 📷 Wed–Sat. 🖥 🔲 🖲

Rooseum was founded in 1988 by the Swedish art collector and financier Fredrik Roos as a showcase for contemporary art. Its exhibitions are often at the cutting edge of modern art, such as the artist Surasi Kuslwong's installation *No Conclusion – Time is the Answer*.

The gallery occupies a former power station built in 1900. It was imaginatively converted by architect Jan Holmgren to provide three galleries on three floors centred around the former steam turbine hall. Renovation work in 2001 added a microcinema and a public auditorium showing alternative and underground films. There is a good café.

🏛 Malmö Konsthall

St Johannesgatan 7. ☎ 040-34 12 93. ⬤ daily. ⬤ Midsummer Eve, Midsummer, 24, 25 & 31 Dec. 🖥 🔲 🖲 🖲 daily. ♿

The Art Hall mounts around ten exhibitions a year, with an international focus spanning the entire spectrum from modern classics to experimental art. The sculptures of Tony Cragg and an installation by Peter Greenaway have featured among the shows. A cornerstone of the gallery's permanent collection is the bequest to the city by private donors Jules and Karin Shyl. During the 20th century they collected more than 100 works, including drawings by contemporary artists Per Kirkeby, Richard Serra and Miroslav Balka.

The Konsthall was designed by architect Klas Anshelm and opened in 1975.

VISITORS' CHECKLIST

Skåne. E6/E22. 🏘 267,000. ✈ 30 km (19 miles) E of centre. 🚊 Skeppsbron. 🚌 Skeppsbron 10. ℹ Central station, 040-34 12 00; Skånegården (E 20, 1 km/half a mile E of Öresund Bridge), 040-34 12 00. 🎭 Malmö Festival (Aug), Flower Festival (mid-Jun), Winterland (Dec–Jan). Ⓦ www.malmo.se

CENTRAL MALMÖ

Jörgen Kocks Hus ②
Kommendanthuset ⑩
Malmö Konsthall ⑦
Malmöhus/
   Malmö Museum ⑨
Residenset ③
Rooseum ⑥
Rådhuset ①
St Petri Kyrka ④
Stadsbiblioteket ⑧
Teknikens och Sjöfartens
   Hus ⑪
Vagnmuseum ⑤

KEY

🚊	Railway station
🚌	Bus terminal
🅿	Parking
✝	Church
ℹ	Tourist information

0 metres   500
0 yards   500

Exploring Malmö

T HE CENTRE OF MALMÖ, where most of the sights are located, is compact and easy to explore on foot. Start at Västra Hamnen, near the fortress of Malmöhus, and walk towards the centre, in the direction of the tower of St Petri Kyrka on Stortorget. Lilla Torg and Möllevångs-torget are lively market squares, and the beautiful parks, such as Slottsparken or Pildammsparken, are a delight to wander through. While the centre retains its old-town atmosphere, futuristic projects are taking shape on the outskirts as part of the visionary new Öresund region.

Malmöhus fortress, built in 1537 and now the home of Malmö Museum

🏛 Stadsbiblioteket

Kung Oscars Väg. 📞 040-660 85 00. ⬤ May–Aug: Mon–Sat; Sep–Apr: daily. ⬤ public holidays. 📷📁🛒

The City Library moved into the "castle" on Kung Oscars Väg in 1946, but even by the 1960s there was talk of expansion. Finally, in 1999, the new state-of-the-art library opened. The architect, Henning Larsen, renovated and extended the old building, introducing large, modern glass panels. He also created the bright and airy Calendar of Light hall.

The library is fitted with the latest modern technology. Electronic, telephone and data connections can be accessed throughout the building and

The spacious Calendar of Light hall in Malmö's award-winning new library

visitors can consult the library's databases, internet and CD-ROM network on 40 computers. The people of Malmö are regular users: eight out of ten residents have visited it, borrowing an estimated 1,500,000 items a year.

🏛 Malmöhus/Malmö Museum

Malmöhusvägen. 📞 040-34 44 37. ⬤ daily. ⬤ 24, 25 & 31 Dec, 1 Jan, Midsummer Eve, Midsummer. 📷 by appointment. 📁 🛒 🛒 partly.

Originally built by Erik of Pomerania in 1434, the fortress of Malmöhus was largely destroyed by war. It was rebuilt by Christian III in 1537. Today it is the oldest preserved Renaissance castle in the Nordic region. Originally, it was a fortified royal manor and mint. After the 17th century the fortress was reinforced with bastions, but it fell into disrepair and through most of the 18th and 19th centuries served as a prison. The solid brick fort is surrounded by a deep moat. Extensive restoration work was carried out in 1932, after which

Malmö Museum moved into the building. The museum's collections cover archaeology, ethnography, the history of art and handicrafts, and zoology.

Stadsmuseet (the City Museum) illustrates the history of Malmö and surrounding Skåne with tools, weapons and domestic objects. It contains models, a large textiles collection and an ethnographical collection.

Some of the rooms in the fortress can also be seen. Another popular attraction is the 18th-century tower with its 7.5-m (25-ft) thick walls and original cannons.

Malmö Museer runs Teknikens och Sjöfartens Hus, Kommendanthuset, Ebbas Hus, Vagnmuseet and Malmö Konstmuseum, which can all be visited on a single ticket.

🏛 Kommendanthuset

Malmöhusvägen. 📞 040-34 44 39. ⬤ daily. ⬤ 24, 25 & 31 Dec, 1 Jan, Midsummer Eve, Midsummer. 🛒 by appointment. 📷 📁 🛒

In the latter part of the 18th century the storage buildings in the Malmöhus courtyard had fallen into disrepair and Gustav III ordered the construction of a new armoury. It was built outside the fortress in the Banér bastion and was completed in 1794. By 1814 the fortress's military days were over and it had become a prison. Kommendanthuset (the Governor's House) became the quarters first for the prison's doctor and priest and later the prison governor.

In the 20th century the city of Malmö took over the building, restored it to its original appearance, and incorporated it into Malmö Museer. Its collections feature military history and the history of weaponry. Temporary exhibitions are also held here.

🏛 Teknikens och Sjöfartens Hus

Malmöhusvägen. 📞 040-34 44 38. ⬤ daily. ⬤ 24, 25 & 31 Dec, I Jan, Midsummer Eve, Midsummer. 🛒 by appointment. 📷 📁 🛒

The Museum of Technology and Seafaring is also part of Malmö Museer. Its exhibits cover virtually everything to do with technological

The 8-km (5-mile) long Öresund Bridge between Sweden and Denmark, carrying a motorway and railway line

development and seafaring, as well as the history of roadbuilding and aviation, engines, and steam engines in particular. Among the exhibits is the delta-winged fighter plane J35 Draken from the 1960s. The technically curious can satisfy their urge to experiment in the *kunskaps-tivoli* interactive test lab.

The museum also covers the industrial and seafaring history of Skåne. Here, the star exhibits include the *U3* submarine and the steam launch *Schebo*. For those who have never been in a submarine, it is an opportunity not to be missed. The shipbuilding and shipping industry and the development of the ports from the 17th century onwards are highlighted, as is ferry traffic, so vital to Skåne. Temporary exhibitions are also held.

Limhamn

5 km (3 miles) SW of the centre.
Malmö Tourist Office, 040-34 12 00.

On the southern edge of Malmö lies Limhamn, a shipping port for lime since the 16th century. Today Limhamn-Bunkeflo is one of the ten districts which make up the city of Malmö.

One of Limhamn's sights is the early-19th century small, blue Soldat-torpet (soldier's house), which shows how a soldier used to live. The cottage was inhabited until 1956. Limhamn Museum Society runs the museum and various events, especially at Midsummer and Christmas.

The Öresund Bridge

E20. 6 km (3 miles) SW of the centre.
The idea of a bridge between Sweden and Denmark had been discussed for more than 100 years, but it was not until 1991 that both countries agreed on how and where this dream could be realized.

Opened in July 2000, the Öresund Bridge is an 8-km (5-mile) long link between Lernacken in Sweden, southwest of Malmö, and the 4-km (2.5-mile) long Danish artificial island of Peberholm, south of Saltholm. The highest part of the bridge rests on four pylons each 204 m (670 ft) tall and the roadway is around 30 m (100 ft) wide. The E20 runs along the upper level of the bridge and the railway along the lower level. It is said to be the longest cable-stayed bridge to carry both a railway and a motorway.

On the west side of Peberholm the link plunges into a 4-km (2.5-mile) long tunnel leading to Copenhagen's international airport, Kastrup. Today the journey by train from Malmö to Copenhagen takes 35 minutes. By 2009 the link will be augmented by a railway tunnel to central Malmö, which will further shorten the journey.

THE ÖRESUND REGION

As part of the EU's vision for a Europe without borders, the Öresund Region project aims to integrate southern Skåne in Sweden with the area around Copenhagen in Denmark, allowing people to cross from one country to another without restrictions. The construction of the Öresund Bridge and tunnel has brought with it enormous benefits for the city of Malmö. It has made the region considerably more attractive to business, the new suburb of Brostaden (Bridge City) has sprung up, cultural exchanges between the two countries are easier and the improved communications have brought more visitors. Architect Santiago Calatrava's Turning Torso housing, due for completion in 2005, is an incredibly bold creation that can be seen as an expression of the region's faith in the future. But the joy is not absolute – there are still many problems to be resolved if the region is to acheive its goal and bring its 3.5 million inhabitants closer together.

The Turning Torso building soaring 190 m (623 ft) high

Trelleborgen, a reconstructed Viking fortress

Trelleborg ⑫

Skåne. E22. 🚶 24,850. 🚗 🚌 ⛴
ℹ️ *Hamngatan 9, 0410-533 20.*
🎷 *Smygehuk Jazz Festival (mid-Jul),
Michaelmas Market.*
🌐 *www.trelleborg.se*

The CENTREPIECE of modern-day Trelleborg is **Trelleborgen**, a remarkable re-creation of a Viking fortress. It is based on the original fortress, thought to have been built by King Harald Blue Tooth in the 10th century and excavated 1,000 years later. The reconstruction opened in 1995.

The town was at its most prosperous in the Middle Ages when German merchants came to trade salt for herring. Some of the old Skåne houses still remain in the quarter around Gamla Torg (Old Square) and in Kloster-gränden, where the ruins of a 13th-century Franciscan monastery still stand. The monastery itself was closed during the Reformation, but its garden is a recreated oasis with a herb, hop and pleasure garden. Stadsparken, the town park with a gorgeous rose garden, is well worth a visit.

Among the other sights is **Trelleborgs Museum**, focusing on local history, **Sjöfartsmuseet** (the Sea-faring Museum) and **Axel Ebbehallen**, which has a large collection of sculptures by Skåne artist Axel Ebbe.

ENVIRONS: A short distance west of Trelleborg lies the village of Skegrie and beside the E6 is **Skegriedösen**, a Stone Age burial mound. The rectangular grave chamber is formed from four stone

blocks with a giant pointed block as a roof, surrounded by 17 footstones. This type of Stone Age burial site is only found in southern and western Sweden.

🏛 **Trelleborgen**
Bryggaregatan. 📞 *0410-460 77.*
⬜ *daily.* 🎟 🅿 📷 ♿
🏛 **Trelleborgs Museum**
Östergatan 1. 📞 *0410-530 50.*
⬜ *Tue–Sun.* 🎟 ♿ 📷 ♿
🏛 **Axel Ebbehallen**
Hesekillgatan 1. 📞 *0410-530 56.*
⬜ *Jun–Aug: Tue–Sun.* 🎟 ♿ ♿

Ystad ⑬

Skåne. E65. 🚶 16,850. 🚗 🚌 ⛴
ℹ️ *St Knuts Torg, 0411-57 76 81.*
🎷 *Ystad Festival (last weekend in
Jul).* 🌐 *www.visitystad.com*

In YSTAD THE IMPACT of Danish rule and contact with the German Hanseatic League is apparent and the medieval church and monastery communities have also left their mark on the town. Among the many old build-

**Apoteksgården, one of Ystad's
many fine half-timbered houses**

ings is the 13th-century **Sta Mariakyrkan**, where every night the watchman in the tower declares that all is well by blowing his horn. In **Karl XII's Hus** on Stora Väster-gatan the warrior king is said to have spent the night in 1715 following his return from Turkey *(see p35)*.

Ystad has a number of museums, including **Ystads Konstmuseum** (Art Museum), **Ystads Hantverksmuseum** (Handicraft Museum) and a military museum. There is a fine theatre on the harbour-side, the home of the Ystad opera company.

ENVIRONS: High above the fishing community of Kåseberga lies the stone ship **Ales Stenar**. The 67-m (220-ft) monument comprises 58 stones and was probably created by the Vikings as a grave or a cult site.

Bollerups Borg, 20 km (12 miles) east of Ystad, is a 13th-century fortress which has been rebuilt several times. The fort is owned by an agricultural college, but is open to the public.

Sandhammaren is best known for its sandy beaches, but in the past was feared by sailors as new reefs were constantly forming around the cape. The lighthouse dates from 1862.

Svaneholm is one of the few Skåne castles which is open to the public. Built on an island in Lake Svanesjön, it was originally a fortress, but was converted into a Baroque castle with magnificent interiors around 1700.

Valleberga Kyrka lies 17 km (11 miles) east of Ystad and is the only round church in Skåne. It has a 12th-century font by Majestatis.

🏛 **Ystads Konstmuseum**
St Knuts Torg. 📞 *0411-577 285.*
⬜ *Tue–Sun.* ⬤ *public holidays.* 🎟 📷 ♿
🏛 **Ales Stenar**
Kåseberga. Road 9, 15 km (9 miles) E
of Ystad. 📞 *0411-57 76 81.* ⬜ *daily.*
🏛 **Svaneholm**
Skurup on E65, 20 km NW of Ystad.
📞 *0411-400 12.* ⬜ *Apr–Jun & Aug:
Tue–Sun; Jul: daily; Sep: Wed–Sun;
Oct: Sat–Sun; Nov–Mar: by
appointment* 🎟 🅿 🏛

A Tour of Österlen ⑭

THE NAME ÖSTERLEN means "the land to the east" and refers to the southeast corner of Skåne from Ravlunda south to Ystad and west to the Linderödsåsen ridge. The land is the most fertile in Sweden and across the rolling plains are many of the country's most treasured ancient monuments, grandest castles and forts and oldest churches. Along the coast, idyllic fishing villages are dotted like pearls on a string and the entire region has become a haven for painters and writers.

Apple orchard in spring, Kivik

Kivik ②
Kivik is best known for its annual market and apple orchards, but it is also a charming fishing village with winding streets and half-timbered houses.

Brösarps Backar ①
This nature reserve is awash with rare flowers. The sight of anemones and cowslips blooming in spring is particularly spectacular. The area has lots of walking trails.

Tomelilla ⑤
Tomelilla is an ideal starting point for a tour of Skåne's rolling countryside. Byagården, the town's Tudor-style farmstead, is considered one of the best examples of its kind in the region.

Simrishamn ③
Old low-rise houses give the town its character. Craftsmen lived around the square, Lilla Torg, and fishermen made their home by the harbour.

Glimmingehus ④
The evocative 16th-century knight's manor offers exciting ghost trails and a taste of medieval cooking.

Map labels: KRISTIANSTAD, Brösarps Backar ①, Ravlunda, Fågeltofta, St Olof, Kivik ②, Rörum, Vik, Baske-mölla, Smedstorp, Simrishamn ③, Hammenhög, Glimmingehus ④, Brante-vik, Skillinge, Glemminge-bro, Löderup, Ales Stenar, Sandhammaren, LUND, Tomelilla ⑤, YSTAD, BALTIC SEA

KEY
▬ Suggested route
═ Other roads

TIPS FOR DRIVERS

Length: around 55 km (34 miles). Major roads are of a good standard, but country roads can be in poorer condition.
Places to eat: cafés and/or restaurants are found in most towns. Hammenhög has a typical Skåne inn, ideal for a lunch break. Äpplets Hus, Kivik, is worth a look.

0 kilometres   10
0 miles   5

Heliga Trefaldighetskyrkan, a Renaissance church, Kristianstad

Kristianstad ⑮

Skåne. E22. 🏃 31,600. ✈ 🚃 🚌
ℹ️ Stora Torg, 044-12 19 88. 🎭
Christianstad Festival (10 days in
Jul). 🌐 www.kristianstad.se

T HE DANISH KING Christian IV
built the town of Kristianstad in the early 17th century
and the original street layout
with two gates can still be
seen today. The town's main
sight is **Heliga Trefaldighets-
kyrkan** (the Church of the
Holy Trinity) from the same
period, an excellent example
of Renaissance architecture. A
more recent attraction is the
eco-museum **Vattenriket**, a
35-km (22-mile) stretch of
wetlands on the Helgeån river.
It is best seen on a guided
river tour. Fishing permits can
be bought at the tourist office.

ENVIRONS: About 15 km (9
miles) to the northeast is
Bäckaskog Slott, a former
monastery dating from the
13th century, which was
rented by the Swedish royal
family during the 19th century.
The castle is set in beautiful
parkland with a herb garden.
    Rinkaby Kyrka lies halfway
between Kristianstad and
Åhus. The 13th-century church

contains paintings from the
15th century depicting the
seasons and farming life.
    Among the most idiosyn-
cratic objects to be seen at the
castle of **Trolle-Ljungby**, 10
km (6 miles) east of Kristianstad, are the Ljungby drinking
horn and pipe, which feature
in a local legend. On Wednes-
days and Saturdays in summer
they are exhibited in a window
facing the courtyard.
    The park of **Wanås Slott**,
20 km (12 miles) northwest of
Kristianstad, is a setting for
international contemporary art.
    Åhus, 14 km (9 miles) south-
east of Kristianstad, is a coastal
community with half-timbered
houses and sandy beaches.
There are 20 golf courses in a
50-km (30-mile) radius.

🪂 **Vattenriket**
ℹ️ Kristianstads Tourist Office, 044-12
19 88. 🅾 daily. 🎫 🛗 (some parts)
🌐 www.vattenriket.kristianstad.se

🏰 **Bäckaskog Slott**
Fjälkinge, 15 km (9 miles) NE of
Kristianstad. 🅲 044-532 20.
🅾 Apr–Sep: daily. 🎫 🔲 🛗
🏰 **Trolle-Ljungby**
Fjälkinge, 10 km (6 miles) NE of
Kristianstad. 🅲 044-550 43. 🅾 (park
& courtyard only) Jun–Sep: Wed & Sat.

Sölvesborg ⑯

Blekinge. E22. 🏃 16,500. 🚃 🚌 🚌
Repslagaregatan 1, 0456-100 88. 🎭
Nogerund Harbour Festival (early Jul).
🌐 www.solvesborg.se

I N THE MIDDLE AGES, Sölvesborg, on the cape of
Listerlandet, was an important
trading centre protected by a
castle. The town has a Danish
feel to it and still retains its
medieval charm. In a former
granary and distillery,
Sölvesborgs Museum traces
the history of Lister. The
town's oldest building is St
Nicolai Kyrka, a church

with parts dating from the
13th century.

ENVIRONS: West of Sölvesborg
and at the far end of the cape
lies the old town of **Hällevik**
with its traditional wooden
houses, fishing harbour,
smokery and guest harbour.
It also has a great little fishing
museum and is well worth
a visit.
    Ferries run from Nogersund
to the island of **Hanö** in
Hanöbukten bay. It's an
attractive place and a popular
destination for sailors. The
island served as an English
naval base in the Napoleonic
Wars in the early 19th century
and there is a graveyard here
for British seamen.

🏛 **Sölvesborgs Museum**
Skeppsbrogatan. 🅲 0456-161 57.
🅾 May–Aug: daily; Sep–Apr: by
arrangement.

Karlshamn ⑰

Blekinge. E22. 🏃 18,900. ✈ 🚃 🚌
ℹ️ Ronnebygatan 1, 0454-812 13
🎭 Baltic Festival (2nd week in Jul).

T HE TOWN OF Karlshamn
was founded in 1664. It
was planned as a naval base
and **Kastellet**, on the island
of Frisholmen, was built to
defend it. However, the naval
port role went to Karlskrona
(see pp188–9) and Karlshamn
became a trading centre with
a reputation for the production
of punsch. A reconstruction of
Punschfabriken, the factory
which produced the delectable
"Flaggpunsch" (see p293),
forms part of **Karlshamns
Museum**. Next to the punsch
factory is **Karlshamns
Konsthall** (Art Gallery).
    Other places of interest incl-
ude **Skottsbergska Gården**,
a merchant's house built in
1763 where both the living

Kastellet on the island of Frisholmen, Karlshamn

◁ **A carpet of white and yellow anemones on a spring day in Stenshuvud National Park** quarters and tobacco shop can be seen as they were in the 18th century. **Asschierska Huset** on Stortorget was Karlshamn's first town hall. The celebrated **Mörrumsån** salmon fishing river runs through the municipality.

ENVIRONS: Around 15 km (9 miles) east of Karlshamn is **Eriksbergs Vilt- och Naturpark**, one of the largest wildlife and nature sanctuaries in Europe and home to golden eagles.

Tjärö, in the idyllic Blekinge archipelago, is a 15-minute boat trip away.

🏛 **Karlshamns Museum**
Vinkelgatan 8. 📞 0454-148 68.
⭕ mid-Jun–mid-Aug: Tue–Sun. 🈺 ♿

Ronneby ⑱

Blekinge. E22. 🚶 11,900. ✕ 🚍 📮
ℹ Västra Torggatan 1, 0457-188 50.
🎪 Tosia Bonnadan Festival (2nd week in Jul). 🅦 www.ronneby.se

F OUNDED IN THE 13th century, Ronneby did not become Swedish until 1658. Prior to that, it was the main town of Blekinge and a busy trading centre. In 1564, during the Seven Years War with the Danes, it was overrun by the army of Erik XIV and burned. About 3,000 inhabitants – the majority of the population –

Renovated spa pavilions at Brunnsparken in Ronneby

were slaughtered in what became known as the Ronneby Bloodbath. In the early 19th century the town gained a new lease of life thanks to the Kockums foundry and enamel works in Kallinge and the Ronneby Brunn spa.

There are a few old buildings in Bergslagen and around Brunnskällan, and the beautiful 18th-century spa park has been restored.

ENVIRONS: Just east of Ronneby is the 13th-century church **Edestads Kyrka**, which once served as a defensive fort. A remarkable 4-m (13-ft) high, 8th-century runestone, **Björketorpsstenen**, lies 7 km (4 miles) east of the town. The text inscribed on the stone is a curse.

Hjortsberga Grave Field on the Johannishus ridge contains 120 ancient burial mounds. About 12 km (7 miles) northeast of Ronneby is **Johannishus Åsar**, a nature reserve set in beautiful pasture land.

Kristianopel ⑲

Blekinge. E22. 🚶 1,500. 📮 📇
ℹ Stortorget 2, 0455-30 34 90. 🎪
Medieval Market (4th week in Aug).

E NJOYING A beautiful location on a peninsula in Kalmarsund, the little fortified town of Kristianopel has become a popular summer haunt with a guest harbour and tourist facilities. It was built by the Danish King Christian IV and gained its town charter in 1600. At the Peace of Roskilde in 1658 it became Swedish. Garden lovers head for **Rosengården**, a private garden filled with more than 500 different varieties of old roses.

ENVIRONS: Brömsebro lies 8 km (5 miles) north of Kristianopel, just inland from the coast. Here on the border between Blekinge and Småland is where peace with Denmark was declared in 1645, when Jämtland, Härjedalen and Gotland once more became Swedish provinces. The negotiations were held on an islet in Brömsebäcken river and a commemorative stone was raised here in 1915. At the mouth of the river are the ruins of Brömsehus, a fortress which was captured in 1436 by Swedish rebel hero Engelbrekt (see p33).

🌹 **Rosengården**
📞 0455-36 62 36. ⭕ mid-May–mid-Sep: daily; other times: by appointment. ♿

SALMON FISHING IN MÖRRUMSÅN

Every year the salmon fishing in the Mörrumsån river attracts enthusiasts from all over the world. Fishing here dates back to the 13th century when the king held all the rights. The river flows through a beautiful landscape from Lake Vrången in the north to the sea at Elleholm via the lakes of Helgasjön and Åsnen.

A fishing permit is required and these cost between 300 and 500 kr per day. During the 2003 season 1,160 salmon were caught here, the record catch weighing in at 17.98 kg (39.6 lbs).

Laxens Hus (Salmon World) in Mörrum gathers together everything to do with fishing and mounts a variety of exhibitions on, for example, the animal life of the river, and the history of the sport.

Fly-fishing for salmon in Mörrumsån

Karlskrona ⑳

Karl XI, the town's founder

THE NAVAL TOWN OF KARLSKRONA is built over several islands in the Blekinge archipelago. Granted a town charter in 1680, it was planned by Erik Dahlbergh and is said to have been inspired by both Versailles and Rome. It centres around the two squares, Stortorget on the island of Trossö, and Amiralitetstorget. The decision to locate Sweden's main naval base in Karlskrona was taken because in winter the fleet was often ice-bound in Stockholm, and an ice-free port was needed further south. Karlskrona has a number of outstanding sights from Sweden's Age of Greatness (*see pp36–7*). In 1998 the town was declared a UNESCO World Heritage Site on account of its naval architecture.

Fredrikskyrkan on Stortorget, designed by Tessin the Younger in Baroque style, 1744

🏛 Grevagården/Blekinge Museum

Fisktorget 2. 📞 0455-30 49 60. ⭘ *mid-Jun–mid-Aug: daily; rest of the year: Tue–Sun.* ⭘ *some public holidays.*

Grevagården on Fisktorget is the main building of Blekinge Museum. The building dates from the early 18th century and was the home of Admiral-General Hans Wachtmeister – the café is set in what was once his kitchen and store room. The museum focuses on the history of Blekinge and Karlskrona's heyday. There is a small Baroque garden reached via a double staircase flanked by two yew trees, believed to date from 1704. Outside on

the square stands the statue of the *Fisherwoman* by Erik Höglund.

🎪 Stortorget

The imposing square – said to be the largest in northern Europe – is flanked, in the Baroque tradition, by two impressive churches, both designed by the architect Nicodemus Tessin the Younger.

Fredrikskyrkan is a large basilica consecrated in 1744, but characterized by the 17th-century taste for Baroque lines. The southern tower has 35 bells which ring three times a day. The other church, Heliga Trefaldighets-kyrkan (Holy Trinity), is also known as the German Church after Admiral-General Hans Wachtmeister who inspired it and is buried in the crypt. It was completed in 1709. After a fire in 1790 the church was rebuilt with a lower dome than its predecessor.

The town hall, completed in 1798, has been rebuilt several times. Today it serves as the seat of Karlskrona district court.

Vattenborgen, the now protected water tower, was built in 1863 to supply Trossö with fresh water. It was replaced by a water tower outside the town in 1939.

🏛 Marinmuseum

Stumholmen. 📞 0455-539 02. ⭘ *Jun–Aug: daily; Sep–May: Tue–Sun.* 🌐 www.marinmuseum.se

The fascinating naval museum, opened in 1997, stands on the harbour on Stumholmen, an island which for almost 300 years has been part of the main base of the Swedish navy. The museum was founded originally in 1752 by King Adolf Fredrik to collect and document naval objects in what was known as Modellkammaren (the Model Room).

Marinmuseum covers every imaginable aspect of maritime activity. It holds a particularly impressive collection of figureheads, weapons and uniforms. From an under-water glass corridor it is possible to see the wreck of an 18th-century ship lying on the bottom of the sea.

One of the world's smallest full-rigged ships, *Jarramas*, a training ship for naval ratings, is moored on the quay outside the museum, along with the minesweeper *Bremön* and the torpedo boat *T38*. The Sloop and Long-Boat Shed contains an exhibition of working boats and often allows visitors the opportunity to see how old wooden boats are restored.

Marinmuseum, showcase for Karlskrona's naval heritage

🎪 Gamla Örlogsvarvet

Högvakten, Amiralitetstorget 1. 📞 0455-30 34 91. ⭘ *Jun–Aug: daily.* 🅿 compulsory.

The Karlskrona shipyard, founded in 1679, became over time one of the country's foremost military shipyards, a position it still holds today. Fortifications and buildings were constructed to build, equip and repair warships. Additional buildings went up on the islands of Lindholmen,

The "Old Man" Rosenbom poor-box outside Amiralitetskyrkan

Söderstjärna and Stumholmen. The only way to see this vast naval harbour and its many 18th-century buildings and workshops is to take a guided tour. Among the most interesting sights in Gamla Örlogsvarvet are the 300-m (984-ft) long Rope Walk, where the rigging for the fleet was manufactured, the Wasa Shed and Polhem Dock on Lindholmen and Five-finger Dock and the Old Mast Crane in the western part of the shipyard. It is the existence of buildings such as these, and the fact that Karlskrona is such a well-preserved example of a late-17th-century planned naval base, that has earned the town World Heritage Site status. Karlskrona was a model for other naval bases throughout Europe in the 18th century.

Close to the entrance to the old shipyard, Högvakten, is Amiralitetskyrkan (the Admiralty church). Consecrated in 1685, it is Sweden's largest wooden church. In front of the church is a replica of the Gubben "Old Man" Rosenbom poor-box.

Today's high-tech shipyard, Karlskronavarvet, run by Kockums, is not open to the public, but new vessels can often be seen along the quay.

🚌 Skärfva Herrgård

5 km (3 miles) W of centre, E 22. **🕿** 0455-490 03. ☐ daily (park). ☐ ☑

In 1785 the ship designer Fredrik Henrik af Chapman built a summer house on the shore between Karlskrona and Nättraby. The building is an unusual mix of a traditional Blekinge cottage open to the roof space and other architectural styles, including an entrance reminiscent of a Doric temple in front of an octagonal cupola crowned with a lantern.

Inside, several rooms are preserved in their original state, including af Chapman's workroom in the form of a ship's cabin. The house is set in an English-style park with a temple-like summer house.

The surroundings are part of Skärfva Nature Reserve which protects the flora and fauna of the manor house estate.

During the summer boats run daily from Karlskrona to Skärfva.

VISITORS' CHECKLIST

Blekinge. 🏠 32,000. ✈ 25 km W of centre. 🚉 🚌 Järnvägsstationsgatan. ⚓ Skeppsbrokajen (Gdynia). 🚩 Stortorget 2, 0455-30 34 90. 🛒 Gardeners' Market (Thu before Midsummer). 🎉 Sail Karlskrona (last weekend in Jul), Bastion Aurora Music Festival (last week in Jul).

KARLSKRONA TOWN CENTRE

Gamla Örlogsvarvet ④
Grevagården/Blekinge Museum ①
Karlskronavarvet ⑤
Marinmuseum ③
Stortorget ②

KEY

🚉	Railway station
🚌	Bus terminal
🅿	Parking
✝	Church
🛈	Tourist information

GOTHENBURG

THE PEOPLE OF GOTHENBURG *have nicknamed their city "the face of Sweden". This maritime metropolis has for centuries been one of Sweden's gateways to the outside world. Historically, the Göta Älv river was the country's only outlet to the west, as can be seen by the remains of fortresses and earthworks that once protected it. Gothenburg is still Sweden's most important port and holds fast to its maritime past.*

With its great harbour and seafaring traditions, it is perhaps only natural that Sweden's second largest city is also its most outward looking. Visitors are always welcome and it is not for nothing that the entertainment on offer and the atmosphere have led to Gothenburg being called "Little London".

Today's Gothenburg (Göteborg in Swedish) was preceded by four earlier towns along the Göta Älv river. These were pawns in a period of constant conflict between Sweden and Denmark. The first town was built by Dutch settlers on the island of Hisingen in the early 17th century. It was hardly established before Gustav II Adolf decided in 1619 that it should be moved to the area where the suburbs of Vallgraven and Nordstaden now stand. The inhabitants still came from Holland and the grid of canals is reminiscent of Amsterdam. Gothenburg's 17th-century incarnation was as a fortified town created by the architect and field marshal Erik Dahlbergh. The 18th century saw Gothenburg become even more cosmopolitan thanks to German, English and Scottish immigration. With the advent of steam power, the shipping industry flourished in the mid-19th century, and the city became a prominent shipbuilding centre. The shipyards have mostly gone, but Gothenburg is still a major industrial city and home of the car manufacturer Volvo.

This vibrant little metropolis of 500,000 people (famous for their particular wittiness) is ideal for sightseeing, and is peppered with green spaces, such as the Botanical Gardens and the amusement park, Liseberg. It is a good starting point for excursions to the west coast islands with their pretty fishing villages and smooth rocks for bathing.

Gothenburg's Botanical Gardens, a green oasis not far from the centre of the city

◁ **An old windjammer, the barque *Viking*, at Lilla Bommen in Gothenburg's inner harbour**

Exploring Gothenburg

A GOOD QUICK WAY to get an overview of Gothenburg is
to see the city from one of the many excellent observation points such as GötheborgsUtkiken, Sjömanstornet
or LisebergsTornet. The central parts of the town lie south
of the Göta Älv river, but it is easy to cross to the large
island of Hisingen by ferry, or by car via the Götaälvbron
or Älvsborgsbron bridges, or the Tingstad tunnel.
Gothenburg has retained its excellent tram network
which provides an ideal way to tour the town, especially
on the vintage carriages of the Ringlinjen line. Paddan's
white tour boats *(see p205)* operate trips along the
17th-century canals and out into the lively harbour.

**Feskekörka fish market reflecting in
the water of the Rosenlund Canal**

SIGHTS AT A GLANCE

KEY

▢	Gothenburg Street-by-Street *see pp194–5*
🚋	Tram stop
🚌	Bus terminal
🚉	Railway station
⛴	Ferry and tour-boat boarding
P	Parking
ℹ	Tourist information

0 metres

0 yards   50

GETTING TO GOTHENBURG

The sea has always been the key to Gothenburg and ferries run daily from Norway, Denmark, Germany and the UK. Fast trains whisk travellers from Stockholm or Malmö in three hours. A well-developed commuter train network and express bus lines ease regional trips. The E6 along the west coast and the E20 from Stockholm meet at the Göta Älv river. Landvetter international airport is Sweden's second largest airport with direct flights to many domestic and international destinations.

Poseidon by Milles in Götaplatsen

CENTRAL GOTHENBURG

0 kilometres 2

0 miles 1

Street-by-Street: Västra Nordstan

T HIS PART OF GOTHENBURG is the pulse of the
seafaring city, encapsulating almost 400 years of
history. On the quayside along the Göta Älv river the
maritime world is ever present, with museum ships at
anchor and the constant to-ing and fro-ing of boats
and ferries. Spectacular new buildings, such as
GöteborgsOperan and GötheborgsUtkiken, contrast
with the city's historic monuments. These include the
East India Company building on Stora Hamnkanalen, a
reminder of the Dutch influence on Gothenburg's
design, and Kronhuset, the city's oldest secular
building. Shoppers should head for nearby Östra
Nordstan and its department stores and galleries.

GöteborgsOperan
*Generous donations
enabled the building of the
long-awaited Opera House,
which opened in 1994* ❸

★ Göteborgs Maritima Centrum
*In the harbour is one of the world's largest
floating ship museums. Both the destroyer*
Småland, *launched 1952 (in the background), and the submarine* Nordkaparen, *1962, can be boarded.* ❹

**Ture
Rinman
footbridge**

Göteborgs Stadsmuseum
*The former East India Company's
classical 18th-century headquarters
building is now the setting for
Göteborgs Stadsmuseum* ❼

STAR SIGHTS

**★ Göteborgs Maritima
Centrum**

★ Barken Viking

KEY

- - - Suggested route

GötheborgsUtkiken

The top of the striped skyscraper provides an excellent view over the river and the bustling harbour below ❶

LOCATOR MAP
See map pp192–3

Lilla Bommen marina

Torsten Henrikssons footbridge

Nordstan shopping mall

★ **Barken Viking**

After a lifetime on the high seas, the 1906 barque, Viking, *lies at anchor in the harbour. It now serves as a restaurant and hotel* ❷

Gustav Adolfs Torg

"The town shall be here," pointed King Gustav II Adolf, as depicted by Bengt Erland Fogelberg's statue (1854). The anniversary of the king's death at the Battle of Lützen on 6 November 1632 is commemorated in the square every year ❻

ÖSTRA HAMNGATAN

POSTGATAN

GUSTAV ADOLFS TORG

NORRA HAMNGATAN

Kungs-torget

0 metres   200

0 yards   200

Kronhuset and Kronhusbodarna

Next to the 17th-century Kronhuset, the Kronhusbodarna sheds are now occupied by craft-workers and restaurants ❺

GötheborgsUtkiken (the"Lipstick"), and the sailing ship *Viking*

Götheborgs-Utkiken ❶

Lilla Bommen 2. **C** *031-15 61 47.* 🚋 *5, 10.* 🚌 *40, 41, 52, 85, 140.* 🏛 *mid-May–mid-Aug: 10am–4pm daily; other times: 11am–4pm Mon–Fri.* 💻 📷

THE CHEEKY RED and white GötheborgsUtkiken office building has dominated the Lilla Bommen harbour area since 1989. Architects Ralph Erskine and Heikki Särg's daring design was soon christened the "Lipstick" by Gothenburg wits. Standing 86 m (282 ft) above sea level, it offers incredible views over the harbour and the city centre from the top floor.

Barken Viking ❷

Gullbergskajen. **C** *031-63 58 00.* 🚋 *5, 10.* 🚌 *40, 41, 52, 85, 140.* 🏛 *daily.* ⬤ *22–31 Dec.* 💻 *summer.* 🍴 ♿ *limited access.*

ONE OF THE WORLD'S few preserved four-masted barques from the great age of sail is permanently moored in Gothenburg. The *Viking* was built in 1906 by the Copenhagen shipyard Burmeister & Wain. She sailed the wheat route to Australia and shipped guano from Chile in South America. A fast and beautiful vessel, she logged a record speed of 15.5 knots in 1909. Her days as a merchant ship ended in 1948. In 1950 she

became a training centre for sailors and chefs.

Today, the *Viking* is an unusual setting for an hotel and conference centre. In summer the 97 m (318 ft) deck becomes a popular harbourside café, restaurant and bar, with a very lively, bustling atmosphere.

Göteborgs-Operan ❸

Christina Nilssons Gata. **C** *031-13 13 00.* 🚋 *5, 10.* 🚌 *40, 41, 52, 80, 85, 140.* 🏛 *mid Aug–Jun: in conjunction with performances; other times: phone for info.* ⬤ *24, 25, 31 Dec, 1 May, Good Friday.* 📷 ♿ 🎫 *book.* 💻 🍴 🏛 **W** www.opera.se

THE 1994 OPENING of the impressive Opera House reflected in the water of the Göta Älv river had been eagerly anticipated by western Sweden's music lovers. This is shown by the vast donation wall listing the names of the 6,000 people who helped to fund the new building.

The theatre is designed on a grand scale in every sense. The octagonal auditorium has the capacity for an audience of 1,300, all able to enjoy the excellent acoustics. The main stage covering 500 sq m (5,380 sq ft) is complemented by a further four equally large

The striking exterior of the riverside GöteborgsOperan, the city's main venue for opera, musicals and ballet

areas for storing sets. Using advanced technology, it is possible to switch quickly between productions, thus enabling the Opera House to stage a repertoire of opera, musicals and ballet.

Architect Jan Izikowitz was inspired by Gothenburg's harbourside location, the aim of his design being for the "building to be possessed by a lightness which encourages thoughts to soar like seagulls' wings over the mighty river landscape".

Gustav Adolfs Torg flanked on its north side by Börsen, built in 1859

The destroyer *Småland*, 1952, in Göteborgs Maritima Centrum

Göteborgs Maritima Centrum **4**

Packhuskajen 8. **C** *031-10 59 50.* **☐** *5,10.* **☐** *40, 41, 52, 85, 140.* **☐** *May–Aug: 10am–6pm daily; Nov: 10am–4pm Fri–Sun; other times: 10am–4pm daily.* **☐ ☐**

A S THE CITY'S new port facilities moved further out towards the sea, Gothenburg's inner harbour became denuded of ships. Fortunately, the situation was rectified in 1987 when Göteborgs Maritima Centrum was set up on the harbour. The museum now has 18 vessels at anchor, comprising what is said to be the world's largest floating ship museum.

Vessels include the destroyer *Småland*, built in 1952 at Eriksbergs shipyard on the other side of the river, the submarine *Nordkaparen* (1962), and the monitor *Sölve* (1875), as well as lightships, fireboats and tugs.

Kronhuset **5**

Postgatan 6–8. **☐** *1, 3, 4, 5, 6, 7, 9, 10, 11.* **☐** *40, 41, 50, 52, 58, 60, 85, 86, 91, 140, 771.* **☐ ☐ ☐**

A GRAND BRICK building in Dutch style, Kronhuset was constructed in 1643–55 and is Gothenburg's oldest preserved secular building. This part of town was originally a storage area for the artillery. The ground floor of Kronhuset was converted into a chamber for the parliament of 1660.

Today, the building is used for concerts and exhibitions. The second floor is devoted to an exhibition illustrating Gothenburg in Sweden's Age of Greatness (see pp36–7).

Around the square are Kronhusbodarna (the Kronhus sheds), which create a

Mid-17th-century Kronhuset, one of Gothenburg's oldest buildings

pleasant setting for crafts people, an old-fashioned country store and glassworks.

Gustav Adolfs Torg **6**

☐ *1, 3, 4, 5, 6, 7, 9, 10, 11.* **☐** *40, 41, 50, 52, 58, 60, 85, 86, 91, 140, 771.* **Rådhuset** **☐** *8am–4.30pm daily.* **☐** *public holidays.* **Stadshuset** **☐** *to the public.* **Börsen** **☐** *to the public.*

G OTHENBURG'S founder, Gustav II Adolf, gave his name to the city's central square. Since 1854 Bengt Erland Fogelberg's statue of the "hero king" has gazed imperiously over the square and Rådhuset (the Town Hall), Börsen (the Stock Exchange) and Stadshuset (the City Hall).

On 6 November, the date on which the king died at the Battle of Lützen in 1632, schoolchildren parade in his honour here and a special marzipan cake is made in the shape of the king's head.

Rådhuset, closest to Norra Hamngatan, was designed by Nicodemus Tessin the Elder (see p24) and completed in 1673. It has a Functionalist extension designed in 1937 by Gunnar Asplund (see p99).

The 18th-century **Stadshuset** and Wenngrenska Villa on the north side of the square are used by the city administration. **Börsen**, designed by P J Ekman in 1849, is the city's main venue for receptions and council meetings.

Ostindiska Huset (East India House) housing Göteborgs Stadsmuseum

Göteborgs Stadsmuseum ❼

Norra Hamngatan 12. 【 *031-61 27 70.* ▤ *1–11.* ▦ *40, 41, 50, 52, 58, 60, 85, 86, 91, 140, 771.* ⏰ *Sep– Apr: 10am–5pm Tue–Sun, 10am–8pm Wed; May–Aug: 10am–5pm daily.* ▣ ▥ *pre-book.* ▤ ⬛ &

T HE CITY MUSEUM is aptly located in the historic Ostindiska Huset (East India House). The building, designed by Bengt Wilhelm Carlberg and Carl Härleman, was constructed in 1747–62 as management premises, auction rooms and a ware-house for the East India

Chinese plate in the collection of Göteborgs Stadsmuseum

Company. When trading ceased in the early 19th century the building became a natural history museum, and in 1861 the City Museum was founded.

The permanent exhibitions show the early history of Western Sweden and the importance of the Göta Älv river as a route to Europe from the Viking period onwards. Displays focus on the history of the first inhabitants of Gothenburg and the industrialization and social upheavals of the 20th century. The work of the East India Company and its trade in exotic goods such as Chinese porcelain, silk and lacquer work, is also featured.

Domkyrkan ❽

Västra Hamngatan. 【 *031-731 61 50.* ▤ *1, 2, 6, 9, 11.* ▦ *60.* ⏰ *daily.* ▥ *pre-book.* ⬛ *summer.* & ⬛ *daily.*

G OTHENBURG'S cathedral, Gustavi Domkyrka, was designed by C W Carlberg in

Neo-Classical style in 1815–25. It stands on the ruins of its two predecessors, which were both destroyed by fire.

In front of the cathedral in Domkyrkoplan is one of the city's preserved watering places: from the late 18th century water was transported here in hollowed-out oak logs from the well of Gustafs Källa to the south of the city.

Gustavi Domkyrka's impressive gilded altar-piece

Trädgårds-föreningen ❾

Slussgatan. 【 *031-365 58 58.* ▤ *1, 3–9, 11, 13, 14.* ▦ *25, 28, 29, 34, 58, 60, 61, 514.* **Park** ⏰ *May–Aug: 7am–9pm daily, Sep–Apr: 7am– 7.30pm.* ▣ ▥ ▤ ⬛ &. **Palm House** 【 *031-41 57 73. Sep–Apr: 10am–4pm daily; May–Aug: 10am–5pm daily.* ⬤ *24, 25 & 31 Dec.* ▣ &.

G OTHENBURG HAS many parks, but Trädgårds-föreningen is in a class of its own. In 1842 work began to transform a marshland south of Vallgraven into beautiful parkland for the benefit of the city's residents.

The flora of five continents are represented in the magnificent Palmhuset (Palm House) built in 1878. The building is filled with flowering camellias, giant bamboo, exotic orchids and plenty of palm trees.

Vattenhuset (the Water House) is carpeted by the twisting roots of mangrove trees and the 2-m (6-ft) wide petals of the giant water-lily.

The Rosarium is not to be missed, especially by rose lovers. It has become a leading world collection with more than 2,000 varieties.

There are cafés in the park and Trägár'n, a restaurant and

THE EAST INDIA COMPANY

Attracted by goods such as tea, silk and porcelain, Sweden was one of the countries which invested in trade with China in the 18th century and Gothenburg became a natural centre for this highly lucrative industry. The Swedish East India Company received its charter in 1731 and operated for 82 years, based in Ostindiska Huset (*see above*). In total, 132

The East Indiaman *Wasa* at Nya Älvsborgs Fästning

expeditions were made to China in 38 different ships. In recent years interest in the work of the Company has resulted in the building of the East Indiaman *Götheborg*. This exact replica of the ship, which sank off Nya Älvsborgs Fästning (*see p205*) on its homeward voyage 250 years ago, was built at the Terra Nova shipyard in Eriksberg. In 2005 the ship set out to sail the traditional trade route to Canton.

Trädgårdsföreningen's Palmhuset, containing plants and trees from five continents in various climatic zones

nightclub which has been entertaining pleasure-seeking locals since the 19th century. It is now housed in a new building with a large open-air terrace for partying.

Ullevi ⑩

Skånegatan. [031- 81 10 20. 🚋 1, 3, 6. 🚌 51, 60. 🔘 during events. 🔲 &

SWEDEN'S LARGEST sporting arena, Ullevi, opened for the 1958 football World Cup and over the years has hosted numerous international events. Architect Fritz Jaenecke's elegant wave-shaped ellipse has been renovated and modernized several times. The arena seats 43,000 spectators for sporting events and can accommodate an audience of 60,000 for concerts.

On the other side of Skånegatan, in front of Gamla Ullevi football stadium, is a statue of Gunnar Gren (1920–91), one of Sweden's greatest-ever footballers.

Röhsska Museet ⑪

Vasagatan 37–39. [031-61 38 50. 🚋 3, 4, 5, 7, 10. 🚌 40, 41, 58, 140. 🔘 noon–9pm Tue, noon–5pm Wed–Sun. ● Good Friday. 📷 pre-book. 🔲 📷 &
🆆 www.designmuseum.se

THE COUNTRY'S leading museum of applied art and design, Röhsska Museet contains a marvellous collection of 20th-century Nordic domestic and decorative items. Other parts of the museum are devoted to European applied art, and antiquities from the ancient world, Japan and China. A

mere fraction of the total of 50,000 objects can be displayed at any one time. Specialist temporary exhibitions are also mounted.

The museum was founded with donations from financiers Wilhelm and August Röhss. It opened in 1916 as the Röhss Museum of Handicrafts in the beautiful brick building designed by architect Carl Westman.

Next to the museum is the University College for Arts and Crafts Design.

Chinese sculpture, Röhsska Museet

Universeum ⑫

Korsvägen. [031-335 64 50. 🚋 4 5, 6, 7, 8, 13, 14. 🚌 50, 51, 52, 61, 761, 771. 🔘 Jan–Apr & mid-Aug–Dec: 11am–6pm Tue, Thu–Sun, 11am–8pm Wed; May–Jun & 1st week in Nov: 10am–6pm Mon–Fri (to 8pm Wed), 11am–6pm Sat–Sun; Jul–mid-Aug: 9am–7pm daily. 📷 🔲
📷 & 🆆 www.universeum.se

ALONG THE Mölndalsån river, not far from Kungsportsavenyn, spreads an area containing several of Gothenburg's major sights

Universeum, designed by Gert Wingårdh and built in 2001

and venues, including Liseberg (see p200), Ullevi and Scandinavium sporting arenas and the conference centre Svenska Mässan.

The Universeum science centre is the latest addition. Opened in 2001, the environmentally friendly building was designed by Gothenburg architect Gert Wingårdh and voted Sweden's best contemporary building in the same year. The centre aims to stimulate the interest of children and young people in science and technology. Here, they can come face-to-face with exotic creatures such as sting-rays and anacondas, study galaxies and moon buggies and conduct ingenious experiments.

Världskulturmuseet ⑬

Södra Vägen 54. [031-63 27 30. 🚋 4, 5, 6, 7, 8, 13, 14. 🚌 50, 51, 52, 61. 🔘 noon–5pm Tue, Sat–Sun, noon–9pm Wed–Fri. 📷 🔲 📷 &
🆆 www.varldskulturmuseet.se

DESIGNED by the London-based architects Cécile Brisac and Edgar Gonzalez, the icecube-like Världskulturmuseet is a new museum of world cultures, completed in 2005. The exhibitions, like the building, are far from traditional; they are intended to surprise, provoke and question stereotyped attitudes towards culture and subculture, and are complemented by a programme of concerts, films, dance and poetry.

Konstmuseet on Götaplatsen, the city's main square, with Carl Milles' statue of Poseidon in the foreground

Liseberg ⑭

Örgrytevägen 1. 🚋 5 🚌 50, 61. 📞 031-400 100. ⏰ last week in Apr–last week in Sep: opening times vary. 📷 🚻 🅿 ♿ 🍴 🌐 www.liseberg.se

THE PEOPLE OF Gothenburg are rightly proud of their amusement park which attracts huge numbers of visitors. Apart from the latest rides, this is the place for dancing and entertainment, shows and theatre performances. It is also a beautiful green park where garden design has always played a major role.

The park's history began in the 18th century when financier Johan Anders Lamberg bought the land and built the first magnificent house, Landeriet, in 1753. He had two passions in life –

Flower Girl by Gerhard Henning in Liseberg park

gardening and his wife Lisa, after whom the new house on the hill was named, Liseberg.

The City of Gothenburg bought the site for the Gothenburg Exhibition in 1923 and founded the amusement park with the installation of an impressive wooden roller-coaster. Other rides followed, attracting 140 million visitors over the past 80 years. In 2003, a new roller-coaster, named after the Norse god "Balder", opened. Also built out of wood, Balder is the biggest roller-coaster in the Nordic countries. It reaches a speed of 90 km/h (56 mph) from a top height of 36 m (118 ft). "Kanonen", opened in 2004, offers another extreme experience, with its rapid acceleration, sharp loops and turns and 360-degree rotation.

Götaplatsen ⑮

🚋 4, 5. 🚌 40, 41, 58. **Konstmuseet** 📞 031-61 29 80. ⏰ 11am–6pm Tue, Thu, Fri; 11am–9pm Wed; 11am–5pm Fri, Sun & public holidays. ⬤ 24, 25 & 31 Dec, Good Friday, 1 May, Midsummer. 📷 ♿ 🚻 🍴 **Konsthallen** 📞 031-61 50 40. ⏰ as Konstmuseet. 📷 ♿ 🚻 🍴 **Konserthuset** ⏰ for concerts. 📞 031-726 53 10. **Stadsteatern** 📞 031-61 50 55. ⏰ for performances.

THE FOCAL POINT of the city is Götaplatsen, the square at the southwestern end of Kungsportsavenyn. Here Gothenburg's bastions of culture, Konstmuseet (the Art Museum), Konsthallen (the Art Hall), Konserthuset (the Concert Hall), Stadsteatern (the City Theatre) and Stadsbiblioteket (the City Library) sit in state. In the centre of this grand square, the water plays around Carl Milles' giant statue *Poseidon*, which has become the symbol of Gothenburg.

Götaplatsen was built for the city's 300th anniversary and the Gothenburg Exhibition in 1923, which is why many of the buildings were exhibition premises from the start. Wide steps lead up from the southeastern side of the square to **Konstmuseet**, designed by Sigfrid Ericson, which became a museum in 1925. It contains a rich collection of Nordic art, with key works by Carl Larsson, Ernst Josephson and the Gothenburg Colourists. The

Liseberg's main stage and venue for shows, bands, acrobats and more

Danish golden age, Dutch and Flemish painting and French Modernists are also represented. Pride of place is taken by Furstenbergska Galleriet, a copy of the gallery which the great patron of the arts had in his private palace in the late 19th century. The neighbouring **Konsthallen** shows temporary exhibitions. The bronze lion on the façade is by Palle Pernevi.

Konserthuset on the south-western side of the square was designed by Nils Einar Eriksson and opened in 1935. The foyer is decorated with murals by Prince Eugen *(Grove of Memories)* and Otte Sköld *(Folk Song)* as well as a large tapestry by Sven X-et Erixson *(Melodies in the Square)*.

Stadsteatern, built in 1934, reopened in 2002 after extensive renovation to highlight the best of Carl Bergsten's elegant 1930's architecture.

Skansen Kronan fortress (1687) on guard high above Gothenburg

Skansen Kronan ⑯

Skansberget. 🚋 6. 🚌 80, 760, 764, 765. ☎ 0705-20 88 08. ◯ Tue noon–2pm, Sat–Sun noon–3pm. ● public holidays. 🎟 📷 pre-book. ♿ limited access.

TOPPED BY A GOLDEN crown, the octagonal Skansen Kronan fortress dates from Sweden's Age of Greatness *(see pp36–7)*. It sits enthroned on the peak of Skansberget. Like its counterpart Skansen Lejonet, near the station area, Kronan is one of the most striking survivors of Erik Dahlbergh's fortifications. It was built in 1687 to protect the city from attack from the south.

The fortress is now a military museum displaying uniforms and weapons. It is surrounded by Skansberget, a leafy park offering excellent views from the top, up steep steps.

Walkers and shoppers in Gamla Haga with its pleasant wooden houses

Gamla Haga ⑰

🚋 1, 3, 6, 9, 11. 🚌 80, 85, 760, 764, 765.

THE FORMER working-class area of the city south of Vallgraven is one of the few places to experience old Gothenburg. The cobbled streets, courtyards and wooden houses of Gamla Haga are home to craftspeople and lined with small shops, cafés and restaurants.

Haga was Gothenburg's first suburb as early as the 17th century and was mainly populated by harbour workers. During the industrialization of the 19th century a shanty town grew up here and tenements filled with people thronging in from the countryside to seek work.

In the 1960s and 70s Haga was fast becoming a slum and threatened with demolition. Widespread public opposition to the plans ensured that important parts were saved and the houses renovated. Some of the *landshövdinge-husen* ("county governor's houses") typical of the area can be seen. These were built in the 1880s, when rules set in 1854 banning wooden houses

in the centre more than two storeys high were circumvented – with the governor's approval. Providing the building had a ground floor in brick, as these do, it could have two wooden floors above and not constitute a fire risk.

Feskekörka ⑱

Rosenlundsgatan. 🚋 3, 6, 9, 11. 🚌 80, 85, 760, 764, 765. ◯ 9am–5pm Tue–Thu; 9am–6pm Fri; 11am–2pm Sat. ● public holidays. 🖥 🍴 ♿

IT IS EASY TO SEE why the wits of Gothenburg nicknamed the fish market Feskekörka (the fish church). Victor von Gegerfelt borrowed from Gothic church architecture when he designed this market hall in 1874, incorporating a steeply pitched roof and large oriel windows.

The catch from the North Sea is brought here directly, guaranteeing the freshest mackerel and the most delicious shellfish. These days there is more to the market than simply selling fish over the counter – the hall provides a colourful setting for restaurant tables at which seafood specialities can be sampled.

Feskekörka fish market, a paradise for lovers of fish and seafood

Sjöfartsmuseet and Akvariet ⑲

Karl Johansgatan 1–3. **(** 031-61 29 00. **☐** 3, 9 and 11. **◯** Sep–Apr: 9am–4pm Tue, Thu & Fri, 9am–9pm Wed; 11am–5pm Sat, Sun & public holidays; May–Aug: 10am–5pm daily. **●** Good Friday, 1 May, Midsummer's Eve, Midsummer. **▨ ✔** phone for info. **ё ⌂ ▢**
Sjömanstornet (0731-81 56 00. **◯** groups only, phone for info. **▨** **W** www.sjofartsmuseum.goteborg.se

Gathenhielmska Huset, once the home of Privateer Captain Lars Gathenhielm

THE MARITIME history of Gothenburg and Bohuslän is the subject of Sjöfartsmuseet (the Maritime Museum). Set up in 1933, it was funded by the Broström shipping family and is situated on Stigberget, high above the Göta Älv river.

The work of Sweden's largest port, changes in the shipbuilding industry over the centuries and the history of Gothenburg's many shipping lines come under the spotlight. Fishing from the medieval herring period to today also features prominently.

Akvariet (the Aquarium) is dedicated to the marine life of the west coast. Here, it is possible to see how crabs, starfish and sea anemones live 40 m (130 ft) below the surface.

Gamla Varvsparken contains various busts including one of the shipbuilder F H af Chapman (1721–1808) (see p77).

Sjömanstornet tower outside the museum is topped by Ivar Johansson's bronze sculpture *Woman by the Sea*, 1933, in memory of the sailors from western Sweden who died in World War I.

The sculpture *Woman by the Sea* topping the "sailors' tower"

Gathenhielmska Huset ⑳

Allmänna Vägen. **☐** 3, 9, 11. **●** to the public apart from the café. **▢**

THE WESTERN side of the Stigberget hill was formerly the site of the Amiralitetsvarvet shipyard and it was here in the early 1700s that Privateer Captain Lars Gathenhielm was granted land by Karl XII. His widow built a two-storey manor house here in 1740. It is one of Sweden's best examples of a Carolian wooden house designed to imitate stone.

Next to the house is an open-air museum of small wooden houses showing what a suburb looked like in 1800.

Slottsskogen and Naturhistoriska Museet ㉑

Linnéplatsen. **▤** 80, 51, 52, 760, 764, 765. **☐** 1, 6. **Naturhistoriska museet (** 031-775 24 00. **◯** Sep–Apr: 9am–4pm Tue–Fri, 11am–5pm Sat–Sun; (Feb–Mar: to 9pm Wed); May–Aug: 11am–5pm daily; 2 May–13 Jun: 9am–5pm Mon–Fri. **●** Good Friday. **▨** **✔** phone to book. **ⓗ ▢ ё** **W** www.gnm.se

SINCE THE 1870s, Slottsskogen has been one of the city's finest green spaces. Criss-crossed by paths, it features dazzling planting, ponds, a zoo and various activities. In spring the azalea valley is ablaze with colour. In 1999, what was then the world's longest border, with over 90,000 flowering bulbs, was created. There are a number of old cottages from western Sweden to be seen in the park. Areas for sport and outdoor activities include Slottsskogsvallen.

Gothenburg's oldest museum, **Naturhistoriska Museet** (the Museum of Natural History), lies in the northern part of the park. Dating from 1833, it moved to Slottsskogen in 1923. Its vast collection of more than 10 million exhibits includes animals from all around the world.

The most famous of its stuffed animals is Malmska Valen, a blue whale measuring more than 16 m (52 ft) long, which was beached in Askimviken in 1865. It was stuffed and mounted on a treetrunk, the upper jaw opens, and inside the whale there is a room with benches and wall hangings where it is said coffee used to be served. Now the whale is only open for visits on special occasions.

Botaniska Trädgården ㉒

Carl Skottsbergs Gata 22 A. **(** 031-741 11 11. **▤** 58. **☐** 1, 7, 8. **◯** 9am–sunset daily. **▨** voluntary. **ⓗ ▢ ё ✔** **W** www.goteborg.se/botaniska

COVERING 1,750,000 sq m (432 acres) and containing 16,000 species, Gothenburg's Botanical Garden is one of the largest of its kind in Europe. Just under a fifth of the area is gardens while the remainder forms a nature reserve partly consisting of primeval forest.

The gardens began to be designed in 1916 and have been expanded continually ever since. The Rhododendron Valley offers a rich tapestry

◁ **Gamla Haga's "county governor's buildings" with a stone ground floor and two wooden storeys above**

ÅMÅL ❷ Karlstad
45
Örebro
ISLAND CANAL
64
Stockholm
E20
24
TIVEDENS
NATIONAL PARK
Stockholm
ND V Ä N E R N
MELLERUD
LÄCKÖ SLOTT ㉑ MARIESTAD ㉓
KINNEKULLE ㉒
48
49
KARLSBORG ㉕
LIDKÖPING ⑳
44
E20
28 SKARA
㉗ SKÖVDE
NERSBORG
HJO ㉖
HÄTTAN 47
V Ä S T E R G Ö T L A N D
42
㉙ FALKÖPING 195
47
30 ALINGSÅS
46
47
48
㉛ ULRICEHAMN
33 BORÅS
157 40 Jönköping
32 TORPA STENHUS
KINNA
27
TRANEMO
Värnamo

Läckö Slott's great hall with its painted
ceiling and historical portraits

Jönköping

HALLAND

ALKENBERG 26

25
38 HALMSTAD

117

39 LAHOLM

E6
E20
Helsingborg

SIGHTS AT A GLANCE

A Tour on the Dalsland Canal ❶

FROM BENGTSFORS THE DALSLAND CANAL carves its way south towards Köpmannebro on Lake Vänern, passing through 19 locks and dropping 45 m (148 ft) to the lake. The scenery varies from beautiful, almost untouched countryside to modern communities, from old ironworks to historic manor houses. The spectacular aqueduct at Håverud is formed from a series of steel plates joined by 33,000 rivets. Both a rail and a road bridge traverse the deep gorge. The canal was designed by Nils Ericsson in the 1860s.

One of the canal's 19 locks making navigation possible

Baldersnäs Herrgård ②
The manor house stands on a promontory in Lake Laxsjö, on the Dalsland Canal. It is set in a romantic park with paths, caves and artificial islands.

Bengtsfors ①
The canal trip begins or ends here. Don't miss Gammelgården open-air museum with its wooden cottages and storehouses.

Högsbyn Rock Carvings ③
Pictures of ships, people and footprints carved in stone 3,000 years ago can be reached by special boat from Håverud, or by car.

Håverud Aqueduct ④
A solution to the problem of crossing a gorge and a 9-m (30-ft) high waterfall was to build four locks and a long steel aqueduct over the waterfall, followed by another lock.

KEY

■ Suggested route by car

-- Route by boat

= Other roads

--- Railway line

TIPS FOR THE TRIP

Length: 5½ hours by boat.
Boat route: from Bengtsfors to Köpmannebro or reverse. The boat stops at several points along the way. Return by bus or train, around 1 hour.

0 kilometres   5

0 miles   3

Hotell Skagerack on the harbourfront in Strömstad

Åmål ❷

Dalsland. Road 45. 👥 9,400. 🚉
🚌 ✈ Karlstad. 🛥 ℹ Marinan,
Hamngatan 1, 0532-170 98. 🎪 Åmål
Blues Festival (second week in Jul).
🌐 www.dalsland.se

DALSLAND'S ONLY TOWN, Åmål, was founded in 1643. Thanks to its strategic location on Lake Vänern, Åmål soon became an important market place, controlling timber exports to Norway and later acting as a transit port for timber and iron to Gothenburg. After several fires in the 17th century and a major fire in 1901, a new town was built on the north side of the Åmålsån river. Little remains of the original buildings apart from a few 18th-century houses around the town park, Plantaget. The local history museum, **Åmåls Hembygds-museum**, whose three floors house a dentist's clinic and a flat furnished in 1920s style, can be found in Snarhögs-gården. The Railway Museum is located in former engine sheds at Åmål Östra.

At **Forsbacka** on the Åmålsän river, 7 km (4 miles) from Åmål towards Bengtsfors, a mechanical hammer for producing iron bars was built at the end of the 17th century. It was used until the end of the 19th century. Today the 18th-century house at Forsbacka ironworks is a hotel and the old buildings are protected. A golf course is on the land.

🏛 **Åmåls Hembygds-museum**
Hamngatan 4 📞 0532-158 20.
🕐 mid-Jun–Aug: daily. 🎫 ♿ partly.

Strömstad ❸

Bohuslän. E6. 👥 6,000. 🚉 🚌
⛴ from Sandefjord, Norway. 🛥
ℹ Norra Hamnen, 0526-623 30.
🎪 Strömstad Festival (2nd Sat in Jul).
Summer music (Jul), Man Must
Dance (last weekend in Jul).

WHEN STRÖMSTAD became Swedish in 1658 it was just a small fishing village, but by 1676 it had become a town, acting as a strategic counter to the Norwegian towns of Halden and Fredrikstad. In the mid-19th century sea-bathing became the fashion and ever since, Strömstad, with its glorious island archipelago and many hours of sunshine, has been one of Sweden's major holiday resorts.

After a fire in the 1870s Strömstad was rebuilt. Today it is a modern town and its proximity to Norway is evident from the number of Norwegian cars and boats.

The **Strömstads Museum** focuses on local history, while **Friluftsmuseet Fiskartorpet** is an open-air museum

Boiled Koster lobster

featuring fishermen's cottages and fishing tackle.

The harbour with bars and shops is in the centre of the town and boats from here serve the islands, including Kosteröarna. Seal safaris operate to waters around the Ursholmarna islands south of Sydkoster. The nature reserves on Rossö and Saltö can be reached by car.

🏛 **Strömstad Museum**
Södra Hamngatan 22. 📞 0526-102
75. 🕐 Mon–Sat. 🔴 public holidays.
🏛 **Friluftsmuseet
Fiskartorpet**
Karlsgatan 45. 📞 0526-617 53.
🕐 summer: daily. 🅿

Koster Islands ❹

Bohuslän. 👥 300. 🚌 from Strömstad.
🛥 ℹ Strömstad Tourist, 0526-623
30. 🎪 Rowing race (2nd Sun in Aug).

THE ISLANDS OF Koster are renowned for their beauty and their flora. Together they form a nature reserve. These are the westernmost Swedish islands to be inhabited: Nordkoster has a permanent population of around 40 people. Sydkoster is the largest island in the group. It is greener than Nordkoster and is best explored by bike. In contrast, Nordkoster is much more barren and can easily be explored on foot.

The highlights of the Koster Islands' calendar include the annual rowing race across the sound between the islands in August and the lobster festival in the autumn.

Made for sunbathing, the polished granite rocks on Nordkoster

Tanum ⑤

Bohuslän. E6. 🏛 *12,000*. 🚌 🚉
ℹ *Tourist Office, Tanumshede, 0525-
183 80.* Ⓦ *www.tanumturist.se*

T HE MUNICIPALITY of Tanum
has an extraordinary 525
km (326 miles) of coastline
indented with fjords and bays.
It stretches from Gerlesborg in
the south to Galtö in the
north, and is sheltered by a
mass of islets and skerries
offshore. Inland, farms nestle
between rocky outcrops.

Above all, Tanum is
renowned for its Bronze Age
rock carvings, with the earliest
dating from around 1000 BC.
Indeed, the concentration of
these pictorial images and
their contribution to the
understanding of Bronze Age
culture is such that they were
designated a UNESCO World
Heritage Site in 1994. Subjects
include human life, animals,
boats and weapons carved
onto smooth rock.

The largest carving, covering
200 sq m (2,150 sq ft), can be
seen at Vitlycke. **Vitlycke
Museum** is well worth a visit
for a fascinating insight into
this form of rock art. The
museum contains exhibitions
and a reconstructed Bronze
Age farm. Guided tours by
night, when carvings that are

not visible by day emerge in
the light of a torch, are
especially enthralling for any
age group.

Around the region, carvings
featuring hunting scenes can
be seen at **Fossum**, east of
Tanumshede; **Tegneby** has
images of ships; and at
Asberget scenes containing
animals, ploughs and axes can
be found.

🏛 **Vitlycke Museum**
3 km (2 miles) S of Tanumshede. 🅲
0525-209 50. ⬭ *Apr–Sep: daily.* 🈂
🅿 🅲 🚻 🛗 🅿 🈂 *by arrangement.* ♿

Fjällbacka's painted wooden houses in the shadow of Vetteberget

Fjällbacka ⑥

Bohuslän. E6/road 163. 🏛 *850*.
🚌 *to Tanum, then bus.* 🚉 ℹ *Torget,
0525-321 20.* 🐟 *Mackerel Fishing
World Championships (last Sat
in Aug).*

O N THE COAST between
Strömstad and Uddevalla
lies the picturesque village of
Fjällbacka. There has been a
settlement here since the 17th
century and like many other
villages along this coast the
community made a living
from herring fishing and
seafaring. Today, holiday-
makers come for the
swimming and boating.

Attractive low-rise wooden
houses and shops line the
narrow streets, but it is the
harbour which is the heart of
the community. This is where
the fishing huts, bars and
tourist services are located.
Fjällbacka has a stunning

BRONZE AGE ROCK CARVINGS

The rock carvings at Tanum represent a high point in the
artistic language of pictures and symbols used by Bronze
Age people more than 3,000 years ago. Images reflect daily
life and hardships, battles won and lost, weapons and
hunting scenes. Mating scenes, fertility symbols and the
afterlife are also common. The importance of the sea is
reflected in the proliferation of ships and fishing scenes. It
is thought that the rock paintings were primarily of ritual
significance, but the depiction
of animals could have acted as
a calendar to show when various creatures could be hunted.
Hands and feet as motifs are
thought to be associated with a
godly being too holy to have
his whole body depicted.

Rock carvings can be found
all over the world, with the
oldest dating from 20,000 BC.
Those in Sweden are younger,
since it wasn't completely free
of ice until 6,500 BC. The
carvings at Tanum date from
1000–500 BC.

**Bronze Age warrior in a state
of sexual arousal, Tanum**

**Bust of actress Ingrid Bergman
(1915–82) in Fjällbacka**

location with islands offshore and the 70-m (230-ft) high mountain, Vetteberget, creating a precipitous backdrop to the village centre and square known as Ingrid Bergmans Torg. Actress Ingrid Bergman spent many summers in Fjällbacka and after her death her name was given to the square and a bust made by Gudmar Olovson (1983).

Vetteberget is divided by a huge gorge, known as Kungsklyfta, named after King Oscar II who visited Fjällbacka in 1887 and had his name carved at the entrance to the chasm. This dramatic setting was also used as a location for the film of Astrid Lindgren's children's book *Ronja Rövardotter* (Ronja the Robber's Daughter).

Nordens Ark ❼

Bohuslän. Road 17, 20 km (12 miles) N of Smögen. 🚌 ☎ 0523-795 90. ⏰ Apr–mid-Jun daily: 10am–5pm; mid-Jun–mid-Aug: 10am–7pm; mid-Aug–Oct: 10am–5pm; Nov–Mar: 10am–4pm. 🏷 🛒 🚻 ☒ www.nordensark.se

THE NATURE PARK and zoo, Nordens Ark, caters specifically for endangered species. Located in Åby Säteri, it contains animals from every corner of the world, including ancient Swedish breeds such as Gotland sheep and mountain cows, Nordic wild

Panda family among the many endangered species at Nordens Ark

animals such as wolves and wolverine, and exotic species such as the Amur leopard and a variety of parrots. Many of the creatures are part of special programmes to protect them from extinction.

To see the animals at close quarters, follow the 3-km (2-mile) walk around the park – and bring binoculars to spot the wide variety of birds. The route takes you between the enclosures via wooden bridges and along gravel paths. Admission in the summer includes a guided tour. The breeding and quarantine areas are not open to the public.

Nordens Ark is a particularly enjoyable outing for families as there are special children's activities throughout the park. Youngsters can find out how animals adapt in relation to their food, enemies and the

environment by being active themselves, trying things out and playing – even adults find these activities entertaining.

Overnight accommodation is also available.

Smögen ❽

Bohuslän. E6/Road 174. 🏠 1,500. 🚌 from Gothenburg. ⛴ 🛈 Sotenäs Tourist Office, Kungshamn, 0523-66 55 50. 🎏 Herring and Shellfish Festival (3rd weekend in Jul), Tradjazz (first weekend in Aug). ☒ www.sotenasturism.se

ONE OF SWEDEN's largest fishing communities, Smögen today is a delightful holiday resort with shrimp trawlers and the daily fish auction providing popular entertainment. Commerce is particularly lively along the wooden quayside.

Ferries operate to the island of Hållö, a nature reserve south of Smögen where there is a lighthouse, **Hållö Fyr**, which has guided seafarers since 1842.

The **Sotenkanalen** links Smögen and Hunnebostrand. Built in the 1930s, the canal is 6 km (4 miles) long and a popular tourist route. **Hunnebostrand** is a typical west coast holiday destination and home to Svenska Hummerakademien (the Swedish Lobster Academy). The village's development was based on stonemasonry.

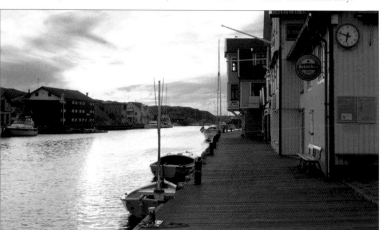

Wooden houses lining the quays of Smögen's well-protected harbour

Uddevalla **9**

Bohuslän. E6, road 44. 🚗 *36,000.*
🚉 🚌 ✈ *Trollhättan.*
ℹ *Kungstorget, 0522-997 20.*
🎭 *Motocross World Championships
(first weekend in Jul), West Coast
Dance Festival (mid-Jul), Fjord Festival
(last weekend in Jul).*
ⓦ *www.uddevallaforum.se*

THE TOWN OF Uddevalla was
famous for shipbuilding
on a grand scale until the
1970s when an economic
crisis forced the closure of its
shipyard. Uddevalla's history
dates from 1496 when it
gained its town charter. Its
strategic location helped trade
to flourish, but also left it open
to attack. It became Swedish
in the Peace of Roskilde in
1658, as the statues of Karl X
Gustav and Erik Dahlbergh in
front of the town hall testify.

Among the town's
attractions, the collections at
Bohusläns Museum focus
on the cultural and natural
heritage of the region. The
museum is by the harbour,
near **Konstgalleriet**, a gallery
for contemporary art. **Sveriges
Sjömanshusmuseum**
concentrates on the history of
seafaring. **Bohusläns
Försvarsmuseum** (Defence
Museum) has a soldier's
cottage among its exhibits.

ENVIRONS: For nature lovers
the unusual shellbanks and
museum devoted to them,
Skalbanksmuseet, are not
to be missed. The museum is
in Kuröd, outside Uddevalla.
The old church of **Bokenäs**
is originally from the 12th
century. The tower and the
church's restored ceiling
paintings date from the 18th
century. The church is on

**Bohusläns Museum in Uddevalla with a
display of old working boats**

Ornate carving on the façade of Restaurang Havsbadet, Lysekil

road 161, 23 km (14 miles)
west of Uddevalla.

🏛 **Bohusläns Museum**
Museigatan 1. 📞 *0522-65 65 00.*
⏰ *Jun–Aug: daily; Sep–May: Sat &
Sun.* 🎭 *by arrangement.* 🖥 🍴 🏠
🏛 **Skalbanksmuseet**
5 km (3 miles) E of Uddevalla. 📞
0522-997 20. ⏰ *Jun–Aug: daily; May
& Sep: Sat & Sun.* 🖥

Lysekil **10**

Bohuslän. E6/road 162. 🚗 *7,300.*
🚉 *to Uddevalla, then bus.* 🚉 🚌
from Fiskebäckskil. ℹ *Södra Hamngatan 6, 0523-130 50.* 🎭 *Hot Bulb
Engine Festival (3rd weekend in Jul).*
ⓦ *www.lysekil.se*

WHEN LYSEKIL gained its
town charter in 1903 the
town was already an established seaside resort.
Buildings in the old part of
Lysekil, Gamlestan, are more
than 200 years old. A walk
along Strandgatan reveals the
charm of this old quarter.
The 19th-century sea-bathing
area has been beautifully
restored. There is a cold bath
house, Oscars Festsal, and the
Nordic-style Curmanska
Villas. The rest of the town is
dominated by the
large, Neo-Gothic
granite church dating
from 1901.
Lysekil lies at the far
end of the Stångenäset
peninsula, with
Gullmarsfjorden –
Sweden's only real
"fjord" in a Norwegian
sense – to the south
and Brofjorden to the
north, and here the
sea has always played
a major role. The

town's aquarium, **Havets
Hus**, is devoted to the marine
and plant life found off the
Bohuslän coast. Around 100
different species of fish can
be viewed in their natural
habitats. There is a walk-
through aquarium and a multi-
media centre. The town's
fishing traditions can also be
experienced at the Hot Bulb
Engine Festival.

🏛 **Havets Hus**
Strandvägen 9. 📞 *0523-196 71.*
⏰ *Feb–Sep: daily.*
🎭 🖥 ♿

Bassholmen **11**

Bohuslän. Road 161 towards
Fiskebäckskil. 🚉 *to Källeviken, then 2
km (1 mile) walk and boat.* 🚢 *from
Uddevalla Tue–Sat.* ⛴ ℹ *Uddevalla
Tourist Office, 0522-997 20.*
Youth Hostel 📞 *0522-65 13 08.*

THE NATURE RESERVE on the
island of Bassholmen,
between Orust and Skaftö, is
one of the highlights of the
Bohuslän archipelago. The
landscape is one of narrow
valleys, leafy meadows and
pine forest, with grazing
horses and sheep. It is a
particularly attractive area for
walking. In the centre of the
island an old farm stands
amid parkland and trees. The
former farm building, with its
many courtyards, is now a
youth hostel.
Bassholmen is also home to
a number of traditional
shipbuilder's yards, which
come under the care of the
Föreningen Allmoge Båtar,
a society which works to
preserve and renovate the
traditional wooden boats of

Bohuslän. Many of these boats can be seen in the museum.

Every summer boating enthusiasts converge on the island for a nostalgic feast to study the craftsmanship involved in greater detail and experience the life of a boatman at the end of the 19th century.

There is a guest jetty in the former shipyard for visiting craft. In summer boats run to Bassholmen from Uddevalla.

Fiskebäckskil, a summer paradise on Skaftö in Gullmarsfjorden

Skaftö ⑫

Bohuslän. Road 161 towards Fiskebäckskil. 🚌 from Uddevalla. 🛈 Lysekil Tourist Office, 0523-130 50.

THE BEST WAY TO see the island of Skaftö is to walk or cycle around it. The scenery varies between fertile agricultural land, pine forests and bare hills. Skaftö's potatoes and strawberries are justifiably famous. In the centre of the island is Gunnesbo, a favourite spot for children where pony rides and a mini-zoo can be found.

In the far south on the slopes running down towards the sea lies **Rågårdsvik**, a small community overlooking the wide Ellösefjorden and the village of Ellöse, site of the internationally successful Hallberg Rassy shipyard. Rågårdsvik Pensionat provides excellent west-coast cuisine.

Between Skaftölandet and Orust are the winding, narrow Malö straits, made famous by the songs of troubadour Evert Taube, while the beautiful Snäckedjupet separates Skaftö

Grundsund harbour, edged with original fishermen's huts

from the mainland. **Fiskebäckskil** in Gullmarsfjorden is a seafaring community established at the end of the 19th century, featuring a captain's house, richly decorated wooden cottages and romantic gardens. It is also the site of Kristineberg Marine Research Station.

The village of **Grundsund** dates from the 17th century. A canal runs through it past the closely packed red fishermen's huts on the lively quayside, so typical of the west coast. The small wooden church, built in 1799, is well worth a look. Delicious fresh seafood is served in the harbourside inn.

Gullholmen ⑬

Bohuslän. 🏠 150. ⛴ from Tuvesvik, Orust. 🛈 Henåns Tourist Office, 0304-311 40. 🌐 www.bastkusten.se

DATING FROM 1585, Gullholmen is one of the oldest fishing communities in Bohuslän. In the mid-19th century one of Sweden's early canning factories was set up here. Line fishing on the Dogger Bank in the North Sea

Weathervane, Fiskebäckskil

produced good catches and in 1910 Gullholmen had a fishing fleet of more than 50 cutters. As the fishing industry declined, so did the population and summer residents have taken over many of the houses. Gullholmen is a typical west-coast summer paradise.

Sights include the church, inaugurated in 1799, and the pilot's lookout which was dismantled in 1916, but is now being rebuilt. **Skepparhuset**, a late 19th-century captain's home with original interiors, is well worth a look. South of Gullhomen, as if thrown out to sea, lies the completely barren **Käringön**. The island is so bare that in the past earth for its small churchyard had to be transported from Orust. The charming tightly-packed houses are almost entirely used by summer visitors and in the season the popular guest harbour is bursting with life. A fishing cottage houses a small museum. The island can be reached by boat from Hällevikstrand on Orust.

🏛 **Skepparhuset**
📞 0304-570 70. ◯ 3rd week of Jun–first week of Aug: Tue & Sun. Other times by arrangement.

Sailing past the picturesque houses of Gullholmen

Mollösund, a typical fishing village on Orust

Orust ⑭

Bohuslän. 🏘 *15,100.* 🚌 *from Stenungsund.* ℹ *Henån Tourist Office, Strandvägen 3, 0304-311 40.* 🎪 *Taube Festival on Flatön (mid-Jul), Boatyard open days (last weekend in Aug).* 🌐 *www.bastkusten.se*

ONE OF SWEDEN'S largest islands, Orust's fortunes over the centuries have been tied to the rise and fall of herring fishing. On the southwest coast, the village of **Mollösund** dates from the 16th century when herring fishing was at its height. A decline in stocks brought poverty, but with the herring's reappearance in the 1750s the population increased, inns opened and refineries for making train oil from herring developed. The bare rocks of Bohuslän are a reminder of this time; the train oil refineries needed lots of wood and the coastline was practically deforested.

Most homes had a fisherman's hut on the harbour and even today the houses and huts are closely packed together. There is a strong smell of stockfish hanging out to dry to produce *Lutfisk* for the Swedish Christmas table.

Today Orust is a centre for the manufacture of superior leisure boats. Half the boats exported from Sweden come from here. The boatyards display their craft in the "Öppna Varv" open days.

Fishing net float

Tjörn ⑮

Bohuslän. 🏘 *15,000.* 🚌 *from Stenungsund.* ℹ *Skärhamn Tourist Office, 0304-67 10 40.* 🎪 *Round Tjörn Yacht Race (3rd Sat in Aug).* 🌐 *www.bastkusten.se*

THE MUNICIPALITY of Tjörn comprises six inhabited islands. Fishing, boat-building and small businesses are the cornerstones of the economy and in summer the population doubles with the arrival of holidaymakers.

Opened in 1960, the **Tjörn Bridges** offer fantastic views over land and water. Tjörnbroleden, the road linking the islands of Tjörn and Orust to the mainland at Stenungsund, crosses the bridges of Stenungsöbron, Källosundsbron and Tjörnbron over Askeröfjorden. In 1980 Tjörnbron collapsed when a ship collided with it in thick fog; a new bridge opened the following year. At its northern end is an ideal site for camping with great views.

Skärhamn, on the west side of Tjörn, is the island's main town. It has a guest harbour, restaurants and hotel. Sights include **Sjöfarts-museum** (the Seafaring Museum), Smedja Volund smithy and the popular **Nordiska Akvarellmuseet** (Nordic Watercolour Museum), a stunning building

Tjörn Bridge, 664 m (726 yd) long, and 45 m (147 ft) high

hosting exhibitions and courses for amateur painters. **Pilane Gravfält**, a burial site with more than 100 Iron Age mounds, stone circles, rings and standing stones, is on northwest Tjörn. Take the road towards Kyrkesund, turn left to Hällene and after 1 km (half a mile) there is a car park.

🏛 **Nordiska Akvarellmuseet**
Skärhamn. Södra Hamnen. 📞 *0304-60 00 80.* ◯ *Jun–Sep: daily; Oct–Apr: Tue–Sun.* ⬤ *some public holidays.* 🎫 ⬛ 🍴 🛍 ♿

The Watercolour Museum, Tjörn, resting on piles in the water

Marstrand ⑯

Bohuslän. Road 168. 🏘 *1,400.* 🚌 🚢 ♿ ℹ *Hamngatan, 0303-600 87.* 🎪 *Fortress Re-enactments, Swedish Match Cup (2nd week in Jul), Marstrand Regatta (4th week in Jul).* 🌐 *www. kungalv.se*

SUN, SAILING and the smell of the sea are what Marstrand is all about. The little town of pastel-coloured wooden houses has its roots in the herring boom of the mid-16th century, which attracted fortune-hunters. But it really took off in the mid-19th century as a fashionable seaside resort. Marstrand built its baths and society arrived.

The town is crowned by the impressive **Carlstens Fästning**, a fortress built in 1666–73 and redesigned in the 1680s by architect Erik Dahlbergh. At one time it was a notorious prison. Tours provide a glimpse into the life and times of the fortress and its inmates in the 18th century. Plays are staged here and feasts held during the summer.

Northwards into the wide waters of Marstrandsfjorden is the rocky island of **Åstol,** almost entirely covered by characteristic white houses and fishing huts. The island can be reached by a 10-minute ferry ride from Rönnäng on Tjörn.

🚩 Carlstens Fästning
[*0303-602 65.* **◯** *daily.* 🏛️ 📷 **▯**
♿ *partly.*

Kungälv ⑰

Bohuslän. E6. 🚶 *20,500.* 🚆 *to Ytterby then bus.* 🚌 ✈️ *Landvetter.*
ℹ️ *Ytterbyvägen 2, 0303-23 92 00.*
🎭 *Medieval Festival (mid-Jul).*
w *www. kungalv.se*

STRATEGICALLY located between the Nordre Älv and Göta Älv rivers, Kungälv occupies the site of the 10th-century Viking settlement of Kongahälla. It is dominated by the ruins of **Bohus Fästning**, a fortress built by the Norwegian King Håkon Magnusson in 1308. Constructed first in wood and later in stone, the fortress was at the frontline in the constant wars between Sweden, Norway and Denmark. At the Peace of Roskilde in 1658 it became Swedish, but it went on to be besieged no less than 14 times without being captured.

In 1678, 900 Swedish defenders faced 9,000 Norwegians and 7,000 German mercenaries, but still the castle didn't fall. In the 18th century it became a prison and in 1789 all the towers were destroyed apart from the main one known as "Fars Hatt" (Father's Hat).

Kungälv church, situated in the market square, dates from 1679.

🚩 Bohus Fästning
[*0303-23 92 00.* **◯** *May–Sep: daily.* ● *Midsummer's Eve.* 🏛️
📷 *by arrangement.*

Bohus Fästning, the impregnable 14th-century fortress at Kungälv

Vänersborg ⑱

Västergötland. Road 45. 🚶 *4,700.*
🚆 🚌 ✕ **ℹ️** *Railway Station, 0521-27 14 00.* 🎭 *Rockadfestival (end Jul). Christmas market (Dec).*
w *www.vanersborg.se*

IN THE SOUTHERNMOST bay of Lake Vänern lies Vänersborg, otherwise known as "Little Paris" after the poems of Birger Sjöberg (1885–1929). A statue of the local poet's muse, Frida, can be seen in the beautiful Skräckleparken on the lake shore, and a reconstruction of his home is in **Vänersborgs Museum**. Other museums focus on medical history, dolls and sport.

The town was founded in 1644 and its Neo-Classical church completed in 1784.

ENVIRONS: Just over 5 km (3 miles) east of the town, the steeply-sided hills of Halleberg and Hunneberg rise up over the landscape. The hillside forests are a nature reserve featuring a large elk population, which is the focus of an annual royal hunt.

On top of Hunneberg is **Kungajaktmuseet Älgens Berg** where the "king of the forest" is presented in interactive displays. The intricacies of elk hunting are explained and visitors can try their hand at shooting an elk themselves, virtually of course.

🏛 Vänersborgs Museum
[*0521-26 41 00.* **◯** *May–Aug: daily; other times: Mon–Fri.* **▯** ♿
🏛 Kungajaktmuseet Älgens Berg
Hunneberg. On road 44.
[*0521-27 79 91.* **◯** *Jun–Sep: daily; other times: Tue–Sun.*
● *eves of public holidays.* 🏛️
📷 *by appointment.* 🅿️ 🛍️ 🍴 ♿

Staircase of locks on the Trollhättan Canal, rising 32 m (105 ft)

Trollhättan ⑲

Västergötland. Road 45. 🚶 *44,000.*
🚆 🚌 ⛴️ **ℹ️** *Innovatum, Åkersjövägen 10, 0520-48 84 72.*
🎭 *Fallens Dagar (3rd weekend in Jul).*
w *www.trollhattan.se*

THE OPENING of the Trollhättan Canal in 1800, linking Lake Vänern and the North Sea, marked the birth of Trollhättan as an industrial town. Today, Trollhättan successfully combines high-tech industries such as SAAB and Volvo Aero with a burgeoning film industry that has earned the town its local nickname, "Trollywood".

The town's main sight is the waterfall area where four locks regulate the once wild 32-m (105-ft) high falls. In summer the sluices are opened several times a week to let the mass of water rush freely down river.

The technology centre **Innovatum Kunskapens Hus** (IKH) features multi-media exhibits on the history and development of Trollhättan. From the centre, a cable car transports visitors 30 m (98 ft) above the canal to the opposite bank. A short walk leads to the Canal Museum.

🏛 Innovatum (IKH)
Åkersjövägen 10. **[** *0520-48 84 80.*
◯ *mid-Jun–mid-Aug: daily; other times Tue–Sun.*
🏛️ 🅿️ 🛍️ 🍴 ♿

Lidköping ⓴

Västergötland. Road 44. 🚶 *24,500.*
✕ 🚌 🚆 ⓘ *Stationshuset, Bangatan
3, 0510-77 05 00.* 🎭 *Arnspelen
Pageant (2nd & 3rd weeks in Jul),
GladJazz Festival (4th weekend in Jul).*
🌐 *www.lidkoping.se*

THE TOWN OF Lidköping lies
at the heart of the area of
Västergötland that is considered to be the cradle of the
Svea Kingdom. Like so many
of Sweden's wooden towns,
Lidköping suffered a devastating fire in 1849, though
some of the 17th-century
buildings around the square
of Limtorget survived.

The Lidan river divides the
town into old and new, and
the two main squares (1446
and 1671 respectively) face
each other across the water.
Nya Stadens Torg (New Town
Square) is the site of a former
hunting lodge, which the
founder of the new town,
Magnus Gabriel de la Gardie,
brought here to serve as a
town hall.

Lidköping is known for the
Rörstrands Porcelain Factory
and **Rörstrands Museum**
attracts visitors in search of
bargain dinner services or
simply to enjoy the show-
pieces in the museum.

Vänermuseet with the
Paleo Geology Centre is an
interactive science museum.

**Rörstrand ceramic stove, now in
the porcelain factory museum**

Läckö Slott, a splendid castle on the shore of Lake Vänern

ENVIRONS: **Husaby**, 10 km (6
miles) east of Lidköping,
encapsulates Swedish history.
It was here at Husaby well
that King Olof Skötkonung
was baptised by the English
monk Sigfrid in 1008. A 12th-
century church now stands at
the site. **Gösslunda Kyrka**,
just west of the town, also
dates from the 12th century.
Outside is a rune stone that
was originally part of the
church wall.

Jan Guillou's popular novels
about the fictional knight Arn
have attracted unexpected
attention to the Lidköping
region. Guided coach tours
are organised in summer.

🏛 **Rörstrands Museum**
Fabriksgatan 4. 📞 *0510-823 48.*
🕐 *daily.* ● *some public holidays.*
🔲 📷 🍴

🏛 **Vänermuseet**
10 min walk from the centre. 📞 *0510-
77 00 65.* 🕐 *Jun–Aug: daily; Sep–May:
Tue–Sun.* ● *some public holidays.*
📷 *by arrangement.* 🔲 📷 🍴 🔲

Läckö Slott ㉑

Västergötland. 20 km (12 miles) N of
Lidköping. 🚌 *from Lidköping.*
📞 *0510-103 20.* 🕐 *May–Sep:
11am–6pm daily.* 📷 🔲 📷 🔲 🔒
🏛 *Medieval Market 3rd week in Jun.*
🌐 *www.lackoslott.se*

JAKOB DE LA GARDIE was the
first to make his mark on
Läckö Slott after it was
assigned to him in 1615. In
2001 Läckö was named the
most beautiful castle in

Sweden. It is surrounded by
water on three sides. Originally built in the 13th century
by Bishop Brynolf Algotsson,
it became the seat of the
bishops of Skara. Count Jakob
and his son, Magnus de la
Gardie, embarked on
remodelling the castle in the
17th century. But in 1681
Läckö was claimed by Karl X
in his recovery of crown
lands from the nobility and its
contents were scattered.

Restoration work in the
20th century has revealed
more than 200 rooms,
including the richly decorated
apartment of Princess Marie
Euphrosyne, wife of Marcus
de la Gardie, and the King's
Hall with its paintings of the
Thirty Years' War.

Läckö is the setting for art
exhibitions and summer
opera performances are held
in the courtyard. The garden
is also open to the public.

Kinnekulle ㉒

Västergötland. Road 44. ⓘ *Götene-
Lidköping Tourist Office, Bangatan 3,
Lidköping, 0510-77 05 00.*

THE 306-M (1,000-ft) high
plateau of Kinnekulle,
known as "the flowering
mountain", rises from the
Västergötland landscape,
providing habitats for wild
flowers, deciduous woods,
pine forests, meadows and
pastures. It is topped with bare
limestone and a 20-m (66-ft)
high lookout tower. Those not

◁ **Sailing boats mooring for the night at Marstrand in Bohuslän** up to the climb can enjoy the views from the restaurant at Högkullen. Limestone has been quarried here since the 12th century. In summer demonstrations at the remaining quarry show how the work used to be carried out.

The area is peppered with ancient Stone Age and Bronze Age sites.

Forshems Kyrka, just to the east, dates from the 12th century and is known for its stone reliefs. The churchyard of the 12th-century church at **Kinne-Vedum,** 2 km (1 mile) north of Götene, has several lily stones, typical of this area.

Mariestad ㉓

Västergötland. E20. 🚗 15,000. 🚉
🚌 ✈ Lidköping. 🚢 🛈 Hamnplan,
0501-100 01. 🔔 Göta Canal Swim
(4th week in Jul).
🆆 www.vastsverige.com

DUKE KARL founded the pretty town of Mariestad in 1583, naming it after his wife, Maria of Pfalz. He built the cathedral and lavishly decorated it in the Baroque style. It is well worth exploring the interesting little streets surrounding the cathedral, lined with buildings from the 18th and 19th centuries.

In 1660 Mariestad became the county town of Skaraborg. The former royal manor of Marieholm, on an island where the River Tidan flows into Lake Vänern, was the governor's residence. It now houses **Vadsmo Museum and Mariestads Industrimuseum** (Industrial Museum).

Mariestad's location on Lake Vänern and the River Tidan makes it an idyllic summer town. The Göta Canal *(see pp146–7)* runs through it and

Marieholm, the former governor's residence in Mariestad

Kanalmuseet (the Canal Museum) is located in Sjötorp just north of the town.

Those keen on rural life should head for **Klockarbolet** in Odensäker, a reconstructed village dating from the 17th and 18th centuries.

🏛 **Vadsbo Museum and Mariestads Industrimuseum**
Mariebolm. 📞 0501-632 14.
⬜ Sep–May: Sat & Sun; Jun–Aug:
Tue–Sun. 🎫 🚻 🅿 🛍 🛗 🍴 🛗 ♿
🏛 **Kanalmuseet**
Sjötorp, off road Rv 26. 📞 0501-512
01. ⬜ Mid-Jun–mid-Aug: daily. 🎫

Tivedens National Park ㉔

Västergötland. Road 49. 🚌 from
Karlsborg. 🛈 Karlsborgs Tourist
Office, 0505-173 50.

ON THE BORDER between Närke and Västergötland lies Tiveden national park, an untouched area of rugged wilderness. It was established in 1983 to protect the remaining primeval forest and lakes, of which Fagertärn is the original habitat of the large red water-lily *(see p17).*

The area is very hilly and demanding for walkers. There is a visitor centre at Stenkälla with information on trails, parking and things to see inside the park.

Giant Ice Age boulders, some up to 10 m (33 ft) high, litter the forest around **Trollkyrka,** the hill east of the road by the visitor centre. The mountain's name is thought to be derived from the fact that the site was used by local people who came here to worship after the ban in 1726 on holding religious services outside churches.

Karlsborgs Fästning, a 19th-century wartime hideaway

Karlsborg ㉕

Västergötland. Road 49. 🚗 4,700.
🚉 🚌 🚢 🛈 Karlsborgs Tourist
Office, Ankarvägen 2, 0505-173 50.
Fortress ⬜ mid-May–Aug: 10am–5pm
daily; other times 10am–3pm Mon–
Fri. 🎫 🍴 Eng by appointment 🅿

IN 1819 KING Karl XIV Johan decided that a fortress should be built at Vanäs on the shore of Lake Vättern. It was named Karlsborg and was to act as an emergency capital in the event of war; a place of safety for the royal family, the national bank and the government. The 90 years it took to build meant that by the time it was finally finished the fortress was out of date and it never had any real significance. Today, however, it is a major tourist attraction. The "town" enclosed within the 3-km (2-mile) long walls is best viewed on one of the guided tours that run daily in the summer. Action fans can watch *Fästningsäventyret,* an adventure depicting life in the fortress in the 1860s complete with stunt men and special effects.

Outside the fortress, the Göta Canal wends its way towards Lake Vänern, passing **Forsviks Bruk,** which offers an interesting glimpse into Sweden's industrial heritage, with a blacksmith's forge, sawmill and working flour mill.

🏛 **Forsviks Bruk**
8 km (5 miles) north of the centre.
📞 Karlsborgs Tourist Office, 0505-
173 50. ⬜ Jun–Aug: daily. 🎫

Hjo's wooden buildings, awarded the Europa Nostra medal in 1990

Hjo ㉖

Västergötland. Road 193/194.
🚆 6,000. 🚌 to Skövde then bus.
🏛 🛈 Floragatan 1, 0503-352 55.
🎭 Craft Fair (2nd weekend in Jul),
Round Vättern cycle race (3rd
weekend in Jun). 🖥 www.hjo.se

MENTION HJO and Swedes immediately think of the exquisite little wooden houses dating from the end of the 19th century with their ornately carved verandas. Hjo is a delightful town to visit. On the shore of Lake Vättern is Stadsparken, a park created when Hjo Spa was founded in the late 19th century. Villa Svea, one of the former spa buildings in the park, houses **Hjo Stadsmuseum** (the Town Museum). It is worth a look for its remarkable calendar clock *Hjouret*, and recreated rooms from the heyday of the spa. The park also contains Fjärilsmuseum (the Butterfly Museum) and Vätternakvarium, an aquarium.

Just like the town, the harbour has medieval origins, but the present one was built in the mid-19th century after the construction of the Göta Canal. In summer, the *Lok-Hjo-Motivet* train takes guided tours (daily except Monday) through the town starting from the harbour. The steamer *S/S Trafik* (1892) runs Sunday tours to Visingö, and jazz cruises to Vadstena across the lake.

The Hjoån river valley, stretching from Lake Vättern to Mullsjön lake 4 km (2.5 miles) west of Hjo has several spectacular waterfalls.

🏛 Hjo Stadsmuseum
Villa Svea, Stadsparken. 📞 0503-351
15. ◐ May–Aug. ♿ partly.

Skövde ㉗

Västergötland. Road 48/49.
🚶 32,500 🚆 🚌 🛈 Sandtorget,
0500-44 66 88. 🎭 Food Festival (last
weekend in Aug), Skövde Film Festival
(mid-Oct).

THE MODERN industrial town of Skövde celebrated its 600th anniversary in 2001. Skövde has been destroyed by fire several times, but after a devastating fire in 1715 little remained other than a single 17th-century house, **Helénsgården**. Today the house is part of Skövde Stadsmuseum (the Town Museum), along with Gamla Rådhuset (the Old Town Hall), 1776, and the neighbouring Gamla Kanslihuset (the Old Government Building), 1915. The museum also holds exhibitions in Hertig Johans Torg.

Kulturhuset, designed by Hans-Erland Heineman in 1964, houses the library, art museum and an art gallery exhibiting Swedish modern art. The library contains Siri Derkert's relief *The Mustard Tree*. In the square in front of Kulturhuset are the sculptures *Monument of an Axeman* by Eric Grate (1965) and *La Mano* by Liss Eriksson. The latter was raised in 1986 in memory of murdered Prime Minister Olof Palme.

ENVIRONS: Rising to the west of Skövde is the 300-m (984-ft) high **Billingen** plateau, with views stretching as far as Lake Vättern. The area is a popular recreation spot with hiking trails, holiday cottages and campsites. The exclusive Billingehus Hotel contains a sports museum.

West of Skövde, on road 49, is the 12th-century church **Våmbs Kyrka**. The church was restored to its original appearance in the 1940s. On the same road, slightly nearer to Skövde, is **Varnhems Klosterkyrka**, a 13th-century three-aisle basilica.

🏛 Helénsgården
Helénsparken. 📞 0500-49 80 69.
◐ summer. 🎫 ♿ by arrangement.
🏛 Kulturhuset
Trädgårdsgatan. 📞 0500-49 85 60.
Konsthallen & Konstmuseet ◐ Sep–
May: Tue–Sun; Jun–Aug: Tue–Sat.
● eves of public holidays. 🖥 🍴

Skara ㉘

Västergötland. E20. 🚶 10,700. 🚆
🚌 🛈 Bladska Huset, Skolgatan 1,
0511-32580. 🎭 Naturum Crane
Dance (end Mar–Apr).

TRADITIONALLY an important seat of learning and a bishopric, Skara is one of Sweden's oldest towns. The 11th-century cathedral lies at its heart, surrounded by a network of streets following a pattern set out in the Middle Ages. On Stora Torget stands Krönikebrunnen, a well which

The nave of Skara's Gothic cathedral, founded in the 12th century

on its exterior chronicles important events in the history of Skara and of Sweden. **Stadsparken** is the site of Västergötlands Museum with its local history collection, and Fornbyn, an open-air museum complete with cottages and animals showing how people lived in the past.

ENVIRONS: Axvall, 10 km (6 miles) from Skara on road 49, is the location for the children's favourite spot, **Skara Sommarland**, a large amusement park with a water park, campsite and holiday cottages.

Around 20 km (12 miles) east of Skara, Lake **Hornborgasjön** is a popular resting place for birds, especially dancing cranes in April–May. There is an observation tower and two information centres.

⚓ **Skara Sommarland**
Axvall, road 49 towards Skövde.
📞 0511-70 300. ⬜ 29 May–22 Aug.

🦋 **Hornborgasjön**
Naturum Hornborgasjön, road 189.
📞 0515-72 70 63. ⬜ daily in season.

Falköping 🟠

Västergötland. Road 46. 🏛 15,400.
🚉 🅸 Odengatan 24, 0515-77 70 50. 🅆 www.falkoping.nu

BETWEEN THE HILLS of Mösseberget and Ålleberg lies the old town of Falköping. Of particular interest are the 12th-century church, St Olofs Kyrka, the medieval wooden houses and the town square, Stora Torget, with Ivar Tengbom's statue *Venus Rising from the Waves* (1931). **Falbygdens Museum** describes the local history.

ENVIRONS: Ekornavallen, 15 km (9 miles) north of Falköping, is an important historic burial site from the Stone, Iron and Bronze Ages.

Dalénmuseet in Stenstorp uses sound-and-light shows to illustrate the life and work of the 1912 Nobel laureate Gustaf Dalén, an innovator in the field of lighting technology and inventor of the AGA oven.

Gökhems Kyrka, west of the town, is a small

Romanesque apse church without a tower. It dates from the early 12th century. Inside, limestone paintings depict *The Creation*.

Gudhems Klosterruin and **Klostermuseum** north of the town are the ruins of a convent founded in 1160. Today it is a museum. **Karleby**, to the east, is one of three villages along a road which probably existed in the Stone Age. Each farm had its burial site and there are 13 passage tumuli here, including one with a burial chamber 17 m (56 ft) long.

Skulls of Stone Age inhabitants from the Falköping area in Falbygdens Museum

🏛 **Falbygdens Museum**
St Olofsgatan 23. 📞 0515-850 50.
⬜ Tue–Fri & Sun. ● some public holidays.

🏛 **Dalénmuseet**
Stenstorp, 10 km (6 miles) N of centre.
📞 0500-45 71 65. ⬜ Mar–Sep: Tue–Sun, Jul also Mon; Oct–Nov: Sat & Sun.
● Dec–Feb, Midsummer Eve. 📷

Alingsås 🟠

Västergötland. E20. 🏛 25,000. 🚉
🚉 🅸 Stora Torget 1, 0322-61 62 00.
🥔 Potato Festival (3rd weekend in Jun), Ljus i Alingsås (Oct).
🅆 www.alingsas.se

JONAS ALSTRÖMER and the textile industry have, between them, left their mark on Alingsås. In the early 18th century, Ahlströmer founded his textile factory and on the proceeds he built **Nolhaga Slott**, a manor which today

has a zoo and bird park. **Alingsås Museum** is housed in the 1730s Ahlströmerska Magazinet. The newly opened **Alingsås Kulturhus** contains an art gallery and library.

ENVIRONS: Gräfsnäs Slottsruin and Park is a ruined castle and park on Lake Anten, 20 km (12 miles) north of Alingsås. An exhibition describes its history. On the road towards Gothenburg lies **Nääs Slott**, a 17th-century castle with an impressive 19th-century interior. Here, the handicraft tradition of western Sweden is cultivated through events and exhibitions. The Midsummer celebrations here are fantastic.

🏛 **Alingsås Museum**
Lilla Torget 1. 📞 0322-61 65 96.
⬜ Tue–Sat.

🏛 **Alingsås Kulturhus**
Sa Ringgtan 3. 📞 0322-61 65 98.
⬜ Wed–Mon. ● some public holidays.

🏯 **Nääs Slott**
Floda, E20, 30 km (19 miles) N of Gothenburg. 📞 0302-318 39.
⬜ May–mid-Jun: Sat, Sun & public holidays; mid-Jun–mid-Aug: daily; mid-Aug–Sep: Sat, Sun & public holidays. 📷

Nolhaga Slott, home of the textile magnate Jonas Ahlströmer, 1727

Ulricehamn Town Hall, 1799, housing the town's tourist office

Ulricehamn ③①

Västergötland. Road 40. 🚶 9,100.
🚃 🚌 🛈 Rådhuset, 0321-271 75.
🎿 Kärringrallyt (all year round: Thu).
🅦 www.ulricehamnsturistbyra.se

T HE TOWN OF Ulricehamn occupies a beautiful setting on Lake Åsunden in an area rich in historic monuments. Originally known as Bogesund, there has been a settlement here since the 14th century. The old coaching road across Västergötland to Halland ran through the town along Storgatan. The local history museum, **Ulricehamns Museum**, is located in an 1868 schoolhouse, while **Ulricehamns Konstoch Östasiatiska Museum**, with its fine collection of Chinese ceramics, is in the old railway station.

Textile enterprises dominate the local economy and in Gällstad the knitwear factories south of the town open their gates to bargain hunters every Thursday afternoon for what is known as *Kärringrallyt* (the "old women's race").

ENVIRONS: Bystad, a farmstead 30 km (19 miles) south of Ulricehamn, has one of Sweden's oldest animal traps, a pit measuring about 5 m (16 ft) in diameter and more than 3.5 m (11 ft) deep.

Along the road between Ulricehamn and Mullsjö lies **Näs Gård**. The manor's six

historic red-painted buildings date from the 17th, 18th and 19th centuries and now form a regional cultural centre and art gallery. Concerts and other cultural events are held here.
Södra Vings Kyrka is a medieval gem of a church, dating in part from the 12th century. The artistic decoration is unusually lavish and includes 15th-century limestone paintings in the nave. The stately lectern was carved in Rococo style in 1748.

🏛 Ulricehamns Konst- och Östasiatiska Museum

Järnvägstorget. 📞 0321-150 90.
⏱ Jan–Dec: Sun. 🎟 🅿 by arrangement. 🚻 🛈

Torpa Stenhus ③②

Västergötland. 26 km (16 miles) N of Borås. 🛈 Borås Tourist Office, 033-35 70 90. ⏱ May–mid-Sep: 11am–5pm. 🎟 Eng 11am; eve in Eng: phone Tourist Office in advance. 🖥

S TANDING ON A promontory at the southern end of Lake Åsunden is the medieval castle Torpa Stenhus. It belonged to the Stenbock family and from the 14th–mid-17th century was an important stronghold for defence against the Danes. The evening guided tour includes thrilling ghost stories from the castle's past. Theatre performances, known as *Torpaspelen*, are staged here in summer.

Painting of Saturn at Torpa Stenhus

Borås ③③

Västergötland. Road 40. 🚶 62,000.
🚉 🚌 🛈 Hallbergsplatsen 1, 033-35 70 90. 🎿 Culture Night (first week in May), Harvest Festival (first week in Sep). 🅦 www.boras.se.

I N 1620 KING Gustav II Adolf decided that the textile pedlars of the Knallebygden area should have a town of

their own and Borås was founded. Textile factories still line the Viskan river, which winds through the town, although the industry has lost ground in recent years.

Borås is a green town with beautiful parks: Stadsparken in the centre is popular, as is Ramnaparken where the open-air Borås Museum is located. Also in the town centre is **Borås Djurpark**, a zoo with more than 80 species from all corners of the world. Large enclosures and attractive grounds make this zoo a pleasant family park.

ENVIRONS: On the road between Borås and Alingsås lies **Hedareds Kapell**, Sweden's only preserved stave church. Apart from its windows and shingled roof, the little, wooden 16th-century church remains as it was when it was built, complete with original 16th-century paintings.
Textilmuseet (the Textile Museum) is a living museum housed in a late-19th-century spinning shed. The history of the textile industry is brought to life with recreated scenes and art and textile exhibitions.

🐾 Borås Djurpark

Boråsparken, bus line 2 from Södra parken. 📞 033-35 32 70. ⏱ May–mid-Sep: daily; Oct & Apr: Sat & Sun; school holidays: daily 🎟 🖥 🛈

🏛 Textilmuseet

Druverforsvägen 8, road 40.
📞 033-35 89 50. ⏱ Tue–Sun.
⏱ some public holidays. 🎟 🅿 by arrangement. 🖥 🛈

Pink flamingo, one of the many exotic species at Borås Djurpark

Gunnebo Slott ㉞

In the 1780s, John Hall, one of the richest men in Sweden at the time, commissioned city architect Carl Wilhelm Carlberg of Gothenburg to design a summer villa and park at Gunnebo. On completion in 1796, Carlberg had created one of the most beautiful and stylistically pure examples of Neo-Classical Swedish architecture. Hall is said to have paid the bill with 38 barrels of gold, but that included everything: the interiors, servants' quarters, orangery, park, kitchen gardens and greenhouse. An adjoining farm made the estate virtually self-sufficient.

The Salon
Three magnificent French windows let in the sunlight, which is reflected on the beautiful parquet floor.

Oval vestibule

Northern Façade
Ionian columns frame the sheltered terrace which opens onto the garden with its neatly clipped trees.

The frieze on the southern gable is made from lead painted to imitate marble.

The staircase leads to the park with its parterres and gravel paths.

The entrance is through the cellar, the starting point for tours.

Ceramic Stoves
The interior design, including exquisite ceramic stoves, is by Carlberg who adopted the light Gustavian style which pervades the entire house.

Park and Gardens
The French-inspired formal garden surrounding the house was also designed by Carlberg, as was the English park, which makes an ideal setting for a walk.

Varberg Fästning, a fortress on the shores of the Kattegat housing a local history museum

Kungsbacka ⑤

Halland. E6/E20. 🏠 17,200. 🚗 🚆
🚶 Storgatan 41, 0300-83 45 95. 🎵
Kungsbacka Chamber Music Festival
(first weekend in Aug).
🅆 www.kungsbacka.se

ALTHOUGH KUNGSBACKA was
an important trading
centre in the 13th century,
almost nothing remains of the
old wooden town. All but two
of the houses were destroyed
in a devastating fire in 1846.
The two survivors are the red
cottage in Norra Torggatan
and the mayor's house at
Östergatan 10. The pretty
pastel-painted wooden houses
that replaced the old at the
end of the 19th century can be
seen around the square. Today,
Kungsbacka is almost a southern suburb of Gothenburg.

ENVIRONS: Around 10 km (6
miles) outside Kungsbacka at
Rydet is **Mårtagården**, a typical 18th-century sea captain's
house. The house is open to
the public in the summer.
Tjolöholms Slott, one of
Sweden's more unusual
buildings, lies 15 km (9 miles)
south of Kungsbacka. This
magnificent English Tudor-
style mansion was built for a
Scottish merchant and completed in 1904. It contained
state-of-the-art features such as
vacuum cleaners, showers and

Tjolöholms Slott, an eccentric English Tudor-
style mansion with Art Nouveau interiors

hot-air heating. The house is
surrounded by beautiful
parkland and also has a
wagon museum.

🚃 Tjolöholms Slott
10 km (6 miles) S of the centre, E6/E20
to Fjärås exit, then road 939. 🕿 0300-
83 45 95. ⏰ May–Aug: daily; Sep: Sat
& Sun; Oct: Sun. **Park** ⏰ daily. 🎫

Varberg ㊱

Halland. E6/E20. 🏠 25,000. 🚗 🚆
🚢 from Grenå. 🚶 Brunnsparken,
0340-887 70. 🎪 Wheels & Wings
motor exhibition (mid-Jul).
🅆 www.turist.varberg.se

THE COASTAL TOWN of Varberg
has, since the 19th century,
been famous for its bathing,
whether the cold curative
baths fashionable of the period
or swimming from the rocks
and sandy beaches. The town
was founded in the 13th century, but little from that time
remains after several fires.
The harbour area is worth a
look and, in particular,
Kallbadhuset, the renovated
cold bath house in Moorish
style with separate sections for
men and women. The oriental
touch is repeated in **Societetshuset**, built in the 1880s
when the town's popularity as
a spa was at its height. Today
it houses a café, restaurant,
pub and disco, playground
and mini-golf. On
summer evenings
concerts are held on
the stage in the park.
Guarding the
approach from the
sea is the mighty
Varbergs Fästning.
Most of the fortress
was built in the 17th
century with parts
dating from the 13th
century. Today it
houses a museum,

**Länsmuseet Varbergs
Fästning**, focusing on the
history of Halland. The
museum's biggest attraction is
the 14th-century Bocksten
Man whose body was discovered in a bog still dressed in a
complete outfit from the
Middle Ages. The notorious
bullet which killed King Karl
XII in 1718 is also on show.
An outpost of the museum is
Båtmuseet, the boat museum
in Galtabäck, 10 km (6 miles)
south of Varberg, displaying
traditional boats and models.

🏛 Länsmuseet Varbergs
Fästning
Varbergs Fästning. 🕿 0340-185 20.
⏰ daily. 🎫 by arrangement.

Falkenberg ㊲

Halland. E6/E20. 🏠 18,600. 🚗 🚆
🚶 Holgersgatan 11, 0346-88 61 00.
🎵 Song festival (first week in Jul).
🅆 www.falkenbergsturist.se

A TOWN WITH medieval roots,
Falkenberg stands at the
mouth of the River Ätran. The
oldest areas of the town
still have their wooden buildings, including St Laurentii
Kyrka (St Laurence's church),
parts of which date from the
14th century.
The pottery **Törngrens
Krukmakeri** (1789) is still in
operation, run by the seventh
generation of potters.
Falkenbergs Museum is
housed in a half-timbered
granary at Söderbron. The
grain dryer is a lofty landmark
in the old town. The museum
features a faithful reproduction
of an apartment from the
1950s and the café has a
working jukebox.
Falkenberg has several
interesting smaller museums,
including **Falkenbergs
Hembygdsmuseum** (Rural

Museum) in St Lars Kyrkogata, a rural museum with a section on salmon fishing. The **Fotomuseet Olympia** in Sandgatan is housed in the town's first cinema (1912) and displays cameras and photos.

ENVIRONS: North of the town is **Morups Tånge**, known for its 28-m (91-ft) high granite lighthouse built in the mid-19th century. The beach below is a nature reserve, a wetland area of international interest and a home for waders.

🏺 **Törngrens Krukmakeri**
Krukmakaregatan 4. ☎ 0346-103 54. ⏰ daily. 🏠 Nygatan 34.
🏛 **Falkenbergs Museum**
Skepparesträtet 2. ☎ 0346-88 61 25. ⏰ Sep–May: Tue, Fri & Sun; Jun–Aug: Tue–Sun. 🏠

Fly-fishing in the salmon-rich River Ätran in Falkenberg

Halmstad ❸❽

Halland. E6/E20. 🚶 53,500. 🚉 🚌 ✈ 🚢 from Grenå. 🛈 Tourist Office, Halmstad Slott, 035-13 23 20. 🎭 Street Theatre Festival (Aug). 🌐 www.halmstad.se

AT THE POINT where the River Nissan flows into Laholmsbukten bay lies Halmstad. In the Middle Ages it was the largest town on the west coast. Today, the medieval inner city with its half-timbered architecture is classified as being of national interest. Kirsten Munk's house on Storgatan is an exceptional 17th-century building in greenglazed Dutch brick. Local craftsmen can be seen at work in **Fattighuset**, Lilla Torg, a former poorhouse dated 1859.

Several modern artists have left their mark on the town and Carl Milles' fountain

The former training ship *Najaden* against a backdrop of Halmstad Slott

Europa and the Bull in Stora Torg and Picasso's *Woman's Head*, which stands between the bridges over the river Nissan, are easily encountered on a stroll.

Halmstad Slott, a 17th-century castle, was built by the Danish King Christian IV. The former training ship *Najaden* is moored on the quayside in front of the castle.

Länsmuseet (the County Museum) has a wide collection of art and cultural history, including painted furniture and tapestries. **Tropikcenter** in Strandgatan is exciting for children with more than 100 species of tropical animals set in their natural habitats. Another hit for children is **Miniland**, a park with models of famous Swedish buildings on a scale of 1:25 and several kids' play attractions such as a BMX track and motorized lorries.

ENVIRONS: To the north, the popular summer resorts of Tylösand, Haverdal and Frösakull spread out along the coast. **Simlångsdalen**, around 20 km (12 miles) from Halmstad on road 25, has several natural attractions including Danska Fall in the River Assman, a 36-m (118-ft) high waterfall.

🏠 **Fattighuset**
Lilla Torg. ☎ 035-21 15 15. ⏰ daily. 🏠
🐾 **Tropikcenter**
Strandgatan. ☎ 035-12 33 33. ⏰ daily. 🏠
🏛 **Miniland**
Ga Tylösandsvägen 1. ☎ 035-10 84 60. ⏰ May–first week of Sep: daily. 🏠 🍴

Laholm ❸❾

Halland. Road 24. 🚶 5,600. 🚉 🚌 🛈 Rådhuset, Stortorget, 0430-154 50. 🎉 Waterfall Day (2nd Sun in Aug), Salmon Festival (3rd Sun in Aug).

HALLAND'S OLDEST and smallest town, Laholm is primarily associated with the long sandy beaches around the bay of Laholmsbukten. Mellbystrand, on the bay 6 km (4 miles) to the west of the town, throngs with holidaymakers in summer. The River Lagan also attracts visitors for the salmon fishing.

Laholm itself is characterized by its winding streets and low houses, reminiscent of Danish rule before 1645. Of the buildings around the square, the 200-year-old **Rådhuset** (Town Hall) is particularly beautiful. Open year round, it houses the Tourist Office, Laholms Teckningsmuseum (the Drawing Museum), a small exhibition on the history of the town and a cell from the time when the building served as a police station. On the western gable there is an automaton symbolizing the meeting in Laholm in 1278 between the Swedish King Magnus Ladulås and Danish King Erik Klipping.

Laholm's tidy rows of houses bearing the hallmarks of the town's Danish past

WESTERN SVEALAND

V ÄRMLAND, NÄRKE AND DALARNA, *with their rich rural heritage, colourful folk costumes, red-painted wooden houses and pastoral scenes, attracted visitors long before the onset of tourism. Stretching from the flatlands of Närke to the mountains of Dalarna, this region is known for its annual ski race and Midsummer festivities, as well as its industrial heritage based on mining and forestry.*

Large expanses of water dominate all three provinces. Southern Värmland encompasses the huge Lake Vänern, which is also the end of the line for the arterial Klarälven river. The beautiful Fryken lakes provided inspiration for one of the province's well-known authors, Selma Lagerlöf *(see p233)*. Her home, Mårbacka, was in this region where so many of her adventures are set. There is plenty of scope for outdoor activities in Värmland, including boating, canoeing, rafting on the Klarälven river and fishing. The forests have exciting trails where walkers are unlucky if they don't see an elk, and on wildlife safaris there is even the chance of glimpsing one of the big four predators – bear, wolf, lynx or wolverine.

Närke, one of Sweden's smallest provinces, is sandwiched between two large lakes, Hjälmaren and Vättern. The centre of the province is dominated by the fertile Närke flatlands, encircled by forest, including the once infamous haunt of bandits, Tiveden, in the south. Örebro, Western Svealand's largest metropolis and Närke's county town, has all the charm of a small town.

Dalarna has the beautiful Siljan lake and the Dalälven river with its arms stretching into the mountains. The province offers more contrasts than most – from the gentle farmland around Siljan to the mountainous north. Every March, these are linked by the Vasaloppet race *(see p245)*, when some 10,000 skiers head from Sälen down to Mora. Midsummer celebrations on Siljan are emblematic of Dalarna. Villages compete to see who has the most stylish maypole, the most accomplished musicians and the best folk dancers.

Rustic interior of Gammelgården in Mora, Dalarna

◁ **Stora Kils church on Nedre Fryken lake, Värmland**

Exploring Western Svealand

FERTILE AGRICULTURAL LAND spreads out around the major lakes, Vänern, Vättern, Hjälmaren and Siljan, and along the river valleys, giving way to a predominantly forested landscape. The region provides ample opportunities for nature lovers, with its abundance of wildlife, and for anglers, who will easily find a good catch. The mountains in Dalarna are the setting for some of the country's most popular ski resorts, walking trails and national parks. Motorists have many attractive small roads to choose from, while the Fryksdalsbanan and Inlandsbanan railway lines guarantee spectacular sights from the train window and leisurely boat trips provide glorious views from the water.

Author and Nobel laureate Selma Lagerlöf's Mårbacka, one of Värmland's many stately homes

GETTING AROUND

Passing through Örebro and Karlstad, the E18 motorway crossing from Stockholm to Oslo is the main artery for traffic to this region. Travelling up into Värmland and Dalarna, the roads follow the river valleys, where the local population is also concentrated. Rail links are good to the southern parts of the provinces, but the northern areas can only be reached by car or bus. Between towns and popular tourist areas the bus services are quite frequent, but they can be patchy in rural areas. In summer, boats ply the major lakes of Vänern, Hjälmaren and Siljan.

KEY

═══ Motorway

▬▬ Major road

═══ Minor road

─── Railway line

SEE ALSO

- **Where to Stay** pp287–8
- **Where to Eat** pp301–2

21 IDRE AND S

Österdalälven

SÄRNA

Trysil (Norway)

71

20

Västerdalälven

62

MA

45

Klara

⊠

TORSBY

HAG

Kongsvinger (Norway)

VÄRMLAND ⊠

FRYKEN LAKES 1

2

Oslo (Norway)

ARVIKA

E18

62

ÅRJÄNG

61

⊠

5

BORGVIKS BRUK 3 **KARLSTAD**

45 **SÄFFLE**

4

Gothenburg **VÄRMLANDS**

VÄNERN

The 16th-century Ornässtugan (in foreground), one of the places associated with Gustav Vasa's adventures in Dalarna

Engelbrekt, champion of liberty, in Örebro, by C G Qvarnström, 1866

SIGHTS AT A GLANCE

A Tour around the Fryken Lakes ❶

AUTHOR SELMA LAGERLÖF called the Fryken lakes the "smiling leaves", and it is the natural surroundings, the glittering waters, the flowering meadows and the dark forests on the horizon that strike visitors most. The author's spirit is a constant presence, and no more so than at the Rottneros estate, which is Ekeby in *Gösta Berling's Saga*, and the author's home, Mårbacka, across the water. The best ways to experience the lakes are aboard the vintage steamer *Freja af Fryken*, or by bicycle or car from Sunne, the main centre of the area.

View across Övre Fryken from Tossebergsklätten

Sunne ②
The regional centre of the Fryksdal valley, Sunne is beautifully situated on the water between Övre Fryken and Mellanfryken. Heritage centres and a host of events in summer, including the Fryksdal Dance, reflect the area's rich folk traditions.

Sahlströmska Gården ①
The home of artist siblings Sahlström in Utterbyn features mementoes of some of the early 20th century's most colourful Swedish artists.

Mårbacka ④
Nobel laureate Selma Lagerlöf's home has been kept just as it was on her death in 1940. Exhibitions linked to the author's work are held in the summer.

Rottneros ③
The estate has magnificent gardens and a large sculpture collection. For children, there is Nils Holgersson's Adventure Park.

KEY

▬ Suggested route

= Other roads

— Fryksdalsbanan railway line

S/S Freja av Fryken ⑤
In 1896, the queen of the Fryken lakes capsized; 98 years later she was salvaged from the lake bed and now sails from the port of Kil, powered by her original 1868 engine.

TIPS FOR THE TRIP

Length: 75 km (47 miles) by road.

Stopping-off point: Tosseberg, 20 km (12 miles) north of Sunne on the road to Torsby.

Other routes: train, Kil–Torsby on Fryksdalsbanan, "Sweden's most beautiful railway". Boat trips: S/S Freja av Fryken (tel: 0554-475 90).

| 0 kilometres | 8 |
| 0 miles | 5 |

*Map labels:* MALUNG, TORSBY, 239, ÖVRE FRYKEN, 45, MELLANFRYKEN, 238, NEDRE FRYKEN, 45, ARVIKA, 61, KIL, KARLSTAD

Arvika ②

Värmland. Road 61. 🏃 14,000.
🚻 🚃 ✈ ⛴ 🛈 Storgatan 22,
0570-817 90. 🎭 Arvika Festival (mid-
Jul), Harbour Festival (Jun).
Ⓦ www.arvika.se

A 1903 Humber in Arvika Fordonsmuseum

THE PEOPLE OF Värmland are known for their wit and ability to tell funny stories, particularly in Jösse, where Arvika is the main town. It is situated on a hill above the bay of Kyrkviken, which is linked to the lake of Glafs-fjorden by a narrow strait.

Arvika Fordonsmuseum, centrally located next to the fire station, has an exciting collection of veteran vehicles, including hundreds of cars, motorcycles and carriages.

The area has long been home to craftworkers and artists, as can be seen in the **Rackstadmuseet** in Taserud just outside the town. This is where sculptor Christian Eriksson set up his studio, Oppstuhage, in the mid-1890s. For many years it was a magnet for artists attracted by the pristine Värmland country-side, such as the painter Gustaf Fjaestad, renowned for his winter scenes.

Klässbols Linneväveri, 20 km (12 miles) south of Arvika, is the Nordic region's only damask weaving mill and a rewarding destination for those who want to see how the linen tablecloths for the Nobel Prize banquets, or fabric for the Royal Family, are made.

🏛 **Arvika Fordonsmuseum**
Thermiavägen 2. 📞 0570-803 90.
⏰ Tue–Sun; Sat–Sun; Jun–Aug:
daily. Group bookings: by appointment. 🚻 🛈 💳 ♿

🏛 **Rackstadmuseet**
Sandgrundsudden. 📞 054-14 31 00.
⏰ Oct–Mar: Thu, Sat, Sun; Apr, May
& Sep: Tue–Sun; Jun–Aug: daily;
other times by appointment. 🚻 🛈

🏛 **Klässbols Linneväveri**
Damastvägen 5. 20 km (16 miles) S of
Arvika. 📞 0570-46 01 85. ⏰ Oct–
Apr: Mon–Fri & Sat; May–Sep: daily.
📷 only pre-booked. 🚻 🛈 ♿

Borgviks Bruk ③

Värmland. 35 km (22 miles) W of
Karlstad. Road 45. 🏃 400. 🚻
Borgvik Byggnadsvård 📞 0555-
743 80, winter: 054-14 31 00.
⏰ Jun–Aug.

THE IRONWORKS IN Borgvik operated from 1600 to 1925. The foundry ruins and works buildings along with the striking manor and 18th-century church make Borgvik one of the leading monu-ments to a bygone industrial age in Värmland. Near Västra Smedbyn is **von Echstedtska Gården**. This impressive 1760s' Carolian manor is known for its murals. Even the privy has burlesque and, to say the least, educational paintings.

🏛 **von Echstedtska Gården**
Västra Smedbyn. 20 km (12 miles) NW
of Säffle. 📞 0533-630 74. ⏰ Jun–
Aug. 📷 📷 only pre-booked. 🚻 🛈

Värmlandsnäs ④

Värmland. 5 km (2 miles) S of Säffle.

JUTTING OUT INTO Lake Vänern is a large peninsula noted for its excellent agricultural land and the medieval churches of **Botilsäter** and **Millesvik**.

From the southernmost tip in Ekenäs it is possible to head out to **Lurö**, Sweden's largest inland archipelago. This is the ideal spot to enjoy countryside well off the beaten track. The boat trip to the main island of Lurö takes an hour.

**Perfect bathing spots along the
shore at Värmlandsnäs**

SELMA LAGERLÖF

In 1909, Selma Lagerlöf (1858–1940) became the first woman to receive the Nobel prize for literature. And despite the passing of a century since she wrote her first masterpiece, interest in the author's captivating adventures continues unabated. Numerous film and TV versions of her works have been produced, including *The Treasure, Thy Soul Shall Bear Witness!*, *The Emperor of Portugallia* and *Jerusalem*. When she made her debut in 1891 with the imaginative novel *Gösta Berling's Saga*, she put the Värmland countryside around the Fryken lakes and the family estate of Mårbacka on the literary map. Even more remarkable was the success of *The Wonderful Adventures of Nils*. The tale of the tiny boy's epic journey with wild geese was translated around the world.

**Selma Lagerlöf,
sculpture by Carl
Eldh, Rottneros**

The Almen quarter, a heritage centre in Karlstad on the Klarälven river

Karlstad ❺

Värmland. E18. 🏠 57,000. ✈ 🚊
🚌 ℹ️ Norra Strandgatan, 054-29 84
00. 🚢 Harbour Festival (Jul/Aug),
Round Vänern Race (Jul/Aug),
Swedish Rally (1st weekend in Feb).
🌐 www.karlstad.se

THE PHRASE *"Sola i Karlsta"*
(Enjoy the sun in Karlstad)
has been used to attract visitors
to the Värmland metropolis.
Yet the truth is that this is no
sunnier a place than any other
in the province. It was, in fact,
a jovial hostess at the town's
inn who brought sunshine into
people's lives in the early 19th
century – her statue now
stands outside the Stadshotell.
But Karlstad has plenty of
other attractions. It was built
on the delta formed by the
Klarälven river before it flows
into Lake Vänern, and was a
market town in medieval
times. It received its charter in
1584 along with its name from
the then king, Karl IX.

Karlstad has been devastated
by fire on many occasions,
most recently in 1865. The
Almen quarter on Västra
Älvgrenen is a heritage centre
comprising traditional wooden
houses which survived the
blaze. Thanks to its large
garden, another survivor was
the bishop's palace, built in
1781. The cathedral was less
fortunate, having to have its
exterior rebuilt along with
its tower. Parts of the early
18th-century interior were
preserved. A well-known
feature of the town is the 12-
arched Östra Bron bridge,
built in 1811. A good insight
into Värmland's history and

folk culture can be gained at
Värmlands Museum down
by the river. The museum also
runs the beautifully situated
Alsters Herrgård, 8 km (5
miles) east of Karlstad, birthplace of poet Gustaf Fröding
in 1860. The manor is a
memorial to him and
other local poets.

The open-air
museum in **Marie-
bergsskogen** has
several historic
buildings, including a
sauna and smoking
hut built by Finnish
immigrants to the
manor of Marieberg.
In the grounds lies
Värmlands Naturum,
featuring the flora and fauna
of the province.

🏛 **Värmlands Museum**
Sandgrundsudden. 400 m (440 yd) N
of the centre. 📞 054-14 31 00.
🕐 Tue–Sun. 🎟 🅿 📷 🍴 📖 🔗 &
🏛 **Alsters Herrgård**
8 km (5 miles) E of Karlstad. 📞 054-
83 40 81. 🕐 May–Aug: daily;
Sep–Dec & Feb–Apr: one weekend a
month. 🎟 🅿 🖼 🔗

**Gustaf Fröding
(1860–1911)**

Hagfors ❻

Värmland. Road 62. 🏠 6,500.
🚌 ℹ️ Folkets Väg 1, 0563-156 50.
🚗 Swedish Rally (early Feb),
Klarhelgen Festival (early Jul),
Klarälvsmässan Fair (3rd week in Aug).

IN THE HEART OF Värmland on
the Klarälven river lies
Hagfors, which has long been
a centre for the steel and
forestry industries. Today,
steel is still manufactured in
Uddeholm just to the west of
the town.

Hagfors is a good starting
point for trips up the Klarälven
valley and out into the forest.
Various places upriver offer raft
trips, which provide the opportunity to spend a few relaxing
days drifting at 1–2 knots,
watching the world go by.
Ekshärad, 20 km (12 miles)
north of Hagfors, has a
red shingled church
built in 1686 with
superb views of the
river. The church-
yard is known for
around 300 iron
crosses with "leaves"
which play in
the wind.
South of the
town is the
Rovdjurscenter,
which specializes in
the big four predators: lynx,
bear, wolf and wolverine. In
addition to its permanent
exhibits, the centre offers
guided tours of the habitats
of these animals.

🐾 **Rovdjurscenter,
Ekshärad**
25 km (16 miles) NW of Hagfors.
📞 0563-54 05 90. 🕐 19 May–
17 Sep: daily. 🎟 🅿 📷 🖼 &

Alsters Herrgård, near Karlstad, birthplace of poet Gustaf Fröding

Filipstad ⑦

Värmland. Road 63. 🚗 6,500. 🚆 🚌
ℹ️ *Stora Torget 3 D, 0590-613 54.*
🎪 *Oxhälja Market (1st week in Sep).*

KARL IX FOUNDED Filipstad in 1611, naming it after his son Karl Filip. Mining, ironworking and blacksmithing were the mainstay of the town, but today it is known for a very different type of industry – it is home to the world's largest crispbread bakery, owned by Wasabröd. Guided tours of the factory show how this very Swedish product is made.

Two of the town's great sons have contrasting memorials. A life-size sculpture by K G Bejemark of the popular poet and songwriter Nils Ferlin (1898–1961) in top hat and tails has been placed on a park bench. Next to Daglösen lake stands inventor John Ericsson's imposing mausoleum. He was a locomotive and warship pioneer and inventor of the screw propeller. Two *Monitor*-type cannons stand next to the monument.

John Ericsson grew up along with his equally illustrious brother Nils in the mining community of **Långban**, 20 km (12 miles) north of Filipstad. Here an entire community built around iron has been

Alfred Nobel's laboratory in the Nobelmuseet, as it was when he died

preserved, including a foundry, now renovated, gaming house and pithead buildings. Mineral hunters investigating the slag heaps of Långban have unearthed an exceptionally diverse collection of no less than 312 minerals.

🚉 Långban

20 km (12 miles) N of Filipstad.
📞 *0590-221 81.* ⏰ *Jun–Aug: daily.*
♿ 🅿️ 🍴 🏛️

Poet Nils Ferlin on his park bench in Filipstad

Karlskoga ⑧

Värmland. E18. 🚗 29,000. 🚆
ℹ️ *Kyrkbacken 9, 0586-614 74.*
🎪 *Swedish Touring Car Championship (end May & mid-Aug); Beach Festival (end Jul).*

IRON ORE has been mined and processed in this area since the 13th century, but it was not until Alfred Nobel *(see p69)* bought the Bofors ironworks and cannon factory in 1894 that the foundation was laid for Karlskoga's expansion. During the 20th century, Bofors grew to become one of the world's leading arms manufacturers.

The **Nobelmuseet** in Björkborns manor, Nobel's last home, shows developments at Bofors and offers an insight into the life of the inventor. Nobel's laboratory is just as he left it when he died. The stable where he kept his Russian stallions is now an industrial museum displaying the history of the ironworks.

Karlskoga's only preserved blast furnace can be found at **Granbergsdals Hytta**, 10 km (6 miles) north of the town.

At the end of the Ice Age water poured out from a lake at **Sveafallen** near Degerfors, 15 km (9 miles) south of Karlskoga. The landscape it created can be seen in the Domedagsdalen (Doomsday valley) and from walking trails through the nature reserve.

Kristinehamn is an idyllic town 25 km (16 miles) west of Karlskoga. Its claim to fame is Picasso's 15-m (50-ft) high sculpture of a Native American head to the south of the town.

🏛️ Nobelmuseet

2 km (1 mile) N of the centre.
📞 *0586-834 94.* ⏰ *Jun–Aug: daily; other times: phone to book.* ♿ 🏛️

THE INVENTOR JOHN ERICSSON

The multi-talented Swedish-American inventor John Ericsson (1803–89) was born in Långban, Värmland, where his father was mine captain. At the age of 13, he was employed in the construction of the Göta Canal *(see p146)*, together with his brother, Nils (1802–70), the father of the Swedish railway. He wrestled with the development of a steam engine and in his early twenties went to England to exploit his invention. He constructed a groundbreaking engine (1829) which, in

John Ericsson's mausoleum

the locomotive *Novelty*, took part in the Manchester-Liverpool race and was narrowly beaten by George Stephenson's *Rocket*. In the USA, Ericsson designed the frigate *Princeton*, and fitted his newly created screw propeller. In competition, the ship claimed victory over the fastest paddle-steamer of the day, the *Great Western*. Ericsson's ultimate triumph came in the American Civil War with the design of the armour-plated warship *Monitor*, with a rotating cannon tower. She overcame the Southern States' *Merrimac* in 1862.

Stjärnsunds Slott, home of Gustaf, the 19th-century "singing prince"

Askersund ❾

Närke. 🚶 4,000. 🚆 🚌 ℹ️ Rådhuset, 0583-810 00. 🎷 Trad Jazz
Festival (2nd week in Jun), Golf Week
(2nd week in Jul), All Car and Bike
Meet (end of Jul).

ON THE NORTH SHORE of Lake
Vättern lies Askersund,
the main town of southern
Närke, offering easy access to
the forests of Tiveden and
islands on the lake. Askersund
received a mention in a Papal
letter dated 1314. A devastating
fire struck the town in 1776,
but many wooden buildings
constructed since then have
been preserved.

The brick-built church,
Landskyrkan, designed by
Jean de la Vallé in 1670,
survived the fire. It is one of
the most splendid religious
buildings from Sweden's Age
of Greatness (see pp36–7),
with its magnificent Baroque
pulpit and altar-piece. The
Oxenstierna-Soopska chapel
designed by Erik Dahlbergh
contains a tin sarcophagus.

ENVIRONS: Lake Vättern's northern archipelago comprises
around 50 islands, most of
which are a nature reserve.
The islands can be reached by
boat from Askersund. Plying
the route is the S/S Motala
Express, which entered service
in 1895 and is known as "the
prisoner of Vättern" as she is
too large to leave the lake via
the Göta Canal.

Stjärnsunds Slott 4 km (2
miles) south of Askersund was
the home of the "singing
prince" Gustaf (1827–52), the
song-writing son of Oscar I.
Built in the early 19th century,
it was so lavishly decorated
that today it is considered to

contain Sweden's finest mid-
19th-century interiors.

🏛 **Stjärnsunds Slott**
4 km (2 miles) S of Askersund.
📞 0583-100 04. 🕐 1 May–31 Aug:
daily; other times by appointment. 🎫
🚶 obligatory. 🖥

Örebro ❿

See pp238–9.

Ludvika ⓫

Dalarna. Road 50. 🚶 14,000. 🚆 🚌
✕ ℹ️ Fredsgatan 10, 0240-860 50.
🎷 Dan Andersson Week (last week in
Jul), Dragon Boat Festival (May/Jun),
Ludvika Festival (1st week in Jul).
🌐 www.ludvika.se

THE WESTERN part of Bergslagen has foundries, mines
and mining magnates' estates
around every corner. The
industry has also left its mark
on the main town, Ludvika.
**Ludvika Gammelgård och
Gruvmuseum** offers a good
impression of mining as it was
in bygone times and more can
be seen out and about in the
surrounding countryside.

ENVIRONS: For many years
Grängesberg, 16 km (10
miles) southwest of Ludvika,

was central Sweden's largest
iron ore mine. It was closed
in 1989. Ore deposits extended beneath the settlement,
and in places buildings had to
be abandoned to allow mining
to continue. The ore was
taken by railway to Oxelö-
sund on the Baltic coast.

**Grängesbergs Lok-
museum** (the Locomotive
Museum) contains the world's
only operational steam
turbine locomotive.

Skattlösberg 35 km (22
miles) northwest of Ludvika,
is where Dan Andersson,
"poet of the forests", was born
in 1888. It is typical of the
villages created by immigrant
Finns in the 17th and 18th
centuries. **Luossastugan**,
where Andersson used to
write, is now a memorial to
the much loved poet.

🏛 **Ludvika Gammelgård
och Gruvmuseum**
Ludvika. 📞 0240-100 19.
🕐 16 Jun–17 Aug: daily; 1–15 Jun
& 18–31 Aug: Mon–Fri. 🎫 🎫 🖥
🏛 **Grängesbergs
Lokmuseum**
Grängesberg. 📞 0240-204 93.
🕐 10 Jun–10 Jul: daily. ● Midsummer's Eve. 🎫 🎫 🖥
🏛 **Luossastugan**
Skattlösberg. 📞 0240-860 50.
🕐 15 May–Aug: daily. 🎫 🎫

Hedemora ⓬

Dalarna. Road 70. 🚶 16,000. 🚆 🚌
ℹ️ Långgatan 1, 0225-343 48.
🎷 Daldansen Dance Festival (last week
in Jul), Hedemora Market (mid-May).

THIS SMALL DALARNA town is
the oldest in the province
with a charter dating from
1459. The 13th-century church
and the pharmacy built in 1779
are among the few buildings
which survived a major fire in

Hedemora, Dalarna's oldest town, granted a town charter in 1459

1849. Another survivor is **Theaterladan** from the 1820s. It was built by a theatre-loving merchant above a granary. Performances take place here in the spirit of the early 19th century and the grain has made way for a museum.

ENVIRONS: Husbyringen, north of Hedemora, is the location for a 60-km (37-mile) circular tour, taking in the countryside and local culture. There are mining centres en route, such as Silvhytteå and Långshyttan. Kloster has the ruins of an abbey. The star feature is Stjärnsund's 18th-century mining settlement, where the father of Swedish mechanics, Christopher Polhem, worked. **Polhemsmuseet** exhibits the work of this inventive genius, including the Stjärnsund clock and ingenious Polhem lock.

Carl Larssongården, a place of pilgrimage for interior designers

ENVIRONS: Stora Tuna, 4 km (2 miles) southeast of Borlänge, is the traditional centre of the flatlands. The medieval church was built at the end of the 15th century with the aim of becoming Dalarna's cathedral, but the province never became a diocese. Its treasures include a 15th-century crucifix.

At **Ornässtugan**, it is said that in the 16th century the future king, Gustav Vasa, fled ignominiously from Danish knights via the privy.

Christopher Polhem (1661–1751)

🖼 **Theaterladan**
Gussarvsgatan 10. 📞 0225-151 15.
🕐 15 May–Sep. 📷 phone for tour.
🏛 **Polhemsmuseet**
Stjärnsund, 15 km (9 miles) S of Hedemora. 📞 0225-800 90, winter 0225-80131. 🕐 Jun: Sat–Sun; Jul–Aug: daily. 🏷 📷 pre-book. 🖼 🏠 ♿

Borlänge ⑬

Dalarna. Road 50. 🚗 45,000. 🚌
🚆 ℹ Sveagatan 1, 0243-25 74 90.
🎿 Darlekarlia Cup (early Jul); Festival salute (1st week in Sep).
🌐 www.borlange.com

DALARNA'S SECOND largest town, Borlänge came to prominence in the 1870s when the Domnarvets Jernverk ironworks was established and several railway lines came together here. But it only received its town charter in 1944. In recent years it has gained a university college to add to its iron and paper industries.
Jussi Björlingmuseet celebrates the town's greatest son, the internationally renowned tenor Jussi Björling (1911–60). All his recordings can be enjoyed here.

🏛 **Jussi Björlingmuseet**
Borganäsvägen 25. 📞 0243- 742 40.
🕐 Sep–May: Tue–Fri; Jun–Aug: daily.
⚫ 1 & 6 Jan, Easter, Ascension Day, Midsummer, 24 & 31 Dec. 🏷 📷 ♿
🏛 **Ornässtugan**
8 km (5 miles) NE of Borlänge.
📞 0243-22 30 72, 745 49. 🕐 Jun–Aug: daily; May, Sep pre-booking. 🏷
📷 obligatory. 🖼 🏠

Sundborn ⑭

Dalarna. 12 km (7 miles) NE of Falun.
🚶 800. 🖼 🖼 ℹ 023-600 53.

SITUATED IN THE village of Sundborn is **Carl Larssongården**, Lilla Hyttnäs, home of the artist Carl Larsson (1853–1919). The interior, containing wooden furniture and traditional Swedish textiles, along with influences from the Arts and Crafts movement and Art Nouveau, has been carefully preserved. Sundborn's shingled wooden church, built in 1755, features paintings by Larsson (1905) and the graveyard contains the artist's family plot.

Nearby, **Stora Hyttnäs** manor is a complete home from the start of the last century with an interesting textile collection and garden.

🏛 **Carl Larssongården**
📞 023-600 53. 🕐 May–Sep: daily; Oct–Apr: Tue. 🏷 📷 🖼 🏠 ♿
limited access.

CARL AND KARIN LARSSON

Through his book *A Home* (1899), the interior design of artist Carl Larsson and particularly his wife, Karin, as expressed in their house in Sundborn, attracted attention worldwide. The couple had lived around Europe before settling with their children in a wooden farmhouse in Sundborn. Here they were able to develop their ideas for home interiors, producing a decorative scheme in traditional rural Swedish style using rustic furniture, home-woven textiles and colourful country patterns combined with a touch of the Arts and Crafts and Art Nouveau movements. This was in strong contrast to the stifled, bourgeois tastes which prevailed at the end of the 19th century. The joy and happiness in the Larsson home can be traced in every brushstroke and line of his book illustrations, which perhaps explains why Carl and Karin's Swedish idyll continues to inspire interior designers (*see pp22–3*).

Karin and Kersti by Carl Larsson

Örebro ⑩

THERE HAS BEEN A TOWN on this site for 750 years, but in 1854 a major fire destroyed the centre of Örebro. This gave scope for a new, more spacious layout on both sides of the Svartån river and elegant buildings coupled with the castle and St Nicolai Kyrka created a particularly fine townscape. A local newspaper described it as "a magnificent 19th-century salon, extravagantly furnished with buildings which proclaim growth and success". But there is also a greener side to Örebro with the promenade that follows the Svartån river to the delights of Wadköping and Karlslund. The river can be explored on foot, by bicycle or in a rowing boat. The free salmon fishing should not be missed.

Örebro Slott on the Svartån river, now the county governor's residence

🏛 Örebro Slott

Kansligatan. ☎ 019-21 21 21.
◯ Sep–May: Sat–Sun; Jun–Aug: daily.
🎟 obligatory. 🖥 🚻 🚹 🔗 limited access. **Northwest Tower** ◯ daily, admission free.

Örebro Slott has dominated the town since Örebro received its charter in the 13th century. In 1347, King Magnus Eriksson gathered the great and the good at Örebro House, as the castle was then called, to adopt a common law for Sweden. At the end of the 16th century, King Karl IX remodelled the castle to create a Renaissance palace. Today's appearance, however, with its mighty round towers, is the result of major rebuilding in the 1890s.

The castle has been the scene of a number of historical events, including the adoption of the first Swedish Parliament Act in 1617 and the election of the French Marshal Jean-Baptiste Bernadotte as heir to the Swedish throne in 1810. Now it is the official residence of the county governor and also houses Örebro Tourist Office. An exhibition in the Northwest Tower highlights the castle's history.

🏛 Örebro Läns Museum

Engelbrektsgatan 3. ☎ 019-602 87 00. ◯ daily. ● public holidays 🎟 phone to book. 🖥 🔗

With its roots in the 1850s, the county museum is Sweden's oldest, although the main collection of more than 100,000 objects from across the county is on show in a 1960s' building in Slottsparken. A permanent exhibition focuses on farming since the Stone Age. The museum's most valuable artifacts, including the Viking silver from Eketorp (see p157), are housed in the Treasury. The museum also runs **Landstingsmuseet** in north Örebro, which is set in an 18th-century hospital building and covers healthcare and mental health through the centuries.

🏛 Rådhuset

Stora Torget. ● closed to the public. Built in 1858–63, the magnificent Neo-Gothic Town Hall was something of a showpiece in its time. King Karl XV didn't think the castle-like building befitted a provincial town, calling it: "...sparkling wine not weak beer!" Today only a fraction of Örebro's administration fits into the Town Hall, although it remains the seat of the Municipal Executive Board. When the clock chimes, automatons from Örebro's history appear, such as reformer Olaus Petri (see p53).

⛪ St Nicolai Kyrka

Nikolaigatan 8. ☎ 019-20 95 30.
◯ daily. 🎟 phone for info.
🔗 🚹 Sun.

The church on Stortorget has origins from the 13th century, but has been restyled many times. The north and south entrances are from the original church and were carved from Närke limestone. The rest is an example of English-inspired Neo-Gothic style, with the tower added at the end of the 19th century.

🏛 Wadköping

On the Svartån river, 1 km (half a mile) from the centre. ☎ Tourist Office, 019-21 21 21. ◯ daily.

The beautiful promenade along the Svartån river through Stadsparken leads to the idyllic wooden houses of Wadköping. This is a cultural centre to which old buildings have been moved to make way for the modern town. It is a vibrant community with craftworkers and small shops, and many people live here. The oldest building is the early 16th-century Kungsstugan (King's Cabin), named after its use by the then Duke

Wadköping, an open-air museum with traditional wooden houses

Karl on his visits to Örebro in the 1580s. His bedchamber has murals painted by his personal artist. Other buildings include Hamiltonska Huset (1844), moved here from the south of the town, where it was the grandest building of its era, and Cajsa Warg's Hus (17th century), the childhood home of the well-known cookery writer Casja Warg. In summer there are concerts and theatre performances.

🏛 Svampen
Dalbygatan 3. [019-611 37 35.] *May–Aug: daily; Sep–Apr: Sat–Sun.* 🏵 🖳 🍴 🚻 ⅙

The mushroom-shaped water tower, which offers a superb view of the town, the flatlands of Närke and Lake Hjälmaren, has become a symbol of Örebro. Since its opening in 1958, 8 million visitors have enjoyed the panorama from a height of 55 m (180 ft). Its construction has set something of a trend – there is a copy in Riyadh in Saudi Arabia.

The tower contains the science centre **Aqua Nova**, where the public has the opportunity to conduct practical experiments with water in all its forms.

🏛 Karlslunds Herrgård
5 km (3 miles) W of Örebro. Diedens Allé 11. [019-27 07 88.] *by appointment.* 🗝 *pre-book.*

Owned by Örebro town, the royal estate of Karlslunds Herrgård dates from the 16th century and brings together nature and culture in perfect harmony. The Gustavian manor house, built in 1804–1809, incorporates wings from the 18th century.

The estate was once a self-sufficient community with around 80 buildings. Craftspeople and artists work here and there are several museums and shops, as well

Karlslunds Herrgård's Gustavian manor house dating from 1804–1809

as nature trails. Carlslunds Kraftstation, built in 1897, is the country's oldest working power station. There is a restored mill housing technological exhibits and an experiment workshop. In the dairy, a museum shows the harsh life of the agricultural labourer in the early 20th century.

Originally, the gardens at Karlslund were remarkably grand and over the past 30 years work has been ongoing to restore them to their former glory, partly in the form of an ecopark.

ÖREBRO TOWN CENTRE

0 metres   400
0 yards   400

KEY

🚉 Train station
🚌 Bus terminal
🅿 Parking
🛉 Church
🛈 Tourist information

The huge Stora Stöten (Great Pit) in the old Falu copper mine outside Falun

Falun ⑮

Dalarna. Road 50. 🚶 *35,000.* 🚌
🚌 ✕ 🚏 *Ttotzgatan 10–12,
023-830 50.* 📷 *Falukalaset (start of
Jun), Falun Då – festival at World
Heritage Site (start of Jul), Falun Folk
Festival (mid-Jul).*

IT GOES WITHOUT saying that
Falun has had a colourful
impact on Sweden. Wooden
buildings painted in the
distinctive Falu red can be
seen everywhere. The paint
has been made since the 17th
century from powdered ore
containing ferrous sulphate
from the Falu mine, on the
back of which the town was
founded. Stora Kopparberget
(Copper Mountain) was the
country's treasure chest – at
its peak, two-thirds of the
world's copper was mined
here. The entire area, including Stora Stöten (the Great
Pit, formed by a collapse in
1687), Falun's historic
buildings and industrial
remains, outlying settlements
and the **Gruvmuseet** (the
Mining Museum), was
designated a UNESCO World
Heritage Site in 2001.
Dalarnas Museum gives a
broad insight into the cultural
history of Dalarna with
extensive collections of folk
costumes, local paintings and
traditional craftwork.

🏛 Gruvmuseet
1 km (half a mile) S of the centre.
📞 *023-78 20 30.* ☐ *Oct–Apr: Sat,
Sun; May–Sep: daily.* ⬤ *1 Jan, Good
Friday, Midsummer, 24 & 25 Dec.*
📷 🚻 🖼 🏛 ♿

🏛 Dalarnas Museum
📞 *023-76 55 00.* ☐ *daily.* ⬤ *Good
Friday, Midsummer, 24 & 25 Dec.*
📷 🚻 🖼 ♿

Leksand ⑯

Dalarna. Road 70. 🚶 *15,500.* 🚌 🚉
🚏 *Norsgatan, 0247-79 61 30.*
📷 *Music on Siljan Lake (Jul), Rowing
race in church boats (1st Sun Jul),
Himlaspelet Pageant (Jul).*
🌐 *www.siljan.se*

THE LANDSCAPE around Siljan
lake is especially beautiful,
but the Leksand area is the
most striking. One of the best
times to see the lake is during
the annual rowing race in
church boats in early July.
Another annual event is
Himlaspelet, one of Sweden's
oldest rural pageants. First
performed in 1941, Rune
Lindström's play about a path
which leads to heaven depicts
the witch trials of the 1670s.
The onion dome of Lek-
sand's 18th-century Baroque
church can be seen from far
and wide. Parts of the church
date from the 13th century.

**ENVIRONS: Karlfeldtsgården –
Sångs i Sjugare** was the
summer retreat of author and
Nobel prize-winner Erik Axel
Karlfeldt (1864–1931). It lies

The folk sculpture *Dalecarlian
Couple* in Leksand

on Opplimen lake just north
of Leksand. Here it is possible
to follow in the footsteps of
the author's heroine, who
came wandering over the
meadows of Sjugare. Also
worth a visit is the garden on
the poet's estate.
Younger visitors to Leksand
will be attracted by **Äventyret
Sommarland**, comprising
three amusement parks on the
banks of Siljan lake: Waterland,
Motorland and Summerland.
Insjön, 8 km (5 miles) south
of Leksand was the birthplace
in 1899 of the Swedish mail
order business run by Åhlén &
Holms. The mail order
tradition lives on with Clas
Ohlson, whose store attracts
so many DIY enthusiasts that
Insjön has become Dalarna's
most visited tourist destination.

**🏛 Karlfeldtsgården – Sångs
i Sjugare**
7 km (4 miles) N of the centre. Road
Rv 70. 📞 *0247-600 28.* ☐ *Jun–Jul:
Tue, Thu & Sat.* 🖼
🎢 Äventyret Sommarland
📞 *0247-13375.* ☐ *May–Aug daily.*
⬤ *Midsummer's Eve.* 🖼
📷 🖼 🏛

Rättvik ⑰

Dalarna. Road 70. 🚶 *4,500.* 🚌 🚉
🚏 *Stationshuset, 0248-79 72 10.*
📷 *Music on Siljan Lake (Jul), Classic
Car Week (late Jul).*

NO ONE CAN FAIL to notice
Rättvik's landmark, Lång-
bryggan pier. After docking at
the pier on the *M/S Gustaf
Wasa*, passengers have a 628-
m (690-yd) walk to reach the
mainland. The pier with all its
fine carpentry was built in
1895 to allow steam boats to

moor near the shallow shore. Rättvik also has a medieval church, beautifully situated on a promontory surrounded by former church stables – the oldest dating from the 1470s.

ENVIRONS: A search for older Dalarna buildings, rural communities and paintings will be rewarded at **Gammelstan** in Norrboda, 35 km (22 miles) north of Rättvik. The village street is lined with old buildings, some of which date back to the 17th century.

Tällberg, 12 km (7 miles) south on the shore of Lake Siljan, has many preserved timber houses in the classic Dalarna style. It is also known for its top-class hotels and guest houses, including the renowned Åkerblads *(see p288)* with its excellent restaurant. At the top of the village, Holens Gammelgård features workshops selling traditional handicrafts.

At **Dalhalla**, 7 km (4 miles) north of Rättvik, a limestone quarry has been converted into an auditorium. The quarry forms an amphitheatre with unique acoustics which have been praised by the world's top opera singers. Concerts are held in summer, and Dalhalla can also be toured in the day. The area was formed 360 million years ago when a meteor landed here, creating a crater which encompasses the whole of the Siljan region.

🏛 Dalhalla
7 km (4 miles) NW of the centre. Road 70. 📞 *0248-79 79 50.* ⭕ *for performances and tours.* 📷 🍴 🔴 ♿

Mora ⓲

Dalarna. Road 70. 🏠 *11,000.* 🚌 🚉 ✈ ℹ *Siljan Tourism Mora, Stationsvägen, 0250-59 20 20.* 🎿 *Vasaloppet Ski Race (1st Sun in Mar), Stora Daldansen Dance Festival (3rd week in May).*

Bedroom in Zorngården, Anders Zorn's home and studio

THE MUNICIPALITY of Mora and the town itself – beautifully situated between Orsasjön and Siljan lakes – offers a wide range of attractions. Mora is particularly associated with King Gustav Vasa (1496–1560) and artist Anders Zorn (1860–1920). Gustav Vasa's travels in Dalarna in 1520 to mobilize local men against the Danish occupation have left many traces. Near Mora, the Utmeland monument (1860) shows several romanticized paintings chronicling Gustav's adventures. It was built over the cellar where he is said to have hidden from Danish scouts. The annual Vasaloppet ski race *(see p245)* is another memorial to the king. At the finishing line in Mora stands Anders Zorn's statue of Gustav Vasa and the nearby **Vasaloppsmuseet** recounts the history of the famous ski race.

Anders Zorn became known internationally not least for his portraits of plump, naked local women. He was genuinely interested in peasant culture and an ardent collector of local handicrafts. In **Zorngården**, which he built himself, he revelled in a world of National Romanticism. On the estate there are a number of older buildings which have been moved here, such as the 12th-century bakehouse which was used as a studio. The nearby Zornmuseet displays Zorn's own art and private collections.

ENVIRONS: Nusnäs, 8 km (5 miles) south of Mora, is where the national symbol of Sweden, the Dala horse, is manufactured. Originally a 19th-century toy, the horses

Zorn's statue of Gustav Vasa in Mora

are carved with a knife and colourfully decorated. It is possible to watch them being made on weekdays.

On the island of **Sollerön** on Lake Siljan is the boatyard where the traditional church boats used for church outings and rowing races between the lakeside villages are made. There is also a pretty church dating from 1785.

Tomteland in Gesunda is the home of Father Christmas and his workshop, which is busy all summer making presents for children. The huge park offers various activities, including the witch's school – strictly for youngsters who want to learn about magic and how to help friends and protect the environment.

🏛 Vasaloppsmuseet
Vasaloppets Hus. 📞 *0250-392 25.* ⭕ *16 Jun–14 Aug: daily; 15 Aug–15 Jun: Mon–Fri.* 🔴 *public holidays.* 📷 📹 ♿

🏛 Zorngården
Vasagatan 36. 📞 *0250-59 23 10, 0250-59 23 16.* ⭕ *daily.* 🔴 *24 & 25 Dec, Good Friday.* 📷 📹

🏛 Tomteland
Gesunda. 12 km (7.5 miles) S of Mora. 📞 *0250-287 70.* ⭕ *varies, phone for info.* 📷 📹

A giant-sized Dala horse, manufactured in Nusnäs

Horse-riding in Dalafjällen, one of the many outdoor activities on offer

Orsa ⑲

Dalarna. Road Rv 45. ⚘ *5,200.* 🚌
🛈 *Dalagatan 1, 0250-55 25 50.*
⚑ *Stone Symposium (Jun), Orsayran Music Festival (Weds in Jul).*

T HE ORSA REGION extends
from the gentle agricul-
tural landscape around Lake
Orsasjön to the desolate lands
of Finnmark in the north.

In the past many of the
local inhabitants made grind-
stones as a sideline, a skill
which can now be studied
at **Slipstensmuseet** in
Mässbacken, 12 km (7 miles)
northeast of Orsa.

In this part of Sweden
animals are still taken to the
mountains for summer
grazing. Around Djurberga,
Fryksås and Hallberg it is
possible to see how dairy-
maids used to live, far from
their villages, churning butter
and making cheese from the
milk of hornless mountain
cattle and goats.

In **Våmhus**, on the western
side of Orsasjön, two crafts
are practised which in the
past were a major source of
income locally: basket weaving
and making jewellery out of
hair. The women used to
walk as far afield as St
Petersburg in Russia, and
Germany, to sell their work.
Orsa Grönklitt, 10 km (6
miles) north of Orsa, is the
main area for outdoor
activities. At Orsa Björnpark
(Orsa Bear Park) special paths
and ramps allow a close-up
view of the bears, wolves,
lynx and wolverine which live
here in large enclosures.

🏛 **Slipstensmuseet**
Mässbacken. 📞 *0250-55 02 55.*
⏱ *summer.* 🅿 ♿ *pre-book.* 🚌 🍴

🦌 Orsa Grönklitt

Grönklitt. 15 km (9 miles) NW of
Orsa. 🛈 *0250-462 00.* ⏱ *daily.* 🅿
🚌 🍴 ♿

Sälen ⑳

Dalarna. Road 71. ⚘ *500.* 🚌 🛈
Centrumhuset, 0280-187 00 ⚑
*Snowboarding World Cup, Speed
Skiing World Cup (May), Vasaloppet
Ski Race (first Sun in Mar).*

L IKE THE MAJORITY of
Dalarna's mountains,
Transtrandsfjällen, with Sälen
at their heart, are rounded
and undulating and less dramatic than the those further to
the north. The highest peak,
Östra Granfjället, is 949 m
(3,114 ft) above sea level.
However, the terrain is
excellent for both downhill
and cross-country skiing and
this, combined with its relative
proximity to Sweden's cities,
has made the area one of the
country's leading destinations
for winter sports enthusiasts.

Whether it's black runs for
advanced skiers, velodrome
curves, spines or jumps for
snowboarders, or family
slopes for children, there is
plenty to choose from in
Sälen. Around 200 km (124
miles) of trails are marked for
cross-country skiers and
summer hikers alike.

Sälen is the starting point of
the 90-km (56-mile) Vasaloppet
ski race to Mora.

Idre and Särna ㉑

Dalarna. Road 70. ⚘ *1,500.* 🚌 🛈
*Framgårdsvägen 1, Idre; Särnavägen 6,
Särna; 0253-200 00.* ⚑ *Mountain
Orienteering (4th week in Jun),
Mountain Festival (2nd week in Jul),
Festival Week (3rd week in Jul).*

N ORTHERNMOST Dalarna,
with the towns of Idre
and Särna, belonged to
Norway until 1644 and the
local dialects still sound
Norwegian. This is a mountainous region and the views
from the peaks are impressive.
In the Nipfjället mountains it
is possible to drive up to a
height of 1,000 m (3,280 ft) for
a good view of Städjan, a
peak 1,131 m (3,710 ft) high.
The STF mountain station at
Grövelsjön on Långfjället, to
the north, is an ideal starting
point for mountain tours.
Idrefjäll is a modern tourist
resort on Idresjön lake with
excellent slopes and lifts.
Särna has a beautiful wooden
church dating from the late
17th century and the rural
museum of Buskgården.
Fulufjället National Park
contains Sweden's highest
waterfall, Njupeskär, with a
drop of 90 m (295 ft). The
effects of a violent storm in
August 1997 can still be seen
here when 400 mm (16 in)
of rain fell in 24 hours.
Streams became torrents and
fallen trees dammed the
water, ploughing wide
furrows through the forest.

The distinctive peak of Städjan in the Nipfjället mountains

◁ **Interior of a traditional mountain pasture hut at Balungen in eastern Dalarna**

The Vasaloppet Ski Race

THE WORLD'S LONGEST and oldest ski race was first held in 1922 when 136 competitors skied the 90 km (56 miles) from Sälen to Mora. Today more than 14,000 skiers take on the challenge on the first Sunday in March. Many more prefer the calmer Open Track race held the previous weekend or special races such as *Tjejvasan* for women. A staff of 3,000 support the skiers by providing blueberry soup, ski waxing and blister plasters. And all

Wreath bearer

because in 1520 Gustav Vasa could not get the men of Dalarna to rise up against the Danes. Disheartened, he fled on skis from the Danish troops towards Norway, but when the local men heard about the Stockholm Bloodbath *(see p58)*, they changed their minds and their two best skiers raced to intercept their future king near Sälen.

In summer, a hiking trail follows the course from Berga in Sälen to the finish at Zorn's statue of Gustav Vasa in Mora.

Berga, just south of the village of Sälen, is the starting point for the 14,000 skiers who are let loose in the early dawn in several stages, top skiers first.

Evertsberg lies halfway between Sälen and Mora. Here, as in many places along the route, the competitors fortify themselves with blueberry soup. Those only skiing half the race can leave the track at this point.

The first steep hills are succeeded by flat marshland.

VÄSTERDALÄLVEN
● Sälen
Smågan
11 km (7 miles)
● Berga
● Transtrand
Mångsbodarna
24 km (15 miles)
VANÅN
Risberg
35 km (22 miles)
Evertsberg
47 km (29 miles)
ÖSTERDALÄLVEN
Oxberg
61 km (38 miles)
Hökberg
70 km (43 miles)
Eldris
80 km (50 miles)
Mora
90 km (56 miles)

0 kilometres   20
0 miles   10

THE FIRST VASALOPPET

At Christmas 1520 Gustav Vasa fled on skis from Mora towards Norway to escape Danish troops. At Lima, near Sälen, local men caught up with him and persuaded the future king to turn back. Since 1922 almost 750,000 skiers have repeated the achievement, albeit skiing in the opposite direction.

Mora marks the end of the race. The winning time is usually just over four hours, but some entrants can take ten hours. The text on the finishing line reads: "In the footsteps of our forefathers for the victories of tomorrow."

SOUTHERN NORRLAND

THE SIX PROVINCES OF SOUTHERN NORRLAND *cover almost a quarter of the country. The character shifts noticeably from the coast with its industry and fishing to the farming communities up along the river valleys, then westwards through forests to the mountains of Härjedalen and Jämtland. Natural resources such as timber and waterpower have had a visible impact on the region.*

In the Middle Ages, the southeasterly province of Gästrikland belonged to Svealand and its gently rolling landscape is more akin to that of neighbouring Uppland than Norrland. An offshoot of the Bergslagen mining district extends into this area and iron-working formed the basis of today's manufacturing industry. The trading port of Gävle has long been a gateway to Norrland.

The pass between Kölberget and Digerberget in the province of Hälsingland is another gateway to the north, beyond which the mountainous Norrland landscape becomes more evident. Huge wooden mansions stand proud with their ornate porches and exquisitely decorated interiors. These houses are evidence of the successful trade in the green gold of the local forests in a landscape of which 80 per cent is covered with productive woodland.

Exploitation of the forests had an even bigger impact on the provinces of Medelpad and Ångermanland. At the end of the 19th century, the timber barons of Sundsvall and Ådalen made themselves a fortune. Today, processing wood into pulp and paper is still a key industry. The smell of sulphur can be quite striking – or could it be the herring dish *surströmming*, best sampled by those who dare at one of the fishing villages along the High Coast, a UNESCO World Heritage Site *(see p256)*.

The provinces of Jämtland and Härjedalen only became part of Sweden in 1645. There is often talk of the "Republic of Jämtland" among diehard locals who seek self-rule. The mountains stretch out to the west, attracting visitors both to the ski resorts and to the upland areas where the wildlife and countryside can still be enjoyed undisturbed.

A reindeer herd round-up for division according to owner, by use of lassos and ear tags

◁ **The mighty Tännforsen Falls on the Åreälven river, with a drop of 26 m (85 ft)**

Exploring Southern Norrland

IN THIS REGION OF IMMENSE CONTRASTS, the coastal provinces of Gästrikland and Hälsingland are home to a colourful rural culture enlivened with traditional folk music and dancing. The High Coast, with its dramatic island archipelago accessible by bridges and ferries, is Ångermanland's contribution to UNESCO's list of World Heritage Sites. Inland, the mountainous provinces of Jämtland and Härjedalen offer wide open spaces for skiing and hiking.

One of the best ways to experience Norrland's varied landscape is to start from the coast and follow one of the river valleys which cut across the country. As the roads wind up-river, they pass through dense forests and on up into the mountains. Alternatively, the Inlandsbanan railway provides a more unusual way of enjoying the hinterland in comfort *(see p331).*

The heather and rushing streams of Helag, with the mountain of Helagsfjället in the distance

GETTING AROUND

The E4 along the coast and the E14 from Sundsvall across the country to Trondheim in Norway are the main arteries for motorists. The inland roads running north-south are of a generally good standard. The roads east-west tend to follow the courses of the rivers. The main railway line runs north-south. Along the coast, the railway goes as far north as Härnösand before heading inland. The Jämtland mountains can be reached by train, but in Härjedalen transport is by car or bus. The Inlandsbanan railway operates in summer. Air travel is an option and the range of domestic flights is good.

KEY

▬▬▬	Motorway
▬▬	Major road
▬▬	Minor road
▬ ▬	Railway line

*Map labels:*
E6 (Norway)
● GÄD
JÄMTLAN
Kallsjön
336
340
Trondheim (Norway)
322
ÅRE 16
E14
Ånnsjön
17 STORLIEN
Indalsälven
Stor-sjön 321
ÖSTERSU
Sylarna 1728 m (5,670 ft)
Helagsfjället 1797 m (5,895 ft)
Ljungan
Röros (Norway)
18 **MOUNTAINS OF HÄRJEDALEN**
84
Ljusnan
HÄRJEDALEN
SVEG 19
Mo

A wooden mansion in Arbro, Hälsingland, typical of the area's traditional architecture

SEE ALSO

- **Where to Stay** pp288–9
- **Where to Eat** pp302–3

Nämforsen Falls and one of
Europe's largest rock
carving sites *(see p255)*

Dorotea

Åsele

STRÖMSUND

ÅNGERMANLAND

Umeå

ÖRNSKÖLDSVIK **12**

SOLLEFTEÅ **11**
ÅDALEN

| 0 kilometres | 50 |
| 0 miles | 30 |

KRAMFORS

13

THE HIGH COAST

HÄRNÖSAND **10**

MEDELPAD

LJUNGA-
DALEN **8**

9 SUNDSVALL

Dellen

DELSBO

6

HUDIKSVALL

Boathouses in Norrfällsviken on the High
Coast in Ångermanland *(see pp256–7)*

7

LSINGLAND

BOLLNÄS
5

4 SÖDERHAMN

GÄSTRIKLAND

SANDVIKEN **3**

GÄVLE **2**

DALÄLVEN DELTA
1

Uppsala

Avesta

SIGHTS AT A GLANCE

The Dalälven delta, one of the top ten fishing spots in Sweden

Dalälven Delta ❶

Gästrikland, Uppland. **i** Gysingö Tourist Office, 0291-210 00. **📷** Weir Day in Älvkarleby (first Sun before Midsummer).

BEFORE THE MIGHTY Dalälven river empties into the bay at Gävle, it forms an expansive delta with hundreds of small islands. The flora and fauna are particularly abundant and the area offers some of the best sport fishing in Sweden.

Least affected by forestry and farming is the area around Färnebofjärden, part of which was declared a national park in 1998. The birdlife is incredibly diverse, with more than 100 breeding species, including several different endangered woodpeckers and owls.

A good place to start exploring the area is Gysinge on road Rv 67, 38 km (24 miles) south of Gävle. The falls between Färnebofjärden and Hedesundafjärden attracted ironworking here at the end of the 17th century. The well-preserved industrial community has a main street dating from the 1770s and a magnificent manor from 1840. Gysinge is also home to **Dalälvarnas Flottnings-museum**, which shows just how important the river once was for timber transportation.

Another important feature of the Dalälven river is hydro-electric power, which manifests itself in **Älvkarleby**, further down-river. The imposing power station, built in 1915, is an attraction in itself, but the most impressive sight is when the water is released at full-flow on Weir Day. Älvkarleby attracts many anglers, who annually land as

much as 20 tonnes of salmon and sea trout.

In **Österfärnebo**, Koversta rural heritage centre is an 18th-century village, offering an insight into local rural life.

🏛 Dalälvarnas Flottningsmuseum
Gysinge Bruk. **📞** 0291-210 00. **○** mid-May–mid-Aug: daily. **📷 ♿**

Gävle ❷

Gästrikland. **👥** 68,000. **🚆 🚌 i** at the central station, 026-14 74 30. **📷** City Festival (1st week in Aug, Wed–Sat), Country Festival (1st week-end in Aug).

GÄSTRIKLAND'S main town has been the gateway to Norrland since the Middle Ages. The mouth of the Gävleån river made an ideal port and traders set up base here to conduct business in the north. The harbourside warehouses along Skeppsbron bear witness to this. Gävle remains one of Sweden's larger ports, although operations have moved further out into the bay. A fire in 1869

destroyed the buildings north of the river, with the exception of the town hall built in 1790 and **Heliga Trefaldighets-kyrkan**, a three-aisle Baroque church dating from 1654. As a result, Gävle has attractive 19th-century buildings and broad tree-lined esplanades as protection against fires. The jewel is the splendid theatre on Rådhusesplanaden, built in 1878. The city park, **Boulog-nerskogen**, which features Carl Milles's famous sculpture, *Five Playing Geniuses*, is the most popular of Gävle's parks.

South of the Gävleån river lies **Gävle Slott**, Sweden's northernmost royal fortification, dating from the 16th century. This is also the location of the old town, "Gamla Gefle", with the streets of wooden houses from the 18th century which have attracted many artists and craftsmen. **Joe Hill Gården** on N Bergsgatan, the birthplace of the Swedish-American union agitator, is now a museum. Other museums include **Länsmuseet Gävleborg** with extensive collections relating to the history of Gästrikland. **Sveriges Järnvägsmuseum** offers a delightful selection of old locomotives and carriages,

The oldest Swedish locomotive (1855) in Sveriges Järnvägsmuseum

from mining titans to neat little narrow-gauge carriages.

Fängelsemuseet is a small but fascinating museum housed in 17th-century prison cells. It gives an insight into prison life at the time.

Furuviksparken attracts families who come to enjoy its Nordic and exotic animals, and live performances, and to swim in a beautiful setting.

🏛 **Länsmuseet Gävleborg**
S. Strandgatan 20. 📞 026-65 56 00.
🕐 Tue–Sun. 🔵 public holidays. 📷 📶
🏛 **Sveriges Järnvägsmuseum**
Rälsgatan 1. 📞 026-14 46 15.
🕐 Jun–Aug: daily; Sep–May: Tue–Sun.
🔵 public holidays. 📷 📶 📶
🏛 **Fängelsemuseet**
Hamiltongatan 1. 📞 026-65 44 30.
🕐 Tue–Thu, Sat–Sun.
🔵 public holidays.
🎪 **Furuviksparken**
10 km (6 miles) E of the centre. Road
Rv 76. 📷 📞 026-17 73 00.
🕐 May–Aug: daily; Sep–Apr: by appointment. 📷 📶 📶 📶

Sandviken ❸

Gästrikland. 👥 23,000. 📷 📷
ℹ Folkets Hus, Köpmangatan 5–7,
026-24 13 80. 📷 Bangen Jazz Festival (end Jun), Chamber Music Festival (end Jul).

THE TOWN OF Sandviken grew up with the establishment of an ironworks on the shore of Storsjön lake in 1860. The new railway line to Gävle was one of the factors in its location. Using the groundbreaking Bessemer production process, Sandviken soon gained a reputation for its steel. In the 1920s it began making stainless steel and by the 1940s it was the world's leading producer of steel for tools and drill bits.

ENVIRONS: Evidence of Sandviken's ironworking roots can be seen in Högbo. Today the community is a centre for recreation and adventure sports. It is also home to the **Textilmuseet**, an offshoot of Nordiska Museet *(see pp88–9)*, with the country's finest collection of textiles and handicrafts.

Opposite Sandviken, on the southern shores of Storsjön,

lies the medieval church of **Årsunda**, with paintings by the master Eghil. Just south of the church is a Viking burial ground, which inspired the Årsunda Viking centre, offering activities with a Viking slant.

🏛 **Textilmuseet**
Högbo, 5 km (3 miles) N of the centre. 📞 026-21 50 01. 🕐 Jul: daily; Aug–Jun: Tue–Sun. 🔵 some public holidays.
📷 📶

Söderhamn ❹

Hälsingland. 👥 12,700. 📷 📷
ℹ Resecentrum, railway station, 0270-753 53. 📷 Family fun evenings at Östra Berget (Thu in Jul), Herring Games (mid-Aug).

SWEDEN'S AMBITIONS for power and the need for armaments lead to the foundation of Söderhamn in 1620. Hälsingland's weapon makers were brought together from around the region to work in the town. The gun and rifle-making factory, built in 1748, now houses the town museum, **Söderhamns Stadsmuseum**.

Russian attacks in 1721 and four disastrous fires have meant that the only remaining building of significance is **Ulrika Eleonora Kyrka**. The

Part of an old furnace in the town of Sandviken, famous for its steel production

pink cruciform church was designed by Tessin the Younger in 1693. The upside of the fires is that a series of parks now creates a green patchwork around the city. Söderhamn's landmark is the **Oscarsborg** tower, which rises proudly on Östra Berget. Anyone braving the 125 steps is rewarded with a breathtaking view of the town and archipelago.

ENVIRONS: The 10 km (6 miles) of the Söderhamnsfjärden inlet were lined with 11 steam-powered sawmills during the industrial boom of the late 19th century. The industrial museum in Ljusne and **Bergviks Industrimuseum** tell the story. A museum featuring more modern technology is **Söderhamns/ F15 Flygmuseum**, which exhibits military aircraft.

The 13th-century church **Tronö Kyrka**, 17 km (11 miles) northwest of Söderhamn, complete with walls, gates and bell tower, is unusually redolent of the Middle Ages. The archbishop and Nobel prize-winner Nathan Söderblom (1866–1931) was born in the rectory, which now houses his memorabilia.

🏛 **Söderhamns Stadsmuseum**
Oxtorgsgatan 5. 📞 0270-157 91.
🕐 May–Aug: daily; Sep–Apr: Sat & Sun.
🏛 **Bergviks Industrimuseum**
15 km (9 miles) west of the centre.
📞 0270-42 32 80. 🕐 by appointment. 📷 📷 voluntary.
🏛 **Söderhamns/F15 Flygmuseum**
Flygstaden, 4 km (2 miles) east of the centre. 📞 0270-142 84.
🕐 Jun–Aug: daily; Sep–Apr: Sun.
📷 📶 📷 by appointment.

Oscarsborg lookout tower, offering a superb view of Söderhamn

Kämpen rural heritage centre at a 16th-century farm in Bollnäs

Bollnäs ⑤

Hälsingland. 🏃 *13,000.* 🚌 🚃
ℹ️ *Stadshustorget, 0278-258 80.*
🎭 *Hälsingehambo Polka Festival (1st Sat after 1st Sun in Jul), Flax Week (1st week Aug).*

LOCATED IN the heart of Hälsingland's rich farming land, Bollnäs is the gateway to the valleys of the Voxnan and Ljusnan rivers. The town itself has a semi-modern centre, with some wooden mansions. The church, built in the 1460s, contains ornate medieval sculpture work. In the Classical-style **Bollnäs Museum** (1929), there is a room devoted to Onbacken, an Iron Age settlement just a stone's throw from the museum. Also worth visiting is **Kämpen** rural heritage centre, a 16th-century farm displaying a wealth of local culture. Bollnäs is on the route of the lively Hälsingehambo marathon dance from Härga to Järvsö in early July.

ENVIRONS: Hälsingland was a major flax-growing area in the 18th century, and local land-owners displayed their wealth in lavishly decorated wooden mansions (*see p18*). Some of Hälsingland's finest estates and farms can be seen around Alfta, about 20 km (12 miles) into the Voxnadalen valley. Alfta rural heritage centre, **Löka**, in Gundbo, comprises three farm buildings, some with beautiful murals. **Hansers** farm has wall hangings from the 15th century. In **Arbrå**, 16 km (10 miles) north of Bollnäs, there is an 18th-century

Log-floater by Per Nilsson Öst (1972)

wooden mansion on the Hans-Andersgården estate where journalist Willy Maria Lundberg (b.1909) created a centre for the preservation of old buildings. As well as being an attraction in its own right, the manor also has exhibitions and specialist gardens. In summer, the tourist office runs guided tours of Hälsingland's farms and manor houses.

Växbo, east of Bollnäs, has the only flax-spinning works in Sweden, which produces and sells items such as tablecloths and napkins.

🏛 **Bollnäs Museum**
Odengatan 17. 📞 *0278-253 26.* ⭘ *Jun–Aug: Tue–Sun; Sep–May: Tue–Sat.* ⬤ *some public holidays.* 🅿️ ♿

Hudiksvall ⑥

Hälsingland. 🏃 *15,000.* 🚌 🚃 ⛴
ℹ️ *Storgatan 33, 0650-191 00.*
🎭 *Delsbo Festival (1st Sun Jul), Music at Dellen (1st week in Jul), Town Festival (last week in Jul).*
🌐 *www.hudiksvall.se/turism*

FISHING, SEAFARING and trade have been the mainstay of Hudiksvall throughout its 400-

year history. In the late 19th century the timber industry boomed and the town became known for its high living, giving rise to the phrase "Happy Hudik".

Despite attacks by Russian forces in the 18th century and numerous fires, a number of older buildings remain, giving the town charm and character. The Sundskanal in the centre, a canal linking Lillfjärden and Hudiksvalls-fjärden inlets, is lined with red huts and merchants' warehouses from the mid-19th century.

East of the inlet is Fiskarstan (Fishermen's Town), with its partly-preserved wooden houses from the early 19th century. Along Hamngatan there are several fine old merchants' yards featuring the elegant wood-panelled architecture of the time. They have terraces on the water-side and shops on the parallel street of Storgatan. An example is the **Bruns Gård** pharmacy, which has an ornate pharmacy entrance on Storgatan and a winged house on the terraces of Hamngatan.

Dominating the skyline is **St Jakobs Kyrka**, a church built in the 17th and 18th centuries, although its onion dome dates from 1888.

Hälsinglands Museum, in an imposing former bank building, provides a good picture of the colourful history of the area.

ENVIRONS: Hudiksvall municip-ality covers a large area of northern Hälsingland, including **Delsbo** and the beautiful Dellensjö lakes to the west. South of the town is **Iggesund**, with its 400 years of ironworking history, and

Picturesque warehouses and quay on Sundskanalen in Hudiksvall

Torpsjön, a typical lake on the mighty Ljungan river, with Fränsta Kyrka on its shore

Enånger, where the 15th-century church contains exquisite medieval ceiling paintings by Andreas Erici and wooden sculptures by master sculptor Håkon Gullesson.

🏛 Hälsinglands Museum

Storgatan 31. ☎ 0650-196 00. ⏰ daily. ● public holidays & eves of public holidays. 🎫 by appointment. 📷 ♿

Ljusdal ❼

Hälsingland. 🚂 🚌 ℹ Turistvägen 29, Järvsö, 0651-403 06. 🎪 Hälsinge-hambo Polka Festival (1st Sat after 1st Sun in July), Butterfly Week (2nd Sun Jul), Bandy World Cup (end Oct). 🌐 www.ljusdal.se

IN THE HEART OF northwest Hälsingland on the Ljusnan river is Ljusdal. Settlers have long been attracted to this fertile valley and their history is explored at **Ljusdals-bygdens Museum**. Christianity came early to the area; parts of the church of **St Olovs Kyrka** are 12th-century.

The Swedish national sport of bandy – similar to ice hockey – is enormously popular in Ljusdal, where teams of bandy players assemble for three days in October to compete for the World Cup.

ENVIRONS: Opportunities for fishing and walking present themselves at every turn. From **Lassekrog**, 40 km (25 miles) upstream from Ljusdal, those who dare can run the rapids on the Ljusnan river. Lassekrog has been an inn since the 17th century. Here, author Albert Viksten's forest camp is a monument to the foresters of old.

South of Ljusdal, at **Järvsö**, wildlife from the north,

including predators such as bear, wolf, wolverine and lynx and their prey, can be seen at **Järvzoo Djurpark** and the adjacent Rovdjurscentret (Predator Centre). Järvsö village itself is known for having Sweden's largest provincial church; when it was completed in 1838 it had space for 2,400 parishioners. On the opposite bank lies **Stenegård**, a 19th-century trading post, now a centre for arts and crafts, with a theatre in the wooden barn.

Stenegård is also the end point for the annual Hälsingehambo Polka Festival, which starts in Hårga, 65 km (40 miles) to the south.

🏛 Ljusdalsbygdens Museum

Museivägen 5, Ljusdal.
☎ 0651-71 16 65. ⏰ Tue–Sat. ● public holidays. 🎫 by appointment. 📷

🐾 Järvzoo Djurpark

1 km (half a mile) south of Järvsö centre. ☎ 0651-411 25. ⏰ daily. 📷 🎫 by appointment. 📷

Ljusdalsbygdens Museum, in a wooden Hälsingland building

Ljungadalen ❽

Medelpad. E14. ℹ Sundsvalls Tourist Office, 060-61 04 50.

THE 350-KM (220-mile) Ljungan river rises at Helagsfjällen mountain and flows into the Gulf of Bothnia just south of the town of Sundsvall. In Medelpad, the river forms an often wide valley with a series of lakes. The E14 follows long stretches of the river, offering spectacular views. The great Norrland forests loom on the horizon and the river was an important timber route.

Stöde Kyrkby on Stödesjön lake, 40 km (25 miles) west of Sundsvall, has a long history, which is illustrated at the Huberget rural heritage centre. The church was built in the 1750s, but contains medieval artifacts from an older, now demolished church.

Borgsjö, 40 km (25 miles) further upriver, has a fine Rococo church built in 1768, with a superb wooden bell tower from 1782. Next to the church is Borgsjö rural heritage centre featuring Jämtkrogen Inn, which was relocated here from the Jämtland border.

Ånge, a railway junction 100 km (60 miles) west of Sundsvall, is an ideal starting point for exploring the area. To the west, the countryside of Haverö spreads out around the Havern and Holmsjön lakes, which are good for canoeing. **Haverö Strömmar** is an 8-km (5-mile) stretch of at times wild rapids with three streams where former dams, mills and fishing huts have been preserved. **Alby**, just off route 83, has a restored eel house showing a fishing method used in the 16th century.

The carefully restored Hotell Knaust's marble staircase

Sundsvall **9**

Medelpad. **50,000.** Midlanda. Stora Torget, 060-61 04 50. Sundsvall Street Festival (1st or 2nd weekend Jul), Dragonboat Festival (1st week in Aug), Selånger market (2nd weekend in Aug). W www.sundsvallturism.com

THE VIEW FROM Norra and Södra Stadsberget hills shows Sundsvall sandwiched between the mouths of the Ljungan and Indalsälven rivers. The sheltered inlets attracted traders to this spot in the 6th century, as can be seen from the Högom burial ground near Selånger. Along-side Selånger's 12th-century church lay St Olofs Hamn, the starting point for trading missions and pilgrimages to Norway's Nidaros (Trondheim).

Sundsvall was founded in 1624. It took off in the mid-1800s with the advent of the steam-powered sawmill. Sweden's first such sawmill was built in 1849 in Tunadal; when the industry was at its height there were 19 sawmills on the island of Alnön alone. In 1888, fire destroyed large parts of the town centre. The railway station survived, and the attractive wooden building is now a casino. A grand "stone town" rose from

the ashes. In Stora Torget stands the statue of the founder King Gustav II Adolf. The square is flanked by the **Town Hall** and the **Hirschska Huset** with its extravagant pinnacles and towers. A notable building on Storgatan is the newly renovated **Hotell Knaust**, built in 1890, with its superb marble staircase. The cultural centre, Kulturmaga-sinet, near the harbour, contains the town library and **Sundsvalls Museum**. On Norra Stadsberget lies **Sundsvalls Stadspark**, which has a collection of buildings from Medelpad, as well as animal enclosures and lookout towers. Södra Stadsberget's outdoor recreation centre has adventure trails for children.

Statues on the roof of Sundsvall town hall

ENVIRONS: Linked to Sundsvall by the Alnöbron bridge, **Alnön** has many monuments to the timber industry. The 13th-century church is interesting for its wooden interior and medieval paintings and sculptures, and the fishing village of **Spikarna** is well worth a visit.

Around 26 km (16 miles) southeast of Sundsvall lies **Galtström**, Medelpad's first ironworks, built in 1695. The works have been restored.

Sundsvalls Museum
Kultumagasinet. 060-19 18 03. Mon–Sat. Easter Mon, Whit Mon, Midsummer's Eve. by appointment.

Sundsvalls Stadspark
Norra Stadsberget. 060-15 40 40. daily. eves of public holidays. by appointment. (by Stads-parken).

Härnösand **10**

Ångermanland. **18,000.** Härnösands Municipality, 0611-34 80 00. Midsummer celebrations at Murberget, Härnösandskalaset (Jul), Park Festival (2nd–3rd week in Jul).

THE COUNTY TOWN of west-ern Norrland has a proud history. It received its town charter from Johan III in 1585, became diocesan capital in 1647 and had an upper secondary school by 1650.

Härnösand's rich history, combined with the fact that, in contrast to other Norrland coastal towns, it was spared major fires for almost 300 years, makes it an interesting place to stroll around. The Russians plundered Härnösand in 1721. A new wooden town replaced the old and charming districts such as Östanbäcken and Norrstan still remain. Standing out among the many public buildings are the town hall from the 1790s on Stora Torget, the old upper secondary school and the county governor's residence.

At Murbergets Frilufts-museum, which is part of **Länsmuseet Västernorr-land**, 18th-century buildings have been preserved, includ-ing the town hall built in 1727. This large open-air museum also reflects farming culture, with crofts and farms, a blacksmith's and sawmill, and a Norrland church village.

Skeppsbron fills with yachts in July when the town's mari-time history is celebrated at the Härnösandskalaset festival.

Länsmuseet Västernorrland
Murberget. 0611-886 10. Tue–Sun. 24, 31 Dec, 1 Jan, Eas-ter Sat. by appointment.

Ådalen ⓫

Ångermanland. Road 90.
🚌 from Örnsköldsvik. 🛈 Kramfors Tourist Office, 0612-801 20.
🎭 Kramfors Town Festival (weekend before Midsummer).

A S THE FORESTRY industry flourished, Ådalen, the river valley leading to Junsele, became a hotbed of trade unionism and earned the nickname "Red Ådalen". In 1931, the year of the Great Depression, a most unlikely event occurred: the military shot indiscriminately into a peaceful strikers' march in Lunde, killing five people. Lenny Clarhäll's powerful sculpture depicting the drama stands on Sandöbron peak.

Already in the mid-18th century, Livonian Johan Kramm set up a water-powered sawmill on the site which in 1947 became the town of Kramfors. Cargo ships were able to navigate 50 km (31 miles) up the river and the lower valley became a magnet for the forestry industry. The line of factories

One of the many rock carvings in Nämforsen from around 4000 BC

is now almost entirely gone. Further up river, however, there are numerous power stations – the Faxälven tributary is home to 36 alone. Particularly worth visiting is **Nämforsen**, where in summer visitors can view the large power station and occasionally see the mighty waterfall burst into life. The islands in the falls are an outstanding site for rock carvings. From 4000–2500 BC, hunters carved out over 2,500 figures.

Örnsköldsvik ⓬

Ångermanland. 🚌 to Sundsvall or Mellansel, then bus/taxi. 🚗 ✕
🚢 🛈 Nygatan 18, 0660-881 00.
🎭 Harbour Festival (1st weekend in Jul), Dragonboat Festival (mid-Aug).
🌐 www.ornskoldsvik.se/turism

N OLASKOGS is one of the names by which this part of northern Ångermanland is known. It means "north of the forest" – the wild frontier forest of Skule (see p256).

Its main town, Örnsköldsvik, or Ö-vik as it is often called, was founded in 1842. Unusually for the time, it was named after a non-royal figure, the county governor Per Abraham Örnsköld. There are good views of the town from Varvsberget and from the top of the ski-jumping tower on Paradiskullen. Many of the town's older buildings

**Arken, designed by architect
Per Eddi Byggstam, 1991**

have been lost to modern developments. A few exceptions include the delightful town hall which, thankfully for Ö-vik's remarkably large artists' colony, was saved as an exhibition space. The beautifully restored junior secondary school houses **Örnsköldsviks Museum**, which displays the history of Nolaskogs.

Attractive new architecture can be seen in the development of the inner harbour, where **Arken** – a centre for offices, university buildings and a library – forms an exciting backdrop. One of its glass-roofed courtyards houses the **Hans Hedbergs Museum** dedicated to the Swedish sculptor (see p22).

ENVIRONS: Next to an excavation site in **Gene Fornby**, 5 km (3 miles) south of the town, a 6th-century farm has been reconstructed, where people come to live and work as they did in the Iron Age.

The most striking medieval church in the area is the octagonal **Själevads Kyrka** from 1880, which was voted Sweden's most beautiful church in a nationwide poll.

🏛 **Örnsköldsviks Museum**
Läroverksgatan 1. 📞 0660-886 01.
◻ Midsummer–Aug: daily; other times: Tue–Sun. ● public holidays. 🔲 🚻
🏛 **Arken**
Strandgatan 21. 📞 0660-785 00.
Public areas ◻ daily. **Hans Hedbergs Museum** ◻ ring Tourist Office 0660-881 00 for info. ● public holidays. 🔲 🚹

SURSTRÖMMING, A FISHY DELICACY

The coast of Southern Norrland has a speciality which many Swedes, not only the people of Norrland, consider to be the ultimate delicacy, although the majority probably detest it. This treat is fermented herring, known as *surströmming*, which, after around eight weeks of fermenting, is canned. When the can is opened it produces what is, to say the least, a characteristic aroma, which aficionados consider absolutely divine. The fishing villages along the High Coast (see pp256–7), such as Ulvöhamn, are the centre of production, and a market is now opening up as far afield as Japan. The fermented herring is eaten reverentially, almost ritually, in early autumn, accompanied by small almond-shaped potatoes and chopped onion. It is best washed down with copious amounts of beer and schnapps.

Can of Surströmming

The High Coast

SWEDEN'S SPECTACULAR HIGH COAST is best experienced on a light summer evening, when the wooded hills are reflected in the calm waters of the bays, or on the quay in Ulvöhamn during the *surströmming* season *(see p255)*, when the peculiar speciality of fermented herring is enjoyed with flat bread, tiny potatoes and schnapps. A boat is ideal for getting around, but the new Högakustenbron bridge provides easy access and ferries sail regularly from several ports. The dramatic landscape is the main attraction. Declared a UNESCO World Heritage Site in 2000, it is the result of the land rising 300 m (984 ft) since the ice receded around 9,600 years ago. At that time Skuleberget hill, north of Docksta, was a tiny island.

Skuleskogens National Park
Watched over by Skuleberget hill, the park covers 30 sq km (12 sq miles) of wilderness, with walking trails through magical ancient forest and over the clifftops along the coast.

Ullångersfjärden
Motorists on the E4 rejoin the Gulf of Bothnia at Ullångersfjärden bay which, with its high, sheer cliffs, is almost fjord-like.

Nordingrå
"Fair Nordingrå" was a tourist destination long before the term High Coast was coined. Beautiful roads lined with steep hills pass through stunning scenery.

Högakustenbron
Since 1997, the 1,800-m (6,000-ft) bridge, suspended on 180-m (600-ft) high pylons, has saved travellers the 13-km (8-mile) detour up the Ångermanälven valley to the Sandöbron bridge.

Skagsudde

The High Coast walking trail stretches 127 km (79 miles) from the mouth of the Ångermanälven to Örnsköldsvik.

VISITORS' CHECKLIST

Ångermanland. E4.
Örnsköldsvik Tourist Office,
0660-881 00. Kramfors Tourist
Office, 0612-801 20. from
Örnsköldsvik.
Skule National Park Skule
Naturum, 0613-401 71.
Skule Song Festival (1st
weekend in Jul).
W www.hogakusten.com

Köpmanholmen

Trysunda

Trysunda
One of the best-preserved villages, Trysunda has a richly-decorated, 17th-century fishermen's chapel. Part of the island is a nature reserve.

N. ULVÖN

ÅLTÖN

Ulvöhamn

GULF OF BOTHNIA

S. ULVÖN

Ulvöhamn
This is the spiritual home of the herring speciality, surström-ming. *Norrland's largest fishing fleet made its home in the sheltered harbour lying between Norra and Södra Ulvön. The chapel dates from 1622.*

Norrfällsviken

nefjärden

Bönhamn

0 kilometres	10
0 miles	5

KEY

— Major road

— Minor road

- - Ferry route

- - High Coast walking trail

National Park

Nature Reserve

Högbonden
The 100-year-old light-house on the island of Högbonden warned shipping of the rocky coastline. Today it is a youth hostel, reached by boat from Bönhamn, the most authentic fishing village on the mainland, and the place to savour local specialities such as fresh river salmon, whitefish and, of course, surströmming.

Thai monument in Utanede, commemorating the King of Siam's royal visit in 1897

Indalsälven ⑭

Jämtland/Medelpad. Road 86. 🚇 to
Sundsvall, then bus. ℹ️ Ragunda
Tourist Office, 0696-68 20 90.
📅 Vildhussen Festival (1st and 2nd
weeks in Jul). 🌐 www.ragunda.se

THE 430-KM (270-mile) long
Indalsälven river rises in
the mountains of Norway and
flows into Klingerfjärden,
north of Sundsvall. The lower
stretch of the river from
Ragunda in Jämtland includes
Döda Fallet (the Dead Falls)
caused by a disastrous attempt
by Vildhussen *(see box)* to
control the river in 1796.

Döda Fallet is now a nature
reserve where it is possible to
walk around the rocky landscape and see the giant basins
carved out by stones in the
falls. An extraordinary open-
air theatre has been created
next to the falls, where the

stand for an audience
of 420 revolves twice
a minute. A stage in
the round is set
against breathtaking
natural scenery.

Utanede features an
exotic Thai pavilion, the
**King Chulalongkorn
Memorial**, erected in
memory of the King of
Siam's trip along the
river in 1897 as a guest
of King Oscar II. The
decorative elements of
the golden pavilion
were built by Thai
craftsmen and seven
million parts were shipped to
Sweden and assembled. The
interior holds a life-sized
bronze statue of the king.

Among the churches along
the river, **Lidens Kyrka**,
dating from 1510, has the
most attractive location (road
86, 37 km/23 miles northwest
of Sundsvall) and contains
medieval sculptures, with a
Madonna from the 13th
century. Vildhussen is buried
in the cemetery here.

Bergeforsen on the coast
is the last of the river's many
power stations. There is an
aquarium where Baltic fish
such as salmon, sea trout and
eel are raised.

🏛 King Chulalongkorn Memorial
Utanede. Road 86, 7 km (4 miles)
south of Bispgården. 📞 0696-321
06. 🕐 mid-May–mid-Sep: daily. 🎫
🕐 hourly. 🅿 🚻 ♿ some facilities.

Östersund ⑮

Jämtland. 🚉 44,000. 🚌 🚆 🛫
ℹ️ Rådhusgatan 44, 063-14 40 01.
📅 Storsjöyran Festival (last weekend
in Jul), Armljot Games (Jul).
🌐 www.ostersund.se/turist

ESTABLISHED ON the shores of
Storsjön lake in 1786, the
county town of Östersund lies
opposite Jämtland's ancient
centre of Frösön. Before
coming under Norwegian rule
in 1178, the people of Jämtland had ruled themselves
and would be happy to do so
again if the Republic of
Jämtland movement had its
way. In a fairly lighthearted
manner, the movement
protects local culture – the
highpoint is the Storsjöyran
Festival at the end of July.

The county museum, **Jamtli**,
with its highly praised
Historieland feature, offers an
exciting picture of life around
Storsjön. This time machine
transports visitors to scenes
from the 18th and 19th
centuries, where history can
be felt, heard and even tasted.
The museum's showpiece are
the oldest preserved Viking
Överbogdal tapestries.

A short bridge leads to the
rolling, green island of Frösön.
Its eastern parts are more like
a part of town, but the views
across Storsjön to the peak of
Oviksfjällen inspired the
composer Wilhelm Peterson-
Berger to create this distinctive
home, **Sommarhagen**, in
1914. The house is now a
museum and the rich interior
with decorative paintings by
Paul Jonze is something of a
companion to Carl Larsson's
Sundborn *(see p240)*. Every

VILDHUSSEN AND THE DEAD FALLS

A drama which was to have a lasting impact unfolded on 6
June 1796 in Ragunda on the Indalsälven river. Magnus Huss,
known as Vildhussen (Wild Huss), a merchant in Sundsvall,
had been building a log flume to bypass the 38-m (125-ft)
high Storforsen waterfall when an unusually high spring flood
put pressure on the lake above the falls. The log flume burst
and the river forged a new route, emptying the 27-km (17-

**Döda Fallet, Vild-
hussen's creation**

mile) long lake in just four hours and send-
ing so much soil and debris downstream
that it formed Sweden's largest delta at the
river mouth. The Storforsen waterfall had
become Döda Fallet (the Dead Falls). Local
people were sceptical of Huss's scheme
from the start and despite the now navig-
able river and fertile land on the old lake
bed, discontent brewed. A year later Huss
died when his boat capsized. Rumour has
it that the oars had been hidden and his
boat pushed out into the fast-flowing river.

**Old stone fireplace in Jamtli
Museum, Östersund**

summer *Arnljot*, Peterson-Berger's drama about the Viking from 11th-century Frösö, is performed in a field a short distance away.

The 12th-century **Frösö Kyrka** is one of Sweden's most popular churches in which to get married. **Frösö Zoo** has 700 animal species from around the world.

ENVIRONS: Storsjön lake is best explored on a steamer, such as the 1875 *S/S Thomeé*, Sweden's oldest steamer still in regular use. Many enthusiasts try to spot the elusive Storsjö Monster, the so-called sister of Scotland's Loch Ness monster.

Brunflo, 15 km (9 miles) south of Östersund, has an 18th-century church with a 12th-century lookout tower.

🏛 Jamtli
Museiplan. 【 063-15 01 10.
⬜ Jun–Aug: daily; Sep–May: Tue–Sun.
⬤ 24, 25, 31 Dec. 🔲 🔲 summer.
🔲 🍴 🔲 ♿

🔲 Sommarhagen
Frösön, 9 km (6 miles from the centre).
【 063-430 41. ⬜ End May–end Aug: daily; other times by arrange-ment. 🔲 by appointment. 🔲 🔲

🦌 Frösö Zoo
3 km (2 miles) south of the centre. 【
063-51 47 53. ⬜ 2nd week in Jun–3rd week in Aug: daily. 🔲 🔲 🔲 🍴 🔲 ♿

Åre 16

Jämtland. E14. 🏃 1,000. 🔲 🔲
🔲 Östersund. 🚹 St Olofs Väg, 0647-177 20. 🎿 Alpine World Cup (Feb), Country Festival (2nd week in Jul).

Åreskutan is Sweden's most visited mountain peak. The cable car lifts passengers from the village of Åre to within 150 m (490 ft) of the summit at 1,420 m (4,658 ft). At this altitude, the skiing season lasts into June. Facilities are plentiful in what has become Sweden's leading ski destination. There are 40 lifts and 100 pistes, some of which are the longest and steepest in the country. Hotels and conference centres rise up into the sky. This is

The 1,700-m (5,600-ft) high Syl, just over a day's walk south of Storlien

in great contrast to how the resort looked at the end of the 19th century with hotels such as Åregården and the Grand. Still here is the Bergbanan run, which has attracted toboganists of all ages. Prominent visitors have included Winston Churchill, who came to hunt elk. Today's range of adventure activities includes scooter safaris, dog sledding, para-skiing, ice-climbing, caving, surfing rapids and mountain biking on Åreskutan.

ENVIRONS: The **Tännforsen** waterfall, 20 km (12 miles) west of Åre, is one of the most impressive in Jämtland, with a drop of 37 m (120 ft).

Narke Samelaäger, on an island on Häggsjön lake, has a Sami camp where visitors can learn how to lasso, or taste delicacies such as reindeer heart. On Åreskutan's eastern spur, 10 km (6 miles) from Åre, lies **Fröå Gruva**, where copper was mined from 1752 to 1916. The countryside is beautiful to wander through, with buildings from various eras. At **Huså Bruk**, another centre for copper mining further to the north, is Huså Herrgård, a manor built in 1838.

Skiers resting at a hut on Åreskutan, Sweden's top ski resort

Storlien 17

Jämtland. E14. 🔲 🔲 🔲 Östersund.
🚹 Åre Tourist Office, 0647-177 20.
🌐 www.storlien.nu

The arrival of the railway in Trondheim in the 1880s opened up new opportunities for Storlien, which is located near the border with Norway. It is only 60 km (37 miles) to the Trondheim Fjord, and the broad pass between Stenfjället and Skurdalshöjden allows mild Atlantic winds to sweep through. The healthy air attracted spa guests to a mountain sanatorium, and with the dawn of the 20th century tourists began arriving.

Today, Storlien is one of Sweden's leading ski centres for both cross-country and downhill. It is also a starting point for walks in the Jämtland mountains, such as via the STF stations of Blåhammaren, Storulvån, Sylarna and Vålådalen. The mountains can also be reached from Enafors on the E14 and by train.

Popular with birdwatchers, nearby **Ånnsjön** lake has a bird station and sanctuary. **Handöl**, on the western shore, has been a site for soapstone mining since the late Middle Ages. It was also where the surviving Carolian forces gathered in 1799 after Carl Gustaf Armfelt's catastrophic retreat from Norway. The Carolian monument on the waterfront is a memorial to the 3,700 men who froze to death in the mountains. Today accommodation and better equipment have prompted more and more people to take up the challenge of completing the 75-km (47-mile) long Carolian March.

The Mountains of Härjedalen

T HE TREE LINE IN HÄRJEDALEN is at 900 m (2,950 ft) and
even in the forested lowlands in the east there are
mountains with bare summits such as Sånfjället and
Vemdalsfjällen. But the mightiest mountains loom
large in the west towards Norway and the province
of Jämtland, with Helagsfjället the highest peak at
1,797 m (5,900 ft). Funäsdalen is the local hub, from
where in summer Sweden's highest road runs via the
Sami village of Mittådalen and the plateau of Flatruet
to Ljungdalen. There are many opportunities for ski-
touring and downhill skiing, fishing in summer and
hiking along the southern part of the Kungsleden trail.

Helags
*STF (see p314) has a
mountain station at the base of
Helagsfjället, Sweden's highest
peak south of the Arctic Circle.*

Ramundberget
*In the summer, this popular
winter sports venue, known for its
early snowfalls, is a good starting
point for mountain hikes to
Helags, Ljungdalen and Fjällnäs.*

The road over the Flatruet
Plateau is only open in summer.

Röros
(Norway)

Fjällnäs

Bruksvallarna

Mittådalen

Ljungo

Tänndalen   84

Tännäs

Funäsdalen
*This lively town in the Härjedalen mountains
has the award-winning Härjedalens Fjäll-
museum, which shows how the Sami and upland
farmers survived the challenges of past times.*

Högvålen

Rogen
*The nature reserve
around Härjedalen's
largest lake system has
unusual flora and
fauna. It is great for
canoeing. The Sami village
of Ruvhten offers ice-fishing
for grayling and char.*

Idre

KEY

▨	Major road
▧	Minor road
- -	Walking trail
▨	Ski resort

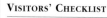

Reindeer Pastures
*The Sami villages of
Mittådalen and Ruvhten
(Tännäs) have summer
pastures in the western
mountains. The winter
pastures stretch as far as
the forests of Sveg and
into Dalarna.*

VISITORS' CHECKLIST

Härjedalen. Road 84. 🚂 to
Ljusdal or Östersund, then bus.
🚌 from Stockholm and Gothen-
burg. ✈ Sveg or Östersund.
ℹ Lofsdalen, 0680-412 33.
Funäsdalen 0684-164 10.
Vemdalen, 0684-302 70.
🎪 Funäsdalen Mountain Market
(Wed). 🌐 www.herjedalen.se

Vemdalsfjällen
*This skiers' paradise has a
joint lift system for the
main resorts: Vemdals-
kalet, Björnrike, Klövsjö
and Storhågna, as well
as great facilities for
cross-country
skiing.*

Klövsjö 🎿

Vemdalsskalet 🎿
Storhågna
Ånge
Vemdalen
Björnrike 🎿
Sveg

Sånfjället
*Parts of this
mountain in the
forest were
declared a
national park
in 1909, partly
to protect the
bear population.
Wolves, lynx
and wolverine
also live here.*

Klövsjö 🎿
Hede
84
sjövålen 🎿
Lofsdalen 🎿
Sveg

0 kilometres   20

0 miles   10

Sveg ⑲

Härjedalen. 🚶 2,700. 🚂 Inlands-
banan (summer), or to Mora or
Ljusdal then bus. 🚌 ✈ ℹ Ljusne-
gatan 1, 0680-107 75. 🎪 Olsmäss
Festival (last weekend in Jul), Julisveg
Festival (Jul).

HÄRJEDALEN'S central town is
Sveg, the gateway to the
mountains. The municipality
of the same name covers an
area larger than many
counties, and with just 11,000
inhabitants it has a population
density of less than one
person per sq km. Forest
stretches in every direction.
Winding waterways provide
opportunities for fishing,
canoeing and beaver safaris.
The nearest mountain for skiing is a 30-minute drive away.

Around Sveg, small villages
such as Duvberg, Ytterberg,
Överberg and Äggen are well-
preserved, with 18th-century
features. **Gammel-Rems-
gården**, 15 km (9 miles)
north of Sveg, is a typical
early-18th-century Härjedalen
manor house with richly
decorated interiors. About 15
km (9 miles) east of Sveg lies
the village of **Älvros**, whose
church has a beautifully
painted bell tower.

Lillhärdal, 30 km (19
miles) south of Sveg, is said
to have been founded in the
9th century by the Viking
Härjulf Hornbrytare. Bildhöst
has one of the last working
crofts, complete with cattle
and milkmaids, while Hamre
Skans is a timbered fortification from the 18th century.

**Älvros church near Sveg, with a
free-standing, painted bell tower**

NORTHERN NORRLAND

STRETCHING FROM THE POPULATED BALTIC *coast through wild forests and marshes to the open expanses of the mountains, Northern Norrland is a vast, almost untouched region. The biting chill and eternal darkness of the long northern winter are compensated for by summer's midnight sun, when nature seizes its short window of opportunity to flourish and the reindeer are moved to new pastures.*

The three provinces of Västerbotten, Norrbotten and Lappland make up Sweden's most northerly region. Västerbotten, on the Gulf of Bothnia, is the most southerly. Its coast and river valleys had booming settlements for many centuries. But today commercial activity is concentrated in towns such as Umeå, with its university and youthful population, and Skellefteå, known as the "Town of Gold" because of its proximity to two of Europe's largest gold deposits. Inland, the wilderness takes hold with vast tracts of forest and marsh. After a journey between Lycksele and Sorsele, Carl von Linné wrote: "A priest could never make Hell sound worse than this." But with modern transport, today's traveller can look forward to outdoor adventures and wildlife in this unspoilt landscape.

North of Västerbotten, Norrbotten's coastline harbours features of rural culture such as the church village in Gammelstad, a UNESCO World Heritage Site. The Norrbotten archipelago is renowned for being the sunniest place in the country and its beach resorts lure holiday-makers. The border with Finland lies along the Torne river, but here the phrase "two countries, one people" is the most applicable.

Lappland borders Norway in the west and Finland in the northeast, but for the Sami (Lapp) people their land extends beyond official boundaries, across the mountains and forests and down to the coast, where their thriving culture of reindeer herding, hunting and fishing prevail. Known as Laponia, this area is also a UNESCO World Heritage Site. National parks such as Sarek protect the alpine landscape with its glaciers and waterfalls. The main towns of Kiruna and Gällivare in northern Lappland owe their existence to the mining industry.

Dog sledding in Jukkasjärvi, Lapland

◁ **Kaitumsjön Lake, Lapland**

Exploring Northern Norrland

A<small>N AREA COVERING MORE THAN</small> one-third of Sweden cannot be explored in a hurry. And things are not made easier by the large areas of wilderness north of the Arctic Circle without roads, in Europe's most sparsely populated region. Despite their northerly latitude, the coastal areas combine a captivating archipelago landscape with rich cultural sights. Spectacular roads lead up into the mountains with romantic names such as "Saga Vägen" (the Saga Highway) and "Blå Vägen" (the Blue Highway). Skiers are tempted by the record-length season, while for hikers, the northernmost section of the 440-km (275-mile) long Kungsleden trail *(see p274)* between Abisko and Hemavan crosses the mountainous <small>UNESCO</small> World Heritage Site of Laponia.

Lake Saggat seen from the Kvikkjokk road in northwestern Lappland

GETTING AROUND

Flying is the most comfortable means of transport. Around a dozen airports offer scheduled flights. Only a few trains travel on the Vännäs–Luleå line and the Malmbanan line running Luleå– Kiruna–Riksgränsen. The Inlandsbanan line through Lappland from Gällivare provides a summer tourist route. The major roads E4, E10 and E12 (the Blue Highway) are of a high standard, but road conditions are variable elsewhere. Bus services between the main towns are usually good, but almost non-existent in the wilder areas. Ferries operate across some mountain lakes in summer, saving time for hikers.

KEY

— Major road

= Minor road

⊶ Railway line

-·- Ferry route

SEE ALSO

- *Where to Stay* p289
- *Where to Eat* p303

Narvik
(Norway)

Akkajaure

Sarektjåkkå
▲
2090 m

KUNGSLEDEN
18

Bodø
(Norway)

KVIKKJOKK ●
Lilla Lu

Piteälven

Skellefteälven

LAPPLA

Mo i Rana
(Norway)

95

Horn-
avan

ARJEPLOG **17**

AMMARNÄS

☒ ● HEMAVAN

Vindelälven

E12

Umeälven

● STORUMAN
☒

● VILHELMINA
☒

45   90

● ÅSELE
92

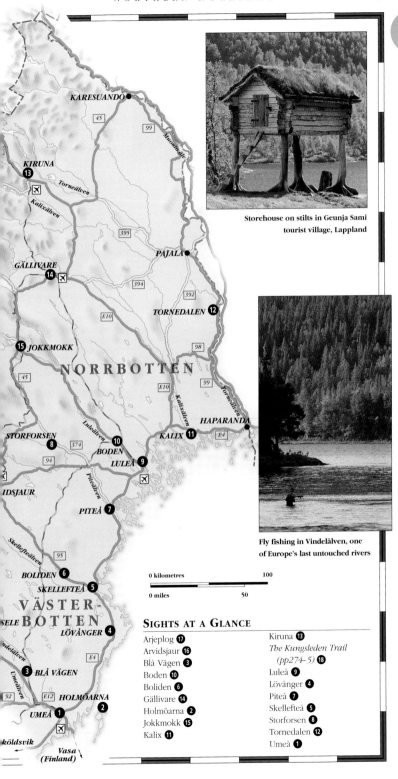

Storehouse on stilts in Geunja Sami tourist village, Lappland

Fly fishing in Vindelälven, one of Europe's last untouched rivers

SIGHTS AT A GLANCE

Birch avenue in Umeå, with the Town Hall in the background

Umeå ●

Västerbotten. 🏠 71,000. 🚉 🚌 ✈
🚢 from Vasa, Finland. ℹ Renmarkstorget 15, 090-16 16 16. 🎭 Int.
Chamber Music Festival (2nd week in
Jun), Film Festival (2nd weekend in
Sep). 🌐 www.visitumea.se

WITH 3,000 BIRCH trees
lining the streets, it is not
surprising that Umeå is known
as "The City of Birches". After
a major fire in 1888, a new
city was built with broad, tree-
lined esplanades and parks to
prevent fires spreading. Post-
fire buildings of interest
include the **Scharinska villa**
on Storgatan, designed by
Ragnar Östberg, and **Moritska
Gården**, Umeå's grandest
residence for a local timber
baron. The city's Neo-Gothic
church was completed in 1894.

Umeå dates back to the 16th
century and became a county
town in 1622. It was an important trading and administrative
centre. The opening of a new
university in 1965 prompted
an expansion that transformed
Umeå into a city – Norrland's
only one. With 30,000 students
and lecturers, it is very much a

young persons' place (average
age 36), which is reflected in
the wide range of entertainment on offer.

In Gammlia, a 10-minute
walk from the centre, the
Västerbottens Museum is
one of Sweden's most rewarding county museums, focusing
on the history of Umeå and
Västerbotten. It includes
Svenska Skidmuseet, which
covers the history of skiing,
and the fishing and maritime
museum Fiske- och Sjöfartsmuseet. In the summer, the
open-air museum **Gammlia
Friluftsmuseum** shows off its
historic farm buildings, complete with pets, and there are
activities for children.

Gammlia is also the location
of **Bildmuseet**, a museum for
contemporary visual arts.

🏛 **Västerbottens Museum**
Gammlia. 📞 090-17 18 00. 🚌
🕐 mid-May–mid-Aug: daily; other
times: Tue–Sun. 🕐 24, 31 Dec. 🚌
🚌 ♿ **Gammlia Friluftsmuseum**
🕐 mid-May–mid-Aug: daily. ♿
🏛 **Bildmuseet**
Gammlia. 📞 090-786 52 27. 🕐 mid-
Jun–mid-Aug: daily; other times: Tue–
Sun. 🎫 by appointment. 🚌 🚹 ♿

Holmöarna ●

Västerbotten. 🏠 90. 🚌 to
Norrfjärden 30 km (19 miles) N of
Umeå, then ferry. ℹ Umeå Tourist
Office, 090-16 16 16. 🎭 Holmö Folk
Festival (last weekend in July).

A 45-MINUTE FREE ferry trip
from Norrfjärden leads to
the Holmö archipelago. There
are four main islands –
Holmön, Grossgrundet,
Angesön and Holmögadd –
and several smaller ones. The
majority of the group forms
part of Sweden's largest archipelago nature reserve. It is an
area of exciting geological
formations and extensive
fields of rubble stones. The
forest and shorelines provide
habitats for 130 species of
birds and a variety of flora.

The islands have been
inhabited since the 14th
century and **Holmöns
Båtmuseum** focuses on the
lives of the local fishermen,
seal hunters and farmers.

The archipelago is ideal for
cycling, bathing and fishing.

🏛 **Holmöns Båtmuseum**
At the ferry quay. 📞 090-552 20
(summer). 🕐 mid-Jun–mid-Aug: daily.
📷 🚹

Encountering a reindeer on
the Blue Highway

Blå Vägen ●

Västerbotten, Lappland. E12. 🚌 ℹ
Umeå Tourist Office, 090-16 16 16.

FROM LAKE ONEGA in Russia
to Träna on Norway's
Atlantic coast, the Blå Vägen
(Blue Highway, E12) stretches
1,700 km (1,050 miles). The
Swedish section follows the
Umeälven river from Umeå
through the towns of
Lycksele, Storuman and

SWEDEN'S 200-YEAR PEACE

Sweden has enjoyed almost 200 years of peace. The last
battles on Swedish soil took place in Sävar and Ratan north
of Umeå in August 1809. Russian troops
had been plundering the coast and a
Swedish expeditionary force landed at the
port of Ratan to attack the Russians from
the rear. The troops marched south towards
Sävar and clashed with the Russians on
19 August. The Swedes were defeated and
withdrew to Ratan, where another battle
was fought the next day. This time the
Swedish troops stood their ground, but
1,000 men died in the conflict. A memorial
in Sävar honours the fallen. As a result of
the war, Finland was lost to Russia.

Infantryman,
model, 1807

Iemavan. Klabböle, near Umeå, is the site of the river's first power station, built in 1899. It now houses the museum of **Umeå Energicentrum**, and is well worth a visit. Children enjoy the "Playing with Energy" exhibit and trying to balance on logs like a log driver. **Stornorrfors**, 6 km (4 miles) upstream, is one of Europe's largest hydroelectric power stations. The immense turbine hall, 90 m (295 ft) underground, is open to the public.

At **Vännäs**, 26 km (16 miles) from Umeå, the unspoilt Vindelälven river joins the Umeälven, and a detour can be made to the mighty **Mårdsele falls** to ride the rapids or fish for salmon, salmon trout and grayling.

Lycksele, the only town in southern Lappland, lies 123 km (76 miles) from Umeå. The local zoo, **Lycksele Djurpark**, specializes in Nordic wildlife.

⛫ Umeå Energicentrum
10 km (6 miles) W of Umeå. 🄲 090-480 28. ⬭ 2nd week in Jun–3rd week in Aug: daily. 🄲 🄲

✹ Lycksele Djurpark
Brännbergsvägen. 🄲 0950-167 10. ⬭ 3rd week in May–Aug: daily. 🄳
🄳🄳🄳🄳🄳

Lövånger ➍

Västerbotten. E4. 🁢 2,400. ⬭ 🄸
Lövånger Tourist Office, 0913-104 80.

THE CHURCH village at Lövånger is one of the largest in the country with 117 cabins. It dates from the Middle Ages, although the oldest surviving cabin is from 1746. The village was built to accommodate churchgoers from remote outlying areas during church festivals. A number of cabins have been restored and are let to visitors. The 16th-century granite church of St Anne is decorated with medieval sculptures.

Sockenmuseet, just north of the church, illustrates how the people of Lövånger lived in the 19th century.

⛫ Sockenmuseet
🄲 0913-100 40. ⬭ odd weeks: Thu–Fri; even weeks: Tue–Wed. 🄳

The church village in Lövånger with accommodation for churchgoers

Skellefteå ➎

Västerbotten. E4. 🁢 34,800. 🄿 to Bastuträsk, then bus. ⬭ 🄳 🄸
Trädgårdsgatan 7, 0910-73 60 20.
🄳 Skellefteå Festival (4th weekend in Jun). 🆆 www.skelleftea.se/English

NORTHERN VÄSTERBOTTEN had to wait until 1845 for its first town, but there had long been a marketplace alongside Skellefteå church. In order to accommodate the large congregation, an impressive Neo-Classical cruciform church was built in 1800 on the site of a 15th-century church. Worshippers came from far afield, staying in Bonnstan, Skellefteå's church village built in the mid-19th century.

It was with the boom in the mining industry in the 1920s that Skellefteå's development took off, fuelled by the huge smelting plant at the mouth of the Skellefteälven river.

The town's green lung is the Nordanå Kulturcentrum, a park stretching along the northern bank of the river. It houses an art gallery, **Skellefteå Museum** and historic buildings.

⛫ Skellefteå Museum
1.5 km (1 mile) W of the centre.
🄲 0910-73 55 10. ⬭ daily. ⬭ some public holidays. 🄳🄳🄳🄳🄳

Boliden ➏

Västerbotten. E4/road 95. ⬭ 🄳
Skellefteå, then bus. 🄸 Skellefteå Tourist Office, 0910-73 60 20. 🄳 Geology Festival (end Aug/early Sep).

THE KINGDOM of Gold is the name given to Skellefteå's ore field which, with Boliden

at its heart, stretches from Bottenviken through northern Västerbotten towards the mountains of Lappland. Europe's two largest gold deposits are mined here, in addition to zinc, copper, silver and tungsten.

Bergrum Boliden, in the old mining office, traces the history of the formation of the sulphide ores more than 4,600 million years ago to their extraction today.

In World War II, the world's longest cable car system was constructed to transport the ore 96 km (60 miles) from the mines in Kristineberg. It is possible to travel along a 13-km (8-mile) long stretch from Örträsk to Mensträsk, swinging over the beautiful countryside at a sedate 10 km/h (6 mph).

⛫ Bergrum Boliden
1 km (half a mile) NW of the centre.
🄲 0910-58 00 60. ⬭ May–Aug: daily; other times by appointment. 🄳
🄳🄳🄳🄳

The Kristineberg cable car system, once used to transport ore

Piteå's sandy beach, and Sweden's best chance of sun

Piteå **⑦**

Norrbotten. E4. 🚶 22,000. 🚉
✈ Kallax. 🚌 🚢 **🛈** Sundsgatan 41,
0911-933 90. 🎭 Piteå Dances and
Smiles Festival (last week Jul).
🌐 www.pitea.se

ORIGINALLY SITUATED next to Öjebyn, Piteå was moved after a fire to the mouth of the Piteälven river. The new town was burned by the Russians in 1721 and rebuilt. Picturesque wooden buildings from the 19th century can be found on the square of Rådhustorget, where the attractive Town Hall dates from 1830. But it is the coast that is the main attraction. The **"Nordic Riviera"** offers extensive sandy beaches and Sweden's best chance of sun. If the weather turns, there is an indoor fun pool.

Öjebyn has a 15th-century church and a well-preserved church village.

ENVIRONS: **Jävre**, off the E4 south of Piteå, has traces of Norrbotten's first settlers from the Bronze Age. The archaeology trail takes in graves, sacrificial stones and labyrinths.

Storforsen **⑧**

Norrbotten. 80 km (50 miles) NW of
Piteå, road 374. 🚌 **🛈** Storforsen
Turism, 0929-72100. **🍴**
🌐 www.storforsen.com

EUROPE'S MIGHTIEST untamed stretch of whitewater can be found on the Piteälven river, 40 km (25 miles) north of Älvsbyn. The rapids drop 82 m (270 ft) over 5 km

(3 miles), at speeds of over 800 cubic metres (176,000 gallons) per second. Efforts to channel the rapids into a single course created Döda Fallet (the Dead Falls), where giant basins can be seen. Log floating has ceased, but a visit to the **Skogs- och Flottnings-museet** will reveal how things looked when Storforsen's huge log jams were formed.

🏛 Skogs- och Flottningsmuseet

Storforsen. **📞** 0929-721 00. ◻ May-
Aug: daily. 🗐 **✓** obligatory. ◻ **🍴**

Storforsen in the Piteälven river, a vast expanse of whitewater rapids

Luleå **⑨**

Norrbotten. E4. 🚶 45,000. ✈ 🚉
🚌 🚢 **🛈** Kulturcentrum Ebeneser,
Storgatan 43 B, 0920-29 35 00.
🎭 Luleå Party (first week in Aug).
🌐 www.lulea.se

THE COUNTY TOWN of Luleå is surrounded by water as the Luleälven river flows into glittering bays with a lush archipelago beyond. A good harbour was the reason for the town's location here in the mid-17th century, when the original site upstream became too shallow.

The church village, **Gammelstads Kyrkstad**, and

its church, Nederluleå Kyrka, form a unique monument to the old trading centre and in 1996 were designated a UNESCO World Heritage Site. The 15th century granite building with its perimeter wall is upper Norrland's largest medieval church. The white steeple towers over a group of 408 small red cabins. This is where churchgoers from remote villages would stay overnight and stable their horses. The church's star vaulting is decorated with paintings from the Albert Pictor school of the 1480s. The magnificent altar-screen from Antwerp dates from 1520.

The cathedral in the new Luleå was built in 1893. **Norrbottens Museum** concentrates on the history of Luleå and Norrbotten.

The ore-loading harbour and SSAB's steelworks are the cornerstones of Luleå. They also influence the science museum, **Teknikens Hus**, where technical experiments can be attempted, such as drilling in a mine and launching a space rocket.

ENVIRONS: **Luleå archipelago**, comprising more than 700 islands and islets, is a favourite place for boat owners. Ferries provide access to places of interest, such as the fishing villages on Rödkallen and Brändöskär.

🛈 Gammelstads Kyrkstad
10 km (6 miles) NW of the centre. 🚌
📞 0920-29 35 81. ◻ 2nd week in
Jun–mid-Aug: daily; other times:
Tue–Thu. 🗐 **✓** ◻ **🍴** 🛗 ♿

🏛 Norrbottens Museum
Storgatan 2. **📞** 0920-24 35 00.
◻ Tue–Sun. ◻ public holidays. 🗐
◻ ♿

🏛 Teknikens Hus
University district, 5 km (3 miles) N of
the centre. **📞** 0920-49 22 01.
◻ Tue–Sun. 🗐 ◻ **🍴** 🛗 ♿

Norrbottens Museum with a Sami summer tent and hut

Boden 🔟

Norrbotten. 35 km NW of Luleå, Road 97. 🚉 ✈ Kallax. 🚌 ℹ Kungsgatan 40, 0921-624 10. 📷 Kanonfestdagen (Festival (end Jul), Harvest Festival (Aug). 🅦 www.boden.se

ITS STRATEGIC LOCATION on the Luleälven river, at the intersection of two main train lines, has made Boden a centre for Sweden's northerly defences. It became the country's largest garrison town at the beginning of the last century and countless young men from across the country have completed their military service here. Five artillery forts circled the town. The nuclear bunker deep in the rock was top secret until only a few years ago. Now **Rödbergsfortet** is a national monument open to the public who can experience life in the fort and even stay in rooms carved out of the rock.

The central Björknäs area is also worth a visit for its open-air heated swimming pool and to see historic Norrbotten farms.

Cannon from Boden fort

About 3 km (2 miles) north of the centre, a Wild West ranch has been built which offers a taste of pioneering life in the 19th century.

🏛 Rödbergsfortet
5 km (3 miles) W of the centre. 📞 070-366 31 62. 🅾 3rd week in Jun–1st week in Aug; other times by appointment. 📷📷📷📷 limited access.

Kalix 🔟

Norrbotten. E4, 50 km (31 miles) W of Haparanda. 🚉 🚌 ✈ Kallax. ⛴ ℹ Töre Tourist Office, 0923-64 10 60. 📷 Grayling Day (end Jul), National River Festival (mid-Aug). 🅦 www.kalix.se

THE KALIX AREA to the north of the Gulf of Bothnia has been inhabited since Stone Age times. **Nederkalix** became a parish in the 15th century, but its church has had a turbulent history, with devastating fires and plundering by the Russians. During the 1809 war, it served as a stable for Russian horses. Englundsgården Cultural Heritage Centre is a good example of Norrland's beautiful wooden architecture.

ENVIRONS: The **Kalixälven** is one of Sweden's few unregulated rivers, ensuring good catches of salmon trout and salmon. The archipelago offers pike and whitefish and the opportunity for seine fishing. Of the islands which can be reached by tour boat, Malören has a timber chapel dating from 1769, an old lighthouse and a pilot station.

Tornedalen 🔟

Norrbotten. Road 99. 🚌 ℹ Haparanda-Tornio Tourist Office, 0922-120 10. 📷 Whitefish Festival in Kukkola (last weekend in Jul), Pajala Market (end Jun).

THE TORNE RIVER and its tributary, Muonio, form the border with Finland, but culturally the areas along both shores are united. Place names are in Finnish, and many of the inhabitants speak a local form of Finnish.

Haparanda, at the mouth of the river, was created as a border town when Torneå became part of Finland in the peace treaty of 1809. A bridge links the sister towns and they share a tourist office.

The disproportionately large train station, which has both normal and Russian wider gauge tracks, is a legacy from its time as a Russian border town.

Fishing is an important part of life on the Torne. Whitefish has been caught in the Kukkola rapids 15 km (9 miles) upstream since the 13th century, using large nets fixed to piers. The best fishing is to be had in late July, when the whitefish festival is held.

Övertorneå, 70 km (43 miles) north of Haparanda, is a fertile horticultural area. The long light summer nights help berries, fruit and vegetables to develop an exceptional flavour. There is a church dating from the 17th century and a good view from the top of the mountain, Luppioberget, where Father Christmas is said to live.

Pajala is the centre of northern Tornedalen. The area is popular for fishing and wilderness camps and it is possible to shoot the rapids on the Torne and Tärendö rivers. The latter is a 50-km (31-mile) long natural link between the Torne and Kalix rivers. **Laestadius Pörte** and museum attract Laestadian Lutherans on a pilgrimage to the simple cabin of the revivalist preacher and botanist Lars Levi Laestadius (1800–61).

🏛 Laestadius Pörte
Pajala. 📞 0978-120 55. 🅾 May–Aug; daily. 📷📷📷

Octagonal church in Övertorneå, the Tornedalen valley's main town

Kalixälven river, one of Europe's few entirely unregulated large rivers

Strikingly shaped church in Kiruna, inspired by a Sami hut

Kiruna ❸

Lappland. E10. 🏔 *19,100.* 🚉 🚌 ✈
ℹ *Folkets Hus, Lars Janssonsgatan 17, 0980-188 80.* ❄ *Snow Festival (last weekend in Jan), Kiruna Festival (4th weekend in Jun).*
w www.lappland.se

I N TERMS OF AREA, Kiruna is one of the world's largest municipalities. It is the site of Sweden's highest mountain, Kebnekaise, 2,111 m (6,925 ft), from where, on a clear day, one can see one-eleventh of the country. For 50 days in summer the sun never sets, and for 20 winter days it never rises. But even in the dark and cold, the people make the best of things. In January they hold a snow festival which is renowned for its ice sculpture competition.

Kiruna's development is due largely to the local iron ore deposits. In 1899 the first ore train rolled out from the mine on the newly laid railway line to Luleå. Ten years later, Kiruna had grown to a town of 7,000 inhabitants. Older buildings include the church, a gift of the mining company LKAB in 1912, whose shape was inspired by a Sami hut, and which is richly decorated by artists of the time, including Prince Eugen, Christian Eriksson and Ossian Elgström.

The Kirunavaara mine is open to visitors for guided tours. **LKAB InfoMine** lies 540 m (1,772 ft) below ground and paints a vivid picture of the development of mining in the region. Shiitake mush-rooms are grown in some of the mine's disused tunnels.

ENVIRONS: The space centre **Esrange**, 40 km (25 miles) east of Kiruna has, since the first rocket was launched in 1966, been a vital link in the European space programme. Guided tours can be arranged.

The former Sami village of **Jukkasjärvi**, 17 km (11 miles) east of Kiruna, has Lappland's oldest chapel, dating from 1607. It houses Bror Hjorth's altar-screen in wood depicting the charismatic 19th-century preacher Lars Levi Laestadius' missionary work among the Sami and Swedish pioneers.

Jukkasjärvi has achieved renown more recently for the **Icehotel**. In November every year, a 5,000 sq m (53,820 sq ft) edifice is built out of ice and snow. Drinks are served in the cool Icebar and guests sleep on ice beds, wrapped in furs, even though it is -40°C outside. Spec-tacular ice sculptures decorate the building. The Ice Globe Theatre, a copy of the Shakes-pearean Globe Theatre in London, is also erected every year and performances are given of *Macbeth* in Sami and Verdi's *Falstaff*. At the end of April everything melts away, but in summer ice sculptures are displayed in the Artcenter, and the restaurant is open all year.

Kiruna's vast mountain landscape is traversed by the **Kungsleden** trail *(see p274).*

Altar-screen by Bror Hjorth, Jukkasjärvi church

🏛 **LKAB InfoMine**
ℹ *Kiruna Tourist Office, 0980-188 80 for bookings.* ◯ *daily.* 🅿 ✔
🏨 **Icehotel Jukkasjärvi**
40 km (25 miles) E of Kiruna. 🚌 *from Kiruna.* **ℹ** *0980-668 00.*
Icehotel ◯ *Dec–Apr.* 🅿 ✔ 🍴 🅰
Ice Globe Theatre 🎭 *Dec–Apr: daily.* **Artcentrum** ◯ *daily.*

Gällivare ❶

Lappland. E10. 🏔 *4,700.* ✈ 🚉 🚌
ℹ *Centralplan 3, 0970-166 60.*
❄ *Winter Market (mid-Mar), Laponia Festival (first weekend in Jul).*
w www.gellivare.se

T HE TWIN communities of Gällivare and Malmberget grew rapidly from the late-19th century as the mining industry developed. But there was a settlement here long before that time: a chapel was built for the Sami in the 17th century and the Sami church on the Vassaraälven river opened in 1751. The arrival of the railway in 1888 sparked an iron ore rush which can be relived at **Kåkstan** in Malmberget and experienced from 1,000 m (3,280 ft) down in the enormous Aitik open-cast copper mine. **LKAB's Gruvmuseum** focuses on 250 years of mining history.

The Gällivare municipality stretches to the Norwegian border, covering parts of the Laponia UNESCO World Heritage Site *(see p275).* The Dundret

Icebar in the 60-room Icehotel, Jukkasjärvi, a creation of ice and snow

◁ **Kebnekaise massif, Lappland, with Sydtoppen, Sweden's highest peak, in the foreground** nature reserve has good cross-country skiing facilities. Dug into the rock here, the adventure centre **Boda Borg** runs activities for families.

Boda Borg
Dundret. 0970-660 68. phone for info.

Jokkmokk ⑮

Lappland. Road 97 & 45. 3,500. Stortorget 4, 0971-222 50. Jokkmokk Market (1st Thu–Sat Feb), Music week in Saltoluokta (early Aug). www.turism.jokkmokk.se

Muddus National Park, part of the Laponia UNESCO World Heritage Site

THE TOWN OF Jokkmokk, celebrating its 400th anniversary in 2005, is best-known for its winter market. For a few days in February, snow, darkness and cold give way to light, warmth and sparkling colours, when more than 30,000 people arrive to browse among the 500 market stalls and join in the festivities. The annual reindeer race through the town often causes chaos, but things are even faster at the reindeer race on the frozen Lake Talvatissjön.

The life of the Sami and the pioneering Swedish settlers is depicted in **Ájtte Fjäll- och Samemuseum**. Unfortunately in 1972 the Sami church built in 1753 burned down. The exterior of the new church replicates the original, but it has a modern interior.

ENVIRONS: The municipality includes the magnificent national parks of Padjelanta, Sarek, Stora Sjöfallet and a section of Muddus, which is part of the Laponia UNESCO World Heritage Site *(see p275)*.

Porjus, 40 km (25 miles) north of Jokkmokk, was Sweden's first major hydro-electric power station (1910–15). Its story is related in **Porjus Expo** which has a power station museum 50 m (164 ft) underground.

In Vuollerim, 43 km (26 miles) south of Jokkmokk, Stone Age settlements have been uncovered on the Stora Luleälv river. The museum **Vuollerim 6000 År** gives visitors the chance to experience Stone Age life.

Ájtte fjäll- och Samemuseum
Kungsgatan 3. 0971-170 70. Jun–Aug: daily; other times: Mon–Fri.

Porjus Expo
Porjus. 40 km (25 miles) N of Jokkmokk, road 45. 0973-776 00. Jun–Aug: daily; other times by appointment.

Vuollerim 6000 År
Vuollerim. 42 km (26 miles) SW of Jokkmokk, road 97. 0976-101 65. Jun–Aug: daily; other times: Tue & Wed.

Arvidsjaur ⑯

Lappland. Road 94 & 45. 4,700. to Jörn, then bus. 0960-175 00. Arvidsjaur Streetmarket (mid-Jul), Sami Festival (last weekend in Aug).

THIS COMMUNITY in central Lapland was founded in the early 17th century when King Karl IX set up a church here to bring Christianity to the Sami. **Arvidsjaur's Sami church village** contains 80 huts and log cabins from the 18th century.

Modern-day Arvidsjaur was experiencing a declining population until when in 1980 it received a boost with the relocation here of Norrland's dragoon regiment from Umeå. Guided tours provide an insight into their physically demanding military training programme (foreign citizens must book in advance).

In the summer a steam train operates on the Inlandsbanan line to the **Rallarmuseet** in Moskosel, which tells of the pioneers who built the railway.

Rallarmuseet
Moskosel, 40 km (25 miles) N of Arvidsjaur, road Rv 45. 0960-175 00. mid-Jun–mid-Aug: daily. limited access.

Arjeplog ⑰

Lappland. Road 95. 4,700. Arvidsjaur. Torget 1, 0961-222 30. Márkan (1st week Mar), Silveryran Festival (Jul). www.arjeploglappland.se

ON THE "Silver Road" between Hornavan and Uddjaur lies Arjeplog, home to the **Silvermuseet**. It was created by the "Lappland doctor" Einar Wallquist, whose home Doktorsgården is open to the public in July. In addition to 16th-century Sami silverwork, the museum looks at the life of the Sami and the pioneering incomers.

The area has much to offer hunting and fishing enthusiasts.

Silvermuseeet
Torget. Tourist Office, 0961-612 90. Jun–mid-Aug: daily; other times: Mon–Sat. limited access.

Traditional huts and log cabins in Arvidsjaur's 18th-century Sami church village

The Kungsleden Trail ⑱

T HE BEST WAY to experience the magnificence of the
Swedish mountains is to hike along a few stages of
the Kungsleden Trail. In 1900, the Swedish tourism
organisation, Svenska Turistföreningen (STF), drew up
plans for a network of marked walking trails and huts
for overnight stays through the mountains from Lappland
south to Grövelsjön lake in Dalarna. Today, the 440-km
(275-mile) long stretch between Abisko mountain station
on the Malmbanan railway line in the north and
Hemavan in southern Lappland forms the Kungsleden
Trail. The simple huts have given way to mountain
stations and rest cabins which offer hikers shelter in bad
weather and overnight accommodation. Some also have
a ferry service to help people on their way.

**Mountain walkers on the well-
marked Kungsleden Trail**

Sarek
*Perhaps the most spectacular of Sweden's national
parks, Sarek has 200 lofty peaks, more than 100
glaciers, wild waterfalls and valleys such as
Rapadalen. It is home to elk, lynx and wolverine.*

Ammarnäs
*The village is located
in the Vindelfjället
nature reserve, created
in 1976 and known
for its fauna. Its
200 inhabitants
mostly live off
tourism and
reindeer herding.*

Hemavan is the final point
for the Kungsleden Trail's
northern section. With the
ski town of Tärnaby close
by, it is a mecca for
alpine skiers.

**Padjelanta
National Park**

Vai
Kutjaure
Låddejåkka
Aras
Stáloluokta
Tuottar
Sårjåsjaure
Staddajåkkå
Tarralu
Sammar
Vaimok
Pieskehaure
Tarre

Vuonatj

Pieljekaise
Båverholmen
Adolfström
Dalovardo
Sjnjultle
Vitnjul
Råvfallsstugan

Skidbäcksstugan

Tärnasjö
Viterskalet
Syter
Serve
Aigert
Ammarnäs
163

Hemavan
Tärnaby

KEY

- ‑ ‑ Kungsleden Trail
- ‑ ‑ Other walking trails
- Major road
- Minor road
- — Railway line
- ⌂ Mountain stations and cabins

0 kilometres

0 miles

Riksgränsen is the last station on the Malmbanan line and a skier's paradise with lifts often operating until as late as Midsummer.

Abisko
Thanks to the E10 and its own train station, the STF tourist facility at Torneträsk in Abisko national park is a natural starting point for mountain walkers.

Nikkaluokta is the end of the road. It is a 19-km (12-mile) walk to the STF mountain station at Kebnekaise; 7 km (4 miles) can be cut by catching the lake ferry.

Kebnekaise
Topping the Kebnekaise massif is Sweden's highest peak at 2,111 m (6,925 ft). Below the summit, the STF station in Ladtjodalen, 690 m (2,264 ft), is a good starting point for tackling the range.

Stora Sjöfallet
This area is impressive for the mountains and glaciers of Akka and the primeval pine forests, but the waterfall is dry due to hydro-electric schemes.

LAPONIA WORLD HERITAGE SITE

The mountainous region of Lappland was designated a UNESCO World Heritage Site in 1996. Laponia has been home to the Sami since prehistoric times and provides the ideal conditions for their traditional nomadic reindeer herding, governed by the seasons. It is also Europe's largest single wilderness area, home to brown bears and alpine flora, as well as being geologically important. These factors contributed to its inclusion on UNESCO's list. The region includes the four national parks Padjelanta, Sarek, Stora Sjöfallet and Muddus, as well as the wetlands of Sjaunja with their rich birdlife.

Sjaunja National Park's extensive wetlands

| **Price categories** for a double room per night, including breakfast unless otherwise stated, plus tax and service.
🔖 Youth hostel *(see pp279)*
Ⓚ under 700 Kr
ⓄⓄ 700–1,400 Kr
ⓄⓄⓄ 1,400–2,100 Kr
ⓄⓄⓄⓄ over 2,100 Kr | **CHILDREN'S FACILITIES**
Cots and highchairs are available and some hotels will also provide a baby-sitting service.
PARKING
Parking is provided by the hotel, either in a private car park or a private garage nearby.
RESTAURANT
The hotel has a restaurant for residents, which also welcomes non-residents – usually only open for evening meals.
BAR
The hotel has a bar that is open to non-residents as well as those staying in the hotel. |

	CREDIT CARDS	CHILDREN'S FACILITIES	PARKING	RESTAURANT	BAR
CITY: *Scandic Sergel Plaza* ⓄⓄⓄⓄ Brunkebergstorg 9, 103 27 Stockholm. **Map** 3 A1. 📞 08-517 263 00. 📠 508-517 263 11. 🌐 www.scandic-hotels.com In the heart of the city, but still in a quiet spot behind Kulturhuset. Mowitz Restaurang & Bar is a cosy place to meet for a coffee or a bite to eat. 🔧 📺 🍸 🏊 🎿 🛗 ⛷ **Rooms:** 403	AE DC MC V	●	▦	●	▦
CITY: *Sheraton Stockholm Hotel & Towers* ⓄⓄⓄⓄ Tegelbacken 6, 101 23 Stockholm. **Map** 1 C5, 3 A2. 📞 08-412 34 00. 📠 08-412 34 09. 🌐 www.sheraton.com/stockholm International deluxe hotel with the largest hotel rooms in Stockholm. Centrally located. Many rooms have great views of Riddarfjärden and Stadshuset. Piano bar and two restaurants. 🔧 📺 🍸 🏊 🛗 🍽 ⛷ **Rooms:** 462	AE DC MC V	●	▦	●	▦
BLASIEHOLMEN & SKEPPSHOLMEN: *af Chapman & Skeppsholmen (STF)* 🔖 Flaggmansvägen 8, 111 49 Stockholm. **Map** 4 D3. 📞 08-463 22 66. 📠 08-611 71 55. 🌐 www.stfchapman.com Perhaps one of the world's most beautiful youth hostels, with beds on board the ship *(see p 77)* or ashore in Hantverkshuset. 🎿 ⛷ **Beds:** 293	AE MC V		▦		
BLASIEHOLMEN & SKEPPSHOLMEN: *Grand Hôtel Stockholm* ⓄⓄⓄⓄ S Blasieholmshamnen, 103 27 Stockholm. **Map** 3 C1. 📞 08-679 35 00. 📠 08-611 86 86. 🌐 www.grandhotel.se A grand hotel in the old style in a magnificent location. The Cadier bar and Franska Matsalen restaurant are renowned. 🔧 📺 🍸 🏊 🛗 🍽 ⛷ **Rooms:** 307	AE DC MC V	●	▦	●	▦
BLASIEHOLMEN & SKEPPSHOLMEN: *Radisson SAS Strand Hotel* ⓄⓄⓄⓄ Nybrokajen 9, 103 27 Stockholm. **Map** 3 C1. 📞 08-506 640 00. 📠 08-506 640 01. 🌐 www.radissonsas.se First-class hotel overlooking Nybroviken. Fantastic city views from the sauna on the top floor. Strand Restaurant & Lounge serves exclusive but uncomplicated meals. 🔧 📺 🍸 🏊 🛗 🍽 ⛷ **Rooms:** 152	AE DC MC V	●	▦	●	▦
DJURGÅRDEN: *Scandic Hotel Hasselbacken* ⓄⓄⓄⓄ Hazeliusbacken 20, 100 55 Stockholm. 📞 08-517 343 00. 📠 08-517 343 11. 🌐 www.scandic-hotels.se/hasselbacken Beautifully restored hotel adjoining Skansen, dating from 1765. Award-winning Hasselbacken restaurant is one of Stockholm's best. Brunch is served at weekends. 🔧 📺 🍸 🏊 🛗 ⛷ **Rooms:** 112	AE DC MC V	●	▦	●	▦
ÖSTERMALM: *Hotel Diplomat* ⓄⓄⓄ Strandvägen 7C, 104 40 Stockholm. **Map** 2 E4. 📞 08-459 68 00. 📠 08-459 68 20. 🌐 www.diplomathotel.com Typical Swedish decor with elegant bathrooms in a well-preserved Jugendstil building from 1907. The T/BAR restaurant is popular. 🔧 📺 🍸 🏊 🛗 **Rooms:** 128	AE DC MC V	●	▦	●	▦
VASASTAN: *Clas på Hörnet* ⓄⓄ Surbrunnsgatan 20, 113 48 Stockholm. **Map** 1 C2. 📞 08-16 51 30. 📠 08-612 53 15. 🌐 www.claspahornet.com Romantic inn with 18th-century atmosphere. Rooms dedicated to Swedish celebrities. Excellent Swedish food in the restaurant. 🔧 📺 🍸 🏊 **Rooms:** 10	AE DC MC V	●		●	▦
VASASTAN: *Ramada Hotel Tegnérlunden* ⓄⓄⓄ Tegnérlunden 8, 113 59 Stockholm. **Map** 1 B3. 📞 08-545 455 50. 📠 08-545 455 51. 🌐 www.hoteltegnerlunden.se Hotel with a casual atmosphere in a quiet location near August Strindberg's residence and museum on Drottninggatan. 🔧 📺 🛗 ⛷ **Rooms:** 102	AE DC MC V	●	▦		▦
KUNGSHOLMEN: *Elite Palace Hotel* ⓄⓄⓄ St Eriksgatan 115, 100 31 Stockholm. **Map** 1 A1. 📞 08-566 217 00. 📠 08-566 217 01. 🌐 www.elite.se Quiet but accessible location in Vasastan. Family-friendly with modern rooms. Full gym, spa and sauna suite. Pub. 🔧 📺 🎿 🛗 🍽 **Rooms:** 216	AE DC MC V	●	▦	●	▦

Price categories for a double room per night, including breakfast unless otherwise stated, plus tax and service.

🝆 Youth hostel *(see pp279)*
Ⓚ under 700 Kr
ⓀⓀ 700–1,400 Kr
ⓀⓀⓀ 1,400–2,100 Kr .
ⓀⓀⓀⓀ over 2,100 Kr

CHILDREN'S FACILITIES
Cots and highchairs are available and some hotels will also provide a baby-sitting service.
PARKING
Parking is provided by the hotel, either in a private car park or a private garage nearby.
RESTAURANT
The hotel has a restaurant for residents, which also welcomes non-residents – usually only open for evening meals.
BAR
The hotel has a bar that is open to non-residents as well as those staying in the hotel.

	CREDIT CARDS	CHILDREN'S FACILITIES	PARKING	RESTAURANT	BAR
KUNGSHOLMEN: *First Hotel Amaranten* ⓀⓀⓀⓀ Kungsholmsgatan 31, 104 20 Stockholm. **Map** 1 A4. 🔲 08-692 52 00. **FAX** 08-652 62 48. 🔲 www.firsthotels.se Newly refurbished full-service hotel near Central Station. Modern Nordic decor using materials such as granite and walnut. Several bars and restaurants. Serves a substantial breakfast. 🔲 🔲 🔲 🔲 🔲 🔲 🔲 **Rooms:** *423*	AE DC MC V	●	▦	●	▦
SÖDERMALM: *Columbus Hotel* ⓀⓀⓀ Tjärhovsgatan 11, 116 21 Stockholm. 🔲 08-503 112 00. **FAX** 608-503 112 01. 🔲 www.columbushotell.se Charming hotel in a listed former barracks dating from 1780. All rooms decorated in Gustavian style. Buffet breakfast in the courtyard in summer. 🔲 🔲 🔲 **Rooms:** *40*	AE DC MC V	●	▦		
SÖDERMALM: *Clarion Hotel Stockholm* ⓀⓀⓀⓀ Ringvägen 98, 104 60 Stockhom. 🔲 08-62 10 00. **FAX** 08-462 10 99. 🔲 www.clarionstockholm.com Söder's largest hotel with exciting architecture and stylish decor. Contemporary Nordic art features in the reception, restaurant and bars. 🔲 🔲 🔲 🔲 🔲 🔲 🔲 **Rooms:** *532*	AE DC MC V	●	▦	●	▦
SÖDERMALM: *Hilton Stockholm Slussen* ⓀⓀⓀⓀ Guldgränd 8, 104 65 Stockholm. **Map** 1 B4. 🔲 08-517 517 00. **FAX** 108-517 517 11. 🔲 www.hilton.com Well-equipped, five-star hotel of modern design with several restaurants and bars. Superb views of Gamla Stan. 🔲 🔲 🔲 🔲 🔲 🔲 🔲 🔲 **Rooms:** *289*	AE DC MC V	●	▦	●	▦
SÖDERMALM: *Långholmen Hotell & Restaurang* ⓀⓀⓀ 🝆 Kronohäktet, Långholmen, 102 72 Stockholm. 🔲 08-720 85 00. **FAX** 08-720 85 75. 🔲 www.langholmen.com This former prison offers accommodation in modernized cells on a leafy island in the city centre. Excellent restaurant and wine cellars. 🔲 🔲 🔲 🔲 🔲 **Rooms:** *102*. Part of the old prison is a youth hostel. **Beds:** *26–125*	AE DC MC V	●	▦	●	▦
FURTHER AFIELD: *IBIS Hotell Stockholm Hägersten* ⓀⓀ Västertorpsvägen 131, 129 44 Hägersten. 🔲 08-556 323 30. **FAX** 08-97 64 27. 🔲 www.ibishotel.com Good-value hotel of high standard located 8 km (5 miles) south of city centre. Near Stockholm International Fairs. 🔲 🔲 🔲 🔲 🔲 🔲 **Rooms:** *190*	AE DC MC V		▦	●	▦
FURTHER AFIELD: *Arlanda Hotellby* ⓀⓀ Bristagatan 22, 190 45 Stockholm-Arlanda. 🔲 08-597 897 00. **FAX** 08-597 898 00. 🔲 www.arlandahotellby.se Comfortable and good-value hotel only 5 min from Arlanda Airport. Transfer to and from the airport 24 hours a day. 🔲 🔲 🔲 🔲 🔲 🔲 🔲 **Rooms:** *148*	AE DC MC V	●	▦	●	▦
FURTHER AFIELD: *Foresta Hotell & Konferens* ⓀⓀⓀ Herserudsvägen 22, 181 25 Lidingö. 🔲 08-505 505 00. **FAX** 08-505 505 90. 🔲 www.foresta.se Near Millesgården *(see p 95)* on the suburban island of Lidingö. Rooms are decorated in light natural materials. 🔲 🔲 🔲 🔲 🔲 🔲 🔲 **Rooms:** *95*	AE DC MC V	●	▦	●	▦
STOCKHOLM ARCHIPELAGO: *Finnhamns Vandrarhem* 🝆 Finnhamns Brygga, 130 25 Ingmarsö. 🔲 08-542 462 12. **FAX** 08-542 461 33. 🔲 www.finnhamn.nu Housed in a grand old merchant's villa, a 10-min walk from the steamer quay. Open all year round. 🔲 **Beds:** *89*	AE MC V	●		●	
STOCKHOLM ARCHIPELAGO: *Sandhamn Hotell & Konferens* ⓀⓀⓀ Box 124, 130 39 Sandhamn. 🔲 08-574 704 00. **FAX** 08-574 504 50. Newly-built hotel next to the Seglar Restaurangen, a restaurant dating from 1897 which is a popular meeting place, particularly during regattas. 🔲 🔲 🔲 🔲 🔲 🔲 **Rooms:** *81*	AE DC MC V	●		●	▦

EASTERN SVEALAND

ESKILSTUNA: *Sundbyholms Slott* ⓚⓚ
635 08 Eskilstuna. 📞 016-42 84 00. FAX 016-965 78. 🅦 www.sundbyholms-slott.se
Just under 10 km (6 miles) north of Eskilstuna, this splendid palace is beautifully
located in the beech woods on the banks of Lake Mälaren. 🛏 TV 🔀 🔋 *Rooms:* 99
AE DC MC V

NORRTÄLJE: *Pensionat Granparken* ⓚⓚ
Gjuterivägen 10, 761 40 Norrtälje. 📞 0176-103 54. FAX 0176-125 02.
🅦 www.pensionatgranparken.se
Charming family-owned guest house with a 100-year history. Quiet location
within walking distance of the centre. Restaurant with several pleasant dining
rooms, all decorated in different styles. 🛏 TV 🔀 🚇 *Rooms:* 16
AE DC MC V

NYKÖPING: *Park Inn Nyköping* ⓚⓚ
Brunnsgatan 33, 611 26 Nyköping. 📞 0155-29 35 00. FAX 0155-29 35 09.
🅦 www.rezidorparkinn.com
Good-value, family-friendly hotel in a convenient location for Kolmårdens
Djurpark *(see p144)* and Skavsta Airport. 🛏 TV 🍽 🔀 🔋 ♿ *Rooms:* 98
AE DC MC V

NYNÄSHAMN: *Skärgårdshotellet* ⓚⓚ
Kaptensgatan 2, 149 31 Nynäshamn. 📞 08-520 111 20. FAX 08-520 105 72.
Located above the harbour, far enough from the centre to enjoy a sense of
the archipelago. Many rooms have sea views and a balcony.
🛏 TV 🔀 🔋 ♿ *Rooms:* 75
AE DC MC V

SIGTUNA: *Sigtuna Stadshotell* ⓚⓚⓚⓚ
Stora Nygatan 3, 193 30 Sigtuna. 📞 08-592 501 00. FAX 08-592 515 87.
Small designer hotel in the heart of Sweden's oldest town. One of the few hotels
with five stars under the Swedish classification system. Classic Scandinavian
interiors, mainly using natural materials. 🛏 TV 🍽 🔀 🔋 *Rooms:* 27
AE DC MC V

SÖDERTÄLJE: *Best Western Hotell Skogshöjd* ⓚⓚⓚ
Täppgatan 15, 151 21 Södertälje. 📞 08-550 926 00. FAX 08-550 926 60.
Well-equipped large hotel with a focus on conferences. Very comfortable
rooms, plus pool and fitness suite. 🛏 TV 🍽 🔀 🔋 🎏 🚇 ♿ *Rooms:* 225
AE DC MC V

UPPSALA: *Hotel Uppsala* ⓚⓚ ♨
Kungsgatan 27, 753 21 Uppsala. 📞 018-480 50 00. FAX 018-480 50 50.
🅦 www.profilhotels.se
Uppsala's largest hotel, newly refurbished and centrally located. Also, there is a
STF youth hostel. 🛏 TV 🔀 🔋 ♿ *Rooms:* 213
AE DC MC V

UPPSALA: *Radisson SAS Hotel Gillet* ⓚⓚⓚ
Dragarbrunnsgatan 23, 753 20 Uppsala. 📞 018-68 18 00. FAX 018-68 18 18.
🅦 www.radissonsas.se
Full-service hotel with a 200-year history in the heart of the city. Two restaurants
offering international and Scandinavian dishes. 🛏 TV 🔀 🔋 🎏 🚇 ♿ *Rooms:* 160
AE DC MC V

VÄSTERÅS: *Elite Stadshotellet Västerås* ⓚⓚ
Stora torget, 721 03 Västerås. 📞 021-10 28 00. FAX 021-10 28 10. 🅦 www.elite.se
High-class, central hotel in a beautiful Jugendstil building. Stadskällaren restaurant
has an interior from the end of the 19th century. 🛏 TV 🔀 🔋 🎏 *Rooms:* 137
AE DC MC V

EASTERN GÖTALAND

GLASRIKET: *STF Ljuders Vandrarhem* ♨
Grimsnäs Herrgård, 360 53 Skruv. 📞 & FAX 0478-204 00.
A manor house in a natural rural setting in the heart of Småland's Kingdom
of Crystal *(see p152)*. 🔀 *Beds:* 64
MC V

JÖNKÖPING: *Elite Stora Hotellet* ⓚⓚⓚ
Norra Flaggstångsgatan 7, 51 12 Jönköping. 📞 036-10 00 00. FAX 036-215 50 25.
🅦 www.elite.se
Beautiful 19th-century building on the southern shore of Lake Vättern. Furnished
in Gustavian style. 🛏 TV 🔀 🔋 ♿ *Rooms:* 135
AE DC MC V

KALMAR: *Slottshotellet* ⓚⓚⓚ
Slottsvägen 7, 392 33 Kalmar. 📞 0480-882 60. FAX 0480-882 66. 🅦 www.slottshotellet.se
A little oasis opposite Kalmar castle. The buildings have been sympathetically
renovated, retaining their old charm. Individually designed rooms with wood
floors, antique furniture and tiled stoves. 🛏 TV 🔀 🔋 *Rooms:* 44
AE DC MC V

<table>
<tr><td colspan="2">
Price categories for a double room per night, including breakfast unless otherwise stated, plus tax and service.
↩ Youth hostel (see pp279)
Ⓚ under 700 Kr
ⓀⓀ 700–1,400 Kr
ⓀⓀⓀ 1,400–2,100 Kr
ⓀⓀⓀⓀ over 2,100 Kr
</td></tr>
</table>

CHILDREN'S FACILITIES
Cots and highchairs are available and some hotels will also provide a baby-sitting service.

PARKING
Parking is provided by the hotel, either in a private car park or a private garage nearby.

RESTAURANT
The hotel has a restaurant for residents, which also welcomes non-residents – usually only open for evening meals.

BAR
The hotel has a bar that is open to non-residents as well as those staying in the hotel.

	CREDIT CARDS	CHILDREN'S FACILITIES	PARKING	RESTAURANT	BAR
LINKÖPING: *Hotell du Nord* ⓀⓀ Repslagaregatan 5, 581 22 Linköping. (013-12 98 95. FAX 013-14 52 91. w www.hotelldunord.se An unusual little hotel with a personal atmosphere. Pleasant location in its own gardens, close to the train station and Stångån river. ⊟ TV ⇆ *Rooms:* 28	AE DC MC V	●	▦		
LINKÖPING: *Scandic Frimurarehotellet* ⓀⓀⓀ St Larsgatan 14, 582 24 Linköping. (013-495 30 00. FAX 013-495 30 11. w www.scandic-hotels.se/frimurarehotellet This classic hotel, which conjures up images of a bygone era, stands right on the town's main street. The Alberts Hall pub serves international food and drink. ⊟ TV ⊟ TV ⛾ ⇆ ≈ & *Rooms:* 84	AE DC MC V	●	▦	●	▦
NORRKÖPING: *Elite Grand Hotel Norrköping* ⓀⓀⓀ Tyska Torget 2, 600 24 Norrköping. (011-36 41 00. FAX 011-36 41 01. Grand building dating from 1906 in a peaceful location on the Motala Ström river within walking distance of the train station. There is a basement spa and in the summer a special playroom for children. ⊟ TV ⇆ & *Rooms:* 206	AE DC MC V	●	▦	●	▦
NÄSSJÖ: *Hotell Högland* ⓀⓀ Esplanaden 4, 571 23 Nässjö. (0380-131 00. FAX 0380-101 25. The hotel stands next to the train station. Well-equipped rooms and a good relaxation suite with a spa pool and solarium. ⊟ TV ⛾ ⇆ & *Rooms:* 104	AE DC MC V	●		●	▦
OSKARSHAMN: *Ramada Hotel Corallen* ⓀⓀ Gröndalsgatan 35, 572 35 Oskarshamn. (0491-76 81 81. FAX 0491-76 81 80. w www.hotelcorallen.se This modern hotel is situated on the harbour with a superb view of the Baltic Sea and the Blå Jungfrun island *(see p 154).* ⊟ TV ⇆ & ≈ & *Rooms:* 74	AE DC MC V		▦	●	▦
VADSTENA: *Vadstena Klosterhotel* ⓀⓀⓀ Klosterområdet, 592 30 Vadstena. (0143-315 30. FAX 0143-136 48. w www.klosterhotel.se Newly refurbished hotel in the former abbey in Vadstena which was planned by St Bridget. ⊟ TV ⇆ & & *Rooms:* 68	AE DC MC V	●	▦	●	●
VÄSTERVIK: *Best Western Västerviks Stadshotell* ⓀⓀⓀ Storgatan 3, 593 30 Västervik. (0490-820 00. FAX 0490-820 01. w www.stadshotellet.nu Next to the harbour and the sea, but still centrally located on Västervik's main street. Newly built with an eye on the past, the exterior is a replica of the former town hotel. ⊟ TV ⇆ & & *Rooms:* 101	AE DC MC V	●		●	▦
VÄXJÖ: *Elite Stadshotellet Växjö* ⓀⓀ Kungsgatan 6, 351 04 Växjö. (0470-134 00. FAX 0470-448 37. w www.elite.se This grand, traditional hotel lies in the town centre. The restaurant serves internationally inspired food with a nod to Småland cuisine. ⊟ ⇆ & & *Rooms:* 132	AE DC MC V	●	▦	●	▦
ÖLAND: *Hotell Borgholm* ⓀⓀ Trädgårdsgatan 15-19, 387 31 Borgholm. (0485-770 60. FAX 0485-124 66. Charming small-town hotel reopening in 2005 after extensive renovations following a fire. ⊟ TV ⇆ *Rooms:* 135	AE DC MC V			●	▦

GOTLAND

	CREDIT CARDS	CHILDREN'S FACILITIES	PARKING	RESTAURANT	BAR
VISBY: *Hotell Gute & Breda Blick* ⓀⓀ Mellangatan 29, 621 56 Visby. (0498-20 22 60. FAX 0498-20 22 62. w www.hotellgute.se Hotel with old-fashioned charm and a central location. Most rooms have broadband access. Sauna and solarium. ⊟ TV ⇆ *Rooms:* 43	AE DC MC V	●			

VISBY: *Hotell St Clemens* ⓚⓚ
Smedjegatan 3, 621 55 Visby. ☏ 0498-21 90 00. FAX 0498-27 94 43.
Ⓦ www.clemenshotell.se
The five buildings of the hotel are linked by gardens alongside the ruins of the medieval church of St Clemens. 🖥 TV ▮ 💱 ▮ & **Rooms:** 30

AE DC MC V

VISBY: *Wisby Hotell* ⓚⓚⓚ
Strandgatan 6, 621 24 Visby. ☏ 0498-25 75 00. FAX 0498-25 75 50.
Like the town, the hotel is a mix of medieval and contemporary. 🖥 TV ▮ 💱
▮ ≋ & **Rooms:** 134

AE DC MC V

KLINTEHAMN: *Pensionat Warfsholm* ⓚⓚ ◇
620 20 Klintehamn. ☏ 0498-24 00 10. FAX 0498-24 14 11. Ⓦ www.warfsholm.se
Charming guest house, set on its own peninsula, 30 km (19 miles) south of Visby. Also cottage and youth hostel accommodation. TV 💱 **Rooms:** 20. **Beds:** 90

AE DC MC V

SOUTHERN GÖTALAND

HELSINGBORG: *Radisson SAS Grand Hotell, Helsingborg* ⓚⓚⓚ
Stortorget 8-12, 251 11 Helsingborg. ☏ 042-38 04 00. FAX 042-38 04 04.
Ⓦ www.radissonsas.se
First-class, newly refurbished hotel, centrally located next to the harbour and station. The restaurant serves Scandinavian cuisine. 🖥 TV ▮ 💱 ▮ & **Rooms:** 117

AE DC MC V

KARLSKRONA: *First Hotel Statt* ⓚⓚⓚ
Ronnebygatan 37-39, 371 33 Karlskrona. ☏ 0455-555 50. FAX 0455-169 09.
Ⓦ www.firsthotels.se
Elegantly designed hotel and banqueting hall from the early 20th century. Popular pub with a range of beers and whiskies. 🖥 TV 💱 ▮ ▮ & **Rooms:** 107

AE DC MC V

KRISTIANSTAD: *Quality Hotel Grand* ⓚⓚⓚ
Västra Storgatan 15, 291 21 Kristianstad. ☏ 044-28 48 00. FAX 044-28 48 10.
Ⓦ www.choicehotels.se
The town's largest hotel, located opposite the church of Heliga Trefaldighets.
Restaurant, nightclub, relaxation suite with sauna. 🖥 TV ▮ 💱 ▮ & **Rooms:** 148

AE DC MC V

LANDSKRONA: *Hotel Öresund* ⓚⓚ
Kungsgatan 15, 261 31 Landskrona. ☏ 0418-47 40 00. FAX 0418-47 40 10.
Ⓦ www.hoteloresund.se
Privately run classic hotel, dating back to the 18th century in a leafy town location. Three restaurants. 🖥 TV 💱 ▮ ▮ & **Rooms:** 130

AE DC MC V

LUND: *Grand Hotel* ⓚⓚⓚ
Bantorget 1, 221 04 Lund. ☏ 046-280 61 00. FAX 046-280 61 50. Ⓦ www.grandilund.se
Built at the end of the 19th century in French Renaissance style. Individually designed rooms. 🖥 TV ▮ 💱 ▮ ▮ & **Rooms:** 84

AE DC MC V

MALMÖ: *Hotell Plaza* ⓚⓚ
Kasinogatan 6, 200 10 Malmö. ☏ 040-33 05 50. FAX 040-33 05 51.
Ⓦ www.hotel-plaza.com
Small, friendly hotel in central Malmö in a quiet location off Södra Förstadsgatan, the city's main pedestrianized street. 🖥 TV 💱 **Rooms:** 48

AE DC MC V

MALMÖ: *Best Western Premier Mäster Johan* ⓚⓚⓚ
Mäster Johansgatan 13, 211 21 Malmö. ☏ 040-664 64 00. FAX 040-664 64 01.
Ⓦ www.masterjohan.se
Modern, award-winning hotel, named best individual business hotel. Newly built in a traditional style in the heart of the city. 🖥 TV 💱 ▮ ▮ & **Rooms:** 69

AE DC MC V

MALMÖ: *Elite Hotel Savoy* ⓚⓚⓚ
Norra Vallgatan 62. Box 880, 201 80 Malmö. ☏ 040-664 48 00.
FAX 040-664 48 50. Ⓦ www.savoy.elite.se
This modern and historically interesting hotel lies in the heart of Malmö within walking distance of the Central Station. 🖥 TV ▮ 💱 ▮ **Rooms:** 109

AE DC MC V

MALMÖ: *Hilton Malmö City* ⓚⓚⓚ
Triangeln 2, 200 10 Malmö. ☏ 040-693 47 00. FAX 040-693 47 11. Ⓦ www.hilton.com
The 20-storey building dominates the shopping district around Triangeln Square. Full service and fantastic views. 🖥 TV ▮ 💱 ▮ ▮ & **Rooms:** 216

AE DC MC V

SKANÖR: *Hotell Gässlingen* ⓚⓚⓚ
Rådhustorget 6, 239 30 Skanör. ☏ 040-45 91 00. FAX 040-45 91 13.
A picturesque exterior in traditional regional style hides the very modern interior of this special hotel. Beautiful countryside close to the sea and beaches. 🖥 TV 💱 ▮ ▮ ≋ **Rooms:** 26

AE DC MC V

For key to symbols see back flap

<table>
<tr><td>

Price categories for a double room per night, including breakfast unless otherwise stated, plus tax and service.

🛏 Youth hostel *(see pp279)*
Ⓚ under 700 Kr
ⓀⓀ 700–1,400 Kr
ⓀⓀⓀ 1,400–2,100 Kr
ⓀⓀⓀⓀ over 2,100 Kr

</td><td>

CHILDREN'S FACILITIES
Cots and highchairs are available and some hotels will also provide a baby-sitting service.
PARKING
Parking is provided by the hotel, either in a private car park or a private garage nearby.
RESTAURANT
The hotel has a restaurant for residents, which also welcomes non-residents – usually only open for evening meals.
BAR
The hotel has a bar that is open to non-residents as well as those staying in the hotel.

</td></tr>
</table>

	CREDIT CARDS	CHILDREN'S FACILITIES	PARKING	RESTAURANT	BAR
YSTAD: *Hotell Continental* ⓀⓀ Hamngatan 13, 271 43 Ystad. 📞 *0411-137 00.* 📠 *0411-125 70.* 🌐 www.hotelcontinental-ystad.se In the heart of Ystad, this hotel was opened in 1829. Thoughtfully refurbished with grand interiors and light rooms. 🛏 📺 ⚡ 🍴 ♿ *Rooms: 52*	AE DC MC V	●	●	●	●

GOTHENBURG

	CREDIT CARDS	CHILDREN'S FACILITIES	PARKING	RESTAURANT	BAR
CENTRE: *Hotel Vasa* ⓀⓀ Viktoriag. 6, 411 25 Gothenburg. 📞 *031-17 36 30.* 📠 *031-711 95 97.* 🌐 www.hotelvasa.se Newly refurbished family-run hotel in the middle of Vasastaden. In summer the breakfast buffet is set up in the inner courtyard. 🛏 📺 ⚡ 🍴 *Rooms: 50*	AE DC MC V	●	●		
CENTRE: *Eggers Hotell & Restaurang* ⓀⓀⓀ Drottningtorget. Box 323, 401 25 Gothenburg. 📞 *031-33 34 44.* 📠 *031-15 42 43.* 🌐 www.hoteleggers.se A listed building in the heart of the city, with early-20th-century character. Located a stone's throw from the train station. 🛏 📺 ⚡ 🍴 *Rooms: 67*	AE DC MC V	●	●	●	●
CENTRE: *Hotel Gothia Towers* ⓀⓀⓀ Mässans gata 24. Box 5184, 402 26 Gothenburg. 📞 *031-750 88 10.* 📠 *031-750 88 82.* 🌐 www.gothiatowers.com Gothenburg's tallest hotel (23 floors) is situated opposite Liseberg amusement park and the Swedish Exhibition Centre. 🛏 📺 🍸 ⚡ 🍴 🛎 ♿ *Rooms: 704*	AE DC MC V	●	●	●	●
CENTRE: *Elite Plaza Hotel* ⓀⓀⓀⓀ Västra Hamng. 3, 404 22 Gothenburg. 📞 *031-720 40 00.* 📠 *031-720 40 10.* 🌐 www.elite.se New five-star hotel in a palatial old building dating from 1889. Exquisitely refurbished, with well-preserved original features combined with modern art and design. 🛏 📺 🍸 ⚡ 🍴 🛎 ♿ *Rooms: 143*	AE DC MC V	●	●	●	●
CENTRE: *Radisson SAS Park Avenue Hotel* ⓀⓀⓀ Kungsportsavenyn 36-38. Box 53233, 400 16 Gothenburg. 📞 *031-758 40 00.* 📠 *031-758 40 01.* 🌐 www.radissonsas.se Luxury modern hotel near Götaplatsen with tastefully decorated rooms, plus conference and banqueting facilities. 🛏 📺 🍸 ⚡ 🍴 🛎 ♿ *Rooms: 318*	AE DC MC V	●	●	●	●
FURTHER AFIELD: *Mölndal/Torrekulla Turiststation* 🛏 428 35 Kållered. 📞 *031-795 14 95.* 📠 *031-795 51 40.* 📧 info@torrekulla.stfturist.se Picturesque, child-friendly location in Sandsjöbacka nature reserve, 10 min by car south of the centre. Outdoor activities nearby, such as swimming. ⚡ ♿ *Beds: 132*	MC V	●	●		

WESTERN GÖTALAND

	CREDIT CARDS	CHILDREN'S FACILITIES	PARKING	RESTAURANT	BAR
BORÅS: *Ramada Hotell Vävaren* ⓀⓀ Allégatan 21, 503 32 Borås. 📞 *033-10 00 20.* 📠 *033-41 18 82.* 🌐 www.hotel-vavaren.se Well-equipped, central hotel with a friendly atmosphere. 🛏 📺 🍸 ⚡ 🍴 🛎 ♿ *Rooms: 97*	AE DC MC V	●	●	●	●
FALKENBERG: *Grand Hotel Falkenberg* ⓀⓀ Hotellgatan 1, 311 31 Falkenberg. 📞 *0346-144 50.* 📠 *0346-144 59.* Built in 1931, this central hotel is Falkenberg's entertainment hub with dance music and nightclub. Set beside the pretty Ätran river. 🛏 📺 🍸 ⚡ 🍴 ♿ *Rooms: 70*	AE DC MC V	●	●	●	●
FJÄLLBACKA: *Stora Hotellet Fjällbacka* ⓀⓀⓀ Galärbacken 3, 450 71 Fjällbacka. 📞 *0525-310 03.* 📠 *0525-310 93.* Charming little hotel with a marine theme inspired by Klassen, a sea captain who set up the hotel in the late 19th century. The rooms are named after people and places from the captain's travels on the high seas and decorated accordingly. 🛏 📺 🍸 ⚡ *Rooms: 23*	AE DC MC V	●	●	●	●

HALMSTAD: *Grand Hotel Halmstad*   (K)(K)(K)
Stationsgatan 44, 302 45 Halmstad. **[** 035-280 81 00. **FAX** 035-280 81 10.
Dating from 1905, the hotel offers a good standard and is located in the middle
of town, near the train station, shopping and restaurants.
🛏 TV 🖥 🍴 ♿ *Rooms: 108*

AE DC MC V

LIDKÖPING: *Best Western Stadt Lidköping*   (K)(K)
Gamla Stadens Torg 1, 531 02 Lidköping. **[** 0510-220 85. **FAX** 0510-215 32.
W www.stadtlidkoping.se
Business and leisure hotel, beautifully situated on the Lidan river in the old
town centre. 🛏 TV 🖥 🍴 ♿ *Rooms: 67*

AE DC MC V

MARSTRAND: *Båtellet*   ♦
Kungsplan, 440 30 Marstrand. **[** 0303-600 10. **FAX** 0303-606 07.
@ marstrandsvarmbadhus@telia.com
The wonderful 19th-century spa house has a restaurant and a youth hostel with
self-catering facilities. 🖥 🏨 ♿ *Beds: 113*

MC V DC

SKÖVDE: *Scandic Hotel Billingen*   (K)(K)(K)
Trädgårdsgatan 10, 541 30 Skövde. **[** 0500-74 50 00. **FAX** 0500-74 50 11.
W www.scandic-hotels.se
Lovely old hotel from the late 19th century with fine architecture and a grand
function suite. 🛏 TV 🖥 🍴 ♿ *Rooms: 107*

AE DC MC V

SMÖGEN: *Hotell Smögens Havsbad*   (K)(K)
Hotellgatan 26, 450 43 Smögen. **[** 0523-66 84 50. **FAX** 0523-66 84 55.
Part listed building and part newly-built hotel in light natural materials
overlooking the water. The restaurant specializes in fish and seafood.
🛏 TV 📺 🖥 ♿ *Rooms: 76*

AE DC MC V

STRÖMSTAD: *Laholmen Hotell*   (K)(K)(K)
452 30 Strömstad. **[** 0526-197 00. **FAX** 0526-100 36.
Situated on a promontory in the harbour. Most rooms have superb views across
Kosterfjorden. The restaurant offers seafood delicacies. 🛏 TV 🖥 🍴 ♿
Rooms: 152

AE DC MC V

TROLLHÄTTAN: *Albert Kök – Hotel och Konferens*   (K)(K)
Strömsberg, 461 57 Trollhättan. **[** 0520-129 90. **FAX** 0520-133 11.
W www.alberthotell.com
The main building from 1856 stands on a hill with wonderful views down the
slope to the town. Top class restaurant. 🛏 TV 📺 🖥 🍴 ♿ *Rooms: 28*

AE DC MC V

VARBERG: *Best Western Varbergs Stadshotell & Asia Spa*   (K)(K)
Kungsgatan 24–26, 432 41 Varberg. **[** 0340-69 01 00. **FAX** 0340-69 01 01.
W www.varbergsstadshotell.com
Attractive early-20th-century decor, offering comfort and a good standard of
technology. Award-winning restaurant and an oriental-style spa.
🛏 TV 📺 🖥 🍴 ♿ *Rooms: 125*

AE DC MC V

ÅMÅL: *Åmåls Stadshotell*   (K)(K)
Kungsgatan 9, Box 2, 662 21 Åmål. **[** 0532-616 10. **FAX** 0532-616 19.
Charming, well-renovated town hotel from 1904. In summer food and drink
are served outside in the hotel garden. 🛏 TV 📺 🖥 🍴 ♿ *Rooms: 29*

AE DC MC V

WESTERN SVEALAND

BORLÄNGE: *Scandic Hotell Borlänge*   (K)(K)(K)
Stationsgatan 21, 784 35 Borlänge. **[** 0243-79 90 00. **FAX** 0243-79 90 11.
W www.scandic-hotels.se
Family-friendly hotel in the heart of Borlänge. Restaurant with good Swedish
fare. 🛏 TV 🖥 🍴 🏨 ♿ *Rooms: 113*

AE DC MC V

FALUN: *First Hotel Grand Falun*   (K)(K)
Trotzgatan 9-11, 791 71 Falun. **[** 023-79 48 80. **FAX** 023-141 43.
W www.firsthotels.com
In central Falun, handy for shopping and entertainment. The same
building has a spa and fitness centre. The restaurant is a popular spot.
🛏 TV 🖥 🍴 🍴 🏨 ♿ *Rooms: 151*

AE DC MC V

KARLSTAD: *Elite Stadshotellet Karlstad*   (K)(K)
Kungsgatan 22, Box 317, 651 08 Karlstad. **[** 054-29 30 00. **FAX** 054-29 30 31.
@ stadshotellet.karlstad@elite.se
Centrally located on the Klarälven river. Traditional atmosphere, individually
decorated rooms and a grand function suite. 🛏 TV 🖥 🍴 🍴 🏨 ♿ *Rooms: 139*

AE DC MC V

Price categories for a double room per night, including breakfast unless otherwise stated, plus tax and service.
🛏 Youth hostel *(see pp279)*
Ⓚ under 700 Kr
ⓀⓀ 700–1,400 Kr
ⓀⓀⓀ 1,400–2,100 Kr
ⓀⓀⓀⓀ over 2,100 Kr

CHILDREN'S FACILITIES
Cots and highchairs are available and some hotels will also provide a baby-sitting service.
PARKING
Parking is provided by the hotel, either in a private car park or a private garage nearby.
RESTAURANT
The hotel has a restaurant for residents, which also welcomes non-residents – usually only open for evening meals.
BAR
The hotel has a bar that is open to non-residents as well as those staying in the hotel.

Hotel	Credit Cards	Children's Facilities	Parking	Restaurant	Bar
MORA: *First Hotel Mora* ⓀⓀ Strandgatan 12, 792 30 Mora. 📞 *0250-59 26 50.* FAX *0250-189 81.* 🌐 www.firsthotels.se Fully refurbished town hotel from the 1830s, right in the centre. Good spa. 🛏 📺 ⚡ 🅿 🍴 ♨ ♿ **Rooms:** *141*	AE DC MC V	●	■	●	
SUNNE: *Quality Hotel & Spa Selma Lagerlöf* ⓀⓀ Box 500, 686 28 Sunne. 📞 *0565-166 00.* FAX *0565-166 20.* 🌐 www.selmaspa.se Hotel and spa on Fryken lake, 60 km (37 miles) north of Karlstad. Cosy setting and good food. 🛏 📺 🍸 ⚡ 🅿 🍴 ♨ ♿ **Rooms:** *340*	AE DC MC V	●	■	●	■
SÄLEN: *Sälens Högfjällsbotell* ⓀⓀⓀ 780 67 Sälen. 📞 *0280-870 00.* FAX *0280-211 61.* 🌐 www.salen-hotell.se Next to the Högfjället/Lindvallen lift system. In addition to hotel rooms, it has a number of self-catering apartments. Activities include skiing and snow-scooter safaris. There is a spa, after-ski and nightclub. 🛏 📺 ⚡ 🅿 **Rooms:** *106*	AE DC MC V	●	■	●	■
TÄLLBERG: *Åkerblads Hotell* ⓀⓀ Sjögattu 2, 793 70 Tällberg. 📞 *0247-508 00.* FAX *0247-506 52.* Pretty, romantic country house dating back to medieval times on Lake Siljan. Many suites and mini-suites. Excellent food. 🛏 📺 ⚡ ♨ ♿ **Rooms:** *69*	AE DC MC V	●	■	●	■
ÖREBRO: *Elite Stora Hotellet* ⓀⓀⓀ Drottninggatan 1, 701 45 Örebro. 📞 *019-15 69 00.* FAX *019-15 69 50.* 🌐 www.elite.se Beautifully situated next to the castle in a mid-19th century building. Slottskällaren restaurant is set in the 14th-century vaults. 🛏 📺 ⚡ 🅿 **Rooms:** *132*	AE DC MC V	●		●	■

SOUTHERN NORRLAND

Hotel	Credit Cards	Children's Facilities	Parking	Restaurant	Bar
GÄVLE: *Scandic Grand Hotel Central* ⓀⓀⓀ Nygatan 45, 803 20 Gävle. 📞 *026-495 84 00.* FAX *026-495 84 11.* 🌐 www.scandic-hotels.se/grandcentral Large business and family hotel in central Gävle. Every child receives a small present at check-in. 🛏 📺 ⚡ 🅿 🍴 ♿ **Rooms:** *220.*	AE DC MC V	●	■	●	■
HUDIKSVALL: *First Hotel Statt Hudiksvall* ⓀⓀⓀ Storgatan 36, Box 85, 824 22 Hudiksvall. 📞 *0650-150 60.* FAX *0650-960 95.* 🌐 www.firsthotels.se Well-equipped hotel in a splendid building in the middle of town. The dance restaurant is the hub of the town's nightlife. 🛏 📺 ⚡ 🅿 🍴 ♨ ♿ **Rooms:** *106*	AE DC MC V	●	■	●	■
HÄRNÖSAND: *First Hotel Stadt Härnösand* ⓀⓀⓀ Skeppsbron 9, 871 30 Härnösand. 📞 *0611-55 44 40.* FAX *0611-55 44 47.* 🌐 www.firsthotels.se A late-20th century hotel in a central location with fine views of the canal and harbour. 🛏 📺 ⚡ 🅿 ♿ **Rooms:** *95*	AE DC MC V	●	■	●	■
HIGH COAST: *Hotell Höga Kusten* ⓀⓀ Hornöberget, 872 94 Sandöverken. 📞 *0613-72 22 70.* FAX *0613-72 22 79.* 🌐 www.hotellhoga-kusten.se A modern hotel at the base of one of the world's longest suspension bridges. It has a superb view across the Ångermanälven river. 🛏 📺 ⚡ 🅿 ♿ **Rooms:** *28*	AE DC MC V	●	■	●	■
SUNDSVALL: *STF Vandrarhem Sundsvall* 🛏 Norra Stadsberget, 856 40 Sundsvall. 📞 & FAX *060-61 21 19.* 🌐 www.stfturist.se Pretty, quiet and leafy location, 20-min walk from the centre. Several double rooms with shower and TV. ⚡ ♿ **Beds:** *137*	MC V	●	■		
SUNDSVALL: *Elite Hotel Knaust* ⓀⓀⓀ Storgatan 13, 851 05 Sundsvall. 📞 *060-608 00 00.* FAX *060-608 00 10.* 🌐 www.elite.se Classic hotel dating from 1891, known for its magnificent staircase. Decor is a combination of old tradition and modern design. 🛏 📺 🍸 ⚡ 🅿 🍴 **Rooms:** *94*	AE DC MC V	●	■	●	■

SÖDERHAMN: *First Hotel Statt Söderhamn*   ⓀⓀⓀ
Oxtorgsgatan 17, 826 22 Söderhamn. 【 *0270-735 70.* **FAX** *0270-135 24.*
W www.firsthotels.se
Newly refurbished, first-class hotel, next to the town hall. 🛏 TV 🏊 🔓 🔥 **Rooms:** *78*

	AE	⬤	▦	⬤	▦
	DC				
	MC				
	V				

UMEÅ: *Royal Hotel Umeå*   ⓀⓀ
Skolgatan 62, Vasaplan, 903 29 Umeå. 【 *090-10 07 30.* **FAX** *090-10 07 39.*
W www.royalhotelumea.com
Film is the theme of this central Umeå hotel, which has its own cinema and is decorated with portraits of Hollywood stars. 🛏 TV 🏊 🔓 🍴 🚌 **Rooms:** *68*

	AE	⬤	▦		▦
	DC				
	MC				
	V				

ÅRE: *Hotel Diplomat Åregården*   ⓀⓀ
Box 6, 890 13 Åre. 【 *0647-178 00.* **FAX** *0647-179 60.* W www.diplomathotel.com
A National Romantic-style building on Åre Torg. Classic hotel accommodation with full service. Open only during the skiing season. 🛏 TV 🏊 🔓 🚌 **Rooms:** *54*

	AE	⬤	▦		▦
	DC				
	MC				
	V				

ÖRNSKÖLDSVIK: *First Hotel Statt*   ⓀⓀ
Lasarettgatan 2, 891 21 Örnsköldsvik. 【 *0660-26 55 90.* **FAX** *0660-837 91.*
W www.firsthotels.se
First-class hotel in the middle of town. Modern creature comforts in a building with old-fashioned charm. 🛏 TV 🏊 🔓 🔥 **Rooms:** *115*

	AE	⬤	▦		▦
	DC				
	MC				
	V				

ÖSTERSUND: *Ramada Plaza Hotel Östersund*   ⓀⓀⓀ
Kyrkgatan 70, 831 21 Östersund. 【 *063-57 57 00.* **FAX** *063-57 57 11.*
Family-friendly business hotel with an Internet-linked TV in every room. Several restaurants and bars. 🛏 TV 📺 🏊 🔓 🍴 🔥 **Rooms:** *126*

	AE	⬤	▦	⬤	▦
	DC				
	MC				
	V				

NORTHERN NORRLAND

ABISKO: *STF Abisko Turiststation*   ⓀⓀ
981 07 Abisko. 【 *0980-402 00.* **FAX** *0980-401 40.* W www.stfabisko.com
Choose between hotel, youth hostel-type accommodation, or self-catering cottages. Hotel offers buffet-style breakfast, lunch and dinner. Open all year, but with full service only during March and April. 🔥 🔥 **Beds:** *300*

	AE	⬤	▦		▦
	MC				
	V				

HAPARANDA: *Haparanda Stadshotell*   ⓀⓀⓀ
Torget 7, 953 31 Haparanda. 【 *0922-614 90.* **FAX** *0922-102 23.*
W www.haparandastadshotell.se
Classic hotel in a splendid late-19th-century building. The Viltkällaren restaurant specializes in using local ingredients. 🛏 TV 🏊 🔓 🔥 **Rooms:** *89*

	AE	⬤	▦		▦
	DC				
	MC				
	V				

JUKKASJÄRVI: *Icehotel*   ⓀⓀⓀⓀ
981 91 Jukkasjärvi. 【 *0980-668 00.* **FAX** *0980-668 90.*
W www.icehotel.com
The world's first ice hotel and a major tourist attraction in its own right *(see p272).* Open mid-Dec to early May. 🏊 **Rooms:** *66*

	AE		▦	⬤	▦
	DC				
	MC				
	V				

KIRUNA: *Scandic Hotel Ferrooms*   ⓀⓀⓀ
Lars Janssonsgatan 15, 981 31 Kiruna. 【 *0980-39 86 00.* **FAX** *0980-39 86 11.*
W www.scandic-hotels.com/ferrooms
Family-friendly hotel of a high standard. One restaurant offering traditional Swedish fare and one for Norrland specialities. 🛏 TV 🏊 🔓 🍴 🔥 **Rooms:** *171*

	AE	⬤	▦	⬤	▦
	DC				
	MC				
	V				

LULEÅ: *Elite Stadshotellet Luleå*   ⓀⓀⓀ
Storgatan 15, 971 28 Luleå. 【 *0920-670 00.* **FAX** *0920-670 92.* W www.elite.se
Elegant modern hotel in central Luleå, but with a 100-year history. Grand ballroom, fine restaurant and pub. 🛏 TV 📺 🏊 🔓 🔥 **Rooms:** *135*

	AE	⬤	▦	⬤	▦
	DC				
	MC				
	V				

LYCKSELE: *Hotell Lappland*   ⓀⓀⓀ
Korpberget 1, Box 34, 921 21 Lycksele. 【 *0950-370 00.* **FAX** *0950-375 15.*
W www.hotelllappland.se
Conference hotel, exhibition centre and the world's largest Sami tent. A selection of fun activities is organised for guests. 🛏 TV 🏊 🔓 🍴 🔥 **Rooms:** *201*

	AE	⬤	▦		▦
	DC				
	MC				
	V				

PITEÅ: *Pite Havsbad*   ⓀⓀ
Box 815, 941 28 Piteå. 【 *0911-327 00.* **FAX** *0911-327 99.* W www.pite-havsbad.se
Huge hotel on the "Norrland Riviera". Pool and many outdoor activities. In addition to traditional hotel accommodation, there are also cottages and a campsite. 🛏 TV 🏊 🔓 🍴 🚌 🔥 **Rooms:** *394*

	AE	⬤	▦	⬤	▦
	DC				
	MC				
	V				

SKELLEFTEÅ: *First Hotel Statt Skellefteå*   ⓀⓀ
Stationsg. 8, 931 31 Skellefteå. 【 *0910-141 40.* **FAX** *0910-71 10 65.* W www.firsthotels.se
Modern, central, full-service hotel dating from 1863. The current building is a typically functional design from the 1950s. 🛏 TV 🏊 🔓 🍴 🔥 **Rooms:** *87*

	AE	⬤	▦		▦
	DC				
	MC				
	V				

WHERE TO EAT

SWEDEN IS ONE OF Europe's liveliest and most varied countries for eating out. Swedish cuisine has won many international awards in recent years, and a number of restaurants have been awarded Michelin stars. Many of the best restaurants are relatively small and informal as a number of top chefs have opened their own establishments. Various ethnic styles of cooking are often combined to create

Swedish hot dog

innovative and delicious dishes in what is called "cross-over" cuisine. Traditional Swedish dishes are frequently served at lunchtime and are excellent value for money. There are also plenty of fast-food outlets, pubs, Chinese restaurants, pizzerias and kebab houses offering inexpensive food. Hot-dog stands, providing filling snacks, can be found practically everywhere.

WHERE TO EAT

SWEDEN HAS a very wide range of restaurants. The majority are found in the larger cities and towns, but there are a number of good places to eat in the smaller towns. Restaurants and cafés can be found in the larger department stores and shopping malls, as well as at most museums. Along the coast and inland there are many friendly restaurants that open just for summer. Larger towns often have market halls with excellent restaurants and cafés, but they are not open in the evening for dinner.

Open sandwiches with a variety of fillings can be bought at cafés and cake shops, which often serve inexpensive hot dishes at lunchtime as well.

Outdoor cafés spring up on many streets and squares with the arrival of summer, and also in parks and green areas such as Djurgården and Kungsports-avenyn in Gothenburg.

TYPES OF RESTAURANT

FASHIONABLE restaurants usually attract a young clientele, and the trendiest places sometimes have a rather stark decor and extremely high noise levels. If you are looking for somewhere quieter, which also has good service, it is often best to choose an established restaurant. There are many specialist restaurants serving cuisine from abroad, or "cross-over" cooking, which is a combination of styles.

Most restaurants charge roughly the same prices, regardless of quality. If you are looking for somewhere cheaper to eat, there are pizzerias, pubs, kebab houses, sushi bars, fast food chains and cafés to choose from.

Those with a sweet tooth shouldn't miss a visit to one of the many modern cafés or traditional cake shops which offer delicious Danish pastries, cinnamon buns, cakes and gateaux.

Inn sign, Gamla Stan

There are few bars as such and the best can be found at the most popular restaurants. Dress is usually informal, even at the more elegant restaurants. Ties are not required but shorts are not acceptable. Most restaurants have a no-smoking section and Government legislation is proposing a total ban on smoking in restaurants.

OPENING TIMES

THE MAJORITY OF restaurants open for lunch at 11.30am and close at around 10pm. Dinner is served from 6pm or even earlier. A number of restaurants are closed on Sundays or Mondays. Smaller restaurants may close for their annual holiday during July.

Prices for lunch are often extremely reasonable, even at the more elegant establishments, so lunchtime is an ideal opportunity to enjoy an inexpensive meal at a pleasant restaurant. *Dagens lunch* (Lunch of the Day) is generally not served after 2pm, even if the restaurant is open in the afternoon.

A number of restaurants and pubs serve food right up to midnight or even later, particularly those which provide entertainment, music

Magnificent interior of Café Opera in Stockholm

Outdoor café in Riddarhustorget in Gamla Stan, Stockholm

or a disco. Anyone still hungry during the night can find hot-dog kiosks which stay open very late, sometimes even round the clock.

VEGETARIAN FOOD

INTEREST IN vegetarian food is increasing in Sweden, and this is reflected by the fact that excellent vegetarian cuisine is now served at most restaurants. There are also several completely vegetarian restaurants in the major cities.

BOOKING A TABLE

RESERVATIONS should be made for evening meals, but many restaurants do not accept bookings for lunch. If you want to be sure of a table at midday, it is best to arrive at the restaurant before 11.30am or after 1pm, by which time most of the lunchtime clientele will have left.

CHILDREN

ALL CHILDREN are welcome in restaurants without exception. They will usually be offered a special children's menu, or half portions from the normal menu. Almost all restaurants have highchairs.

PRICES

PRICES OF MEALS in Sweden are very similar. At most places hot dishes cost from about 100 kr, or 200 kr or more at expensive restaurants. Lunch prices are around 60–70 kr, and that often includes a non-alcoholic drink and coffee. However, the price of beer, wine and other alcoholic drinks can vary considerably. It generally follows that the more expensive the restaurant, the higher the price of the wine. The house wine is usually the cheapest, with a bottle normally costing from 150 kr. Beer is cheaper in pubs than in restaurants. Tap water is free of charge, and Sweden's drinking water is of excellent quality.

Tips are always included in the price, but if you want to reward good service you can round up the bill. If the restaurant has a manned cloakroom, the normal price is 10 kr per person. A number of restaurants do not allow guests to take outdoor clothing into the dining room. Credit cards are accepted in virtually every restaurant.

READING THE MENU

DINNER AT A Swedish restaurant usually includes a starter (*förrätt*), hot main course (*varmrätt*) and dessert (*efterrätt*). Most offer one or more fixed-price meals with a choice of two or three dishes at a lower price than the à la carte menu. It is perfectly acceptable to have just a starter or main course. At lunchtime most people order only one course. The meal is nearly always served on the plate, but the more elegant restaurants often have dessert or cheese trolleys. Many restaurants have menus in English; if they don't, the waiters and waitresses are usually familiar with English and will be pleased to explain the menu to you.

Some restaurants serve a typical Swedish *smörgåsbord*, usually on Sundays. Some specialize in a fish or shellfish buffet. During December a *Julbord* is usually available. This is similar to the normal *smörgåsbord*, but with a lavish buffet selection of traditional seasonal dishes. You can eat as much as you like at a fixed price, but drinks are not included.

WHAT TO DRINK

WINE AND BEER are the normal accompaniments to a meal, as well as mineral water. The wine list often features wine from countries outside Europe, along with a house wine. Vintage wines are usually not available at medium-price restaurants.

Many pubs and restaurants offer a wide selection of beers, often with one or more on draught. A few small Swedish breweries make an excellent non-filtered beer. Beer is graded into three classes, with Class I the weakest.

Herring or "home-cooking" is usually washed down with beer, sometimes accompanied by one of the many different flavoured schnapps.

Spirits and wines are more expensive in Swedish restaurants than in most other countries because of the high duty on alcohol and the State retail alcohol monopoly.

Grythyttan, a gastronomic haven with a well-stocked wine cellar which also offers tastings

What to Eat in Sweden

Crisp-bread

Sweden offers some very special gastronomic ingredients such as elk, reindeer, bleak roe, shellfish and local fish. Thanks to strict regulations, Sweden's food is among the purest in Europe. Salmon can be caught in the heart of Stockholm, and zander, pike, Baltic herring and perch in the archipelago. Char is fished in Lake Vättern and freshwater crayfish are plentiful in lakes and rivers in autumn. Varieties of mushrooms, and lingonberries, blueberries and cloudberries all grow wild.

Cheese
Swedish cheese goes well with herring, such as cheese spiced with cumin (left) or the nutty Västerbotten cheese (right).

Pickled herring, chopped onion and sour cream.

"Gubbröra" (anchovies, beetroot, onion, capers, egg yolk).

Pickled herring

Herring marinated in mustard

"Jansson's temptation", a gratin of anchovies, potatoes, sliced onion and double cream.

Böckling, smoked herring.

Bleak roe with chopped onion and sour cream.

SMÖRGÅSBORD

This typically Swedish buffet has a variety of dishes, but often starts with a selection of herring *(sill)* prepared in different ways. Cold dishes come next, then hot dishes and desserts. Diners help themselves and change plates between courses.

Herring, fried and pickled in vinegar and chopped onion.

Shellfish Soup
Fresh shellfish such as oysters, mussels, lobster, shrimps and prawns come from Sweden's west coast.

Gravad Lax
Salmon marinated for two days in sugar, salt and dill, is served with a cold sweet and sour mustard sauce and dill.

Quiche with Salad
Many cafés serve inexpensive lunches with, for example, a quiche filled with shellfish, ham, cheese or vegetables.

PEAS WITH PORK

Traditionally served on Thursdays, this national dish is yellow pea soup with lightly salted meat or sausage accompanied by mustard. Hot punsch is served on festive occasions. It is followed by pancakes with jam.

Mustard

Hot punsch

Grilled Salmon
Sweden has a rich variety of fish from the sea and the lakes, and they are prepared in more different ways than in most countries. Salmon is served as a starter as well as a main course. It can be boiled, fried, grilled, poached and served cold, marinated, smoked or salted. Here the grilled salmon is served with a selection of blanched vegetables.

Grilled Zander
Freshly caught zander from the Stockholm archipelago or Lake Mälaren is served with shrimps and grated horseradish.

Swedish Meatballs
Always part of a smörgåsbord, this national dish is also eaten hot with mashed potato, preserved lingonberries and gherkins.

Brisket of Beef
Boiled salted brisket of beef with root vegetables is one of the most common Swedish "home-cooked" dishes.

Reindeer Calf Fillet
Reindeer meat is very tender, lean and delicious. Here it is grilled with chanterelles, black salsify and cranberries.

Cheesecake and Cloudberries
A traditional dessert made with eggs and almonds, served here with cloudberries from the north or the archipelago.

Rosehip Soup
This can be eaten hot or cold, with whipped cream or ice cream. Served here with vanilla parfait and almond biscuits.

Hot Chocolate and Cinnamon Buns
A bun is popular with hot chocolate or coffee.

DRINKS

Sweden imports a huge variety of wine from all over the world, but people usually drink beer or schnapps with herring or a *smörgåsbord*. Punsch (a sweet arak spirit) is often served with coffee, or hot with pea soup. Swedish vodka is popular worldwide, but there are also some 60 types of local schnapps flavoured with different herbs and spices. Swedish beer is enjoying a renaissance, with products such as non-filtered beer, light ale and blueberry beer being produced at new small breweries.

Mineral water   **Non-filtered beer**   **Akvavit schnapps**   **Swedish punsch**

Choosing a Restaurant

THIS LISTING COVERS some 120 restaurants in all price categories selected for their good value, excellent food and/or location. The restaurants, bars and cafés are listed alphabetically, area by area, starting with those in central Stockholm. For map references in Stockholm, see the Street Finder map, *pp112–17*. The key to the symbols is on the back flap.

	CREDIT CARDS	OPEN LUNCH-TIME	OPEN LATE	FIXED-PRICE MENU	GOOD WINE LIST

STOCKHOLM

		CREDIT CARDS	OPEN LUNCH-TIME	OPEN LATE	FIXED-PRICE MENU	GOOD WINE LIST
GAMLA STAN: *Den Gyldene Freden* ⓚⓚⓚ Österlånggatan 51, 103 17 Stockholm. **Map** 3 C3. ⓒ *08-24 97 60.* An artists' restaurant with a long tradition. Swedish/French cuisine, as well as modestly priced traditional Swedish fare. 🔀 ✚ 🆅 🆈		AE DC MC V		▦		▦
GAMLA STAN: *Pontus in the Greenhouse* ⓚⓚⓚⓚ Österlånggatan 17, 111 31 Stockholm. **Map** 4 C3. ⓒ *08-545 273 00.* One of Stockholm's virtuoso young chefs creates culinary masterpieces with prices to match. Affluent clientele and comfortable location on first floor. Pleasant bistro with lower prices at street level. 🔀 ✚ 🆅 🆈		AE DC MC V	●	▦	●	▦
CITY: *Bistro Jarl* ⓚⓚ Birger Jarlsgatan 7, 111 45 Stockholm. **Map** 2 D4. ⓒ *08-611 76 30.* Small, luxurious restaurant, a favourite spot for sophisticated city folk. Mediterranean and Swedish dishes. The city's only champagne bar. 🔀 🆈		AE DC MC V	●	▦		▦
CITY: *Prinsen* ⓚⓚⓚ Mäster Samuelsgatan 4, 111 44 Stockholm. **Map** 2 D4. ⓒ *08-611 13 31.* Hundred year-old restaurant with a noisy, arty clientele. The menu is traditional with a modern twist. Swedish and Continental dishes. 🔀 ✚		AE DC MC V	●	▦		▦
CITY: *Restaurangen* ⓚⓚⓚ Oxtorgsgatan 14, 111 57 Stockholm. **Map** 2 D4. ⓒ *08-22 09 52.* Choose five dishes at a fixed price and try various wines as well. Beautifully presented food and stylish decor. ♿ 🔀 🆅 🆈		AE DC MC V	●	▦	●	
CITY: *Fredsgatan 12* ⓚⓚⓚⓚ Fredsgatan 12, 111 52 Stockholm. **Map** 2 D5. ⓒ *08-24 80 52.* Star chef Melker Andersson offers a gastronomic experience with his "world cooking", combining the cuisines of many countries. Austere modern decor and trendy clientele. ♿ 🔀 ✚ 🆅 🆈		AE DC MC V	●	▦	●	▦
CITY: *Operakällaren* ⓚⓚⓚⓚ Operahuset, Karl XII's Torg, 111 86 Stockholm. **Map** 2 D5, 3 B1. ⓒ *08-676 58 01.* The capital's classic temple of gastronomy. The chefs are young and creative, the dining room with its lavish 19th-century ceiling paintings and the Jugendstil bar are attractions in themselves. Café Opera has lower prices and a famous afternoon cake buffet. One Michelin star. ♿ 🔀 ✚ 🆅 🆈		AE DC MC V				▦
BLASIEHOLMEN & SKEPPSHOLMEN: *Berns' Salonger* ⓚⓚⓚ Näckströmsgatan 8, Berzelii Park, 103 27 Stockholm. **Map** 2 D4. ⓒ *08-566 322 22.* Sir Terence Conran designed this spacious new restaurant in a building rich in tradition. The restaurant, seating 248, focuses on seafood. The Bar & Grill can seat 110 people. ♿ 🔀 🆅 🆈		AE DC MC V	●	▦		
BLASIEHOLMEN & SKEPPSHOLMEN: *Grands Veranda* ⓚⓚⓚⓚ Södra Blasieholmshamnen 8, 103 27 Stockholm. **Map** 3 C1. ⓒ *08-679 35 86.* A popular meeting place with views over Strömmen, Gamla Stan and the Royal Palace. Hotel guests, locals and tourists enjoy breakfast, lunch and dinner here every day of the year. ♿ 🔀 ✚ 🆅 🆈		AE DC MC V	●	▦	●	▦
ÖSTERMALM: *Ett Litet Hak* ⓚⓚⓚ Grev Turegatan 15, 114 46 Stockholm. **Map** 2 D4. ⓒ *08-660 13 09.* Atmospheric local bar with trendy Continental food and considerate staff. 🔀 🆅 🆈		AE DC MC V	●	▦		
ÖSTERMALM: *Halv Grek Plus Turk* ⓚⓚⓚ Jungfrugatan 33, 114 44 Stockholm. **Map** 2 E3. ⓒ *08-665 94 22.* Excellent tasty food and a friendly atmosphere. Choose from a variety of hot and cold Greek and Turkish dishes. ♿ 🔀 🆅 🆈		AE DC MC V		▦		▦

Average prices for a three-course meal for one, half a bottle of house wine and unavoidable charges such as service and cover:
Ⓚ under 300 Kr
ⓀⓀ 300–400 Kr
ⓀⓀⓀ 400–500 Kr
ⓀⓀⓀⓀ over 500 Kr

OPEN LUNCH-TIME
These restaurants are open for lunch and usually serve inexpensive meals.
OPEN LATE
Restaurants which remain open with their full menu after 10pm.
FIXED-PRICE MENU
A fixed-price menu is available for lunch, dinner or both, usually with three courses.
GOOD WINE LIST
Restaurant has a wide choice of good wines, or a more specialized range.

Restaurant	Price	Credit Cards	Open Lunch-time	Open Late	Fixed-price Menu	Good Wine List
ÖSTERMALM: *Brasserie Godot* Grev Turegatan 36, 114 38 Stockholm. **Map** 2 E3. **(** 08-660 06 14. Fashionable restaurant offering classic French and Swedish cuisine. Highlights include duck-thigh confit with orange sauce. Good value. 🔵 V 🍷	ⓀⓀⓀ	AE DC MC V		■		
ÖSTERMALM: *Paul & Norbert* Strandvägen 9, 114 56 Stockholm. **Map** 2 E4. **(** 08-663 81 83. A gastronomic jewel for gourmets. Elegant, discreet and modern decor, superb service and delicious seasonal food. ✂ V 🔧	ⓀⓀⓀⓀ	AE DC MC V	●		●	■
ÖSTERMALM: *Villa Källhagen* Djurgårdsbrunnsvägen 10, 115 27 Stockholm. **(** 08-665 03 00. One of Stockholm's best restaurants with a beautiful waterfront location. The cuisine is international with the accent on Swedish ingredients. Pleasant outdoor terrace. 🔵 ✂ 🔧 V 🍷	ⓀⓀⓀⓀ	AE DC MC V	●		●	■
DJURGÅRDEN: *Värdshuset Ulla Winbladh* Rosendalsvägen 8, 115 21 Stockholm. **(** 08-663 05 71. Beautifully located restaurant with olde-worlde atmosphere and well-prepared food. Swedish specialities and some more modern dishes. The outdoor café is very popular in the summer. 🔵 ✂ 🔧 V 🍷	ⓀⓀⓀ	AE DC MC V	●	■		
DJURGÅRDEN: *Restaurant Hasselbacken* Hazeliusbacken 20, 100 55 Stockholm. **(** 08-517 343 00. Well-prepared traditional restaurant fare is served in a finely restored 1850s setting. In summer there is an outdoor café. 🔵 ✂ 🔧 V 🍷	ⓀⓀⓀⓀ	AE DC MC V			●	
KUNGSHOLMEN: *Roppongi* Hantverkargatan 76c, 113 38 Stockholm. **(** 08-650 17 72. A high-class sushi restaurant offering a range of Japanese delicacies. ✂ 🔧 V	ⓀⓀ	AE DC MC V	●		●	
KUNGSHOLMEN: *Spisa Hos Helena* Scheelegatan 18, 112 28 Stockholm. **Map** 1 A5. **(** 08-654 49 26. Atmospheric and award-winning eatery where the food is good and the staff welcoming. 🔵 ✂ V 🍷	ⓀⓀ	AE DC MC V			●	
VASASTAN: *Rolfs Kök* Tegnérgatan 41, 111 61 Stockholm. **Map** 1 C3. **(** 08-10 16 96. Reliable local spot with stylish interior and great food. Cross-over and Swedish cuisine in perfect harmony. Faithful clientele. 🔵 ✂ 🍷	ⓀⓀⓀ	AE DC MC V	●	■		■
VASASTAN: *Wasahof* Dalagatan 46, 113 24 Stockholm. **Map** 1 A3. **(** 08-32 34 40. Brasserie-style restaurant popular among theatre and opera folk. The speciality is seafood, but Swedish and international dishes are also on the menu. Adjoins an oyster bar. 🔵 ✂ 🍷 ♪	ⓀⓀⓀ	AE DC MC V		■	●	■
VASASTAN: *Storstad* Odengatan 41, 113 51 Stockholm. **Map** 1 C2. **(** 08-673 38 00. This is where people go if they want to be seen, and the bar is usually packed. Minimalist decor, comfortable seating, imaginative food and courteous staff. 🔵 ✂ V 🍷	ⓀⓀⓀ	AE DC MC V		■		■
SÖDER: *Bistro Humlebof* Folkungagatan 128, 116 30 Stockholm. **(** 08-641 03 02. Traditional pub food with German and Czech beer on tap. Great atmosphere and caring staff. 🔵 ✂ 🍷	Ⓚ	AE MC V				
SÖDER: *Östgötakällaren* Östgötagatan 41, 116 25 Stockholm. **(** 08-643 22 40. Local restaurant serving excellent food at low prices. Fantastic staff. V 🍷 ● *Jul*	ⓀⓀ	AE DC MC V	●	■		

For key to symbols see back flap

Average prices for a three-course meal for one, half a bottle of house wine and unavoidable charges such as service and cover:
Ⓚ under 300 Kr
ⓀⓀ 300–400 Kr
ⓀⓀⓀ 400–500 Kr
ⓀⓀⓀⓀ over 500 Kr

OPEN LUNCH-TIME
These restaurants are open for lunch and usually serve inexpensive meals.

OPEN LATE
Restaurants which remain open with their full menu after 10pm.

FIXED-PRICE MENU
A fixed-price menu is available for lunch, dinner or both, usually with three courses.

GOOD WINE LIST
Restaurant has a wide choice of good wines, or a more specialized range.

	CREDIT CARDS	OPEN LUNCH-TIME	OPEN LATE	FIXED-PRICE MENU	GOOD WINE LIST
SÖDER: *Lo Scudetto* ⓀⓀⓀ Åsögatan 163, 116 32 Stockholm. 08-640 42 15. Top-class traditional and innovative dishes, cheerful service and football pictures on the walls.	AE MC V				▓
SÖDER: *Texas Long Horn* ⓀⓀ Sankt Paulsgatan 4a, 118 46 Stockholm. **Map** 3 B5. 08-702 06 82. A tiny establishment which serves perfectly grilled juicy steaks at unbeatable prices. Often full with queues for admission.	AE DC MC V				
FURTHER AFIELD: *Stallmästaregården* ⓀⓀⓀ Norrtull, 113 47 Stockholm. 08-610 13 00. A 17th-century inn in an idyllic location on Brunnsviken and close to WennerGren Centre. Barbecue, rotisserie and top Swedish dishes. Outdoor terrace.	AE DC MC V	●		●	▓
FURTHER AFIELD: *Edsbacka Krog* ⓀⓀⓀⓀ Sollentunavägen 220, 191 35 Sollentuna. 08-96 33 00. International cuisine at an inn dating from 1626, with a setting and service to match. Food is based on the best Swedish ingredients, expertly prepared and beautifully presented. Two Michelin stars.	AE DC MC V			●	▓
FURTHER AFIELD: *Ulriksdals Wärdshus* ⓀⓀⓀⓀ Ulriksdals Slottspark, 170 79 Solna. 08-85 08 15. Legendary inn in a stunning location with beautiful interior. Elegant and ambitious food. According to the *Guinness Book of Records*, it has the world's best wine list. Famous for its excellent *smörgåsbord*.	AE DC MC V	●	▓	●	▓
ARCHIPELAGO: *Utö Värdshus* ⓀⓀⓀ Gruvbryggan, 130 56 Utö. 08-504 203 00. A boat is required to reach this island, either your own or the regular ferry. The restaurant is large and often busy in the summer. Traditional, value-for-money menu. Overnight accommodation. ● *Jan–Feb*	AE DC MC V	●	▓		
EASTERN SVEALAND					
HÖLÖ: *Oaxen Skärgårdskrog* ⓀⓀⓀⓀ Oaxen, 153 93 Hölö. 08-551 531 05. Archipelago restaurant open in the summer, which has become a popular destination thanks to good food with local ingredients and an emphasis on fish dishes. Reached by own boat or car ferry via Mörkö.	AE DC MC V			●	▓
JÖNÅKER: *Wreta Gestgifveri* ⓀⓀⓀ Wretas Gård, 610 50 Jönåker. 0155-720 22. Romantic Gustavian dining room with period decor, but modern top-class food. Overnight accommodation.	AE MC V	●			
NYKÖPING: *Mickes Skafferi* ⓀⓀⓀ Västra Storgatan 29, 611 32 Nyköping. 0155-26 99 50. Great cooking with Swedish and Continental touches. Outdoor terrace in the summer, but can be difficult to get a table.	AE DC MC V			●	
SIGTUNA: *Sigtuna Stads Hotell* ⓀⓀⓀⓀ Stora Nygatan 3, 193 30 Sigtuna. 08-592 501 00. Genuine Swedish cuisine in a modern guise served in the restaurant of this Scandinavian-style designer hotel.	AE DC MC V	●		●	▓
SÖDERTÄLJE: *St Ansgars Källare* ⓀⓀⓀ Kaplansgatan 1, 151 72 Södertälje. 08-550 325 25 Classic food served in the brick-lined cellar of one of the town's oldest stone houses. One of the better restaurants in Södertälje.	AE DC MC V				▓

TROSA: *Bomans Hotel & Restaurant*
Östra Hamnplan, 619 30 Trosa. [0156-525 00.
Menu almost entirely Swedish with some French touches. Even though it
may not appear particularly original, the food is excellent and good value
for money. Helpful staff. Christmas and New Year.

UPPSALA: *Hambers Fisk*
Fyristorg 8, 753 10 Uppsala. [018-71 00 50.
Charming combination of delicatessen and restaurant. The delicatessen
platter is a safe bet, but otherwise the atmosphere, the staff and the
champagne are possibly the biggest attractions.

UPPSALA: *Wermlandskällaren*
Slottsgatan 2, 753 09 Uppsala. [018-13 22 00.
Traditional restaurant in smart period setting. A great menu, including
truffles and foie gras and all that goes with them. July.

VÄSTERÅS: *Avenue*
Kopparbergsvägen 3, 721 09 Västerås. [021-10 11 90.
Swedish cuisine with French and Italian twists served in a bright open space
with lighting designed by Poulsen. Somes tables are in glass booths for
undisturbed conversation. 6 weeks in summer.

EASTERN GÖTALAND

BORGHOLM: *Bakfickan, Hotell Borgholm*
Trädgårdsgatan 15, 387 31 Borgholm. [0485-770 60.
Small, high-class restaurant, which has developed its own special cuisine
based on well-seasoned quality ingredients. It has been renovated after a
fire in 2004.

JÖNKÖPING: *Svarta Börsen*
Kyrkogatan 4, 553 16 Jönköping. [036-71 22 22.
Classic eatery located behind the town hall. Traditional menu highlighting
Vättern char, game and lamb. 6 weeks in summer.

KALMAR: *Helen & Jörgens*
Olof Palmes Gata 2, 392 33 Kalmar. [0480-288 30.
Friendly restaurant with a personal style and a menu that hits the spot;
the empahsis is towards Mediterranean cooking. Fresh lobsters from the
restaurant's aquarium.

LINKÖPING: *Stångs Pm & Co*
Södra Stånggatan 1, 582 73 Linköping. [013-31 21 00.
Linköping's trendiest place to eat is located in a warehouse by the Stångån
river. Ambitious food, often local game. Christmas and New Year.

MOTALA: *O'Learys Bar & Restaurang*
Platensgatan 15, 591 35 Motala. [0141-21 04 00.
Well-cooked, good food. Menu covers everything from hamburgers and salads
to chicken and steaks. Sporting events shown on the screen.

NORRKÖPING: *Pappa Grappa Trattoria & Bar*
Gamla Rådstugegatan 26, 600 46 Norrköping. [011-18 00 14.
Jolly Italian trattoria in a rustic setting, known for its huge portions and
excellent desserts.

NÄSSJÖ: *Entré Bar & Restaurang*
Borgmästargränd 10, 553 20 Jönköping. [036-16 14 40.
This restaurant in an old wooden building near Storgatan has a sober interior
and modern art on the walls. Value-for-money menu with many exotic
dishes from all corners of the world. Warm and friendly.

SÖDERKÖPING: *Stegeborgs Hamnkrog*
Stegeborg, 614 97 Söderköping. [0121-420 01.
Archipelago restaurant on a small island. Large outdoor terrace in the summer.
Popular and pleasant "local restaurant" with good food to suit every pocket.
Open from end of April to mid-September.

VADSTENA: *Valven*
Storgatan 18, 592 30 Vadstena. [0143-123 40.
Centrally located in Vadstena, close to the main square of Stora Torget, and set
in the historic building Helgeandshuset. The fried Lake Vättern char with dill
potatoes and crayfish sauce is much in demand.

For key to symbols see back flap

	CREDIT CARDS	OPEN LUNCH-TIME	OPEN LATE	FIXED-PRICE MENU	GOOD WINE LIST
Average prices for a three-course meal for one, half a bottle of house wine and unavoidable charges such as service and cover: Ⓚ under 300 Kr · ⓀⓀ 300–400 Kr · ⓀⓀⓀ 400–500 Kr · ⓀⓀⓀⓀ over 500 Kr **OPEN LUNCH-TIME** These restaurants are open for lunch and usually serve inexpensive meals. **OPEN LATE** Restaurants which remain open with their full menu after 10pm. **FIXED-PRICE MENU** A fixed-price menu is available for lunch, dinner or both, usually with three courses. **GOOD WINE LIST** Restaurant has a wide choice of good wines, or a more specialized range.					

VÄXJÖ: *Fiskepiren* ⓀⓀ

Båtsmanstorget 1, 352 30 Växjö. ☎ 0470-156 56.
Value-for-money fish restaurant in minimalist setting. Pike-perch fillet and shellfish platters are the top items on the menu. 🍴 Ⓨ ♿

| | AE DC MC V | ● | | ● | |

GOTLAND

VISBY: *Bakfickan* ⓀⓀ

Stora Torget 1, 621 56 Visby. ☎ 0498-27 18 07.
Charming, simple and cosy restaurant with the emphasis on fish and shellfish. The food is simple but good and the wine list mainly features white wines, many by the glass. Busy in the summer. 🍴 🧒 Ⓥ Ⓨ

| | AE DC MC V | ● | | | ▦ |

VISBY: *Donners Brunn Restaurang & Bar* ⓀⓀⓀ

Donners Plats 3, 621 57 Visby. ☎ 0498-27 10 90.
Well-known restaurant in the heart of Visby serving dishes with a Gotland touch. Welcoming staff. 🍴 🧒 Ⓥ Ⓨ ● Christmas and New Year.

| | AE DC MC V | | | ● | ▦ |

SOUTHERN GÖTALAND

BILLEBERGA: *Farbror Elofs Skafferi* ⓀⓀ

Kvarnvägen 1, 260 21 Billeberga. ☎ 0418-43 11 77.
A restaurant with a difference which can get quite chaotic. The dining room is packed with knick-knacks. Seasonal menu; good, well-cooked food. 🍴 Ⓨ

| | AE MC V | ● | ▦ | ● | |

BRANTEVIK: *Branteviks Bykrog* ⓀⓀⓀ

Mästergränd 2, 272 38 Brantevik. ☎ 0414-220 69.
Village restaurant, often full in summer, which can mean a long wait for food. Impressive wine cellar. ♿ 🍴 Ⓨ

| | AE DC MC V | ● | | ● | ▦ |

GENARP: *Häckeberga Slott* ⓀⓀⓀ

240 13 Genarp. ☎ 040-48 04 40.
A gastronomic experience in a captivating castle setting. The menu is constantly changing and the chef aims high. ♿ 🍴 Ⓥ

| | AE DC MC V | | | ● | ▦ |

HELSINGBORG: *Gastro* ⓀⓀⓀⓀ

Södra Storgatan 11-13, 252 23 Helsingborg. ☎ 042-24 34 70.
The menu offers an interesting and unexpected mix of flavours and ingredients. The wine list and sommelier are just two of the restaurant's highlights. ♿ 🍴 Ⓨ

| | AE DC MC V | | ▦ | | ▦ |

HELSINGBORG: *Niklas* ⓀⓀⓀⓀ

Norra Storgatan 16, 252 20 Helsingborg. ☎ 042-28 00 50.
Commended, elegant restaurant with delicacies such as frogs' legs and foie gras. Impressive and exciting wine cellar. ♿ 🍴 Ⓨ

| | AE DC MC V | | | ● | ▦ |

KARLSKRONA: *PM Pub & Mat* Ⓚ

Ronnebygatan 46, Kronanhuset, 371 33 Karlskrona. ☎ 0455-818 80.
Centrally located eatery on Karlskrona's main street with a typical pub menu. ♿ Ⓥ Ⓨ 🧒 🎵

| | AE MC V | ● | | ● | |

KRISTIANSTAD: *Bar-B-ko* ⓀⓀ

Tivoligatan 4, 291 31 Kristianstad. ☎ 044-21 33 55.
A popular, central restaurant with outdoor tables in summer. Barbecued meat, fish and vegetarian options. ♿ 🍴 Ⓥ Ⓨ ● Christmas and New Year.

| | AE DC MC V | | ▦ | | |

KRISTIANSTAD: *Tomarp Gårdshotell* ⓀⓀⓀ

Helmershusvägen 105, 291 94 Kristianstad. ☎ 044-931 18.
Charming country-hotel restaurant. Menu focuses on hearty home-cooking. Considerate staff. ♿ 🍴

| | AE MC V | ● | | ● | |

LANDSKRONA: *Akropolis Rådhusrestaurangen* Ⓚ

Nygatan 2, 261 31 Landskrona. ☎ 0418-102 86.
Traditional Greek food, including meat and fish, served on a plank.
♿ 🍴 🧒 🎵 Ⓥ Ⓨ

| | AE DC MC V | ● | | | |

LUND: *EBar* ⓚⓚ
Mårtenstorget 9, 223 51 Lund. 📞 046-211 22 88.
Typical restaurant in medium-sized town, with minimalist decor and excellent value-for-money food. Enthusiastic staff and small, but interesting wine list. 🔳🔳🔳

AE / DC / MC / V

LÖDERUP: *Mötesplats Österlen* ⓚⓚⓚⓚ
Örum 52, 276 40 Löderup. 📞 0411-55 66 88.
Exquisite gourmet restaurant in a renovated former school. Exciting flavours and impressive fresh ingredients, many sourced locally. 🔳🔳

AE / MC / V

MALMÖ: *Tempo Bar & Kök* ⓚⓚ
Södra Skolgatan 30a, 214 23 Malmö. 📞 040-12 60 21.
Value-for-money bar with excellent food and adventurous chefs. Starters the size of a main meal. Great atmosphere and popular with the younger crowd. 🔳🔳🔳🔳

AE / MC / V

MALMÖ: *1 R.O.K.* ⓚⓚ
St Pauli Kyrkogata 11, 211 49 Malmö. 📞 040-30 20 24.
Small gourmet restaurant alongside a brasserie. Exciting, innovative cuisine with a touch of the East. 🔳🔳🔳🔳⬤ *Christmas and New Year.*

AE / DC / MC / V

MALMÖ: *Lemongrass* ⓚⓚ
Grynbodgatan 9, 211 33 Malmö. 📞 040-30 69 79.
In-restaurant with a Continental atmosphere and dishes representing various countries and cuisines of Asia. 🔳🔳🔳🔳⬤ *4 weeks in summer.*

AE / DC / MC / V

MALMÖ: *Sturehof* ⓚⓚ
Adelsgatan 13, 211 22 Malmö. 📞 040-12 12 53.
A touch of nostalgia with brown walls and black-and-white service. Traditional food, including herring buffet and steak Rydberg. 🔳⬤ *Christmas and New Year.*

AE / DC / MC / V

MALMÖ: *Johan P Saluhallens Fiskrestaurang* ⓚⓚⓚ
Landbygatan 3, 211 34 Malmö. 📞 040-97 18 18.
Restaurant combined with a fishmonger's and chocolate shop. One of the best fish restaurants in Malmö with a menu featuring eel, herring and shellfish dishes. 🔳🔳🔳🔳

AE / DC / MC / V

MÖLLE: *Maritime* ⓚⓚⓚ
Bökebolsvägen 11, 260 42 Mölle. 📞 042-36 22 30.
Beautiful dining room overlooking the harbour and Kullaberg. Set menu of three to eight dishes. 🔳🔳🔳⬤ *Sep–Jun, except to guests who make a booking.*

AE / DC / MC / V

NYHAMNSLÄGE: *Rut På Skäret* ⓚⓚⓚ
Gläntan 6, Skäret, 260 41 Nyhamnsläge. 📞 042-34 61 88.
Delicacies from Skåne and more modern dishes served in a rustic cottage in the countryside. 🔳🔳🔳⬤ *Jan–Mar.*

AE / DC / MC / V

TRELLEBORG: *Dannegården* ⓚⓚⓚ
Strandgatan 32, 231 62 Trelleborg. 📞 0410-481 80.
Restaurant with slightly old-fashioned decor and high-class food. Large range of whisky, Calvados and Armagnac. 🔳🔳🔳

AE / MC / V

YSTAD: *Restaurang Bryggeriet* ⓚⓚ
Långgatan 20, 271 43 Ystad. 📞 0411-699 99.
Varied menu from around the world. Also a focus on Skåne cuisine with dessert menu featuring *spettkaka*, the local pyramid cake from Nedraby. 🔳🔳🔳🔳🔳

AE / DC / MC / V

GOTHENBURG

CENTRE: *Mañana* ⓚ
Lasarettsgatan 6, 411 19 Gothenburg. 📞 031-711 72 90.
Minimalist modern interior and menu based on the simple ingredients of Mediterranean cuisine. Excellent food and pleasant bistro atmosphere. 🔳🔳🔳🔳

AE / MC / V

CENTRE: *Fond* ⓚⓚⓚ
Götaplatsen, 412 56 Gothenburg. 📞 031-81 25 80.
Located on Gothenburg's main square. The restaurant uses purely Swedish ingredients in its dishes and has a good wine list. One Michelin star. 🔳🔳🔳🔳

AE / DC / MC / V

CENTRE: *Trägår'n* ⓚⓚⓚ
Nya Allén, 411 38 Gothenburg. 📞 031-10 20 80.
There may be a nightclub next door, but this restaurant is peaceful and ambitious. The food is inspired, with Asian influences.
🔳🔳🔳🔳🔳🔳

AE / DC / MC / V

Average prices for a three-course meal for one, half a bottle of house wine and unavoidable charges such as service and cover: Ⓚ under 300 Kr ⓀⓀ 300–400 Kr ⓀⓀⓀ 400–500 Kr ⓀⓀⓀⓀ over 500 Kr	**OPEN LUNCH-TIME** These restaurants are open for lunch and usually serve inexpensive meals. **OPEN LATE** Restaurants which remain open with their full menu after 10pm. **FIXED-PRICE MENU** A fixed-price menu is available for lunch, dinner or both, usually with three courses. **GOOD WINE LIST** Restaurant has a wide choice of good wines, or a more specialized range.				

	CREDIT CARDS	**OPEN LUNCH-TIME**	**OPEN LATE**	**FIXED-PRICE MENU**	**GOOD WINE LIST**
CENTRE: *Herr Dahls Mat & Martinis* ⓀⓀⓀ Kungstorget 14, 411 10 Gothenburg. ℂ 031-13 45 55. Trendy restaurant with a modern menu. Mr Dahl himself is renowned as a member of the Swedish culinary Olympic team. 🖰 ⚡ 🍷 ● *last week in Jul.*	AE DC MC V	●	■	●	■
CENTRE: *Kock & Vin* ⓀⓀⓀ Viktoriagatan 12, 411 25 Gothenburg. ℂ 031-701 79 79. Restaurant and wine bar. The wine bar serves light small dishes and all wines by the glass. The dining room offers excellent value-for-money food in a congenial setting. 🖰 ⚡ 🍷	AE DC MC V		■	●	■
CENTRE: *28+* ⓀⓀⓀ Götabergsgatan 28, 411 34 Gothenburg. ℂ 031-20 21 61. One of the city's best restaurants with a style all of its own. It also features one of the better wine cellars in town. Professional staff. One Michelin star. 🖰 ⚡	AE DC MC V		■	●	■
CENTRE: *Fiskekrogen* ⓀⓀⓀⓀ Lilla Torget 1, 411 18 Gothenburg. ℂ 031-10 10 05. Famous fish restaurant, renowned for its turbot, and shellfish buffet. Popular for lunches. Large wine cellar with a wide range of champagne. 🖰 ⚡ 🍷 ● *Jul.*	AE DC MC V	●	■	●	■
CENTRE: *Thörnströms Kök* ⓀⓀⓀⓀ Teknologgatan 3, 411 32 Gothenburg. ℂ 031-16 20 66. Fine dining for an adult clientele. Faultless decor and staff. ⚡ 🇻 🍷 ● *Jul.*	AE DC MC V		■	●	■
CENTRE: *Tvåkanten* ⓀⓀⓀⓀ Kungsportsavenyn 27, 411 36 Gothenburg. ℂ 031-18 21 15. Relaxed, top-end restaurant with an adult clientele. Food served outdoors in the summer, making for a livelier atmosphere. Good, simple Swedish fare, and great value. 🖰 ⚡ 🇻 🍷	AE DC MC V	●	■	●	■
FURTHER AFIELD: *Hos Pelle* ⓀⓀⓀ Djupedalsgatan 2, 413 07 Gothenburg. ℂ 031-12 10 31. Local restaurant with art exhibitions. Ambitious menu. Professional staff and a great wine list. 🖰 ⚡ 🇻 🍷 ● *Jul.*	AE DC MC V		■	●	■
FURTHER AFIELD: *Sjömagasinet* ⓀⓀⓀ Klippans Kulturreservat, 414 51 Gothenburg. ℂ 031-775 59 20. Popular fish restaurant with fried crab, smoked mussels, lobster and other delicious seafood as its biggest sellers. Good wine list. One Michelin star. 🖰 ⚡ 🇻 ● *Jul.*	AE DC MC V	●		●	■
WESTERN GÖTALAND					
BORÅS: *Oliven* Ⓚ Lilla Brogatan 11, 503 30 Borås. ℂ 033-10 10 65. Friendly local restaurant offering a largely Mediterranean menu, with a special emphasis on Greek cuisine. 🖰 ⚡ 🇻 🍷	AE MC V	●		●	■
GREBBESTAD: *Grebys* ⓀⓀ Strandvägen 1, 457 72 Grebbestad. ℂ 0525-140 00. Shellfish restaurant in a former jam factory. Great atmosphere and fresh seasonal shellfish. Very busy in the summer, when it can be difficult to get a table. ⚡ 🐟 🍷	AE DC MC V			●	■
HALMSTAD: *Akvarell* ⓀⓀⓀⓀ Hotell Tylösand, 301 16 Halmstad. ℂ 035-305 01. Non-smoking dining room with renovated minimalist design and fantastic views. Exciting menu and great wine list, many served by the glass. 🖰 ⚡ 🍷	AE DC MC V		■	●	■

KVÄNUM: *Bjertorp Slott*	Ⓚ Ⓚ Ⓚ	AE DC MC V	●		●	▦
535 91 Kvänum. 【 0512-203 90. Grand castle dining room with original fittings. Three-course menus change daily. Famous for its wine cellar and expert staff who can be relied upon to recommend the right wine for every meal. 🕭 ⚡ ♿						
SKÖVDE: *Husaren*	Ⓚ	AE DC MC V		▦		
Sta Helena Gata 10, 541 30 Skövde. 【 0500-41 79 79. Classic restaurant with good food. Dishes include chicken marinated in soya and ginger. Live music, usually Fri–Sat. 🕭 ⚡ �V 🎵 ❢						
STRÖMSTAD: *Gusto Restaurang*	Ⓚ Ⓚ	AE DC MC V	●			
Norra Hamngatan 9a, 452 31 Strömstad. 【 0526-600 62. Small town restaurant with limited menu. Emphasis on tapas, but grilled meat and some fish dishes also served. ⚡ ♿ �V ❢ ● *weekdays Dec–Feb.*						
TROLLHÄTTAN: *Aquavit Grill och Bar*	Ⓚ Ⓚ	AE DC MC V			●	▦
Kungsgatan 24, 461 30 Trollhättan. 【 0520-187 33. Popular restaurant for business lunches with an emphasis on home-cooking. Less busy in evenings and at weekends when the menu is more sophisticated. Wine tastings also arranged. ⚡ ♿ �V ❢						
TROLLHÄTTAN: *Albert Kök*	Ⓚ Ⓚ Ⓚ	AE DC MC V			●	▦
Strömsberg, 461 57 Trollhättan. 【 0520-129 90. Seasonal menu using local ingredients. Elegant restaurant with magnificent views from the terrace. 🕭 ⚡ �V						
UDDEVALLA: *Agassis Restaurang*	Ⓚ	AE DC MC V	●	▦	●	
Kungsgatan 31, 451 30 Uddevalla. 【 0522-301 55. Meat, fish and pasta, plus vegetarian dishes. Important sporting events shown on the wide screen. 🕭 ⚡ ♿ 🎵 �V ❢						
VARBERG: *Restaurang Borggården*	Ⓚ Ⓚ Ⓚ	MC V	●		●	▦
Fästningen, 432 44 Varberg. 【 0340-108 66. Themed medieval or Viking-style banquets set in Varberg's fortress. Open for lunch in the summer with no need to pre-book. 🕭 ⚡ ♿ 🎵						
WESTERN SVEALAND						
BORLÄNGE: *Ulfshyttans Herrgård*	Ⓚ Ⓚ Ⓚ	AE DC MC V			●	▦
781 96 Borlänge. 【 0243-25 13 00. Good food served in a historical manor house. Also spa/relaxation centre and live music. 🕭 ⚡ ♿ �V 🎵						
FALUN: *Mariann's Pub och Restaurang*	Ⓚ	AE DC MC V	●	▦		
Stigaregatan 6, 791 60 Falun. 【 023-201 01. Classic à la carte and pub menu. Bar, dining room and veranda. In the centre of town with alfresco dining in the summer. 🕭 ⚡ ♿ �V ❢						
FALUN: *Banken Bar & Brasseri*	Ⓚ Ⓚ Ⓚ	AE DC MC V	●	▦		▦
Stadshusgränd 2, 791 12 Falun. 【 023-17 19 11. A varied menu is on offer at this centrally located restaurant. ⚡ �V ❢						
HÄLLEFORS: *Sikfors Herrgård*	Ⓚ Ⓚ Ⓚ	AE DC MC V			●	▦
Sikfors, 712 93 Hällefors. 【 0591-151 15. A stylishly decorated 19th-century manor house offering a set three-course menu with a rural touch. ⚡ ♿ �V						
KARLSTAD: *Glada Ankan*	Ⓚ	AE DC MC V		▦		
Kungsgatan 12, 652 24 Karlstad. 【 054-21 05 51. Restaurant and night club serving Mexican food, soup and pasta. Live music. 🕭 ⚡ 🎵 ❢						
KARLSTAD: *Blå Restaurang & Bar*	Ⓚ Ⓚ Ⓚ	AE MC V		▦	●	▦
Kungsgatan 14, 652 24 Karlstad. 【 054-10 18 15. Elegant restaurant with modern interior and views over the square. Expert staff and beautifully served food from an interesting, innovative menu. 🕭 ⚡ ❢						
MORA: *Jernet Bar och Matsal*	Ⓚ Ⓚ	AE DC MC V	●			
Strandgatan 6, 792 30 Mora. 【 0250-150 20. The restaurant is housed in Mora's oldest industrial building dating from the late 19th century. Dishes include Swedish classics and international cuisine. 🕭 ⚡ 🎵 ❢ ● *2 weeks in Jan.*						

For key to symbols see back flap

Average prices for a three-course meal for one, half a bottle of house wine and unavoidable charges such as service and cover: Ⓚ under 300 Kr ⓀⓀ 300–400 Kr ⓀⓀⓀ 400–500 Kr ⓀⓀⓀⓀ over 500 Kr	**OPEN LUNCH-TIME** These restaurants are open for lunch and usually serve inexpensive meals. **OPEN LATE** Restaurants which remain open with their full menu after 10pm. **FIXED-PRICE MENU** A fixed-price menu is available for lunch, dinner or both, usually with three courses. **GOOD WINE LIST** Restaurant has a wide choice of good wines, or a more specialized range.			

	CREDIT CARDS	OPEN LUNCH-TIME	OPEN LATE	FIXED-PRICE MENU	GOOD WINE LIST
SÄLEN: *Lammet och Grisen* ⓀⓀⓀ Lindvallen, 780 67 Sälen. 📞 *0280-210 90.* Satisfying restaurant where guests can eat as much meat as they like and select delicacies from the buffet. 🔣	AE DC MC V		■	●	■
SÄLEN: *Olarsgården* ⓀⓀⓀ 780 67 Sälen. 📞 *0280-210 29.* Considered to be the best restaurant in the ski resort with specialities such as elk heart, air-dried capercaillie and venison on the game menu. Large wine list. On Sälfjällstorget, 1 km (half a mile) from Lindvallen. 🔣	AE DC MC V	●		●	■
SÄLEN: *Onkel Jean* ⓀⓀⓀⓀ Sälens Högfjällshotell, 780 67 Sälen. 📞 *0280-870 20.* Luxury restaurant at the Högfjällshotellet, complete with white tablecloths and chandeliers. Russian caviar and champagne as well as local ingredients from the mountains feature on the menu. 🔣	AE DC MC V			●	■
ÖREBRO: *Slottsskänken* ⓀⓀ Örebro Slott, 701 42 Örebro. 📞 *019-12 23 39.* Good cooking and a delightful atmosphere at Örebro Slott. Dine à la carte with a glass of wine or a beer. 🔣	MC V	●	■	■	■
ÖREBRO: *Drängen* ⓀⓀⓀ Oskarsvägen 1, 702 14 Örebro. 📞 *019-32 32 96.* Rustic and friendly cottage setting with Falu red walls and the buzz of guests. The food is simple, uncomplicated, good and value for money, especially the desserts. 🔣	AE DC MC V	●	■		

SOUTHERN NORRLAND

	CREDIT CARDS	OPEN LUNCH-TIME	OPEN LATE	FIXED-PRICE MENU	GOOD WINE LIST
BRUNFLO: *Mikado* ⓀⓀⓀ Grytan, 834 98 Brunflor. 📞 *063-209 08.* Remarkably exotic gem of a restaurant in Jämtland. Orders should be placed in advance when a table is booked. Many dishes are fondues and prepared at the table, accompanied by sake, green tea or Japanese beer. 🔣	AE DC MC V		■	●	
GÄVLE: *Skeppet* ⓀⓀⓀ Nygatan 45, 803 11 Gävle. 📞 *026-12 99 50.* Restaurant in the vaults below the Grand Central Hotell. Relaxed, professional atmosphere with a menu of classic dishes. 🔣	MC			●	
HUDIKSVALL: *Gretas Krog* ⓀⓀ Västra Tvärkajen, 824 12 Hudiksvall. 📞 *0650-966 00.* Traditional Swedish à la carte menu served in a wood-pannelled restaurant. Large windows overlook the waterfront and harbour. Outdoor seating in summer. 🔣	AE DC MC V	●	■		
SANDVIKEN: *Högbo Brukshotell* ⓀⓀⓀⓀ Hans Hiertas väg 20, 811 92 Sandviken. 📞 *026-24 52 31.* Hotel restaurant which has gained a name for its top-class cuisine under Gert Klötzke, a member of the Swedish Culinary Olympic team. The food is really something out of the ordinary and well worth the price. 🔣	AE DC MC V	●	■	●	■
SUNDSVALL: *Il Barone* ⓀⓀ Kyrkogatan 14, 852 31 Sundsvall. 📞 *060-17 66 04.* Famously the best restaurant in Sundsvall. Friendly Italian bistro with large portions and reasonable prices. Known for its excellent pasta and long wine list, many by the glass. 🔣	AE DC MC V		■		■
UMEÅ: *Rex Grill och Bar* ⓀⓀ Rådhustorget 1, 903 26 Umeå. 📞 *090-12 60 50.* This former town hall houses Rex bar, which also has a quieter restaurant. Simple cuisine. 🔣	AE DC MC V	●	■	●	■

UMEÅ: *Viktor* ⓀⓀ
Vasagatan 11, 902 29 Umeå. 📞 *090-71 11 15.*
High quality through and through. Menus change often and ingredients are
always fresh. Good wine cellar and friendly setting. ♿ ❄ 🅥 🍸
AE DC MC V

ÅRE: *Villa Tottebo* ⓀⓀ
Parkvägen 1, 830 13 Åre. 📞 *0647-506 20.*
Unpretentious eatery reminiscent of a local restaurant in Southern Europe. The
food is excellent. Star chefs often invited to cook. ♿ ❄ 🔨 🅥 🍸
AE DC MC V

ÅRE: *Marmite Matsal* ⓀⓀⓀⓀ
Årevägen 72, 830 13 Åre. 📞 *0647-502 40.*
Small restaurant with big ambitions. Four menus offering exciting tastes:
Swedish, French, Spanish and Italian. Great wine list and selection of liqueurs.
Expert staff. ♿ ❄ 🅥
AE DC MC V

ÖRNSKÖLDSVIK: *Restaurang Mammamia* ⓀⓀ
Storgatan 6, 891 27 Örnsköldsvik. 📞 *0660-147 00.*
Traditional Italian restaurant with the focus on pizza and pasta.
♿ ❄ 🅥 🍸 🎵
AE DC MC V

ÖSTERSUND: *Innefickan* ⓀⓀ
Postgränd 11, 831 31 Östersund. 📞 *063-12 90 99.*
Local ingredients are successfully combined with the flavours of Italy and the
Mediterranean and served in a cellar dining room. Welcoming atmosphere.
♿ ❄ 🅥 🍸
AE DC MC V

NORTHERN NORRLAND

BODEN: *Pär & Mickes* ⓀⓀ
Kungsgatan 20, 961 31 Boden. 📞 *0921-538 35.*
Varied menu featuring international dishes and local ingredients.
♿ ❄ 🅥 🍸
MC V

GAMMELSTAD: *Margaretas Wärdshus* ⓀⓀ
Lulevägen 2, 954 33 Gammelstad. 📞 *0920-225 42 90.*
Typical Norbotten restaurant with the emphasis on local cuisine. Try grouse,
elk, capercaillie and bear, or smoked reindeer and mountain char, and finish
off with cloudberries or Arctic raspberries. ♿ ❄ ● *Christmas and New Year.*
AE DC MC V

JUKKASJÄRVI: *Icehotel Restaurang* ⓀⓀⓀⓀ
981 91 Jukkasjärvi. 📞 *0980-668 84.*
This famous restaurant offers gastronomic specialities in the unusual setting of
a restaurant built of ice. ♿ ❄ 🅥 🍸 ● *May–Sep.*
AE DC MC V

KIRUNA: *3nd Baren & Restaurang Landström* ⓀⓀ
Föreningsgatan 11, 981 32 Kiruna. 📞 *0980-663 80.*
Good food in a congenial location in the centre of Kiruna. Many Norrland
specialities on the menu. ♿ ❄ 🍸
AE DC MC V

LULEÅ: *Nautiska Kompaniet* ⓀⓀⓀ
Storgatan 28, 972 32 Luleå. 📞 *0920-22 78 80.*
Well-designed à la carte menu based on seasonal ingredients from Norrland.
♿ ❄ 🍸 ● *July–Sep.*
AE DC MC V

LYCKSELE: *Restaurang Lorentus* Ⓚ
Verkstadsvägen 11, 921 45 Lycksele. 📞 *0950-107 11.*
Swedish traditional cooking, plus pizza, fish, meat and Mexican dishes. Live
music some evenings. ♿ ❄ 🎵 🍸
AE DC MC V

PITEÅ: *Piteå Stadshotell* ⓀⓀ
Olof Palmes gata 1, 941 33 Piteå. 📞 *0911-23 40 00.*
Food from all corners of the world accompanied by cool beer from the cellar.
♿ ❄ 🎵 🍸
AE DC MC V

SKELLEFTEÅ: *Restaurang Vitberget* ⓀⓀ
Mossgatan, 931 70 Skellefteå. 📞 *0910-77 58 00.*
The wonderful views across the town of Skellefteå are matched by the star
turn on the menu, barbecued meat. Only Swedish ingredients used. ❄ 🍸
AE MC V

VILHELMINA: *Hotell Wilhelmina* ⓀⓀⓀ
Volgsjövägen 16, 912 34 Vilhelmina. 📞 *0940-554 20.*
Excellent dinners in a relaxing setting. Many of the ingredients are gathered
from the countryside of southern Lapland.
♿ ❄ 🔨 🅥 🍸
AE DC MC V

For key to symbols see back flap

SHOPPING IN SWEDEN

NOWADAYS SWEDEN IS worth visiting for the shopping alone. In all Swedish towns, and even in the big cities, the shops are within easy walking distance of each other. The city centres offer a good range of small, trendy boutiques for fashion and interiors, shops for antiques and curios, luxury international designer outlets and well-stocked department stores. Cameras, mobile phones, furs, children's clothing, toys and Swedish glass

Dala horse
(see p306)

and designer goods are cheaper in Sweden than in many other countries. Those looking for a typical Swedish souvenir could buy a Dala horse or a proper Swedish schnapps glass from one of the factories in the Kingdom of Crystal. Although Lapland is a long way north, Sami handicrafts can be bought in most craft shops, including knives with carved bone handles and silverwork. Leather and fur goods are also good value.

OPENING TIMES

MOST SHOPS USUALLY open at 10am and close at 6pm, although many in Stockholm city centre remain open until 7pm. Most shops are open until 2pm on Saturdays, while the major department stores stay open until 5pm. Large stores, shopping malls and some city-centre shops are open on Sundays. Market halls are closed on Sundays and public holidays. Many larger supermarkets are open daily until 8pm.

PAYMENT

ALL THE MAJOR credit cards and traveller's cheques are accepted at most Swedish shops. You may be asked for proof of identity. Some larger shops also accept euros *(see p324)*. Goods can be exchanged if you produce the

receipt. Purchases can be made on a sale-or-return basis if this is noted on the receipt.

VALUE ADDED TAX

VALUE ADDED TAX ("moms" in Swedish) is charged on all items except daily newspapers. The VAT rate is 25 per cent; but only 12 per cent on food and 6 per cent on books. VAT is always included in the total price.

TAX-FREE SHOPPING

RESIDENTS OF countries outside the European Union are entitled to a refund of the VAT paid on their purchases. Look for the "Tax-free shopping" sign in shop windows. Keep your receipts and on departure from the EU go to the Global Refund office at the airport or ferry terminal to obtain a 15–18 per cent refund.

NK, Stockholm's most exclusive department store

Sale-time at an elegant shoe shop in Stockholm

SALES

TWICE A YEAR Sweden's shops and department stores have sales with reduced prices on clothing, shoes and other fashion goods. Sales are indicated by the *rea* sign. The year's first sales period starts after Christmas and continues throughout January. The second sales period lasts from late June to the end of July.

SHOPPING CENTRES AND DEPARTMENT STORES

THE BEST-KNOWN Swedish superstore internationally is **IKEA**, which has 14 outlets across the country from Sundsvall in the north to Malmö in the south, and has become a popular tourist attraction in its own right. It sells not only furniture, but everything else for the home. The textiles section is particularly good, as well as

IKEA's home furnishings stores can be found in many parts of Sweden

the kitchenware and china departments.

Another well-known store is the fashion house **H&M** (Hennes & Mauritz), which has branches in many towns. It stocks the latest fashions at low prices. H&M has its own designers and makes clothing for women, men, teenagers and children. The shops also sell accessories, underwear, perfume and cosmetics.

NK (Nordiska Kompaniet) in Stockholm and Gothenburg is Sweden's leading department store, in which many well-known names in fashion and cosmetics have their own outlets. NK is a practical choice for those in a hurry. It stocks everything from Swedish-designed products, jewellery, handicrafts and souvenirs to cameras, films, books and CDs.

Åhléns, which has stores in many towns and cities, offers most items at good prices.

British chain **Debenhams** offers a slightly different range from other department stores.

Almost every large town has its own shopping centre or mall with a standard range of stores such as H&M, Lindex, Kappahl, Twilfit and Dressmann (clothing), Guldfynd (jewellery), Duka (glass and china), Hemtex (textiles), Expert (cameras, stereos, TVs) and Teknik-magasinet (electronics).

In Stockholm, **Gallerian** on Hamngatan is the largest mall and the prices are lower than in the elegant **Sturegallerian** near Stureplan with its many trendy boutiques.

Nordstan, off Brunnsparken in Gothenburg, is a mall with department stores such as Åhléns and specialist shops.

HansaCompagniet in central Malmö is a modern shopping centre.

A few examples of the larger shopping centres around the country include **Kungspassagen** in Umeå, **Forumgallerian** in Uppsala and **Krämaren** in Örebro.

Most towns have local markets selling flowers, fruit, vegetables and sometimes also handicrafts. Smaller places only have an outdoor market once a week, but in Hötorget in Stockholm, trading carries on every day except Sundays.

WINES AND SPIRITS

THE ONLY SHOPS selling alcohol in Sweden are run by Systembolaget, the state monopoly chain. They are open Mon–Fri 10am–6pm and Sat 10am–2pm (except public holiday weekends). The minimum age for buying alcohol at Systembolaget shops is 20 and staff are entitled to ask for proof of age (see also p321).

Åfors glassworks store, Kingdom of Crystal, Småland (see pp152–3)

What to Buy in Sweden

Elk candlestick

THE DALA wooden horse must be the most typical Swedish souvenir. But it is facing strong competition from the elk, which has become a symbol for a nation with vast tracts of unspoilt countryside. The Swedes love the great outdoors, so there are plenty of shops selling top-class sporting equipment. Swedish glass and crystal are renowned around the world. Orrefors and Kosta are just two of several glassworks producing both classic and modern glassware. Educational toys in natural materials are a Swedish speciality and so are clogs, which can be found in most shoe shops.

Hand-painted clogs

HANDICRAFTS & DESIGN

Modern Swedish design is a familiar concept worldwide, even for simple everyday items *(see pp22–3)*. Handicrafts have a long tradition in Sweden and contemporary designers often use old crafts such as wrought-iron work, weaving, pottery and woodcarving.

Dala Horse and Cockerel
Originally the brightly painted Dala horses and cockerels were toys carved from left-over fragments of wood. Later the horse became a national symbol, now sold in many variants.

Swedish Glass
Hand-blown sets are made in Småland's glassworks, as well as artistic crystal creations and objects for daily use.

Nobel **glass carafe from Orrefors by Gunnar Cyrén**

Traditional schnapps glasses

Tray with design by Josef Frank, Svenskt Tenn

Cheese slicer and knife by Michael Björnstierna

Objects for the Home
The larger department stores often commission well-known designers for porcelain, glass, textiles and household items which make highly desirable gifts.

Mama, **a humorous clothes hanger**

Crux **rug by Pia Wallén**

Children's Toys
Colourful wooden toys from Brio are worldwide favourites. Educational picture books, games and puzzles are all excellent gifts for children.

OUTDOOR GEAR

Many Swedes enjoy outdoor pursuits such as fishing, hunting, sailing, golf, camping and all types of winter sports, so there are plenty of well-equipped sports shops around. Unique items include Sami handicrafts beautifully made from reindeer horn or skin.

Hand Knits

Caps and gloves with attractive designs, known as lovikka, *are made from a special wool which gives good protection in cold or wet conditions.*

Drinking vessel in carved wood

Reindeer Skin Rucksack

Rucksacks have always been popular in Sweden. This exclusive leather model is made in Lapland.

Sami Handicrafts

A hunting knife with a sheath of reindeer horn, or a kåsa, *a drinking vessel carved in birch, are not only attractive, but useful when out walking in the wild.*

Spinning Reel and Lures

ABU-Garcia makes top-quality fishing tackle, perfect for Sweden's long coastline, countless lakes and rivers with their rich and varied fishing.

SWEDISH DELICACIES

Among the many Swedish goodies are preserves made from wild berries, such as lingonberries (served with meatballs or pancakes) and cloudberries (delicious with whipped cream). Ginger biscuits are for Christmas while crispbread is great year-round, especially with herring.

Lingonberry preserve   **Cloudberry jam**

Pickled Herring

Pickled herring should be enjoyed with new potatoes cooked with dill, chopped chives and sour cream. Versions flavoured with mustard, dill or other herbs or spices are also available.

Swedish schnapps gift-pack miniatures

"Raspberry boat" candy   **Salt liquorice**   **Crispbread**   **Ginger biscuits**

Where to Shop in Sweden

CLOTHING FROM ALL the well-known international fashion houses can be found in Stockholm, Malmö and Gothenburg. If you want something rather different, it is worth seeking out the creations of younger Swedish fashion designers. Swedish interior design is famous for its clean lines, functionalism and the use of pale wood, and the country is a paradise for anyone interested in design. Handicrafts are of a high quality. Leisurewear and sports goods offer excellent value for money.

FASHION

STOCKHOLM'S top places for fashion are in the "golden triangle" bounded by Stureplan, Nybroplan and Norrmalmstorg. Clothing at more moderate prices can be bought in department stores and shopping centres across the country. **GeKås** in Ullared and **Knalleland** in Borås have become popular attractions due to their low prices and large number of stores and factory outlets, not least in the "mail-order town" of Borås, with its weaving and textile traditions.

If you are looking for Swedish designers, **NK** in Stockholm and Gothenburg (*see p305*) has a good selection of clothing created by younger designers as well as mainstream Swedish brands. Classic men's clothing of high quality is designed by Oscar Jacobsson, while Stenström shirts are sold in department stores and the more elegant menswear boutiques. **Björn Borg** has his own shops selling men's and women's clothing and underwear, perfume and accessories. The designer **Filippa K** produces smart clothing for fashionable women and men.

DESIGN AND INTERIOR DECORATION

STOCKHOLM, Gothenburg and Malmö have a number of interior decoration shops selling the products of young designers and well-known artists. To see the latest on offer, it is worth visiting **DesignTorget**, which has stores in all three cities displaying designers' work. Stockholm's **R.O.O.M** on Kungsholmen and **Asplund**

in Östermalm, and **Norrgavel** in Stockholm, Gothenburg, Malmö and Lammhult, are just a few of the shops with the most up-to-the-minute selection of products. **Svenskt Tenn** is Stockholm's oldest shop for interiors, with both new and classic designs. **Nordiska Galleriet** in Stockholm has exclusive modern furniture and decorative items, while **Blås & Knåda** on Hornsgatan displays and sells the largest selection of contemporary Swedish ceramics and glass, both objects of art and items for everyday use. **Nordiska Kristall** on Kungsgatan has a wide choice of Swedish glassware, which can also be found in department stores.

MUSIC AND MULTIMEDIA

MANY SWEDISH POP bands now have an international reputation. Exciting new talents continue to find their way into the charts, and the latest products can often be bought in the large record shops before they become available outside Sweden. Apart from pop and rock, Sweden has a long folk-music tradition, as well as many jazz musicians and opera singers. **MEGA Skivakademien** in Stockholm stocks a wide selection of CDs, as do the large department stores.

SPORT AND LEISURE

THE SWEDES devote a lot of time to outdoor sports and activities. With shops all over the country, **Naturkompaniet** and **Peak Performance** have an exclusive selection of sportswear and equipment. **Stadium** and **Team Sportia** have a varied choice of sports

clothing and equipment at attractive prices and are also nationwide. Good equipment and exclusive clothing for hunting and fishing can be bought at **Walter Borg** in central Stockholm. **Löplabbet** countrywide specializes in running and jogging.

SOUVENIRS AND HANDICRAFTS

SCHNAPPS GLASSES, silver jewellery, hand-painted clogs, Sami crafts, hand-knitted garments, candles, Christmas decorations and wrought-iron products can all be bought in department stores and shops specialising in Swedish handicrafts.

At Skansen open-air museum in Stockholm, visitors can shop for handicrafts in attractive little houses.

Nusnäs in Dalarna is the place to buy the original Dala horse, which can be found at **Nils Olsson Hemslöjd AB**.

Yllet in Visby sells hand-spun wool, woollen garments and sheepskin goods.

MARKETS

SMALL LOCAL markets can be found almost everywhere, but a few have become so big that they have attracted international attention.

Jokkmokk's winter market (1st Thu–Sat in Feb) is a major Sami market. The Kivik market (mid-Jul) is like an amusement park. Skänninge market (1st Wed–Thu in Aug) is a classic affair dating back to the Middle Ages. Michaelmas markets are held in central Sweden in autumn.

The bustling flea market in Skärholmen, Stockholm, is the place to find a bargain every day of the week. Entrance fee Sat–Sun, free on other days.

GLASS AND CHINA

MOST DEPARTMENT stores and gift shops sell glass from Swedish manufacturers. Visitors to the Kingdom of Crystal in Småland have a choice of no fewer than 14 glassworks within a radius of a few miles (*see pp152–3*). At **Orrefors** and **Kosta**, there are bargains to be had among the everyday glassware and the studio glass. **Reijmyre** in Östergötland is also popular among bargain-hunters. For porcelain, the factory shop at **Rörstrand** offers value for money.

SWEDISH DELICACIES

THE CAPITAL HAS three market halls – **Östermalms-hallen**, **Hötorgshallen** and **Söderhallarna** – which are a joy to just wander around. Salmon, bleak roe, smoked eel and smoked reindeer meat are all delicious culinary souvenirs. Malmö's **Johan P** and Gothenburg's **Briggen** are also pleasant market halls offering mouth-watering Swedish delicacies.

On the west coast, seafood is a must and whether you are after prawns, crab or autumn's black gold, lobster, it is best purchased at the harbourside when the boats come in. In the north, game of various kinds is the big attraction and you can often find smoked reindeer and reindeer heart in grocery stores, along with fermented Baltic herring and Norrland cloudberry jam.

Swedish crispbread is another delicacy and the bakery in Leksand has a factory shop. Traditional red and white striped candy rock originates from Gränna, which has a large number of shops selling rock.

DIRECTORY

FASHION

Björn Borg
Sergelgatan 12,
Stockholm. **Map** 1 C4.
(08-21 70 40.

Champagne
Fredsgatan 1, Gothenburg.
Map see p92.
(031-15 73 71.

Filippa K
Grev Turegatan 18,
Stockholm. **Map** 2 D4.
(08-545 888 88.

Ge-Kås i Ullared
Danska Vägen, Halmstad.
(0346-375 00.

Imperium
Vallgatan 22, Gothenburg.
Map see p192.
(031-711 13 36.

Knalleland
Borås.
(033-14 03 35.

MQ
Södra Tullgatan 3, Malmö.
(040-12 01 31.
Strömpilsplatsen 1, Umeå.
(090-786 36 80.

Olsén Mode
Södergatan 21, Malmö.
Map see p179.
(040-12 10 50.

DESIGN AND INTERIORS

Asplund
Sibyllegatan 31,
Stockholm. **Map** 2 E3.
(08-662 52 84.

Blås & Knåda
Hornsgatan 36,
Stockholm.
Map 3 A5.
(08-642 77 67.

DesignTorget
Kulturhuset,
Sergels Torg 3, Stockholm.
Map 1 C4.
(08–508 315 20.
Götgatan 31, Stockholm.
(08-462 35 20.
Vallgatan 14, Gothenburg
Map see p192.
(031-774 00 17.

House
Humlegårdsgatan 14,
Stockholm.
Map 2 E3.
(08-545 853 40.

Nordiska Galleriet
Nybrogatan 11,
Stockholm.
Map 2 E4.
(08-442 83 60.

Nordiska Kristall
Kungsgatan 9,
Stockholm.
Map 2 E4.
(08-10 43 72.

Norrgavel
Birger Jarlsgatan 27,
Stockholm.
Map 2 D3.
(08-545 220 50.
Engelbrektsgatan 20,
Malmö. **Map** see p179.
(040-12 22 46.

R.O.O.M
Alströmergatan 20,
Stockholm.
(08-692 50 00.

Svenskt Tenn
Strandvägen 5,
Stockholm. **Map** 2 E4.
(08-670 16 00.

MUSIC

MEGA Skivakademien
Sergelarkaden 6,
Stockholm.
Map 1 C4.
(08-566 157 00.

Skivhuset CDmedia
Lilla Klädpressaregatan 7,
Gothenburg.
(031-15 55 05.

SPORT AND LEISURE

Löplabbet
Rundelsgatan 16, Malmö.
(040-12 35 70.

Naturkompaniet
Kungsgatan 4A,
Stockholm. **Map** 2 D4.
(08-723 15 81.

Peak Performance
Biblioteksgatan 18,
Stockholm.
Map 2 D4.
(08-611 34 00.
Södergatan 9,
Malmö.
Map see p179.
(040-97 02 20.

Stadium
Fredsgatan 8,
Gothenburg.
Map see p192.
(031-711 06 09.

Team Sportia
Bruksgatan 6, Umeå.
(090-71 79 70.

Walter Borg
Klara Norra Kyrkogata 26,
Stockholm. **Map** 1 C4.
(08-14 38 65.

SOUVENIRS AND HANDICRAFTS

Nils Olsson Hemslöjd AB
Edåkersvägen 17, Nusnäs.
(0250-372 00.

Svensk Hemslöjd
Sveavägen 44, Stockholm.
Map 1 C3.
(08-23 21 15.

Yllet
St Hansgatan 19, Visby.
(0498-21 40 44.

GLASS AND CHINA

Kosta Glasbruk
Kosta. (0478-345 00.

Orrefors Glasbruk
Orrefors. (0481-341 89.

Reijmyre
Reijmyre.
(011-871 84.

Rörstrand
Lidköping.
(0510-823 46.
Gustavsberg.
(08-570 356 55.

SWEDISH DELICACIES

Briggen
Linnéstaden, Gothenburg.
(0247-448 20.

Hötorgshallen
Hötorget, Stockholm.
Map 1 C4.

Johan P
Saluhallen, Malmö.

Östermalmshallen
Östermalmstorg,
Stockholm.
Map 2 E4.

ENTERTAINMENT IN SWEDEN

THE RANGE OF CULTURAL events and entertainment in Sweden is large and richly varied. The whole spectrum is covered from outdoor celebrations to mark local customs to top international acts performing in giant arenas. The seasons have an effect on what's on: large city theatres tend to close during the summer and launch their new programmes of plays, opera and dance in late August or early September. Meanwhile, summer reviews, popular comedies and local historical plays are staged across the

country. In parks, palace gardens and amusement parks, summer is a particularly eventful time, with artists of every imaginable kind putting on a performance. Added to that are the countless markets, festivals covering film, jazz, music, food, theatre, folklore, and much more besides. Winter brings ski races and skating, indoor fairs and Christmas markets. Nightlife continues all year. There are excellent nightclubs and casinos in the major cities. Jazz clubs and pubs offer a wide range of live music to suit all tastes.

Folk Dancers,
Rättvik

SOURCES OF INFORMATION

A RELIABLE SOURCE of information is **Sveriges Rese- och Turistråd**'s official tourist and events guide on the Internet. This provides listings for everything from music and sport to seasonal events such as Medieval Week in Visby or the Vasaloppet ski race in Dalarna. The site has links to the websites of Stockholm, Gothenburg and Malmö, but also has details of events across the country.

Daily newspapers and free local papers are an excellent source for regional events such as concerts, theatre performances and nightclubs. The tourist information offices and most hotels also have listings and can often help with advice and booking tickets.

BOOKING TICKETS

TICKETS FOR most events can usually be bought at the box office of the theatre or sports arena in question, but to ensure admission it may be more practical to book in advance, with the help either of the hotel or a tourist information office. Another alternative is to use a booking agency, such as **Biljett Direkt**, which, for a small fee, will take telephone bookings for tickets to stage shows, concerts and sports events. At **Box-office** in Stockholm, tickets can be purchased over the counter for various events in Sweden and beyond, and tickets ordered via the event organizer can be collected. Many tickets are also sold via the gaming agent ATG across the country.

Dalhalla's music stage (see p241) in a dramatic quarry near Rättvik

MAJOR ARENAS AND CULTURAL CENTRES

IN ADDITION TO the long-established, traditional theatres, many towns and cities have more recently built multi-purpose cultural complexes offering a wide spectrum of public events. Often such centres are home to the local theatre company and orchestra.

The major entertainment and event arenas such as **Globen** in Stockholm and **Scandinavium** in Gothenburg have a huge audience capacity. International rock and pop concerts, charity galas and major sporting events are usually held at these enormous venues.

In the summer, the large outdoor stages, for example at Skansen and Gröna Lund in Stockholm, Liseberg in Gothenburg and Dalhalla, between Rättvik and Mora, attract a wide range of jazz, folk and classical artists alike.

Sea of people at the Philharmonic's annual outdoor concert, Stockholm

THEATRE

SWEDEN HAS almost 500 theatres spread across the country. Many are town or county theatres, but there are also private theatres with long traditions and small park and amateur theatres.

Sweden's national theatre is **Kungliga Dramatiska Teatern** *(see p71)*, which has six stages. It regularly mounts international and Swedish classics, including Shakespeare and Strindberg, as well as modern foreign and Swedish works.

Lighter plays and musicals are often performed at **ChinaTeatern** in Stockholm and **Lorensbergsteatern** in Gothenburg. Venues such as **Konsertteatern** in Sundsvall and **Göta Lejon** in Stockholm often stage performances suitable for children and families.

CLASSICAL MUSIC, DANCE AND OPERA

WORLD-CLASS music can be heard at **Berwaldhallen** in Stockholm, the home of Sveriges Radios Symfoniorkester and the Radiokören choir, considered one of the internationally leading a cappella ensembles. **Konserthuset** *(see p68)* is the base of for Kungliga Filharmoniska Orkestern. The season runs from August to May.

Konserthuset in Gothenburg is home to Göteborgs Symfoniker. Norrköping has the **De Geerhallen** venue and Folkets Park in Sundsvall has **Tonhallen**, one of Sweden's best concert halls.

Classical opera and ballet of the highest quality can be seen at **Kungliga Operan** *(see p66)*. Every season at

Sundsvalls Teater, an ambitious, go-ahead regional theatre

GöteborgsOperan, with a wide repertoire of opera and musicals

least three major ballets delight packed houses. This venue also stages traditional performances of most operas in their original language. During the summer, popular opera performances are held at **Drottningholms Slottsteater** *(see p109)*. All the operas staged here are from the 18th century, with an orchestra of the period.

The spectacular modern **GöteborgsOperan** *(see p196)* is an exciting, internationally-renowned venue for opera, ballet and musicals. Norrlandsoperan in Umeå and Malmö Opera och Musikteater are two of the country's other major venues for opera and ballet.

Dansens Hus in Stockholm, which has taken over the National Theatre's former venue, often hosts top-name dance companies from Sweden and abroad.

FOLK MUSIC

SWEDISH FOLK music is enjoying a resurgence in popularity. Skansen in Stockholm *(see p92)* is the prime venue, where musicians and folk dancing troupes perform regularly at traditional events. However, there are local folk groups and regional clubs covering practically every corner of the country. The easiest way of finding out where and how to enjoy Swedish folk music is to check at the local tourist information office or in the local press.

There are a few permanent venues for folk music: **Folkmusikhuset** in Stockholm,

Folkmusikkaféet in Gothenburg and **Folkmusikens Hus** in Rättvik are just some of the places offering a wide programme of performances and information about forthcoming events.

CHURCH MUSIC

MANY CHURCHES in the cities hold organ recitals at lunchtime, for example Jacobs Kyrka in Stockholm *(see p66)*, where visitors can take a breather in a tranquil setting. Storkyrkan *(see p53)* also holds concerts on Saturday and Sunday afternoons in the spring and autumn. The cathedrals of Uppsala Domkyrka *(see p128)* and Västerås Domkyrka *(see p138)* stage organ recitals every Saturday. Many churches also have a concert programme, particularly in conjunction with major religious festivals.

ROCK AND POP

THE LARGEST of the venues for rock and pop music are **Globen** in Stockholm and **Scandinavium** in Gothenburg. These attract top international artists, along with the many successful Swedish bands. **Cirkus** in Stockholm is a well-established venue for music and theatre in a beautiful old setting. More modern rock venues include **Munchenbryggeriet** in Stockholm, **Kulturbolaget** in Malmö and **Trädgår'n** in Gothenburg. Around the country there are smaller theatres, students' unions and clubs where groups and artists perform.

Concert in the ruins of Bohus Castle in Kungälv

JAZZ CLUBS

JAZZ HAS ENJOYED a renaissance in recent years and the range on offer increases annually. One venue of repute is **Fasching** in Stockholm, with performances almost daily. Another jazz haunt in the capital is **Stampen**, which attracts a rather more mature audience. Gothenburg has **Nefertiti** and in Malmö there is **Jeriko**. Across the country there are jazz clubs holding concerts once a month or so.

Jazz cruises have become popular in the summer. The Stockholm archipelago is plied by *S/S Blidösund*. Cruises are also organized elsewhere in the country, for instance across Lake Vättern and the Åland river and out into the Gothenburg archipelago.

MUSIC PUBS

SWEDISH PUB culture has changed enormously and it is becoming increasingly common to follow the Continental pattern of slipping into a bar or pub for a while after work, having a beer and listening to music.

Many pubs have introduced live music – some have folk singers performing on a regular basis, while others have a DJ. The best way of being sure to hear live music is to scan the local press entertainment (*nöjen*) pages.

In Stockholm, the Irish pub **The Dubliner** offers live Irish music. The popular **Engelen** bar has live music several days a week. Gothenburg's finest pubs include **Sticky Fingers** and Jameson's pub, and Helsingborg has its own English pub, Charles Dickens, where the clientele can enjoy karaoke, live music, singers, bands and various other forms of entertainment.

There are a number of traditional English and Irish-style pubs spread across the country, usually offering a wide range of beer and spirits and serving a selection of bar snacks.

NIGHTCLUBS, CASINOS AND SHOWS

GENERALLY SPEAKING, nightclubs hold traditional disco nights on Friday and Saturday. During the rest of the week the venue is usually hired by various clubs focusing on different styles of music. Almost all the larger towns and cities have one or two nightclubs, but the quality varies, as does the music on offer. In Stockholm,

A traditional folk music festival in Tällberg on Lake Siljan in Dalarna

the majority and the best of the capital's nightclubs are located around Stureplan. At the rear of the Opera House is **Café Opera**, Stockholm's longest-established nightclub, with an international style. The crowd is usually quite mixed – young, trendy types and older, smartly-dressed folks. **Sturecompagniet** is a large club on several floors. At street level there is also a rock bar. Swedish celebrities and visiting foreign stars mingle at top celeb hangout **Spy Bar**, but it can be difficult to get in on certain nights. Other well-known nightclubs include **Crown** in Malmö and **Gutekällaren** in Visby.

A relative newcomer to the entertainment scene is the state-run casino chain **Casino Cosmopol**, which to date has opened branches in Stockholm, Gothenburg, Malmö and Sundsvall.

A combination of good food and top-flight entertainment is on offer at **Hamburger Börs** in Stockholm, with its shows featuring the best Swedish artists. **Wallmans Salonger**, which can be found in Stockholm and Malmö, offers musical entertainment with dinner served by waiters and waitresses who are, in fact, professional performers.

In Gothenburg, **Rondo** is a classic show venue.

FESTIVALS

COUNTLESS festivals large and small are organized all across Sweden in the summer. Almost every town has its own festival, some with a specific focus, such as folk, jazz or rock.

Among the most renowned of the local festivals are Göteborgskalaset in Gothenburg, Storsjöyran in Östersund and Gatufesten in Sundsvall.

There are numerous music festivals, the largest of which – for example the Hultsfred Festival – attract huge audiences. Other famous music festivals include the Falun Folk Music Festival, the Sweden Rock Festival in Sölvesborg, the Gotland Chamber Music Festival in Visby, the Stockholm Jazz Festival and the Umeå International Jazz Festival.

The best-known film festivals are the **Gothenburg Film Festival** (Jan/Feb) and the **Stockholm International Film Festival** (Nov), but several other cities and towns hold their own film festivals with a different focus, such as Umeå (Sep).

DIRECTORY

SOURCES OF INFORMATION

Sveriges Rese- och Turistråd
W www.visit-sweden.com
C 08- 789 10 00.

BOOKING TICKETS

Biljett Direkt
W www.ticnet.se
C 077-170 70 70.

Box-office
Palmhuset, Norrmalmstorg, Stockholm. **Map 2 D4.**
C 08-10 88 00.

ARENAS, CULTURAL CENTRES

Globen
Globentorget 2, Stockholm.
C 077-131 00 00.

Scandinavium
Valhallagatan 1, Gothenburg. C 031-81 10 20.

THEATRE

China Teatern
Berzelii Park 9, Stockholm.
Map 2 D4.
C 08-566 323 50.

Göta Lejon
Götgatan 55, Stockholm.
C 08-643 67 00.

Konsertteatern
Köpmangatan 11, Sundsvall. C 060-61 32 62.

Kungliga Dramatiska Teatern
Nybroplan, Stockholm. **Map 2 E4.** C 08-667 06 80.

Lorensbergsteatern
Lorensbergsparken, Gothenburg. C 031-708 62 00.

CLASSICAL MUSIC, DANCE, OPERA

Berwaldhallen
Dag Hammarskjölds Väg 3, Stockholm.
C 08-784 50 00.

Dansens Hus
Barnhusgatan 12–14, Stockholm. **Map 1 C3.**
C 08-508 990 90.

De Geerhallen
Dalsgatan 15, Norrköping.
C 011-15 50 30.

Drottningholms Slottsteater
Drottningholms Slott, Lovön, W of Stockholm.
C 08-660 82 25.

GöteborgsOperan
Christina Nilssons Gata, 41, Gothenburg.
C 031-13 13 00.

Konserthuset
Götaplatsen, Gothenburg.
C 031-726 53 00.

Konserthuset
Hötorget, Stockholm.
Map 1 C4.
C 08-786 02 00.

Kungliga Operan
Gustav Adolfs Torg, Stockholm. **Map 2 D5.**
C 08-791 43 00.

Tonhallen
Fabriksgatan 14, Sundsvall.
C 060-19 88 00.

FOLK MUSIC

Folkmusikens Hus
Dalagatan 7, Rättvik.
C 0248-79 79 50.

Folkmusikhuset
Skeppsholmsgården, Stockholm. **Map 2 E5.**
C 08-411 99 88.

Folkmusikkaféet
Allégården, Gothenburg.
C 031-701 76 61.

ROCK AND POP

Cirkus
Djurgårdsslätten, Stockholm. C 08-587 987 00.

Kulturbolaget
Bergsgatan 18, Malmö.
C 040-30 20 11.

München-bryggeriet
Söder Mälarstrand 29, Stockholm.
C 08-658 13 00.

Trädgår'n
Nya Allén, Gothenburg.
C 031-10 20 80.

JAZZ CLUBS

Fasching
Kungsgatan 63, Stockholm. **Map 1 B4.**
C 08-534 829 60.

Jeriko
Spångatan 38, Malmö.
C 040-611 84 29.

Nefertiti
Hvitfeldtsplatsen 6, Gothenburg.
C 0318-711 15 33.

Stampen
Stora Nygatan 5, Stockholm. **Map 3 B4.**
C 08-20 57 93.

MUSIC PUBS

Engelen
Kornhamnstorg 59 B, Stockholm. **Map 3 B4.**
C 08-505 560 00.

Sticky Fingers
Kaserntorget 7, Gothenburg.
C 031-701 07 17.

The Dubliner
Smålandsgatan 8, Stockholm.
Map 2 D4.
C 08-679 97 02.

NIGHTCLUBS, CASINOS, SHOWS

Café Opera
Operahuset, Stockholm.
Map 3 B1.
C 08-676 58 07.

Casino Cosmopol
Kungsgatan 65, Stockholm. **Map 1 B4.**

C 08-781 88 00.
Packhusplatsen 7, Gothenburg.
C 031-333 55 00.
Slottsgatan 33, Malmö.
C 040-664 18 00.
Casinoparken 1, Sundsvall.
C 060-14 11 00.

Crown
Amiralsgatan 19, Malmö.
C 040-611 80 88.

Gutekällaren
Stora Torget, Visby.
C 0498-21 00 43.

Hamburger Börs
Jakobsgatan 6, Stockholm. **Map 2 D5.**
C 08-787 85 00.

Rondo
Örgrytevägen 5, Gothenburg. C 031-40 02 00.

Spy Bar
Birger Jarlsgatan 20, Stockholm. **Map 2 D3.**
C 08-545 037 01.

Sturecompagniet
Sturegatan 4, Stockholm.
Map 2 D3.
C 08- 611 78 00.

Wallmans Salonger
Teatergatan 3, Stockholm.
Map 2 E5.
C 08-505 560 00.
Generalsgatan 1, Malmö.
C 040-749 45.

FESTIVALS

Gothenburg Film Festival
Heurlins Plats 11, Gothenburg.
W www.filmfestival.org
C 031-339 30 00.

Stockholm International Film Festival
Slupskjulsvägen 3, Stockholm. **Map 4 E2.**
W www.filmfestivalen.se
C 08-677 50 00.

SPORTS AND OUTDOOR ACTIVITIES

Sweden has countryside in abundance and the *"allemannsrätt"* (Right to Roam) makes it accessible in a way rarely found elsewhere in the world. No wonder an active outdoor life has become such a staple of the Swedish lifestyle. Constantly rising demand for outdoor activities has led to an increasing range of trails for hiking, canoeing and cycling, and the construction of hundreds of new ski lifts, golf courses and

Recommended cycle trail

guest harbours. There has also been a boom in adventure sports – from challenging hikes in remote mountain regions and sea kayaking in the outer archipelagos to competing in the long-distance Vasaloppet skiing race, the Vansbrosimningen swimming race or the Vätternrundan cycling race, which together make up what is known as the "Swedish Classic". More leisurely pursuits include horse riding and fishing.

GENERAL INFORMATION

In addition to the tourist information offices, there are a number of organizations to assist outdoors enthusiasts. The state-run **Naturvårdsverket** has an excellent website, which also provides useful information about Sweden's 28 national parks. **Friluftsfrämjandet** is a 100-year-old voluntary organization – the backbone of outdoor life for its many activities and operations.

HIKING TRAILS

Although it is possible to pitch a tent almost anywhere, it is often more practical to follow one of the many well-tended hiking trails. There are numerous lowland trails, such as the Skåneleden, which runs south to north through Skåne. Mountain trails

proliferate, the best of which is the renowned Kungsleden stretching 450 km (280 miles) *(see pp274–5).*

Maps of the trails usually provide information about stopping-off points, attractions, accommodation and services along the way.

The most popular mountain areas have marked trails for day trips and longer hikes with overnight accommodation in huts and at mountain stations. For more than 100 years, **Svenska Turistföreningen (STF)** has been the main provider of services in the mountains in summer and winter.

The mountain trails mainly run through road-free land. There are STF mountain stations at strategic locations from Abisko in Lapland to Grövelsjön in Dalarna. Although out in the wilds, these are relatively easy to access and make an excellent

Walking with poles, a popular form of exercise

starting point for hiking tours in the mountains. The stations have hotel-standard accommodation, restaurants, self-catering kitchens, shops and equipment hire.

Along the trails, there are simple huts in which to stay, with a self-catering kitchen and in some cases provisions for sale. Space cannot be booked in advance, but everyone usually gets a roof over their head. In the summer, STF has special hosts to help with tips and advice.

The trails crossing the high mountains can be extremely demanding for the uninitiated. It is important not to be too ambitious and to have appropriate equipment.

Whatever the time of year, the weather changes quickly, so keep up to date with the forecast, which is usually posted at stations and huts. The summer season for mountain hiking is from about mid-June to mid-September.

A hiker en route to the Sylarna mountain station, Jämtland

One of STF's many huts across the mountains

ENDURANCE TESTS

COMPETITIONS for elite athletes and fitness enthusiasts alike have become increasingly popular in Sweden, attracting thousands of participants of all levels. Some enter the "Swedish Classic", in which over one year competitors ski the Vasaloppet *(see p245)* or Engelbrektsloppet (60 km/37 miles), cycle the Vätternrundan (300 km/190 miles), swim the Vansbrosimningen (3 km/2 miles) and run the Lidingöloppet (30 km/19 miles). Other events include the Stockholm Marathon *(see p27)* and the O-ringen in orienteering.

SWIMMING

THERE ARE generally no restrictions for anyone wanting to take a dip in lakes, rivers and the sea. However, there is no need to take any risks as there are thousands of public bathing areas where the water quality is checked by the health authorities. Even in the north,

there are plenty of opportunities to swim, for example at Pite Havsbad, where the sunny beaches are known as "The Nordic Riviera" *(see p268)*. In many places, the natural bathing spots are supplemented by water parks and fun pools offering all kinds of watery activities, such as at Skara Sommarland *(see p223)* and Sydpoolen in Södertälje.

Generally, water quality is high in Sweden and even in the cities it is sometimes possible to swim from rocks and beaches. Långholmen in central Stockholm is a favourite spot for a dip. In hot summers, however, poisonous algae sometimes blooms along the coast, so take advice locally on whether swimming is advisable.

Indoor pools are a popular choice. Stockholm has the historic Centralbadet and Sturebadet among others.

The spa and bathing culture has a long tradition in Sweden, particularly in places such as Loka *(see p141)*, with its modern facilities.

CYCLING

PEDAL POWER is a great way to experience towns and countryside alike. The bicycle has enjoyed something of a renaissance in Sweden and Stockholm in particular has invested heavily in cycle paths and special cycle routes.

Cycling holidays have long been popular on islands with little traffic such as Öland and Gotland. However, there are now cycle trails following minor roads and disused railway lines, often marked by green cycle-trail signs. A wide range of cycling packages is available and there are plenty of places to hire bicycles, tandems and trailers.

There are 30 or so regional cycle trails around the country, which require one or more stopovers to complete the distance. They can often be combined with the extensive Sverigeleden national trail which runs 2,590 km (1,600 miles) from Helsingborg in the south to Karesuando in the far north. The trail is well-signposted and special maps are available.

On the easier routes, 97 per cent of which are paved, those who have the time for a really long cycling holiday can experience Sweden's ever-changing landscape. Information about cycling trails is available from **Svenska Cykelsällskapet**.

Another option for those who fancy pedalling is to take a trolley trip on several railway tracks across the country where rail traffic has ceased.

A cycling trip on Visingsö in Lake Vättern, offering easy routes, fascinating sights and beautiful countryside

Trekkers heading for Storsylen in the Jämtland mountains

WINTER ACTIVITIES

IT IS NO SURPRISE that Swedish skiers have dominated the World Cup at times, both in downhill and cross-country skiing. In winter, much of the country is covered in snow and there is some great skiing to be had.

There is an extensive network of cross-country skiing trails, many of which are floodlit, a necessity during the long dark evenings. It is also possible to ski on snow-covered golf courses or on iced-over lakes and the frozen waters of the archipelagos. The ice is also ideal for skating, an enjoyable experience on a sunny winter's day. Check the safety information first, as things can quickly turn serious if the ice cracks.

Sweden has hundreds of lifts for downhill skiers, which

Snowboarding and skiing are popular in the Swedish mountains

are listed on the website for the skiing organization **SLAO**. The two largest ski resorts are Åre, 600 km (370 miles) north of Stockholm, and Sälen, just over 400 km (250 miles) north of the capital. Most people on mountain holidays stay in self-catering cottages or apartments. Accommodation must be booked well in advance, particularly during the high season, and usually for complete weeks (Sun–Sun), weekends (Thu–Sun) or short weeks (Sun–Thu). It is easiest to buy lift passes and hire skis or snowboards at the resort.

GOLF

SWEDISH GOLFERS have achieved major successes in recent years, particularly in the ladies' events, with Annika Sörenstam leading the way. This golfing phenomenon is partly due to the ambitious junior programme supported by many of the country's golf clubs. Under the umbrella of the **Svenska Golfförbundet**, there are more than 400 golf courses, an extremely high figure in relation to the population size. Although the climate in parts of the country may be considered unsuitable for golf, the courses offer high quality during the summer. Almost all courses are open

to guest players, but demand is great and it can be difficult to find a suitable teeing-off time in high season at many clubs. Green fees vary from 150 kr on basic courses to more than 500 kr at exclusive city clubs. You must be a member of a golf club to play as a guest on a Swedish course.

HORSE RIDING

HORSE RIDING is a popular sport in Sweden, and there are almost 1,000 riding clubs. There is a wide range of riding available, from trips for beginners on Icelandic ponies to mountain trekking for those with experience. The tourist offices can provide local contacts.

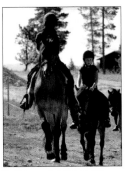

Trekking on Icelandic ponies

BOATING, CANOEING, WHITE-WATER RAFTING

THE LONG coastline, inviting archipelagos and numerous lakes make exploring the country by water particularly rewarding. There are almost 500 classified guest harbours offering good facilities for sailors. The classification is administered by **Svenska Kryssarklubben**, which is also a good source of information about natural harbours and boating in general. All types of craft from simple rowing boats to large motor boats and yachts can be hired from marinas around the country.

Although there are no specific requirements for sailing smaller boats, you will need basic knowledge of boating even for a day trip. As a rule, documented qualifications equivalent to the Swedish skipper's certificate *"förarintyg"* are required for taking out larger boats.

There are great opportunities for canoeing, with almost 20,000 km (12,500 miles) of trails on inland waters and around the archipelagos. The website for **Kanotleder i Sverige** lists 400 tours in Canadian canoes and kayaks, along with canoeing centres and rental sites across the country. For more advanced canoeists, there are plenty of opportunities to try sea kayaks in the outer archipelagos and white-water canoeing on the Norrland rivers. White-water rides are also possible, heading down the rapids in large rubber rafts or up on jetskis.

HUNTING AND FISHING

SWEDEN HAS more than 300,000 hunters and during the elk hunting season some forest villages are packed. Around 100,000 elks are shot every year. As a guest of land owners and hunting teams, foreign hunters can take part in small game and elk hunts. However, in the latter case, a special elk shooting test is required as well as a hunting permit. Taking your own weapon requires a great deal of bureaucracy, so hiring a weapon is recommended. Details about conditions, hunting times and hunt organizers are available from **Svenska Jägareförbundet**.

A third of all Swedes go fishing at least once a year, and no wonder with access to

Rod fishing, often free along Sweden's lengthy coastline

the most extensive fishing waters in Europe. There are more than 200 species of saltwater fish on the west coast, some of which also venture into the brackish water of the Baltic Sea. Added to this are around 40 species of freshwater fish in the lakes and rivers.

Rod fishing in coastal waters is often free. In other waters, the necessary fishing permit can be purchased locally. The **Sveafiskekortet** permit is a nationwide option offered by Sveaskog, which administers the national forests and land covering a fifth of the country. Sweden's leading and most traditional salmon fishing waters in Blekinge's Mörrum *(see p186)* are also state-owned.

Salmon and sea trout can even be fished in the heart of Stockholm, where Strömmen has unusually clean water for a city of a million people.

Fishing trips by boat are offered widely. **Sportfiskarna** provides information about sport fishing.

DIRECTORY

GENERAL INFORMATION

Friluftsfrämjandet
C 08-447 44 40.
@ info@frilufts.se

Naturvårdsverket
C 08-698 10 00.
W www.naturvardsverket.se

Svenska Turistföreningen (STF)
C 08-463 21 00.
W www.svenskaturistforeningen.se

CYCLING

Svenska Cykelsällskapet
Sweden's cycle trails.
W www.svenska-cykelsallskapet.se

WINTER ACTIVITIES

Skistar
Central reservations for ski resorts of Sälen, Vemdalen and Åre.
W www.skistar.com

SLAO
Swedish ski lifts. @ slao@slao.se

GOLF

Svenska Golfförbundet
C 08-622 1500.
@ info@sgf.golf.se

BOATING, CANOEING

Kanotleder i Sverige
Canoe trails and canoe hire.
W www.kanotguiden.com

Marinliv
Boat hire. @ info@marinliv.com

Svenska Kryssarklubben
C 08-448 2880. @ info@sxk.se

HUNTING, FISHING

Sportfiskarna
C 08-704 44 80.
@ hk@sportfiskarna.se

Sveafiskekortet
C 08-704 44 80.
@ info@sveaskog.se

Svenska Jägarförbundet
C 0155-24 62 00.
@ info@jagareforbundet.se

Experiencing the Swedish countryside by canoe

SURVIVAL
GUIDE

PRACTICAL INFORMATION

Tourist office symbol

WEDEN IS a country of huge distances – it is as far from Malmö in the south to Treriksröset in the north as it is from Malmö to Rome. So, it is worth planning any trip in advance. The local tourist offices publish useful information on the Internet. All types of accommodation from luxury hotels to bed-and-breakfasts can be booked online. Once you have arrived in Sweden, there are more than 300 authorized tourist information offices nationwide which can provide help. The towns all have modern facilities for the traveller, including banking services and emergency medical care, and the public telephone system is first-class. Customs and border controls now apply mainly to travellers from countries outside the EU. For EU citizens and Norwegians, the entry procedure is relatively straightforward.

TOURIST INFORMATION

SWEDEN HAS a number of tourist offices abroad, run by **Sveriges Rese- och Turistråd**. An overview of what's on offer for tourists and links to all the local tourist offices can be found at www.visit-sweden.com.

Another user-friendly general website is **Svensk TuristGuide** at www.sverige turism.se. Visitors can click on the map to reach regional tourism organizations and obtain detailed information about accommodation, eating out, attractions and events. Brochures and travel tips can also be requested by e-mail or phone.

In addition to the 300 official tourist information offices, information points open in summer, often attached to larger attractions. Offices with the blue and yellow "i" sign usually offer a broader service than those with the green and white "i".

The hub of Stockholm's tourist information is the **Tourist Centre Stockholm** in Sverigehuset.

PASSPORTS AND CUSTOMS

CITIZENS OF virtually all countries can enter Sweden as tourists without a visa. Norwegians and visitors from European countries which have signed the Schengen agreement do not, in principle, need a passport. However, all airlines require passports for passengers flying from countries outside the Nordic region, so it is always wise to carry your passport.

Different customs regulations apply to travellers from the European Union (EU) and those from other countries. Citizens of EU countries can take an unlimited amount of alcohol and tobacco products into Sweden without having to pay tax, provided they are for personal use. Citizens from non-EU countries can take in 1 litre of spirits or 2 litres of fortified wine, including sparkling wine, 2 litres of wine and an unlimited amount of strong beer, 200 cigarettes, or 100 cigarillos, or 50 cigars or 250 g tobacco. But they can only take in goods up to a value of 1,700 Kr in addition to normal travel-related items. To import alcohol, you must be 20 years old, and for tobacco, 18.

Items such as milk, cheese, butter, eggs and potatoes may not be taken into Sweden by private individuals. Norwegians and EU citizens may only take in a maximum of 15 kg (33 lb) of meat or fish. Visitors from some other countries are permitted to bring in 1 kg (2.2 lb) of meat and 1 kg (2.2 lb) of fish, but sometimes a certificate from a recognized exporter is required.

Dogs and cats from EU countries can be taken into Sweden, providing they have a veterinary certificate from the animal's home country. The animal must also have an identification marking, as well as an import permit issued by the Swedish Board of Agriculture (available from Swedish embassies).

Tax-free sales in Sweden are permitted only for travellers with a final destination outside the EU.

Tullverket provides up-to-date information in several languages by telephone and on its website.

OPENING HOURS

MOST MUSEUMS and major sights are open between 10am and 6pm all year, and they often have longer opening hours in the summer. Many museums close on Mondays. Some have extended opening hours one evening in the week. Admission to a number of state-run museums is free of charge. Admission charges for other museums

Tourist information office, Stockholm

◁ **A ferry bringing summer visitors to the isolated Baltic island of Gotska Sandön, north of Gotland** vary between about 30 and 70 Kr. There is usually a discounted price for children, students and senior citizens. In many places, churches are only open for services, although some have opening hours for visitors.

Stockholm and other cities have special discount cards for tourists. They can be purchased from tourist information offices and many hotels and are valid for one or more days. A family card is usually also available. The card gives free travel on public transport, free or discounted admission to museums and other attractions and events, and may also offer discounts at restaurants and shops.

Discos and nightclubs generally charge an entrance fee of 60–120 kr. Tickets for the theatre, concerts and sporting events can be bought locally, in the cities at special ticket offices, or at the gambling service ATG's outlets via **BiljettDirekt**, www.ticnet.se.

DISABLED VISITORS

IN SWEDEN, public areas have to be accessible for physically or visually disabled people, as well as those suffering from allergies. Sweden is a long away ahead of many other countries in this respect. Wheelchair ramps and spacious toilets for disabled people are fitted in all new buildings.

Disabled car drivers with a disability permit from their home country can park in special areas.

In Stockholm, the Tunnelbana underground network and local trains are adapted for disabled passengers. Buses "kneel" at bus stops to give a reasonable height for passengers to get on or off. Visitors from abroad can

The GöteborgPass, giving free admission to museums

obtain information in English before their stay from **De Handikappades Riksförbund** by telephone or via the Internet. Brochures with information about facilities for disabled visitors at theatres, cinemas, museums and libraries are available from tourist information offices.

ETIQUETTE

BANS ON SMOKING are increasingly common throughout Sweden. Smoking is generally not permitted in public places, including all local transport and queues at bus stops and railway stations. Restaurants are obliged to provide no-smoking areas.

The Swedes queue patiently, but guard their place jealously. They are usually friendly and pleased to help foreign tourists. The use of first names is the norm and a friendly *"Hej!"* is the common greeting.

Casual clothing is acceptable almost everywhere, including restaurants, particularly in the summer.

Service is always included in restaurant prices, but it is usual to round up the bill by up to 10 per cent for good service.

The logo of Systembolaget, the state-owned liquor store

ALCOHOL

SWEDISH POLICY towards alcohol is restrictive. Wines and spirits can be bought only in the relatively few shops of the state monopoly **Systembolaget**. They are open Monday–Friday 10am–6pm, and Saturday 10am– 2pm. The minimum age for buying alcohol in these shops is 20, and young people may be asked to produce proof of their age. In restaurants, the minimum age for buying alcohol is 18. Most restaurants and pubs stop selling alcohol at 1am, but some bars stay

open till 5am. With a maximum permitted blood alcohol level of only 0.2 per mil, drinking is effectively banned for car drivers.

The Swedish custom of *"skåling"* confounds many visitors. To *"skål"*, look the person in the eye, raise your glass, drink, then repeat the eye contact before putting down your glass. If the glasses are full of schnapps, then Swedes like to sing their special schnapps songs.

Personal Security and Health

Police symbol

Sweden is a safe destination compared with most countries in the world. You needn't worry about natural disasters such as earthquakes or hurricanes. Crime does occur, with some cities suffering more than others, but this is rarely a concern for tourists. However, it is important to lock the car and hide valuables when parked. Look out for pickpockets in the summer and avoid the empty, commercial parts of city centres late at night. Sweden has a well-developed network of emergency services which travellers can call on. Rescue services and hospital emergency clinics are highly efficient.

Policeman   **Guard**

Police car

Protecting Property

Although Sweden is a comparatively safe place, tourists can still run into trouble at times. Especially in the summer months, the many popular events attract bag-snatchers and pickpockets. In the cities and in crowded public areas visitors should be particularly careful to keep an eye on their property, especially handbags and cameras. Avoid using unmanned cloakrooms at restaurants and museums.

Valuables and personal documents should always be locked in the hotel safe. It is equally important not to leave any valuables in your car; ideally, choose a hotel with its own parking facilities.

There is no need to carry large amounts of cash. All major credit and debit cards are accepted in virtually all shops and restaurants, and cash machines are common, at least in larger places. When taking out cash, watch out for conmen who may offer to help, but are actually after your money or card.

Personal Safety

The Swedish police are generally extremely helpful and speak good English. Police patrolling on foot or in cars are a routine sight in the cities, and mounted police are often in evidence at special events. In the suburbs, however, police can be thin on the ground. Out in the country, the police presence is low. Not all towns

Mounted police

have evening and night police patrols and even fewer have open police stations.

In many places, uniformed security guards have taken over the function of the police. They are a common feature in department stores, at train and Tunnelbana stations and as car patrols.

Stockholm, Gothenburg and Malmö are safe to stroll around on foot. Stockholm's Tunnelbana (underground railway) is efficient and comfortable, as well as being safe at most times. CCTV security systems are installed at some stations, squares, department stores and shops.

Beware the strict rules regarding alcohol, drugs and some medications when driving. A driver is guilty of drunk driving with a blood alcohol level of only 0.2 per mil and gross drunk driving (from 1.0 per mil) is punishable by imprisonment. The possession of drugs is illegal.

Breaking traffic rules, particularly speed limits, may lead to hefty fines.

For some years it has been illegal to buy sexual services in Sweden so it is the buyer, not the prostitute, who is prosecuted. Street prostitutes are now a very rare sight in the inner cities.

Lost Property

Lost or stolen property should be reported to the nearest police station. A police report will be needed for any insurance claim. In addition to the police lost property offices (Polisens

Hittegodsexpedition), large towns and cities have lost property offices (Hittegodsavdelning) at railway stations, bus stations and airports. They are often only open during the day and not all of them will give information over the phone. There is usually a good chance of recovering lost goods.

Visitors from abroad should contact their embassy or consulate if they lose their passport.

EMERGENCIES

The emergency telephone number for police, fire or ambulance is **112**. It can be dialled free of charge from all public telephones, but should be used only in emergencies.

HEALTHCARE

No special vaccinations are needed to visit Sweden. Medical assistance is available across the country from doctors and district nurses at the local medical centre open surgeries.

There are duty clinics in the evenings and at weekends, but you must make an appointment by phone. Many hospitals have accident and emergency departments, some of which are privately run. Patients should not report to emergency clinics with minor ailments. First, contact the healthcare information service **Sjukvårdsrådgivningen** for instructions in English. Its staff have up-to-date knowledge about the current situation in the city's hospitals and can assign patients to a suitable hospital or duty doctor. Particularly during the holiday period, it is always advisable to use this central information service, to avoid

unnecessarily long waiting times. For severe toothache, patients can usually receive the help of a local dentist and larger places have special duty dentists.

Citizens of other EU and EEA countries are entitled to emergency medical care at the same low rate as Swedes if they produce form E111 and a valid passport or other form of identification. More extensive treatment costs extra so it is advisable to take out separate medical insurance covering specialist care, hospital expenses and repatriation before travelling.

MEDICINES

In Sweden, medicines are only sold at pharmacies. Medicines for minor ailments are available without a prescription, but many medicines which are available over the counter abroad require a prescription in Sweden. There is also a risk that the medication prescribed at home may not be approved in Sweden. It is best to ensure that you pack sufficient medication for the duration of your trip.

Pharmacy staff are well trained and can give good advice. Unfortunately, pharmacies can be hard to find in the countryside and they are not open on Sundays. A limited number of natural remedies are also sold in health food stores.

Pharmacy sign

OUT AND ABOUT

Sweden has a varied landscape and climate and it is important to respect the forces of nature. In the mountains, the weather can change very quickly from still and sunny one moment to fog

or a storm the next. If you have the right equipment and follow the rules, a trip in the mountains need not be dangerous. The STF mountain stations offer good advice about safe trails.

Along the coast drowning accidents claim many lives every year. Avoid going out in flimsy craft and boats which are beyond your capabilities. Take advice from local people about the weather.

There is no need to worry about the forest predators – bears, wolves, lynxes and wolverines. They are shy creatures and prefer to avoid people. The same applies to Sweden's only poisonous snake, the adder. However, anyone bitten by a snake should seek medical advice.

Mosquitoes can be a nuisance from June to autumn, especially at dusk, along waterways and in the mountains. Pharmacies stock mosquito repellent. In the archipelagos, there is also a risk of being bitten by ticks, which carry a number of diseases. Ticks should be removed from the skin with tweezers as quickly as possible. If the redness around the bite area persists, consult a doctor.

Ambulance

Banking and Local Currency

SWEDEN HAS RETAINED its own currency, the Swedish krona, rather than adopting the euro. A number of shops in major tourist areas will accept euros, but goods are almost exclusively priced in kronor. Visitors can change currency in banks, but better rates of exchange can often be obtained at bureaux de change in the main towns, which have longer opening hours. Automatic cash machines can be found outside most banks and in shopping centres across the country. Credit and debit cards are accepted virtually everywhere, and the larger stores will take traveller's cheques.

Bankomat, the joint cash-machine system of the business banks

BANKS

THERE ARE plenty of banks in the towns, all providing a good service. Their opening times vary, but the normal hours are 9.30am–3pm. Some banks stay open until 6pm at least once a week. All banks are closed at weekends and on public holidays, as well as the day before a public holiday.

Svenska Kassaservice, which handles the Swedish post office Posten's cash transactions, has almost 1,000 offices around the country. They are agents for certain banks and accept withdrawals on a debit card.

There are nearly 3,000 automatic cash machines throughout the country. They come in two types: Bankomat machines are the joint system of the business banks, while Uttag machines belong to FöreningsSparbanken. Foreign visitors can use all cash machines provided that they have a bank card with a PIN code that is linked to, for example, Visa or MasterCard. Machines usually have instructions in several languages. The charge for withdrawing cash varies according to the type of card.

CURRENCY EXCHANGE

VARIOUS BUREAUX de change chains are represented in Sweden. Generally they provide a better exchange rate than the banks, and in city centres there is always a bureau de change office close by. Changing money in your hotel is the most expensive option. It is worth checking exchange rates and commission charges, because the differences can be significant. Currency can be changed at international airports from 5.30am, and from 7am at city train stations seven days a week.

The head office of Handelsbanken on Kungsträdgårdsgatan, Stockholm

Forex bureau de change, situated in large towns and at airports

CREDIT CARDS

ALL THE WELL-KNOWN credit cards, such as **Visa**, **Diners Club**, **Eurocard** and **MasterCard**, are accepted across Sweden, but not all places accept American Express because of opposition to the relatively high charges which the retailer has to pay.

Cards can be used not just at larger hotels and restaurants, but at nearly all shops and services. If you pay by credit card, most shops will ask you to produce proof of identity. Some shops also offer a cash withdrawal service for small amounts in conjunction with purchases.

Cash machines can be used to make withdrawals using an internationally accepted credit card with a PIN code.

TRAVELLER'S CHEQUES

TRAVELLER'S CHEQUES are one of the safest ways of carrying large amounts of money. They are not accepted in all shops, but can be changed at banks. It is sensible to keep a receipt showing the serial numbers of the cheques in a separate place. When buying cheques in your home country, it is worth checking the procedure if you lose any of your cheques.

CURRENCY

SWEDEN'S CURRENCY is the krona (plural kronor). The krona (abbreviated as SEK or Kr) is divided into 100 öre. The smallest coin is 50 öre and the largest note is 1,000 kronor, which is not used much. If possible, it is advisable not to carry notes of more than 500 Kr.

Although Sweden has not adopted the euro, many shops in tourist areas and border towns will accept payment in euros, but will usually give change in kronor.

20 Kr (Selma Lagerlöf)

Notes
Swedish currency notes are issued in denominations of 20, 50, 100, 500 and 1,000 kronor. They depict famous Swedes, including monarchs, scientists and authors.

50 Kr (Jenny Lind)

100 Kr (Carl von Linné)

500 Kr (King Karl XI)

1000 Kr (King Gustav Vasa)

Coins
Coins are issued in values of 50 öre, and 1, 5 and 10 kronor. The 1 Kr and 10 Kr coins depict Sweden's monarch on the obverse side while the 5 Kr has his monogram on the reverse side. The 50 öre piece incorporates the state "three crowns" symbol.

50 öre   1 krona   5 kronor   10 kronor

Telecommunications, Post and Media

Sweden has a first-class public telephone system. A top-ranking telecommunications industry and high living standards have placed the Swedes among the world's biggest users of telephones. Although the fixed telephone system is well developed, there are now nearly as many mobile phone users as there are people in the country. With the advent of the 3G system allowing video telephony and advanced data services, the aim is for 99 per cent of the population to have coverage by the end of 2004. Internet use is widespread, with impressive investment in broadband.

A modern Swedish phone kiosk

Making a Phone Call

Sweden is divided into 250 dialling code areas. The prefix for international calls from Sweden is 00. Then dial the country code and the phone number without the initial zero of the area code. To dial Sweden from abroad, the country code is 46. For enquiries such as whether your phone will operate in the mountains, call Telia's customer services on 0046 771 99 02 00. For directory enquiries in Sweden, call 118 118. This also provides listings of mobile numbers.

The number of public telephone kiosks has shown a marked decline, as most Swedes have a mobile phone. The remaining public phones are mainly card-operated. They are owned by Telia and are cheapest to use with a Swedish phonecard. These can be bought at newspaper kiosks and in shops, and are available for 50 or 120 units. For a local call, the minimum charge is four units to a landline, with higher charges for calls to mobile phones and international calls. Some credit cards, petrol cards and international phonecards such as Access can be used, but at a higher rate. Instructions on how to use public telephones are also shown in English. It is possible to make reverse-charge (collect) calls within Sweden from all public phones by dialling 2#. The emergency number is 112. Some 020 and 0200 numbers can be called free of charge.

Coin-operated phones are very rare. Should you find one, they also have instructions in English and accept 1 Kr, 5 Kr and 10 Kr coins.

Mobile Phones

The Nordic countries have long had the analogue NMT network, which was known for its good coverage. Now the digital GSM network has taken over, offering a broader range of mobile services, and good coverage outside the cities.

Next-generation mobile telephony, 3G, was introduced in 2003 and offers even more advanced services. Coverage has so far been poor in many places, but plans are in place to rectify this. Having a mobile phone is a good idea even out in the wilderness, but there is no guarantee that you will be able to call for help when you need it.

In most cases, European visitors can use their GSM and 3G phones in Sweden.

Using a Card Telephone

1 Select instructions in the language of your choice.

2 Lift the receiver.

3 Insert the card and wait for the dialling tone.

4 Dial the number and wait to be connected. If your phonecard credit is running out, you will hear a signal. Press the cardswitch button and insert a new card to continue the call.

5 Remove the card. If you forget, you will hear a signal.

Telephone cards
for 50 units.

Fax, E-Mail, Internet

The majority of hotels, airports, train stations and large shopping centres offer fax, telegram, e-mail and Internet services. There are

Internet cafés dotted around the country. Hotels which focus on business travellers may have computers available for use in your room.

Swedish postage stamps

Post

THE SWEDISH POSTAL service has an almost 400-year history, but many Swedes think the service has deteriorated in recent years. Post offices have been closed and replaced by a few large postal centres, mainly for companies. For the general public, there are small service points, primarily in supermarkets and at petrol stations. They have the advantage of longer opening hours in the evenings and at weekends. The disadvantage is a frequent lack of space and services. Cash transactions have also been split off into a special company with its own offices, Svensk Kassaservice *(see p324)*. Perhaps the best service is provided in the really remote areas by mobile postal workers. Stamps can be

Yellow postbox for national and international, blue for local mail

bought at post offices, Pressbyrån kiosks and tourist information offices. The basic postage for a postcard or letter under 20 g within Sweden is 5 Kr (non-denominated stamp) or 5.50 Kr (denominated stamp); for abroad the postage is 10 Kr. Postboxes are painted blue for local letters and yellow for other domestic and international mail. Collection times are shown on the postbox and sometimes take place in the early afternoon. In large towns there are last-minute postboxes, which are emptied in the evenings.

Most international courier services are represented in the cities and special services are also operated by the Swedish post office, Posten.

TV and Radio

MOST HOTELS provide a television in the room with both national and foreign channels. The most frequently used are the Swedish SVT1, SVT2, TV3, TV4 and Channel 5, as well as the international CNN, Sky News, BBC and Eurosport channels. SVT1 and 2 are state-run public-service channels. SVT2 and TV4 broadcast local programmes in the morning and evening, including weather forecasts.

There are also a number of local radio stations, broadcasting mainly international and Swedish music. P6, Stockholm International, has English and German-language programmes on 89.6 MHz.

Post office logo

Newspapers and Magazines

MAJOR FOREIGN newspapers and magazines can be bought in the cities, at airports and at other transport hubs. Pressbyrån kiosks, tobacconists, department stores

One of the country's many Pressbyrån kiosks

and some tourist information offices stock a limited selection of foreign publications. See the directory below for a range of newsagents.

DIRECTORY

TELECOMMUNICATIONS

Telia customer services
📞 020-41 10 10. 🌐 www.telia.se

Directory Enquiries
📞 118 118 (Sweden).
📞 118 119 (International).

POST OFFICE

Postens customer service
📞 020-23 22 20.
🌐 www.posten.se

COURIER SERVICES

DHL
📞 020-345 345.
🌐 www.dhl.se

Federal Express
📞 0200-252 252.
🌐 www.fedex.com/se

TNT
📞 020-960 960.
🌐 www.tnt.com/se

FOREIGN NEWSPAPERS

Press Stop Gothenburg
Drottninggatan 58.
📞 031-15 84 45.

Press Stop Malmö
Södergatan 20. 📞 040-12 52 02.

Press Center, Stockholm
Gallerian, Hamngatan 37.
Map 2 D4. 📞 08-723 01 91.

Press Specialisten, Stockholm
Sveavägen 52. **Map** 1 C3.
📞 08-21 91 13.

TRAVEL INFORMATION

Stockholm Arlanda is the busiest of Sweden's international airports, although a number of other airports have international flights, notably Gothenburg's Landvetter and Sturup, near Malmö, in the south. Since summer 2000, Sweden has been linked with Continental Europe by a bridge over the Öresund Strait to Denmark for road and rail traffic. It is now possible to fly to

Aircraft of Scandinavian Airlines (SAS)

Copenhagen and take a short train journey across the bridge to Malmö. There are still a number of car ferry services operating between Denmark and Sweden, as well as across the Baltic Sea from Finland and the Baltic States, and across the North Sea from Norway and Great Britain. In summer, an increasing number of cruise liners call into Swedish ports. Express buses operate services from cities across Europe.

ARRIVAL BY AIR

Most major European cities have direct flights to one of Stockholm's three airports: Arlanda, Skavsta and Bromma. Landvetter near Gothenburg and Sturup outside Malmö also have international traffic. Arlanda is served by around 60 international airlines. It is also possible to fly via Copenhagen in Denmark. The leading Scandinavian airline **SAS** dominates. Other operators include **Lufthansa**, **British Airways** and **Finnair**. **Delta Air Lines** operates from the US to Paris with onward flights to Stockholm via Air France; **American Airlines** flies to the UK with onward connections via British Airways or Finnair.

Arlanda is 40 km (25 miles) north of central Stockholm and is also a hub for Swedish domestic flights and charter services. Bromma, close to the centre, may only be used by environmentally friendly aircraft. Skavsta lies 100 km

Arlanda Express linking Arlanda Airport with central Stockholm

(60 miles) south of Stockholm, near Nyköping. Low-cost airline **Ryanair** flies to Skavsta and Gothenburg, from London Stansted and Glasgow, and also serves Malmö from Stansted and Skavsta from Glasgow.

GETTING FROM AND TO THE AIRPORT

All the international airports are served by airport buses to the city centre in conjunction with

arrivals and departure times. Stockholm's Arlanda Airport has a "Flygbussarna" bus service, which operates every five minutes at peak times. Journey time is 45 minutes to the City Terminal at Central Station. An onward journey by taxi can be booked on the bus. The taxi ride into town from the airport is quicker, but more expensive. Most taxi firms have a fixed charge to the city centre. Avoid unauthorized taxis and check the fare before departure. The shortest journey time is by the pricier Arlanda Express train, a 20-minute trip to Central Station. Trains depart every 15 min from the two stations, Arlanda South (serving terminals 2, 3 and 4) and Arlanda North (for terminal 5).

AIR FARES

Fare options are many and varied, particularly if you are flexible about departure and arrival dates, or can book well in advance.

Increased competition between the airlines has made it considerably cheaper to fly to Sweden from many European destinations, and now SAS offers low-cost tickets with a no-frills service to meet the competition. It is possible to find return flights from London, Paris or Frankfurt for less than £80. Tour operators often have packages with attractive air fares and accommodation included. Newspaper advertisements and travel companies' websites have details of last-minute deals.

Terminal 5 (International) at Stockholm's Arlanda Airport

Ferry from Finland on the way to its terminal in Stockholm

ARRIVAL BY FERRY

A NUMBER OF FERRY companies operate direct services across the North Sea and the Baltic to Sweden. The large car ferries used on most routes offer plenty of passenger comforts, good food, entertainment and shopping.

From Newcastle in the UK, **DFDS** sails to Gothenburg via Kristiansand in Norway.

Although the new Öresund Bridge has reduced ferry traffic from Denmark, the short Helsingør–Helsingborg hop still has several ferries an hour operated by **Scandlines** and **HH-Ferries**. **Stena Line** has the routes Grenå–Varberg and Fredrikshavn–Gothenburg.

The busiest route in terms of passenger numbers is from Finland with regular crossings from Helsinki, Turku and Mariehamn to Stockholm and Kapellskär. Both **Viking Line** and **Silja Line** have terminals in Stockholm at Stadsgården and Värtahamnen respectively. The crossing takes about 15.5 hours from Helsinki and 11 hours from Turku. Silja also operates ferries between Vaasa in Finland and Umeå in northern Sweden. From Estonia, **Tallink** operates the

routes Tallinn– Stockholm and Paldiski– Kapellskär. **Riga Sea Line** operates between Riga in Latvia and Stockholm.

Polferries has the routes Świnoujście–Ystad and Gdansk–Nynäshamn. **Stena Line** operates the Gdynia–Karlskrona route.

Trelleborg is the major port for traffic from Germany. **TT-Line** goes from Rostock and Travemünde, **Scandlines** from Rostock and Sassnitz. **Stena Line** sails the Kiel–Gothenburg route.

ARRIVAL BY TRAIN OR EXPRESS BUS

T HERE ARE EXCELLENT train links from Continental Europe and Norway and a large network of express bus routes. **Tågplusguiden/ Expressbussguiden** is a good online search service providing an overview of train and long distance bus services.

ARRIVAL BY CAR

M OTORISTS ARRIVING from Denmark can use the spectacular Öresund Bridge between Copenhagen and Malmö *(see p181)*. On the Swedish side, the toll bridge connects with the E4 motorway to Stockholm and the north. Alternatively, there are car ferries.

Car ferries are also the most practical option from Finland and the Baltic States, as driving around the Baltic Sea can take two days.

The borders with Finland and Norway have customs posts which are often unmanned. However, the entry regulations still apply *(see p320)*.

Arrival hall at the Central Station in Stockholm

DIRECTORY

AIRLINES

American Airlines
☎ 800-433 7300.
W www.americanair.com

British Airways
☎ 0200-77 00 98.
W www.britishairways.com

Delta Air Lines
☎ 800-241 4141.
W www.delta.com

Finnair
☎ 020-78 11 00.
W www.finnair.nu

Lufthansa
☎ 0770-727 727.
W www.lufthansa.se

Ryanair
☎ 0900-200 40 40.
W www.ryanair.com

SAS
☎ 0770-727 727.
W www.scandinavian.net

FERRY COMPANIES

DFDS
☎ 020-650 650.
W www.dfdsseaways.se

HH-Ferries
☎ 042-19 80 00.

Polferries
☎ 040-12 17 00.
W www.polferries.se

Riga Sea Line
☎ 08-510 01 500.

Scandlines
☎ 042-18 61 00.
W www.scandlines.se

Silja Line
☎ 08-22 21 40.

Stena Line
☎ 031-704 00 00.
W www.stenaline.se

Tallink
☎ 08-666 60 01.

TT-Line
☎ 0410-562 00.
W www.balticships.co.uk

Viking Line
☎ 08-452 40 00.
W www.vikingline.se

TRAIN, EXPRESS BUS

Tågplusguiden/ Expressbussguiden
W www.resplus.se

Getting Around Sweden

Flying within sweden has its advantages considering the enormous distances between places, and in many cases the fares are reasonably priced. The high standard of overnight sleeper trains makes long journeys by train a comfortable option. The X2000 Express train running between the major cities often competes well in terms of time and comfort with domestic flights. Elsewhere in the country, buses provide much of the public transport. Travelling by boat offers exciting opportunities to discover Sweden's magnificent archipelagos and waterways.

Skyways, one of many companies offering domestic flights in Sweden

DOMESTIC FLIGHTS

The vast length of Sweden makes domestic flights a convenient option, and deregulation and increased competition in recent years have made prices more reasonable. Of the 47 airports offering scheduled flights, the 19 largest are state-run by **Luftfartsverket**. Its website contains information about the airports, flights and current arrivals and departures.

Stockholm/Arlanda dominates the domestic flight scene, but several companies have chosen to fly from the capital's more centrally located Bromma Airport. Landvetter, outside Gothenburg, and Sturup, outside Malmö, are other major airports.

Flight times are generally short: Stockholm–Gothenburg takes 55 minutes. The longest direct flight, Stockholm–Kiruna, takes 1 hr 50 mins.

SAS is still the leading airline in terms of passenger numbers, but with its 27 destinations, **Skyways** reaches most parts of the country. Other operators include **Malmö Aviation** and **Nordic Airlink**. Tickets can be bought at travel agents or directly from the airlines. Tickets booked online can generally be paid for with a credit card and collected at the airport. It is worth searching for the lowest prices, particularly if you book a long way in advance. Young people under 26 can buy cheap standby tickets.

Travellers to Malmö could consider flying to Kastrup in Copenhagen, as there is a fast train transfer to central Malmö across the Öresund Bridge.

Larger airports are served by airport buses, which operate in conjunction with arrivals and departures.

TRAVELLING BY TRAIN

There is a well-developed train network covering parts of Sweden from the Öresund Bridge in the south to Riksgränsen in the north. Stations and services are good by international standards. The trains are run by a number of competing companies. The state-run **SJ** operates most long-distance routes. Other major players include **Connex** and **Tågcompaniet**, which have parts of the lines in Norrland. At county level, train services are run by local train companies in partnership with bus services and in some cases ferry services.

Travel involving different companies and forms of transport is administered by **Samtrafiken**, which is part-owned by each of the transport companies. SJ offers a booking service for Tågplus tickets for English-speaking travellers.

In recent years, airlines have experienced tough competition from the X2000 Express train which links the cities of Copenhagen/ Malmö, Gothenburg, Härnösand and Mora to Stockholm. The journey time is around 5 hours from Malmö and 3 hours from Gothenburg. The trains offer a business class service similar to that of airlines.

SJ logo

InterCity is the main long-distance alternative to the X2000, offering first- and second-class seats. The overnight sleeper trains are recommended for longer journeys such as Gothenburg–Östersund and Connex routes in northern Norrland. The standard is high and you can often have your own compartment with shower, if you wish. Normal compartments contain three berths, but there are also six-berth compartments. Ticket prices vary

Malmbanan line from Kiruna to Narvik in northernmost Norrland

considerably depending on the type of train. Discounts are worth searching for.

Tickets can be bought via ATG's outlets around the country and at larger stations. Buying tickets on the train attracts a fee of around 30 kr. Note that seat/berth reservations are necessary for the X2000 and night trains.

The **Inlandsbanan** line operates in summer, offering the opportunity to travel through the Swedish wilderness, forests and mountains. It runs 1,300 km (800 miles) from Kristinehamn on Lake Vänern north to Gällivare in northern Lapland.

TRAVELLING BY BUS

I N MANY PLACES buses are the only public transport available and although services are patchy in rural areas, it is possible to get about. Local timetables are on **Samtrafiken**'s website.

Express buses compete with trains and airlines on longer routes. Journey times are longer, but ticket prices are lower and the buses are modern. See Samtrafiken's Expressbussguiden for routes and times. Some bus companies, such as **Swebus Express**, do not require pre-booking. If one bus is full, another one is laid on.

Many express bus companies arrange special excursions in the tourist season. Contact the tourist information offices for information. Trips are also arranged to the southern Fjällen where there is no train line. **Fjällexpressen** is one of the operators running ski buses from Stockholm and Gothenburg.

Abisko's modest station building on the Malmbanan line

TRAVELLING BY BOAT

S WEDEN'S LONG coastline, vast lakes and extensive archipelagos make for busy boat services. In addition to the scheduled services, sightseeing trips and tours are offered in summer, occasionally on classic old steamers.

The Dalsland, Strömsholm and Kinda canals attract some charming boats, but the tourist trail to beat them all is the Göta canal (see pp146–7). Sweden's blue ribbon takes you 611 km (380 miles) in a relaxed three days, negotiating 65 locks, the country's three largest lakes and some of Sweden's most attractive scenery.

Boat services to the Baltic Sea's largest island, Gotland, are run by **Destination Gotland**, with its modern high-speed ferries, which take less than three hours on either of the Nynäshamn–Visby or Oskarshamn–Visby routes. In peak summer season, there are up to eight departures a day. Although the ferries can take 500 cars per trip, it can be difficult to get a place for a car during public holidays and other holiday periods if you have not booked in advance.

Gotland's high-speed catamaran service approaching Visby

Road Travel in Sweden

DᴵˢᵀᴬNCES WITHIN SWEDEN are huge, and in the rural areas travelling in your own or a rented car is often the only way of getting about. The well-developed road network varies in quality, but the major roads are generally of a good standard. State-run ferries operate a free service in the archipelagos. Although traffic can be heavy in the cities in rush hour, it is never on the same scale as in the UK and on the Continent, and Swedish motorists are generally good-natured. For advice on driving in Stockholm, *see page 334.*

Elk on the road, a hazard for motorists in the forests

ROAD STANDARDS

SᴡᴇᴅᴇN HAS an extensive road network, with more than 210,000 km (130,000 miles) open for public use. Almost the same again is not accessible, primarily forestry roads which are closed with a boom. The majority of the public roads are sealed and of a good standard. The exceptions can be found in the forested counties of the northwest, where ice and heavy traffic can make the roads difficult to negotiate.

The national road network comprises *europavägar* ("European motorways"), *riksvägar* (national roads) and *länsvägar* (county roads). Motorways such as the E4 and stretches of the E20 and E6 make up less than 1,200 km (700 miles). With the exception of the Öresund Bridge, roads are toll-free.

The three-lane highways require some attention for the uninitiated. The traffic runs in opposite directions along one or two lanes with a wire barrier to separate the flow.

TRAFFIC RULES

GᴇNERALLY, SWEDISH traffic is comparatively well organized and the majority of motorists follow the rules of the road. Road safety is good, despite occasionally dense traffic and severe weather conditions. The number of road fatalities is less than 500 a year, the same level as in the 1940s.

The most common breach of the rules relates to speed limits, despite the presence of speed cameras and radar patrols. The fines are high and there is a risk of losing your licence for serious speeding offences.

The maximum permitted speed on motorways is 110 km/h (68 mph), but the limit is more often 90 km/h (55 mph). On country roads the limit is usually 70 km/h (43 mph) and in built-up areas the limit is 50 km/h (31 mph). The limit is reduced to 30 km/h (19 mph) around all schools and nurseries. Residential areas often have traffic calming measures such

as road narrowing and speed bumps. By law, the driver and all passengers must wear seatbelts. Children up to the age of six must use child seats.

Beware of the strict rules regarding alcohol and driving. A driver is guilty of drink-driving with a blood alcohol level of only 0.2 per mil and gross drink-driving (from 1.0 per mil) is punishable by imprisonment.

Motorists must give way to pedestrians at crossings not controlled by lights. Vehicles must stop at junctions onto major roads, even if there is no Stop sign. At roundabouts, vehicles already on the roundabout always have right of way. Traffic lights with a continuous amber light mean "stop" and there are hefty fines for driving through a red light. Side-lights or dipped headlights must be used even during daylight hours.

Winter tyres must be used from 1 Dec–31 Mar. Studded tyres may be used, but not during the period 1 May–30 Sep, unless the road conditions require them.

CAR FERRIES

Sᴛᴀᴛᴇ-RUN CAR ferries operate free of charge in the archipelagos and across some of the larger rivers. Some places also have private ferries, which do levy a charge. You rarely need to book, but check the timetable carefully as the ferries may not run late at night unless in emergencies. **Vägverket** can provide information.

Sunnerstabron on the E6, one of Sweden's many road bridges

ROAD SIGNS

SWEDISH ROAD SIGNS mostly follow the European standard, but the country also has some signs of its own. Signs carrying the symbol for elk, reindeer or deer warn drivers that there is a major risk of colliding with wildlife. Thousands of accidents involving animals occur every year and a collision between a car and a full-grown elk is often fatal. The risk is particularly high in the summer around 5am–8am and 10pm–2am, when visibility is poor. Fences along the roadside are no guarantee that animals won't suddenly appear on the road.

Warning sign for elk

As in the rest of Europe, brown signs with white symbols indicate recommended tourist routes, heritage sites, tourist areas and attractions along the road such as a national park or a historic building.

Individual attractions may be indicated by a sign with a white "pretzel" on a blue background.

PARKING

THERE IS USUALLY a charge for parking in towns and built-up areas, especially in the centre of towns and cities. City car parks and on-street parking are often expensive. Sometimes charges apply 24-hours a day and at weekends, too. Many ticket machines accept credit cards and petrol cards, but they may not always work, so it is best to keep a good number of 10 Kr coins to hand.

Diligent traffic wardens hunt out illegally parked cars and the fines can be high, particularly if you have parked illegally in a space reserved for disabled drivers.

Where parking is free during the night, there is sometimes a parking ban on certain days for cleaning, so it is always important to check the signs – otherwise your

car may be towed away. Supermarkets and other large stores often have free parking for a few hours, but be aware that sometimes they require a special parking ticket for your windscreen showing your arrival time.

FUEL AND SERVICES

THERE ARE PLENTY of service stations along the major roads and in built-up areas, but they may be few and far between in rural areas. Although some stations are manned 24-hours a day, drivers are often directed to automatic pumps which take cards and notes. It is sensible to fill up before a night drive.

In the event of technical problems, there are few places which can help outside working hours – garages are usually closed in the evenings and at weekends.

Assistancekåren and **Falck** offer emergency roadside assistance. They often have an agreement with motoring organizations and insurance companies abroad.

RENTING A CAR

IN ADDITION TO the familiar international car hire chains, there are a number of local options, including the petrol companies' extensive rental service. Most places will have some form of car rental.

It is possible to pre-book cars at airports and major train stations, often for one-way rental where you leave the car at your destination.

Bookings can be made from abroad via the Internet or by phone. You generally only need a valid driving licence to rent a car, but there may be an age limit of 20, or even 25 for exclusive vehicles. Prices vary considerably, so it is worth shopping around. Special weekend deals are common and considering Sweden's long distances, it is best to opt for offers which include unlimited mileage.

Traffic warden

DIRECTORY

TRAFFIC INFORMATION

Vägverket
@ vagverket@vv.se

CAR RENTAL

Avis
C 08-78 82 00.
W www.avis.com
@ reservation-office@avis.se

Europcar
C 020-78 11 80.
W www.europcar.com

Hertz
C 020-211 211.
W www.hertz.com

OKQ8
C 020-850 850.
@ kundservice@okq8.se

Statoil
C 020-25 25 25.

CAR FERRIES

Vägverket, Färjerederiet
C 08-544 415 00.
@ vagverket.farj@vv.se

VEHICLE RECOVERY

Assistancekåren
C 020-912 912.

Falck
C 020-38 38 38.

ROAD MAPS

Stanfords, London
C 020-7836 1321.
W www.stanfords.co.uk

WINTER DRIVING

ROAD CONDITIONS in the winter vary depending on the severity of the weather and the location. Studded tyres are permitted in Sweden and their use is recommended, at least from central Sweden northwards.

Anyone not used to winter driving should not venture out if there is a risk of snow and ice. The major roads are treated with salt, and ploughing is generally good, but even in Skåne in the far south, snow storms can cause traffic chaos and in some years military tracked vehicles have had to be called out.

Getting Around Stockholm

Pedestrians and bicycles

S TOCKHOLM IS A PERFECT CITY for pedestrians. Distances between sights are short, and there is always something interesting to discover among the eye-catching vistas and waterfront scenes. Cycling is popular and there are many cycle lanes throughout the city, although for the visitor a green area such as Djurgården might be more relaxing for a cycle trip. Public transport on buses, trams, underground trains, local trains and ferries is efficient. Apart from Gamla Stan, and during the rush hours, driving a car in Stockholm is relatively easy, although parking can be difficult.

Taking a waterfront stroll along Djurgårdsbrunnsviken

STOCKHOLM ON FOOT

I N CENTRAL Stockholm, walking is the best way to see the sights and get a feel for the place. Road users are more disciplined here than in many other cities. Pedestrians are not allowed to cross a road against a red light, but motorists must stop and give way to pedestrians at zebra crossings without traffic lights.

The clear street signs make it easy to find one's way around, and Stockholmers are always glad to help visitors. There are walking and cycling routes everywhere in the city. Take care not to step out in the cycle lane, which is often marked just with a white line to separate it from the walking lane.

Gamla Stan is a popular area for exploring on foot, and there is always something to see around Kungsträdgården as well. In good weather, nothing beats Djurgården, with its host of attractions set in beautiful parkland only a short distance from the centre.

There are pleasant waterfront walks along the quays, for example from Stadshuset along Norr Mälarstrand and the Riddarfjärden bay.

Walks with multilingual guides are organized regularly, often with a special theme – history, architecture or parks, for example.

CYCLING

T HE CAPITAL'S network of cycle paths is increasing all the time, but you need to be an experienced city cyclist if you want to explore the central area from the saddle. Otherwise Stockholm and its surrounding area are tailor-

made for cycling. There are plenty of places to hire bicycles and mopeds.

DRIVING IN STOCKHOLM

A NYONE FAMILIAR with driving in large cities will have no problems in Stockholm. It is relatively easy to get about by car, except during the rush hours (7.30am–9.30am, 11.30am–1pm, and 3.30–6pm). Cars are not really necessary in the city centre because of the short distances between sights and excellent public transport. However, a car is an advantage if you want to explore further afield.

Congestion charges are being introduced on a trial basis during weekdays at the approaches to the city centre.

The speed limit is usually 50 km/h (31 mph), but near schools it is 30 km/h

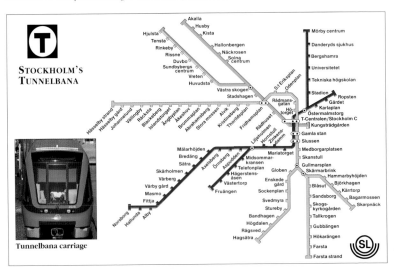

Tunnelbana carriage

(19 mph). Speeds up to 70 km/h (43 mph) are permitted only on the main roads in and out of the city.

It is often hard to find a parking space. In some areas parking charges apply 24-hours a day, but usually parking is free in the evenings, at night and at weekends. Check for street cleaning times when parking is prohibited.

The city's traffic wardens are diligent. Being wrongly parked could cost you a fine of 450 kr or more. Do not leave valuables in your car, particularly in a car park.

TAXIS

Distances between places in the city centre are short and brief journeys by taxi rarely cost more than 100 Kr. There are usually plenty of taxis available, particularly at taxi ranks and major sights, with the exception of the rush hours. You can also hail an empty taxi, indicated by the illuminated sign on the car roof. The best method is to order a taxi by phone or book one in advance. It is always worth enquiring what the fare is likely to be, as many companies charge a fixed rate. Be careful about using unauthorized taxis without a taxi sign on the outside, or a taxi identity card on display inside, especially at night.

PUBLIC TRANSPORT

All public transport in the county of Stockholm is under the control of **Stockholms Lokaltrafik**, but the actual services are run by several companies. An extensive network of local trains, underground trains, buses and ferries carries hundreds of thousands of commuters in from the

suburbs every day. In the city centre, the Tunnelbana (T-bana) underground system's green, red and blue lines are the mainstay, supplemented by city buses, a few tramlines and ferry routes.

The Stockholm area is divided into five zones, one of which is the city centre. There is a choice of tickets – single trip, one-day, three-day, one-month. It is worth buying a book of 10 or 20 discount coupons if you are planning several trips. Each zone costs 30 kr, but the coupons cut the price to 16 kr. Tickets for a single journey can be bought on departure, while the books of coupons are sold at Pressbyrån outlets, SL stations and T-bana stations.

The network of red city buses is built around a number of blue "feeder" routes

Ferry linking Gamla Stan and Djurgården

which run more frequently. Many streets in the city centre have special bus lanes which speed up the traffic. The best routes for sightseeing are 3, 4, 46, 47, 62 and 69.

Run by **Waxholmsbolaget**, public transport in the archipelago is good all year round, with more frequent services from June to August. An excellent way to explore the archipelago is to take the ferries from Strömkajen, which stop off at countless picturesque jetties along the way.

Other recommended trips include Birka, Drottningholm and Mariefred/Gripsholm *(see pp110–11)* A popular way of getting to Djurgården is on the ferry from Slussen to Allmänna Gränd. SL's one-day and three-day cards are valid on the Djurgården ferry.

Red city bus and blue "feeder" bus

DIRECTORY

TRAFFIC INFORMATION

Stockholms Lokaltrafik
- 08-600 10 00.
- www.sl.se

TAXIS

Taxi Kurir
- 08-30 00 00.

Taxi Stockholm
- 08-15 00 00.

Taxi 020
- 020-20 20 20.

ARCHIPELAGO AND SIGHTSEEING BOATS

Waxholmsbolaget
Strömkajen, Vaxholm, Stavsnäs.
- 08-679 58 30.
- www.waxholmsbolaget.se

Strömma Kanalbolaget
Nybrokajen, Stadshusbron.
- 08-587 140 20.
- www.stromma.se

Open Top Tours
- www.opentoptours.com

SIGHTSEEING

A pleasant way of enjoying Stockholm from the water is to take an excursion run by Stockholm Sightseeing (**Strömma Kanalbolaget**). A "Round Kungsholmen" tour departs hourly from the quayside near the City Hall. The "Under Stockholm's Bridges" and "Round Djurgården" tours depart from Strömkajen near the Grand Hotel, and passengers are also picked up from Nybroplan. Tickets can be bought at both these points. A commentary is provided on headsets in several languages. The tours generally run once an hour. Most tours are only available in the summer, but some run until December.

Sightseeing tours by bus include the **Open Top Tours** double-deckers, which run between strategic stops close to attractions in central Stockholm. Passengers can hop on and off along the way.

Acknowledgments

STREIFFERT FÖRLAG would like to thank the following staff at Dorling Kindersley:

PUBLISHER
Douglas Amrine

PUBLISHING MANAGERS
Jane Ewart, Anna Streiffert

SENIOR EDITOR
Christine Stroyan

MAP CO-ORDINATOR
Casper Morris

DTP MANAGER
Jason Little

PRODUCTION CONTROLLER
Linda Dare

DORLING KINDERSLEY would like to thank all those whose contributions and assistance have made the preparation of this book possible.

MAIN CONTRIBUTORS
ULF JOHANSSON has produced Swedish guidebooks such as *Sverigeboken* and *Sverigevägvisaren*. He has also been a publisher and year-book editor at the Swedish tourist association Svenska Turistföreningen.

MONA NEPPENSTRÖM is an editor and travel journalist and has written a large number of Swedish guide-books, including *Sverigeboken*, *Sverigevägvisaren*, *Turisttoppen* and rail company SJ's travel guide series *Längs spåret*.

KAJ SANDELL wrote the *Eyewitness Stockholm* travel guide. He is a journalist and formerly wrote for Swedish publishers Åhlén & Åkerlunds Förlag and Swedish daily broadsheet *Dagens Nyheter*.

FACTCHECKING
Lena Ahlgren

PROOFREADER
Stewart J Wild

INDEX
Helen Peters

ARTWORK REFERENCE
Svenska Aerobilder AB

PHOTOGRAPHY PERMISSIONS
The publishers would like to thank all those who gave permission to photograph at museums, palaces, churches, restaurants, hotels, stores and other sights too numerous to list individually. Particular thanks go to the Guild of Museum Directors in Stockholm for permitting access to picture archives as well as making additional photographing of objects and exhibitions possible.

PICTURE CREDITS
t = top; tl = top left; tlc = top left centre; tc = top centre; trc = top right centre; tr = top right; cla = centre left above; ca = centre above; cra = centre right above; cl = centre left; c = centre; cr = centre right; clb = centre left below; cb = centre below; crb = centre right below; bl = bottom left; bc = bottom centre; br = bottom right; b = bottom.

Every effort has been made to trace the copyright holders. Dorling Kindersley apologizes for any unintentional omission and would be pleased, in such cases, to add an acknowledgment in future editions.

Commissioned by the publisher, the book's main photographers, Peter Hanneberg, Erik Svensson and Jeppe Wikström, produced the majority of the photographs reproduced in this book. They have also contributed archive pictures which have been listed among the other picture credits. The publisher would like to thank the photographers and all the other individuals, organizations and picture libraries for permission to reproduce their photographs and illustrations:

AMAROK AB:
Magnus Elander 16t, 16clb.

ARMÉMUSEUM:
266bl.

ÁTTJE FJÄLL- OCH SAMEMUSEUM:
Jan Gustavsson 20tr.

©DACS:
Märta Måås-Fjetterström 22br; *Concrete*, Jonas Bohlin 23tr; Hans Hedberg 22tr; Sigurd Persson 23tl; *Breakfast Outdoors*, Pablo Picasso 78tr; *The Dying Dandy*, Nils Dardel 78bl; *Monogram*, Robert Rauchenberg 78crb; *The Child's Brain*, Giorgio De Chirico 79cl; Einar Forseth 100tr; Simon Gate 153tr; *Visby Wall*, Hanna Hirsch-Pauli 164tr; *Altarpiece in Jukkasjärvi Church*, Bror Hjort 272c.

DANSMUSEUM:
64tr.

DROTTNINGHOLMS SLOTTSTEATER:
Bengt Wanselius 109tr, 109bc.

ETNOGRAFISKA MUSEET:
Bo Gabrielsson 93c.

FJÄRILS & FÅGELHUSET:
97cl.

GREAT SHOTS:
Peter Gerdehag 118–119.

GUNNEBO SLOTT:
225tl.

GÖTEBORGS KONSTMUSEUM:
Karin and Kersti, Carl Larsson 237b.

PETER HANNEBERG:
2–3c, 4t, 13t, 16cla, 16cra, 17tc, 17cl, 17br, 19cr, 20tl, 20b, 21cb, 123b, 135b, 161bc, 161br, 246, 247b, 248c, 258bl, 259tr, 262, 263b, 268c, 269br, 270–271, 274ca, 275cb, 312b, 314b, 315t, 315b, 318–319.

CHRISTER HÄGG:
East Indiaman Wasa, Jacob Hägg 198b.

IMS BILDBYRÅ:
43tl.

JÖNKÖPINGS LÄNS MUSEUM:
Bianca Maria in Among Elves and Trolls, John Bauer 21bl.

KOSTA BODA:
Ann Wåhlström 23b; Ulrika Hydman Vallien152b; Kjell Engman 153bc.

KUNGLIGA BIBLIOTEKET:
36br, 70b.

KUNGLIGA HUSGERÅDSKAMMAREN:
Alexis Daflos 4b, 56tr, 56clb, 57tr, 107tc; 106cl, 106bl, 107bl, 108tr, 108clb; *The Triumph of Karl XI*, Jacques Foucquet 37tl; 46b; Håkan Lind 54cra, 54crb, 54br; 54tl, 55tc, 55cr, 56cla, 107cr; 135c.

KUNGLIGA MYNTKABINETTET:
51crb; Jan Eve Olsson 52cl, 69tr.

KUNGLIGA OPERAN:
Mats Bäcker 64bc, 67tl, 67c.

KÄLLEMO AB:
23c.

LIVRUSTKAMMAREN:
37bl, 41br; Göran Schmidt 41cla, 51tl; Nina Heins 52bl.

MEDELHAVSMUSEET:
Ove Kaneberg 64cla.

METRIA KIRUNA:
8cr.

MODERNA MUSEET:
Per Anders Allsten 78br.

MUSEUM TRE KRONOR:
56br.

MUSIKMUSEUM:
Nina Heins 70cra.

NATIONALMUSEUM:
22clb; *Flowers on the Windowsill*, Carl Larsson 22–23c; *Gustav Vasa*, Cornelius Arendtz 30; *Ansgar Preaches Christianity*, Georg Pauli 32bl; *Stockholm Bloodbath*, Dionysius Padt-Brügge 33t; *The Entry of King Gustav Vasa of Sweden into Stockholm, 1523*, Carl Larsson 34t; *Portrait of Erik XIV*, Steven van der Meulen 34c; *The Fire at the Royal Palace 7th May 1697*, Johan Fredrik Höckert 35tr; *Portrait of Queen Kristina*, David Beck 35cl; *The Death of Gustav II Adolf of Sweden at the Battle of Lutzen*, Carl Wahlbom 36bl; *The Crossing of the Belt*, Johan Philip Lemke 36–37c; *Karl X Gustav*, Sébastien Bourdon 37cr; *Bringing Home the Body of King Karl XII of Sweden*, Gustaf Cederström 37br; *King Gustav III of Sweden*, Lorens Pasch d.y. 38tl; *Portrait of the Bernadotte Family*, Fredrik Westin 38crb; *The Coronation of Gustav III*, Carl Gustav Pilo 40cla; *The Battle at Svensksund*, J T Schoultz 40clb; *A Noisy Dinner*, Johan Tobias Sergel 40bc; *Conversation at Drottningholm*, Pehr Hilleström 40–41c; *The Murder of Gustav III*, A W Küssner 41tr; *Bacchanal on Andros*, Peter Paul Rubens 47tl; 55br; *The Conspiracy of the Batavians under Claudius Civilis*, Rembrant 80cla; *David and Bathsheba*, 80bl; *The Love Lesson*, Antoine Watteau 80tr; *The Lady with the Veil*, Alexander Roslin 81tl; *The Faun*, Johan Tobias Sergel 81cb; *Karl XIV Johan's Visit to Berga*, A C Wetterling 146t; *Valdemar Atterdag Plunders Visby 1361*, Carl Gustaf Hellqvist 167b.

NATURHISTORISKA RIKSMUSEET:
Staffan Waerndt 96c.

NORDISKA MUSEET:
47tr; Birgit Brånvall 88tr; Mats Landin 88cl; Sören Hallgren 88bc; *Snowstorm at Sea*, August Strindberg 89cra; 89tr; *The Proposal*, Knut Ekwall 89tl.

POSTMUSEUM:
59crb.

PREMIUM PUBLISHING:
Anders Hanser 24b.

PRESSENS BILD:
5tr, 6–7c, 10, 11b, 12t, 14t, 15b, 21tr, 24tr, 25t, 25c, 25b, 27b, 43cr; Hans T. Dahlskog 43br; 54bl; Jan Delden 68br; Gunnar Seijbold 71tl; 87tl; Axel Malmström 99tr; 105br, 120t, 206, 259b, 304cr, 305tr, 310cr, 316tl.

REDERI AB GÖTA KANAL:
147cra.

LAILA REPPEN:
18–19c.

RIKSANTIKVARIEÄMBETET:
3c.

SJÖHISTORISKA MUSEET:
94c.

SKANSEN:
Marie Andersson 92c.

SKOGSKYRKOGÅRDEN:
105c.

SKYWAYS:
Jonas Kosunen 330t.

INGALILL SNITT:
18t.

STATENS HISTORISKA MUSEUM:
84cla, 84clb, 84bl, 84br, 85tc, 85ca, 85cb, 85br, 85bl, 130b.

STENINGE SLOTT:
130t.

STOCKHOLMS AUKTIONSVERK:
41bl.

STOCKHOLMS STADSBYGGNADSKONTOR:
95c.

STOCKHOLMS STADSHUS:
Jan Asplund 100br, 101tl.

STOCKHOLMS STADSMUSEUM:
32t; *Tre Kronor Palace*, Govert Camphuysen 36cl; *Newspaper Readers*, J A Cronstedt 39tl; *The Regicide Anckarström Punished in Front of the House of Nobility*, 41cr; 42bl, 43clb.

STRINDBERGSMUSEET:
24tl; Per Bergström 69bc.

SVENSKA AKADEMIEN:
Leif Jansson 40tr.

ROLF SØRENSEN:
16bl, 17bl.

THIELSKA GALLERIET:
Hornsgatan, Eugène Jansson 93tr.

LARS TUFVESSON:
Lars Tufvesson 181b.

INGRID VANG NYMAN:
14c.

VASALOPPSMUSEET:
244t, 244cla, 244cra, 244bl.

VASAMUSEET:
Hans Hammarskiöld 47br, 90tr, 90cla, 90bl, 90br, 91tc, 91cra; 91crb, 91bl.

VIN & SPRITHISTORISKA MUSEET:
98c.

CLAES WESTLIN:
22cla.

JEPPE WIKSTRÖM:
26b, 27t, 29b, 44–45, 48, 52tr, 62, 64clb, 65crb, 65bl, 68tl, 72, 76br, 77ca, 82, 83t, 86t, 87tr, 97br, 99tl, 99b, 100bl, 102t, 103t, 103cl, 103b, 104tl, 110cr, 110cra, 111tl, 111br, 276–277, 290b, 310bl, 329t, 334t.

ÖSTASIATISKA MUSEET:
Erik Cornelius 74cla, 76bl.

JACKET: Front: CORBIS: Freelance Consulting Services Pty Ltd, bl; DK IMAGES: Jeppe Wikström, br; WWW.PIXGALLERY.COM: Bo Jansson, main; STATENS HISTORISKA MUSEUM: c. Back: DK IMAGES: Peter Hanneberg, tr; ZEFA VISUAL MEDIA: F Damm, bl. Spine: WWW.PIXGALLERY.COM: Bo Jansson.

Phrase Book

When reading the imitated pronunciation, stress the part which is underlined. Pronounce each syllable as if it formed part of an English word, and you will be understood sufficiently well. Remember the points below, and your pronunciation will be even closer to the correct Swedish.

ai:	as in 'fair' or 'stair'
ea:	as in 'ear' or 'hear'
ew:	like the sound in 'dew'
EW:	try to say 'ee' with your lips rounded
oo:	as in 'book' or 'soot'
OO:	as in 'spoon' or 'groom'
r:	should be strongly pronounced

Swedish Alphabetical Order
In the list below we have followed Swedish alphabetical order. The following letters are listed after **z**: **å, ä, ö**.

You
There are two words for 'you': 'du' and 'ni'. 'Ni' is the polite form; 'du' is the familiar form. It is not impolite to address a complete stranger with the familiar form.

IN AN EMERGENCY

Help!	**Hjälp!**	*yelp*
Stop!	**Stanna!**	*stanna!*
Call a doctor!	**Ring efter en doktor!**	*ring efter ebn doktor*
Call an ambulance!	**Ring efter en ambulans!**	*ring efter ebn ambewlanss*
Call the police!	**Ring polisen!**	*ring poleesen*
Call the fire brigade!	**Ring efter brandkåren!**	*ring efter brandkawren*
Where is the nearest telephone?	**Var finns närmaste telefon?**	*vahr finnss nairmasteh-telefawn*
Where is the nearest hospital?	**Var finns närmaste sjukhus?**	*vahr finnss-nairmasteh shewkhews*

COMMUNICATION ESSENTIALS

Yes	**Ja**	*yah*
No	**Nej**	*nay*
Please (offering)	**Varsågod**	*vahrsbawgOOd*
Thank you	**Tack**	*tack*
Excuse me	**Ursäkta**	*ewrsbekta*
Hello	**Hej**	*hay*
Goodbye	**Hej då/adjö**	*haydaw/ahyur*
Good night	**God natt**	*goongtt*
Morning	**Morgon**	*morron*
Afternoon	**Eftermiddag**	*eftermiddabg*
Evening	**Kväll**	*kvell*
Yesterday	**Igår**	*ee gawr*
Today	**Idag**	*ee dahg*
Tomorrow	**I morgon**	*ee morron*
Here	**Här**	*hair*
There	**Där**	*dair*
What?	**Vad?**	*vah*
When?	**När?**	*nair*
Why?	**Varför?**	*vahrfurr*
Where?	**Var?**	*vahr*

USEFUL PHRASES

How are you?	**Hur mår du?**	*hewr mawr dew*
Very well, thank you.	**Mycket bra, tack.**	*mEWkeh brah, tack*
Pleased to meet you.	**Trevligt att träffas.**	*treavligt att traiffas*
See you soon.	**Vi ses snart.**	*vee seas snahrt*
That's fine.	**Det går bra.**	*dea gawr brah*
Where is/are . . .?	**Var finns ...?**	*vahr finnss...*
How far is it to . . .?	**Hur långt är det till?**	*hewr lawngt ea dea till*
Which way to . . .?	**Hur kommer jag till ...?**	*hewr kommer yah till ...*
Do you speak English?	**Talar du/ni engelska?**	*tablar dew/nee engelska*
I don't understand	**Jag förstår inte.**	*yah furshtaur inteh*
Could you speak more slowly, please?	**Kan du/ni tala långsammare, tack.**	*kan dew/nee tabla lawngssamareh tack*
I'm sorry.	**Förlåt.**	*furrlawt*

USEFUL WORDS

big	**stor**	*stOOr*
small	**liten**	*leeten*
hot	**varm**	*varrm*
cold	**kall**	*kall*
good	**bra**	*brah*
bad	**dålig**	*dawleeg*
enough	**tillräcklig**	*tillraikleeg*
open	**öppen**	*urpen*
closed	**stängd**	*staingd*
left	**vänster**	*vainster*
right	**höger**	*burger*
straight on	**rakt fram**	*rahkt fram*
near	**nära**	*naira*
far	**långt**	*lawngt*
up/over	**upp/över**	*EWp/urver*
down/under	**ner/under**	*near/eunder*
early	**tidig**	*teedeg*
late	**sen**	*sehn*
entrance	**ingång**	*ingawng*
exit	**utgång**	*EWtgawng*
toilet	**toalett**	*too-alett*
more	**mer**	*mehr*
less	**mindre**	*meendre*

SHOPPING

How much is this?	**Hur mycket kostar den här?**	*hewr mEWkeh kostar debn hair*
I would like . . .	**Jag skulle vilja . . .**	*yah skewleh vilya*
Do you have?	**Har du/ni ...?**	*habr dew/nee ...*
I'm just looking	**Jag ser mig bara omkring**	*yah sear may babra omkring*
Do you take credit cards?	**Tar du/ni kreditkort?**	*tahr dew/nee kredeetkoort*
What time do you open?	**När öppnar ni?**	*nair urpnar nee*
What time do you close?	**När stänger ni?**	*nair stainger nee*
This one.	**den här**	*debn hair*
That one.	**den där**	*debn dair*
expensive	**dyr**	*dewr*
cheap	**billig**	*billig*
size (clothes)	**storlek**	*stOOrlek*
white	**vit**	*veet*
black	**svart**	*svart*
red	**röd**	*rurd*
yellow	**gul**	*gewl*
green	**grön**	*grurn*
blue	**blå**	*blaw*
antique shop	**antikaffär**	*anteek-affair*
bakery	**bageri**	*babgeree*
bank	**bank**	*bank*
book shop	**bokhandel**	*bOOkhandel*
butcher	**slaktare**	*slaktareb*
cake shop	**konditori**	*konditoree*
chemist	**apotek**	*apoteak*
fishmonger	**fiskaffär**	*fisk-affair*
grocer	**speceriaffär**	*spesseree-affair*
hairdresser	**frisör**	*frissurr*
market	**marknad**	*marrknad*
newsagent	**tidningskiosk**	*teednings-cheeosk*
post office	**postkontor**	*posstkontOOr*
shoe shop	**skoaffär**	*skOO-affair*
supermarket	**snabbköp**	*snabbchurp*
tobacconist's	**tobakshandel**	*tOObaks-handel*
travel agency	**resebyrå**	*reasseb-bEWraw*

SIGHTSEEING

art gallery	**konstgalleri**	*konnst-galleree*
church	**kyrka**	*chEWrka*
garden	**trädgård**	*traidgawrd*
house	**hus**	*hews*
library	**bibliotek**	*beebleeotek*
museum	**museum**	*meuseum*
square	**torg**	*tobrj*
street	**gata**	*gabta*
tourist information office	**turist-informations-kontor**	*tureest-informashbOOns-kontOOr*
town hall	**stadshus**	*statshews*
closed for holiday	**stängt för semester**	*staingt furr semester*
bus station	**busstation**	*bewss-stashOOn*
railway station	**järnvägsstation**	*yairnvaigs-stashOOn*

STAYING IN A HOTEL

Do you have any vacancies?	**Har ni några lediga rum?**	*habr nee negra leadiga rewm*
double room with double bed	**dubbelrum med dubbelsäng**	*doobelrewm med doobel-seng*

twin room	**dubbelrum**	*doobelrewm*
	med två	*med tvaw*
	sängar	*sengar*
single room	**enkelrum**	*enkelrewm*
room with	**rum med**	*rewm med*
a bath	**bad**	*bahd*
shower	**dusch**	*dewsh*
key	**nyckel**	*nEWckel*
I have a	**Jag har**	*yah bahr*
reservation	**beställt rum**	*bestellt rewm*

EATING OUT

Have you got a	**Har ni ett**	*hahr nee ett*
table for...	**bord för...?**	*bOOrd furr ...*
I would like	**Jag skulle vilja**	*yah skewleh vilya*
to reserve	**boka ett**	*bOOka ett*
a table.	**bord.**	*bOOrd*
The bill, please.	**Notan, tack.**	*nOOtan, tack*
I am a	**Jag är**	*yah air*
vegetarian	**vegetarian**	*vegetariabn*
waitress	**servitris**	*sairvitregss*
waiter	**servitör**	*sairviturr*
menu	**meny/**	*menEW/*
	matsedel	*mabtseadel*
fixed-price	**meny med**	*menEW med*
menu	**fast pris**	*fast prees*
wine list	**vinlista**	*veenlista*
glass of water	**ett glas**	*ett glabss*
	vatten	*vatten*
glass of wine	**ett glas vin**	*ett glabss veen*
bottle	**flaska**	*flaska*
knife	**kniv**	*k-neev*
fork	**gaffel**	*gaffel*
spoon	**sked**	*shead*
breakfast	**frukost**	*frewkost*
lunch	**lunch**	*lewnch*
dinner	**middag**	*middahg*
main course	**huvudrätt**	*bEWvEWdrett*
starter	**förrätt**	*furrett*
dish of the day	**dagens rätt**	*dahgens rett*
coffee	**kaffe**	*kaffeh*
rare	**blodig**	*blOOdee*
medium	**medium**	*medium*
well done	**välstekt**	*vailstehkt*

MENU DECODER

abborre	*abborreh*	perch
ansjovis	*ansbOOvees*	anchovies
apelsin	*appelseen*	orange
bakelse	*bahkelse*	cake, pastry, tart
banan	*banabn*	banana
biff	*biff*	beef
bröd	*brurd*	bread
bullar	*bewllar*	buns
choklad	*shooklahd*	chocolate
citron	*sitrOOn*	lemon
dessert	*dessair*	dessert
fisk	*fisk*	fish
fläsk	*flaisk*	pork
forell	*fooraill*	trout
frukt	*fruckt*	fruit
glass	*glass*	ice cream
gurka	*gewrka*	cucumber
grönsaksgryta	*grurnsabks-grEWta*	vegetable stew
hummer	*hummer*	lobster
kallskuret	*kall-skuret*	cold meat
korv	*koorv*	sausages
kyckling	*chEWkling*	chicken
kött	*churtt*	meat
lamm	*lamm*	lamb
lök	*lurk*	onion
mineralvatten	*minerahl-vatten*	mineral water
med/utan	*mehd/ewtan*	still/sparkling
kolsyra	*kawlsEWra*	
mjölk	*m-yurlk*	milk
nötkött	*nurtchurtt*	beef
nötter	*nurtter*	nuts
ost	*oost*	cheese
olja	*olya*	oil
oliver	*oleever*	olives
paj/kaka	*pa-y/kabka*	pie/cake
potatis	*potabtis*	potatoes
peppar	*peppar*	pepper
ris	*rees*	rice
rostat bröd	*rostat brurd*	toast
räkor	*raikoor*	prawns
rökt skinka	*rurkt sheenka*	cured ham
rött vin	*rurtt veen*	red wine
saft	*safft-*	lemonade
salt	*sallt*	salt
sill	*seell*	herring

skaldjur	*skabl-yewr*	seafood
smör	*smurr*	butter
stekt	*stehkt*	fried
strömming	*strumming*	baltic herring
socker	*socker*	sugar
soppa	*soppa*	soup
sås	*saws*	sauce
te	*tea*	tea
torr	*torr*	dry
ungsstekt	*ewngs-stehkt*	baked, roast
vinäger	*vinaiger*	vinegar
vispgrädde	*veesp-graiddeh*	whipped cream
vitlök	*veet-lurk*	garlic
vitt vin	*veett veen*	white wine
ägg	*aigg*	egg
älg	*ail-y*	elk
äpple	*aippleb*	apple
öl	*url*	beer

NUMBERS

0	**noll**	*noll*
1	**ett**	*ett*
2	**två**	*tvaw*
3	**tre**	*trea*
4	**fyra**	*fEWra*
5	**fem**	*fem*
6	**sex**	*sex*
7	**sju**	*shEW*
8	**åtta**	*otta*
9	**nio**	*nee-oo*
10	**tio**	*tee-oo*
11	**elva**	*elva*
12	**tolv**	*tolv*
13	**tretton**	*tretton*
14	**fjorton**	*f-yoorton*
15	**femton**	*femton*
16	**sexton**	*sexton*
17	**sjutton**	*shewton*
18	**arton**	*abrton*
19	**nitton**	*nitton*
20	**tjugo**	*chEWgoo*
21	**tjugoett**	*chEWgoo-ett*
22	**tjugotvå**	*chEWgoo-tvaw*
30	**trettio**	*tretti*
31	**trettioett**	*tretti-ett*
40	**fyrtio**	*furti*
50	**femtio**	*femti*
60	**sextio**	*sexti*
70	**sjuttio**	*shewti*
80	**åttio**	*otti*
90	**nittio**	*nitti*
100	**(ett) hundra**	*(ett) bewndra*
101	**etthundraett**	*ett-bewndra-ett*
102	**etthundratvå**	*ett-bewndra-tvaw*
200	**tvåhundra**	*tvawbewndra*
300	**trehundra**	*treabewndra*
400	**fyrahundra**	*fEWrabewndra*
500	**femhundra**	*fembewndra*
600	**sexhundra**	*sexbewndra*
700	**sjuhundra**	*shEWbewndra*
800	**åttahundra**	*ottabewndra*
900	**niohundra**	*nee-oobewndra*
1,000	**(ett) tusen**	*(ett) tEWssen*
1,001	**etttusenett**	*ett-tEWssen-ett*
100,000	**(ett) hundra-**	*(ett) bewndra*
	tusen	*tEWssen*
1,000,000	**en miljon**	*ebn milyOOn*

TIME

one minute	**en minut**	*ebn meenEWt*
one hour	**en timme**	*ebn timmeb*
half an hour	**en halvtimme**	*ebn balvtimmeb*
ten past one	**tio över ett**	*teeoo urver ett*
quarter past one	**kvart över ett**	*kvabrt urver ett*
half past one	**halv två**	*balv tvaw*
twenty to two	**tjugo i två**	*chEWgoo ee tvaw*
quarter to two	**kvart i två**	*kvabrt ee tvaw*
two o'clock	**klockan två**	*klockan tvaw*
13.00	**klockan tretton**	*klockan tretton*
16.30	**sexton och trettio**	*sexton ock tretti*
noon	**klockan tolv**	*klockan tolv*
midnight	**midnatt**	*meednatt*
Monday	**måndag**	*mawndabg*
Tuesday	**tisdag**	*teesdabg*
Wednesday	**onsdag**	*oonssdabg*
Thursday	**torsdag**	*toorsdabg*
Friday	**fredag**	*freadabg*
Saturday	**lördag**	*lurrdabg*
Sunday	**söndag**	*surndabg*

FOR PEACE OF MIND ABROAD,
WE'VE GOT IT COVERED

DK INSURANCE PROVIDES YOU WITH QUALITY WORLDWIDE INSURANCE COVER

For an instant quote
go to **www.dk.com/travel-insurance**

Stockholm
Transport Map